ANTHROPOLOGICAL RELIGION

MAX MÜLLER

AMS PRESS
NEW YORK

ANTHROPOLOGICAL

RELIGION

The Gifford Lectures

DELIVERED

BEFORE THE UNIVERSITY OF GLASGOW
IN 1891

BY

F. MAX MÜLLER, K.M.

FOREIGN MEMBER OF THE FRENCH INSTITUTE

LONDON

LONGMANS, GREEN, AND CO.

AND NEW YORK: 15 EAST 16TH STREET

1892

Library of Congress Cataloging in Publication Data

Müller, Friedrich Max, 1823-1900.
  Anthropological religion.

  Reprint of the 1892 ed. published by Longmans, Green,
London, New York, which was issued as Gifford lectures,
1891.
  Includes index.
  1. Religion. 2. Religions. 3. Soul. I. Title.
II. Series: Gifford lectures; 1891.
BL48.M76   1975   291   73-18822
ISBN 0-404-11428-8

Reprinted from the edition of 1892, London and New York
First AMS edition published in 1975
Manufactured in the United States of America

AMS PRESS INC.
NEW YORK, N. Y. 10003

PREFACE.

——◆——

In lecturing before the Members of the University of Glasgow, on the origin and the growth of religion my chief object has been to show that a belief in God, in the immortality of the soul, and in a future retribution can be gained, and not only can be, but has been gained by the right exercise of human reason alone, without the assistance of what has been called a special revelation. I have tried to prove this, not, as others have done, by reasoning *à priori* only, but by historical investigation; I have tried to gather in some of the harvest which is plenteous, but which requires far more labourers than are working in this field at present. In doing this, I thought I was simply following in the footsteps of the greatest theologians of our time, and that I was serving the cause of true religion by showing by ample historical evidence, gathered from the Sacred Books of the East, how what St. Paul, what the Fathers of the Church, what mediaeval theologians, and what some of the most learned of modern Divines had asserted again and again was most strikingly confirmed by the records of all non-Christian religions which have lately become accessible to us by the patient researches of Oriental

scholars, more particularly by the students of the
ancient literature of India.

I could not have believed it possible that in under-
taking this work, I should have exposed myself to
attacks from theologians who profess and call themselves Christians, and who yet maintain that worst
of all heresies that during all the centuries that have
elapsed and in all the countries of the world, God *has*
left Himself without a witness, and has revealed Himself to one race only, the most stiff-necked of all the
Semitic races, the Jews of Palestine. I was glad to
hear that these attacks emanated chiefly from Roman
Catholic priests, carrying on at present an active pro-
paganda at Glasgow, from men who consider not only
the heathen, but all who are not Roman-Catholics,
more particularly all honest searchers after truth, as
outside the love of God. Yet, they are the same men
who represent John H. Newman as the highest pattern
of Christian orthodoxy. But I must be permitted to
doubt whether they have ever had time to read his
writings. For who has spoken more frankly and
more powerfully of what has been achieved by Natural,
as distinguished from Supernatural religion than Newman? Who knew better than Newman how near
the wisest and best among Greeks and Romans had
come to the truths of Christianity? 'I know,' he
writes in his *Apologia* (p. 243), 'that even the unaided
reason, when correctly exercised, leads to a belief in
God, in the immortality of the soul, and in a future
retribution.' Is this so very different from what I
have said, and what I have tried to prove by historical
evidence? Whatever Newman may have been, he

knew at all events Greek and Latin, and to know these languages and the thoughts contained in their literature is an excellent preservative against that narrow-mindedness and un-Christian intolerance which one hoped would by this time have become extinct, at least among the more highly educated members of the Roman-Catholic priesthood.

But it seems that I have given still greater offence by what I have said about the naturalness of miracles than by my defence of Natural Religion. I do not see, however, after reading all that my adversaries have written, that I can retract a single word or modify in the least what I have said about certain miracles. To believe in miracles seems to be in the eyes of my opponents the one great test of orthodoxy. But they ought surely to know, if they are acquainted with the recent theological literature on miracles, that the whole controversy about miracles turns on the definition which is given of that term. Let me refer my opponents again to Dr. Newman, who says in so many words: 'Most miracles are a continuation or augmentation of natural processes. For instance, there is said[1] to be something like manna in the desert ordinarily, and the sacred narrative mentions a wind as blowing up the waters of the Red Sea, and so in numerous other miracles'; that is to say, the manna from heaven was not a physical miracle, but an ordinary event, ignorantly mistaken for. a miracle, and the passing of the Red Sea was simply the effect of the wind blowing up the waters. Surely to admit so much is to admit everything; or

[1] *Contemporary Review*, July, 1891, p. 48.

at all events, to admit the fundamental principle of
what is contemptuously called the German or critical
school.   It is true that Dr. Newman excepts some
miracles, but who is to judge which miracles are to be
excepted, and which are to be interpreted as natural
events, misapprehended by those who witnessed and
those who recorded them, whether in the Old or in the
New Testament?   It should be remembered also that
the miracle of the Manna in the Desert is a miracle to
which Christ referred (St. John vi. 31), but which as
usual He interpreted in a higher sense, when He said:
'Verily, verily, I say unto you, Moses gave you not
that bread from heaven, but my Father giveth you
the true bread from heaven.   For the bread of God is
he which cometh down from heaven, and giveth life
unto the world.'

    But let us now turn to Protestant theologians.   The
present Bishop of London can hardly be considered a
very dangerous heretic.   But what does he say about
miracles in his Bampton Lectures, preached before the
University of Oxford in 1884?   First of all, with regard to the old question of historical evidence, he waves
aside the whole of the miracles of the Old Testament.
He shows what historical evidence there is for the
miracles of the New Testament, and then proceeds: 'No
such evidence can now be produced on behalf of the
miracles of the Old Testament.   The times are remote,
the date and authorship of the Books not established
with certainty; the mixture of poetry with history,
no longer capable of any sure separation, and, if the
New Testament did not exist, it would be impossible
to show such a distinct preponderance of probability

as would justify us in calling on any to accept the miraculous parts of the narrative as historically true.'

From a purely historical point of view he rightly considers the evidence for the miracles in the New Testament far stronger than the evidence for the miracles in the Old Testament, but even of these he admits (p. 150) 'that without the satisfaction which the Bible gives to the conscience, no miracles, however overwhelmingly attested, no external evidence whatever, would have compelled intellects of the highest rank side by side with the most uncultivated and the most barren, to accept the Christian teaching as divine.' And again (p. 157) he lays it down as a general principle that 'the supernatural in the form of miracles can never be the highest kind of evidence.'

When the Bishop proceeds to discuss certain classes of miracles, he goes nearly as far as Cardinal Newman. 'The miraculous healing,' he writes (p. 195), 'may be no miracle in the strictest sense at all. It may be but an instance of the power of mind over body, a power which is undeniably not yet brought within the range of Science, and which nevertheless may be really within its domain. In other ways what seems to be miraculous, may be simply unusual.'

Here we see how everything depends on the definition of a miracle or of what is usual and not usual. Miracle, like all words, has had a long history. There is a time in the history of human thought when such a distinction is altogether unknown. Then follows a time when all is supernatural, when the blue sky and the daily rising of the sun are marvels. After that, with the increase of human knowledge, certain segments of our experience are separated and labelled natural. And why? Because they return with great regularity, and thus lead us to suppose that we understand them and can account for them. As these segments become larger and larger, the residue of what we cannot understand and account for grows smaller and smaller, and if once the human mind has arrived at the conviction that *everything* must be accounted for, or, as it is sometimes expressed, that there is uniformity, that there is law and order in everything, and that an unbroken chain of cause and effect holds the whole universe together, then the idea of the miraculous arises, and we, weak human creatures, call what is not intelligible to us, what is not in accordance with law, what seems to break through the chain of cause and effect, a miracle.

Every miracle, therefore, is of our own making, and of our own unmaking. In one sense every sunrise is a miracle. Mohammed speaks of it as the greatest of all miracles. But very soon it became a matter of course and ceased to be a miracle. Then, when the daily rising and setting of the sun had ceased to be a miracle, the sudden darkening of the sun or of the moon struck the human mind as irregular, till solar and lunar eclipses too could be accounted for. But as their regular recurrence could be understood and predicted by the few only, it is not surprising that these few, call them sages, or prophets, or priests, should occasionally have appealed to these startling events as manifestations of a divine will, or as a confirmation of the authority which they wished to exercise over the less enlightened masses.

Even in our days, suppose a miracle had been worked, would it not be the greatest presumption for science to say that it was a miracle? 'To prove it to be a miracle,' to quote Dr. Temple's words once more (p. 30), 'would require not a vast range of knowledge, but absolutely universal knowledge.'

A comparative study of religions shows that there is hardly any religion which in its later, if not in its original stages, has not been infected by miracles.

Dr. Stokes has lately called attention to the fact that in the history of the Christian religion also we see that one of the earliest, if not the earliest known apologist of Christianity, the philosopher Aristides, at the beginning of the second century, does not lay any stress on ordinary miracles or prophecy in support of the truth of Christianity. In his lately discovered Apology before Hadrian, or Antoninus Pius, Aristides speaks of Jesus Christ as the Son of God Most High, and he adds, '*it is said* that God came down from heaven, and from a Hebrew virgin took and clad Himself with flesh, and in a daughter of man there dwelt the Son of God.' And again: 'He was pierced by the Jews, and He died and was buried, and *they say* that after three days, He rose and ascended to heaven.' His own faith in God still breathes a purely Platonic spirit. He begins his Apology by saying:

'I, O king, by the grace of God came into this world: and having contemplated the heavens and the earth and the seas, and beheld the sun and the rest of the orderly creation, I was amazed at the arrangement of the world; and I comprehended that the world and all that is therein are moved by the impulse of another, and I understood that He that moveth them is God, who is hidden in

them and concealed from them ; and this is well known that that
which moveth is more powerful than that which is moved. And
that I should investigate concerning this mover of all, as to how
He exists—for this is evident to me, for He is incomprehensible in
His nature—and that I should dispute concerning the steadfastness
of His government, so as to comprehend it fully, is not profitable
for me ; for no one is able perfectly to comprehend it. But I say
concerning the mover of the world, that He is God of all, who
made all for the sake of man ; and it is evident to me that this
is expedient, that one should fear God and not grieve Him. Now,
I say that God is not begotten, not made ; a constant nature, without
beginning and without end ; immortal, complete, and incomprehensible ; and in saying that He is complete, I mean this—that
there is no defining in Him, and He stands in need of nought, but
everything stands in need of Him : and in saying that He is without beginning, I mean this—that everything which has a beginning
has also an end, and that which has an end is dissoluble. He has
no name, for everything which has a name is associated with the
created. He has no likeness, nor composition of members, for he
who possesses this, is associated with things fashioned. He is not
made, nor is He male or female. The heavens do not contain Him,
but the heavens and all things visible and invisible are contained
in Him. Adversary He has none, for there is none that is more
powerful than He. Anger and wrath He possesses not, for there is
nothing that can stand against Him. Error and forgetfulness are
not in His nature, for He is altogether wisdom and understanding,
and in Him consists all that consists. He asks no sacrifice and no
libation, nor any of the things that are visible : He asks not anything from any one, but all ask from Him.'

We can easily distinguish three classes of miracles.
Some · miracles are ideas materialised, others facts
idealised, while a third class owes its origin to a simple
misunderstanding of metaphorical phraseology. When
we are told that Lao-tse was born as an old man with
grey hair, can we doubt for a moment that this was
only meant to express an idea, namely a belief in his
extraordinary wisdom ? The miracle here is simply
an idea materialised. Yet a follower of Lao-tse would

cling to this miracle, nay, his belief in Lao-tse's teaching might possibly suffer shipwreck, if his faith in the miraculous birth of his teacher were destroyed.

The idea from which the miracle sprang may be quite true and intelligible; turned into a material miracle, it becomes absurd.

Miracles due to the idealisation of material facts are very frequent in all religions. Nearly all the miracles of healing belong to it. We have no reason to doubt that a powerful mind can influence a weaker and suffering mind. We all know what faith-cures mean. When a doctor tells us that there is nothing the matter, or that after taking some often quite harmless medicine we shall be all right again, how many have felt encouraged and reinvigorated. Can we doubt that many of the cures wrought at the shrines or on sight or touch of relics of Roman Catholic saints belong to this class?

There are men and women even now whose very face seems to drive out evil thoughts—what wonder if their friends and grateful patients speak of them as having the power of healing and driving out devils! These miracles occur in all religions, both ancient and modern, and there are few persons who have not witnessed them. To call them all intentional frauds is an insult to humanity.

As to the third class of miracles, those which owe their origin to a misunderstanding of language, they are particularly frequent when the sober thought of the West tries to interpret the more vivid language of the East. But they are by no means restricted to that one cause. Every language becomes more and more forgetful of its antecedents, and is apt to interpret old language by new thought, though not always correctly.

I have no doubt that many Christians, both young and old, believe, that when Jesus had been baptized, a real dove in a bodily shape was let loose and sent down from heaven. They have read it, they have seen it represented in ever so many pictures. And yet, who can doubt that the Gospels themselves speak of it as a vision only, and not as a material fact. St. Matthew says (iii. 16) that ' the heavens were opened unto Him, and that He saw the Spirit of God descending *like* a dove, and lighting upon Him.' St. Mark says (i. 10), 'And straightway coming up out of the water, He saw the heavens opened, and the Spirit *like* a dove descending upon Him.' It is only when we come to St. Luke that we meet with the narrative of a material fact, that the Holy Ghost descended in a bodily shape like a dove from heaven upon Him. In the Gospel of St. John the vision is no longer represented as a vision of Christ Himself; but it still remains a vision of John, who says, ' I saw the Spirit descending from heaven, *like* a dove, and it abode upon Him.' Who can doubt that the expression of the Spirit descending *like* a dove, or even *as* a dove, is but an Eastern simile, and that the whole meaning and the real truth of the event would be destroyed, if we changed the simile into a material fact, and the Spirit into a feathered biped!

I know there are Christians who would not even surrender their belief in a miraculous cock, crowing after Peter had denied his Lord thrice. And yet what serious student of the New Testament can doubt, that when Christ said, 'Verily, I say unto thee, that this night before the cock crow, thou shalt deny me thrice,' He meant no more than what we should mean if we said, 'Before cock-crow,' that is, before the morning.

It could easily be shown that by materialising an idea we generally lose an important lesson, while by idealising a fact we destroy its reality or misinterpret it altogether. In either case we lose far more than we gain.

There is one miracle, however, in the New Testament which stands by itself, and on which the belief in miracles, nay, the whole belief in Christ's teaching has often been made to hinge. Has not St. Paul declared, 'If Christ is not risen, our faith is in vain'? Yes, but what did 'risen' mean to St. Paul? Was it the mere resuscitation of a material body, or was it the eternal life of the spirit? It required courage, no doubt, for a Bishop to apply the same reasoning to this as to all other miracles. 'It is quite possible,' Dr. Temple writes (p. 196), 'that our Lord's resurrection may be found hereafter to be no miracle at all in the scientific sense.' 'But this new discovery,' he adds (p. 199), 'if once made, would not affect the place which our Lord's Resurrection holds in the records of revelation. It is not the purpose of revelation to interfere with the course of nature ; if such interference be needless, and the work of revealing God to man can be done without it, there is no reason whatever to believe that any such interference would take place.'

How different is this from the language of Dr. Liddon, when speaking of the resurrection. Many will remember the almost gruesome eloquence with which he described the idea of our Lord's sacred body rotting in the soil. Why have recourse to such appeals to our imagination? Why not use the more simple and more scriptural language of dust returning to dust, or the body being changed into the elements out of which it had been framed?

Taking the evidence such as it is, I can honestly follow Dr. Temple and others in accepting the bodily resurrection of our Lord as a real historical fact, as a fact which from very early days was miraculised and misinterpreted, while on the other hand, our Lord's ascension will have to be understood, as I tried to show, as a sublime idea, materialised in the language of children. Is not a real fact that happened in a world in which nothing can happen against the will of God, better than any miracle? Why should we try to know more than we can know, if only we firmly believe that Christ's immortal spirit ascended to the Father? That alone is true immortality, divine immortality; not the resuscitation of the frail mortal body, but the immortality of the immortal divine soul. It was this rising of the Spirit, and not of the body, without which, as St. Paul said, our faith would be vain. It is the Spirit that quickeneth, the flesh profiteth nothing (St. John vi. 63).

I have little doubt that sooner or later these very simple truths will be accepted by all honest Christians, though at present they are still violently attacked, and stigmatised by very offensive names. Was it not said by Archdeacon Wilson at the Church Congress this year that 'modern criticism is practically unanimous in saying that a non-historical element, no

longer separable, has mixed with the narrative, and
that in this respect the sacred books of Christianity
are like those of Mosaism, of Buddhism, or Islam, or
other religions, and that modern criticism is practically
unanimous in saying that an atmosphere of the
miraculous in a certain stage of the human mind is an
inseparable accompaniment of the profound reverence
with which a great Teacher and Prophet and Saint
is regarded by his followers, and the necessary literary
form in which such reverence would express itself. It
is impossible, therefore, that such an atmosphere
should not have gathered round the memory of
Christ.' This was spoken in the presence of Bishops
and Archbishops, and not one of them cried Ana-
thema. Was it then so grave an outrage when I declared that miracles, so far from being impossible, are
inevitable in the early stages of almost all religions ?
I have long professed these convictions, and I know
they are shared by thousands, aye, by hundreds of
thousands. But I have no wish to shield myself
behind the Bishop of London or any other eccle-
siastic dignitary. I am by no means certain that
Dr. Temple would approve of all that I have said,
nay, I am quite willing to admit that in selecting
certain passages of his Bampton Lectures, I have
taken those only which scientific honesty extorted
from the Bishop. It can easily be said that my extracts are garbled, but I can only admit that they were
carefully selected. Those who listened to his Bampton Lectures, know the strong qualifications which
the Bishop added, and the considerate way in which
he tried not to give offence to any of his hearers,

But qualifications may modify the aspect of certain statements, they can never contradict or annihilate them.

On one point only I must confess my complete divergence from the Bishop. 'It is not God's purpose,' he says (p. 214), 'to win the intellectually gifted, the wise, the cultivated, the clever, but to win the spiritually gifted, the humble, the tender-hearted, the souls that are discontented with their own short-comings, the souls that find happiness in self-sacrifice.' If I ventured to speak of God's purpose at all, I should say the very contrary, that it is not God's purpose to win only the spiritually gifted, the humble, the tender-hearted, the souls that are discontented with their own shortcomings, the souls that find happiness in self-sacrifice—those are His already—but to win the intellectually gifted, the wise, the cultivated, the clever, or better still, to win both. It would be an evil day for Christianity if it could no longer win the intellectually gifted, the wise, the cultivated, the clever, and it seems to me the duty of all who really believe in Christ to show that Christianity, if truly understood, can win the highest as well as the humblest intellects. Dr. Temple himself has done much in showing that this is possible. He has likewise shown how much of the mere outworks of Christianity cannot hold the ground on which they have been planted, that they have to be given up by force at last, when they ought to have been given up long before, and that, when given up at last, they often tear away with them part of the strength of that faith of which they had previously been not only

the buttress outside, but a part of the living framework. He makes no secret that he includes in
these outworks the verbal and even literal inspiration of the whole Bible and, as we have seen, much
of the miraculous element of the Old, and even
in the New Testament. Dr. Temple has thus removed
many a stone of stumbling in the way of the most
honest disciples of Christ. But it will be to many of
them a real day of Damascus, when the very name
of miracle shall be struck out of the Dictionary of
Christian theology. The facts will remain exactly as
they are, but the Spirit of truth will give them a
higher meaning. What is wanted for this is not less,
but more faith, for it requires more faith to believe in
Christ without than with the help of miracles. The
signs and wonders which He wrought will remain just
the same, but they will no longer obscure the greatest
of all His signs and wonders—Himself. Let a per-
verse and adulterous generation seek for other signs.
It is those only who cannot believe unless they see
signs and wonders who are told to believe for the very
works' sake (St. John xiv. 11). Nothing, I feel sure,
has produced so much distress of mind, so much
intellectual dishonesty, so much scepticism, so much
unbelief as the miraculous element forced into Christianity from the earliest days. Nothing has so much
impeded missionary work as the attempt to persuade
people first of all not to believe in their own miracles,
and then to make a belief in other miracles a condition
of their becoming Christians. It is easy to say, ' You
are not a Christian if you do not believe in the
Christian miracles.' I hope the time will come when

we shall be told, 'You are not a Christian if you cannot believe in Christ without the help of miracles.' If I have in the slightest way helped towards that end, I shall feel that I have been loyal to the spirit of the founder of this lectureship, loyal to those who have twice entrusted me with the delivery of these lectures, loyal to the Spirit of truth, and, what is the same, loyal to the spirit of the Founder of our religion, whatever obloquy many who profess and call themselves Christians, many who ought to know better, nay, some who do know better, have poured on my head.

Painful as these charges have been to me, I must not conclude this preface without expressing my sincere gratitude to the Glasgow Presbytery for having thrown them out by a majority of 17 to 5, and to the General Assembly for having declined even to entertain them.

F. MAX MÜLLER.

OXFORD, *Oct.* 21, 1891.

TABLE OF CONTENTS.

———•+———

LECTURE III.

SUMMARY OF THE RESULTS OF PHYSICAL RELIGION.

LECTURE IV.

THE HISTORICAL PROOF OF THE EXISTENCE OF GOD.

LECTURE V.

About the True Character of Ancestor-Worship.

LECTURE VI.

The Untrustworthiness of the Materials for the Study of Religion.

LECTURE VII.

The Discovery of the Soul.

LECTURE VIII.

DISCOVERY OF THE SOUL IN MAN AND IN NATURE.

LECTURE IX.

FUNERAL CEREMONIES.

LECTURE X.

WHAT WAS THOUGHT ABOUT THE DEPARTED.

APPENDICES.

—◆◆—

APPENDIX I.

APPENDIX II.

APPENDIX III.

APPENDIX IV.

APPENDIX V.

Appendix VI.

Appendix VII.

Appendix VIII.

LECTURE I.

ON FREEDOM OF RELIGIOUS DISCUSSION.

Difficulty of lecturing on Religion without giving offence.

DO you think it is possible to lecture on religion, even on natural religion, without giving offence either on the right or on the left? And do you think that a man would be worth his salt who, in lecturing on religion, even on natural religion, were to look either right or left, instead of looking all facts, as they meet him, straight in the face, to see whether they are facts or not; and, if they are facts, to find out, if possible, what they mean, and what they are meant to teach us?

Religion, I know full well, differs from all other subjects. It appeals not only to our head, but to our heart. And as we do not like to hear those who are very near to our heart, those whom we love and revere, criticised, or even compared, it is but natural that many people should object to a criticism of that religion which they love and revere, nay, even to a comparison of it with other religions.

But let us ask ourselves, Does this attitude with regard to those whom we love and revere, really prove that we have an undoubting faith in them? If we

(3)   B

had, should we not rather wish to hear our friends compared and criticised, if only in order to have an opportunity of defending them, and of showing how infinitely superior they are to all others?

Why then should we not have the same feeling with regard to our religion as with regard to our friends, always supposing that we can give a good account of the faith that is in us, and of the reasons for which we love and revere our own religion? For if our own religion comes out victorious from the trial, and superior to all the rest, surely we shall have gained, not lost. And if other religions should after all appear not so infinitely inferior to our own, not altogether of a different stuff, should we be really poorer, because others are richer than we supposed? Would our religion be less true, because some of its truths are found in other religions also?

We may, I think, go a step further. Our own self-interest surely would seem to suggest as severe a trial of our own religion as of other religions, nay, even a more severe trial. Our religion has sometimes been compared to a good ship that is to carry us through the waves and tempests of this life to a safe haven. Would it not be wise, therefore, to have it tested, and submitted to the severest trials, before we entrust ourselves and those most dear to us to such a vessel? And remember, all men, except those who take part in the foundation of a new religion, or have been converted from an old to a new faith, have to accept their religious belief on trust, long before they are able to judge for themselves. Hence a child of Mohammedan parents invariably believes in Mohammed and the Korân. An Italian child never doubts the miraculous achievements of the Saints, and follows his mother in kneeling in adoration before the image of the Virgin Mary. And while in all other matters an independent judgment in riper years is encouraged, every kind of influence is used to discourage a free examination of religious dogmas, once engrafted on our intellect in its tenderest stage. A Mohammedan who should renounce the prophet, knows that he risks his life. And a Roman Catholic who should doubt the truth of the legends of the Saints, or look upon the adoration of any image as idolatry, would soon be called a sceptic and an infidel, or, what is even worse, a Protestant. We condemn an examination of our own religion, even though it arises from an honest desire to see with our own eyes the truth which we mean to hold fast; and yet we do not hesitate to send missionaries into all the world, asking the faithful to re-examine their own time-honoured religions. We attack their most sacred convictions, we wound their tenderest feelings, we undermine the belief in which they have been brought up, and we break up the peace and happiness of their homes. And yet, if some learned Jew, like Mendelssohn, if some subtle Brâhman, like Rammohun Roy, aye, even if some outspoken Zulu, like Colenso's friend, turns round on us, asks us to re-examine the date and authorship of the books of the Old or the New Testament, presses us to explain some portions of the Athanasian Creed, or challenges us to produce the evidence on which we also are quite ready to accept certain miracles, we are surprised and offended, forgetting that with regard to these questions we can claim no privilege, no immunity.

Private Judgment.

When I say *we*, I only mean those who have rejected once for all every infallible human authority, whether the infallibility of the Pope, or the infallibility of the Church, or the infallibility of the Bible, or, lastly, even the infallibility of the immediate disciples and apostles of Christ, who, as you know, are the very last to claim such infallibility. If we have once claimed the freedom of the spirit which St. Paul claimed, ' to prove all things and to hold fast that which is good,' we cannot turn back, we cannot say that no one shall prove our own religion, no one shall prove other religions and compare them with our own. We have to choose once for all between freedom and slavery of judgment, and though I do not wish to argue with those who prefer slavery, yet one may remind them that even they, in deliberately choosing slavery, follow their own private judgment, quite as much as others do in choosing freedom. In claiming infallibility for Bible, Popes, or Councils, they claim in reality far greater infallibility for themselves in declaring by their own authority Bible, Popes, or Councils to be infallible.

How easily people deceive themselves with regard to what is private judgment and what is not, may be seen in the case of Cardinal Newman. When he was still a member of the Church of his own country, he wrote, May 5, 1841 (*Apologia*, p. 188):

' We have too great a horror of the principle of private judgment to trust it in so immense a matter as that of changing from one communion to another. We may be cast out of our communion, or it may decree heresy to be truth,—you shall say whether such contingencies are likely; but I do not see other conceivable causes of our leaving the Church in which we were baptised.'

Now between the year 1841 and 1845 the English Church, as far as I know, did neither the one nor the other, it did not invent any new heresy, nor cast out Newman and his friends; and yet—Cardinal Newman followed his private judgment, and submitted to an infallible Pope.

Comparative Study of Religions.

In choosing between Romanism and Protestantism, or in choosing between Christianity and Judaism, or any other religion, we must necessarily compare these religions with our own. I do not mean to say, therefore, that a comparative study of all religions forms part of the duty of every Christian man and woman, but it seems to me that to condemn such studies, and to throw discredit on those who honestly devote themselves to this examination and comparison of all religions, is contrary to the spirit of St. Paul, and contrary to the highest command of Christianity to do unto others as we wish they should do unto us.

Lord Gifford's Foundation.

And yet, do not suppose that those who have entered on this branch of historical research, and in particular those who have accepted the responsibility imposed upon them by Lord Gifford's bequest, are insensible to the dangers and difficulties with which their work is beset. It may be quite true that they are relieved of some part of their responsibility by the very fact that Lord Gifford's bequest has been

accepted by the great Universities of Scotland. It
was quite possible that, under the conditions which
he had attached to it, some of the Universities might
have declined to accept Lord Gifford's bequest. Their
acceptance of the bequest, therefore, implied their
general approval of its objects, and thus became
really more important even than the bequest itself.
They admitted thereby that a treatment of religion
in the spirit prescribed by the founder of these
lectureships, would prove advantageous to the young
students committed to their care, and that nothing
should be kept back from them that had received the
approval of competent scholars.

But it seems right nevertheless to listen to the
objections that have been made against granting a
place among academic studies to the Science of
Religion, and to weigh at all events what has been
said and written against it by men whose judgment
and sincerity cannot be doubted.

Timid Counsels.

There are persons of very sound judgment who,
though they fully approve of a comparative treatment
of religions, and of the freest criticism of our own
religion, still insist that it is wise to keep such studies
for the few. They expressed this opinion years ago in
the case of *Essays and Reviews*, and more recently in
the case of *Lux Mundi*. Such books, they hold,
ought to be written in Latin. Religion, they say, is
common property. It belongs by its very nature to
the young and to the old, to the wise and to the
unwise, to men, women, and children. Unless it fulfils that condition, unless it is open to little children,

as well as to the wisest of the wise, it may be philosophy, it may be absolute truth, but it ceases to be religion. Now in lectures on any other subjects, we are told that the technical character of the language which is employed, restricts their influence to those who can judge for themselves. No one would think of putting restrictions on lectures on botany, because people might learn from what plants they could extract poisons. No one would prevent Professors of chemistry from lecturing to large classes, because some of their pupils might wish to learn how to prepare dynamite. But while every other subject is thus by its very nature restricted to a professional class, we are reminded that a study of religion, or, at all events, an interest in religion, appeals to every human heart, and that a treatment of religion that may be quite harmless, nay, quite legitimate with advanced students and hard-headed thinkers, may prove very hurtful to younger minds, not prepared as yet for such strong diet.

I know quite well that there is some truth in all this. I do not even deny that the use of the Latin language in theological discussions, which are likely to prove a stumbling-block to the uninitiated, had its advantages. But it seems to me perfectly useless to discuss such proposals now. We must learn to accept the times in which we live, and make the best of them. Whatever is now treated of in academic precincts, is preached the next day in the streets, and there is neither palace nor cottage that is not reached by the million arms of the public press. Latin is no longer any protection; I doubt whether it was so altogether even in the middle ages.

The discovery of Copernicus (1473–1543) that the earth moves round the sun and does not form the centre of the universe, may indeed have been kept back for nearly a century, remaining known to those only who could read Latin. But it burst forth all the same in the Italian writings of Galileo (1567–1642), and people soon recovered from the shock, even though deprived of that much cherished conviction that they formed the centre of the universe.

Artificial protection of any kind is out of date in the century in which we live, and in which we must learn to act and to do as much good as we can. To expect that religion could ever be placed again beyond the reach of scientific treatment or honest criticism, shows an utter misapprehension of the signs of the times, and would, after all, be no more than to set up private judgment against private judgment. I believe, on the contrary, that if the inalienable rights of private judgment, that is, of honesty and truth, were more generally recognised, the character of religious controversy would at once be changed. It is restriction that provokes resentment, and thus embitters all discussions on religious topics.

I have had to discuss this question many times with some of the leading theologians of our time. I do not mean with men who simply acted their part on the stage of the world, but with men who were honestly convinced that freedom of thought and freedom of discussion were wrong and mischievous within the sphere of religion, and ought to be restrained by authority.

One of them declared to me that it had been his lot during a long life to read more heresy than any other living man, and he dwelt in the most forcible language on the abyss, both intellectual and moral, into which he had gazed again and again, but from which he had at last turned resolutely away. He considered it his duty for the rest of his life to keep others from the mental agonies through which he himself had passed, and he would have welcomed any measures by which that abyss could have been enclosed, and public discussion of religious problems could have been prevented once for all.

All I could say to him in reply was, if such a terrible abyss really existed, it must have its purpose in the world in which we have been placed, like many other things which entail suffering and agony, and are nevertheless meant to serve a good purpose. To shut our eyes will not remove that abyss, while courage and faith may possibly help to throw a bridge across the dark chasm that seems to separate man from those bright regions for which his heart is always yearning.

When I read a few days ago a letter from Cardinal Newman, which Canon Maccoll has published in the *Contemporary Review* (January, 1891, p. 144), I seemed once more to hear almost the same voice to which I had often listened at Oxford. Speaking of the authors of *Essays and Reviews*, Newman writes : 'Some of them, I trust, were urged by a sincere feeling that it is not right to keep up shams. Yet did they really see the termination, or rather the abyss, to which these speculations lead, surely they would see that, before attempting to sift facts, they ought to make sure that they have a firm hold of true and eternal principles. To unsettle the minds of a generation, when you give them no landmarks and no causeway across the morass, is to undertake a great responsibility.

'The religion of England depends, humanly speaking, on belief in the Bible, the whole Bible, etc., and on the observance of the Calvinistic Sabbath. Let the population begin to doubt in its inspiration and infallibility—where are we? Alas! whole classes do already; but I would not be the man knowingly to introduce scepticism into those portions of the community which are as yet sound. Consider the misery of wives and mothers losing their faith in Scripture; yet I am told this sad process is commencing.'

But the most curious part is, that while Cardinal Newman—he was already a member of the Roman Catholic Church when he wrote this—considers a belief in the plenary inspiration of the whole Bible, the Old as well as the New Testament, and the observance of the Calvinistic Sabbath, essential to the faith of Protestants, he does not think that the Roman Catholic faith requires the same elaborate support.

'The volume in question,' he continues, namely *Essays and Reviews*, 'is levelled at Revelation as a whole, but is especially a blow at the Old Testament. Now the plenary inspiration of Scripture is peculiarly a Protestant question, not a Catholic. We, indeed, devoutly receive the whole Bible as the Word of God; but we receive it on the authority of the Church, and the Church has defined very little as to the aspects under which it comes from God, and the limits of its inspiration. Supposing, for argument sake, that it could be proved that some passage in the Pentateuch about Egyptian history was erroneous; nay, let the universality of the deluge over the globe, or the literal interpretation of Genesis be, for argument sake, disproved, it would not affect a Catholic, for two reasons—(1) Because the Church has not made them points *de fide*, and (2) because not the Bible, but the Church, is to him the oracle of Revelation; so that, though the whole Scripture were miraculously removed from the world as if it had never been, evil and miserable as would be the absence of such a privilege, he would still have enough motives and objects of his faith, whereas to the Protestant the question of Scripture is one of life and death.'

Thus, according to Cardinal Newman, the Roman Catholic may be trusted to criticise the Bible, particularly the Old Testament. He would not be affected if, for argument sake, the universal deluge or the crossing of the Red Sea, could be disproved. And why? Because the Church is to him the oracle of Revelation. And who speaks in the name of the Church? Popes and Cardinals. And who are Popes and Cardinals? Men such as Mr. John Newman himself, who followed his own private judgment in leaving the Church in which he was born, the Church of England, for the Church of Italy. There is no escape, you see, from private judgment, as little as there is from our own shadow.

Another great theologian whom I knew at Oxford, and whose recent death is still in all our memories, would draw in eloquent and touching words the picture of a child sleeping in his cradle, and dreaming happy dreams of God and His angels. Who would wake such a child, he said. I knew full well what he meant. There is certainly no happier life than a life of simple faith, of literal acceptance, of rosy dreams. We must all grant that, if it were possible, nothing would be more perfect. Nay I go further still, and I gladly acknowledge that some of the happiest, and not only some of the happiest, but also some of the best men and women I have known in this life, were those who would have shrunk with horror from questioning a single letter in the Bible, or doubting that a serpent actually spoke to Eve, and an ass to Balaam.

But can we prevent the light of the sun and the noises of the street from waking the happy child from his heavenly dreams? Nay, is it not our duty to wake the child, when the time has come that he should be up and doing, and take his share in the toils of the day? And is it not well for those who for the first time open their eyes and look around, that they should see by their side some who have woke before them, who understand their inquiring looks, and can answer their timid questions, and tell them in the simple-hearted language of our old poet:

> 'There lives more faith in honest doubt,
> Believe me, than in half the creeds.'

No, however excellent the motives of these faint-hearted theologians may be, not only are the remedies which they propose impossible, but it is easy to see that they would prove much more dangerous than the diseases which they are meant to heal. To encourage people, and particularly theologians, not to speak the truth openly, though they know it, must be fatal to every religion. Who could draw the line between the truth that may, and the truth that may not be communicated? I have known theologians, occupying now the highest positions in the Church, who frankly admitted among their own intimate friends, that physical miracles, in the ordinary sense of the word, were once for all impossible, but who would not have considered it right to say so from the pulpit. I do not question their motives nor do I doubt their moral courage, I only question the soundness of their judgment. I feel convinced that to many of their hearers, an open statement of the conviction at which they had themselves arrived would have been far more helpful than many an apologetic sermon. If their own faith in Christianity is not shaken, because they have ceased to believe in miracles as mere miracles, nay, if their belief in Christ's teaching has grown all the stronger since they discarded these crutches, why should it be different with others whom they profess to guide? There exists at present a very wide-spread impression that preachers do not preach all they know, that they will not help others to face the abyss, which all have to face, and that they will not open the shutters to let in the light of the sun and the fresh air of the morning, which we are all meant to breathe; but that they are keeping the truth to themselves, I will not say from any unworthy motives, but from fear that it might do more harm than good to others. To all this I know but one reply. Can there be anything higher and better than truth? Is any kind of religion possible without an unquestioning trust in truth? No one knows what it is to believe who has not learnt to believe in truth, for the sake of truth, and for the sake of truth only. The question of miracles is no longer, as it was in the days of Hume, a mere question of historical evidence. A comparative study of religions has taught us that miracles, instead of being impossible, are really inevitable, that they exist in almost every religion, that they are the natural outcome of what Mr. Gladstone has well called ' imperfect comprehension and imperfect expression.' Why should such well-established results of scientific enquiry be withheld from those whom they most concern, and, what is still worse, why should they reach the people at large, as it were, through unauthorised channels, and not from the mouths of their recognised teachers ?

It ought, I think, to be clearly understood that restrictions on religious discussions have in our days, and in this country, at all events, become perfectly impossible, and that such palliatives as the use of Latin would be simply futile. But for that very reason the question becomes all the more important, what we have a right to expect and to demand from those whose duty it is to treat religious questions.

It has always been considered as one of the essential conditions of civilised life that the religious convictions of every citizen should be respected and protected against insult and injury. Whether a state should recognise and support an established Church, is a question that admits of debate. But what admits of no debate is that the law should prevent or punish any insults offered to individuals or societies on account of their religious convictions. A state in which religious convictions entail civil disabilities, or in which religious professions lead to social advantages, cannot be called a civilised state in the highest sense of the word. Every creed is sacred to those who hold it. Whether a fetish-worshipper calls on his fetish for food and drink, or chastises it if his

prayer is not fulfilled, or whether an atheist exclaims
in despair, ' O God, if there be a God, save my soul,
if I have a soul,' they both hold their belief and their
unbelief sacred, and they have a right to see their
religious convictions, if not respected, at all events
protected against insult. These are no doubt extreme cases, but even in such extreme cases toleration
and charity are far more likely to prove efficient
remedies than scorn and insult. If we can respect a
childlike and even a childish faith, we ought likewise
to learn to respect even a philosophical atheism
which often contains the hidden seeds of the best and
truest faith. We ought never to call a man an
atheist, and say that he does not believe in God, till
we know what kind of God it is that he has been
brought up to believe in, and what kind of God it is
that he rejects, it may be, from the best and highest
motives. We ought never to forget that Socrates was
called an atheist, that the early Christians were all
called atheists [1], that some of the best and greatest
men this world has ever known, have been branded
by that name. Men may deny God for the very sake
of God. You remember what old Plutarch said, that
it was better not to believe in Gods at all, than to
believe in Gods, such as the superstitious believe them
to be. ' I, for my own part,' he continues, ' would

---

[1] Athenagoras (Legatio, 10) gives an elaborate defence of the
Christians against the charge of atheism. ' I have sufficiently
demonstrated,' he says, ' that they are not atheists who believe in
One who is unbegotten, eternal, unseen, impassible, incomprehensible and uncontained ; comprehended by mind and reason only,
invested with ineffable light and beauty and spirit and power, by
whom the universe is brought into being and set in order and held
firm, through the agency of his own Logos.'—(Hatch, *Hibbert Lectures*,
p. 253.)

much rather have men say of me that there never was a Plutarch at all, nor is now, than to say that Plutarch is a man inconstant, fickle, easily moved to anger, revengeful for trifling provocations, vexed at small things [1].'

This is as true to-day as it was in Plutarch's time, and it is right that it should be said, however much it may offend certain ears. One of our greatest theologians has not hesitated to say: 'God is a great word. He who feels this and knows it, will judge more mildly and justly of those who confess that they dare not say, "I believe in God [2]."'

When people speak in a truly honest and kind spirit, they will understand one another, however widely they may stand apart in their religious opinions. But for that object it is absolutely necessary that discussion and controversy should be completely unfettered. You cannot have a good fight or a fair fight, if you tie the hands of the two combatants; least of all, if you tie the hands of one combatant only.

Lord Gifford's Conditions.

It was the object of Lord Gifford's bequest to untie the hands of combatants, but at the same time to fix the conditions on which the combat should be conducted. What was wanted for that purpose, as he declared in his will, were 'reverent men, true thinkers, sincere lovers, and earnest enquirers after truth.' These words are not used at random. Each sentence seems to have been carefully chosen and attentively weighed

---

[1] Sir John Lubbock, *Pleasures of Life*, ii. p. 217.
[2] Rothe, in his *Stille Stunden*.

by him. He felt that religion was not a subject like other subjects, but that, whether on account of its age or owing to its momentous bearing on human welfare, it ought to be treated with due care and respect. *Reverence* alone, however, would not be sufficient, but should be joined with true thinking. *True thinking* means free thinking, thinking following its own laws, and unswayed by anything else. Think what thinking would be, if it were not free! But even this would not suffice. There ought to be not only loyal submission to the laws of thought, there ought to be a *sincere love*, a deep-felt yearning for truth. And lastly, that love should not manifest itself in impatient and fanatical outbursts, but in *earnest enquiry*, in patient study, in long-continued research.

Men who have passed through these four stages are not likely to give offence to others or to be easily offended themselves. I am sorry to have to confess it, but among the many lessons which a comparative study of religions teaches us, there is one that seems very humiliating, namely, that religious intolerance has been much more common in modern than in ancient times. I know the excuse which is made for this. It is said, that as our convictions become deeper and stronger, our intolerance of falsehood also must assume a more intense character, and that it would show an utter want of earnestness if it were otherwise. There may be some truth in this, but it is a dangerous truth. It is the same truth which led the Inquisition to order the burning of heretics, because it would be better for their souls, and which inflicted in our own times a less violent, though perhaps a not less painful martyrdom on such 'reverent men, true thinkers, sincere lovers, and earnest inquirers after truth' as Dean Stanley, Bishop Colenso, and Charles Kingsley.

Toleration in other Religions.

Let us see how the problem of toleration has been solved in other religions. Perhaps on this point also a comparative study of religions may have some useful lessons for us. For the difficulty is one that besets them all. The religion of the young can never be quite the same as that of the old, nor the religion of the educated the same as that of the ignorant. We all know it. Bishop Berkeley was a Christian; so is Mr. Spurgeon. But think of the gulf that separates the two. And yet it is the object of religion that it should serve as a bond between all classes, and should supply a language in which all should be able to join without dishonesty.

Toleration in Ancient India.

I tried to explain on a former occasion how this problem has been solved in ancient India. The Indian Law recognised four stages in the life of every man. The first stage was that of the pupil, which lasted till a man had reached the age of manhood. A pupil had to show implicit obedience to his superiors, and to learn without questioning the religion of his forefathers.

The second stage was that of the householder, which lasted till a man had grown-up children. A householder had to marry, to earn his living, to bring up a family, to perform daily sacrifices, and all this again without questioning the teaching of his religious guides.

Then followed the third stage, that of the dweller in the forest, the Vânaprastha, the ascetic. In that stage a man was not only released from his household duties, but his sacrificial observances also were much reduced, and he was allowed to indulge in the freest philosophical speculations, speculations which often ran counter to the theological system of the Brâhmans, and ended by replacing religion altogether by philosophy.

The last stage was that of the hermit, who withdrew himself from all human society, and willingly went to meet his death, wherever it would meet him [1].

To us it seems difficult to understand how a religion, not only so full of different shades of thought, but containing elements of the most decidedly antagonistic character, could have lasted; how neither the father should have contemptuously looked down on his son who performed sacrifices which he himself had surrendered as useless, nay as mischievous, nor the son should have abhorred his father who had thrown off his belief in the gods or devas, and adopted a philosophy that taught the existence of something higher and better than all these gods. And yet this system seems to have answered for a long time. Recognising the fact that the mind of man changes from childhood to old age, it allowed the greatest freedom to old age, provided always that old age had been preceded by the fulfilment of all the duties of a pater familias, and by an unquestioning submission to the discipline of youth.

I do not say that we see here the best solution of our problem. I only call your attention to it as one

---

[1] *Hibbert Lectures*, p. 348.

out of many solutions, based on the principle of toleration for diversities of religious faith, which are inevitable so long as human nature remains what it is, and what it always has been. No society can exist without different classes. Our own society at all events, as it has grown up during thousands of years, cannot exist without them. I do not think so much of classes differing from each other by wealth or titles. I mean classes differing by education, and consequently by culture and intelligence. It is impossible to expect that these different classes, differing from each other so much in all other respects, in their education, their occupations, their manners, their tastes, their thoughts and language, should not differ in their religion also. It is the ignoring of this simple fact which has wrought so much mischief. It has led to hypocrisy on one side, and to an unreasoning dogmatism on the other. I know there are some who hold that, however much people may differ in other respects, they are all alike in religion. We are told that the faith of the child is as good as that of the sage; and that an old ignorant woman, who cannot even read her Bible, may be a far better Christian than a young curate who has just taken a first class at Oxford. It is the old story of using words in different senses, or ignoring what Mr. Gladstone calls 'the changes which the lapse of time works in the sense of words.' So far as practical religion goes, so far as doing good is concerned, no doubt many a poor widow who throws in her two mites is better than the scribes and rich men who cast their gifts into the treasury. And who that ever saw an innocent child dying—stretching her arms towards angel-faces above, and giving her last parting look to all whom she loved on earth—can doubt that of such is the kingdom of heaven ?

But we are speaking of something quite different, though it is called by the same name of religion. We are speaking of what educated and highly educated men believe, what conceptions they form of the Deity, of the relation of the human to the divine, of the true meaning of revelation, of the true nature of miracles, nay of the date of MSS., and the value of the various readings in the Hebrew or Greek text of the Bible. All these are questions which hardly exist for millions of human beings, of which they need not take any cognisance at all, but which nevertheless to those for whom they once exist, are questions of the deepest import. It is on these questions that we must claim the same freedom which even the most orthodox of Brâhmans allowed to their fellow-creatures. Only, we must claim it, not only for the aged who retire into the forest, but for all whose mind has been awakened, and who mean to do their duty in this life.

Esoteric and Exoteric Religion.

I know how strong a feeling there is against anything like a religion for the few, different from the religion for the many. An esoteric religion seems to be a religion that cannot show itself, that is afraid of the light, that is, in fact, dishonest. But so far from being dishonest, the distinction between a higher and a lower form of religion is in reality the only honest recognition of the realities of life. If to a philosophic mind religion is a spiritual love of God and the joy of his full consciousness of the spirit of God within him,

what meaning can such words convey to the millions
of human beings who nevertheless want a religion, a
positive, authoritative, or revealed religion, to teach
them that there is a God, and that His commands must
be obeyed without questioning.   And do not think
that this appeal for freedom of conscience comes from
the educated laity only.   The educated clergy are
sighing for it even more.   Let me quote the words of
one whose right to speak on this subject can hardly
be questioned, considering that thousands of families
in England have confided to him the care of their
sons, just at that critical period of life when childish
faith has to grow into manly conviction; considering
also that one of our most orthodox Bishops has
entrusted him with the examination of candidates for
Holy Orders, I mean the Ven. James M. Wilson, Archdeacon of Manchester, the late Headmaster of Clifton,
Examining Chaplain to Bishop Moorhouse, and Private
Chaplain to Bishop Temple.

'I say at once,' he writes[1], 'that we, educated
Christian men, have a distinct duty to perform in
this direction, always remembering the great law of
charity.   I think that the Church ought to provide
meat for her strong men, as well as secure that her
babes shall get milk.   One of our failures is in this
duty.   I do not think that it can be denied that the
popular Christianity of the day, whether among
priests or people, in church or chapel, is for the most
part far less tolerant than is the Spirit of Christ, or of
St. Paul, or of the great minds among Christians of all
ages.   That it should be so among the people is for

---

[1] *Essays and Addresses*, p. 162.

the present unavoidable. It ought not to be so, and it need not be so among the educated laity and clergy, and they ought not to permit the intolerance of ignorance to pass unchecked, as it often does. We clergy ought to stem the tide more bravely than we do, and we ought to have done so in time past. We, as a rule, regard differences of opinion on speculative questions, and even on the terms in which we choose to present them, as very serious matters; and expect old and young, philosophers and simple men and women, to accept unquestioningly the same terms. I think this is wrong. I do not at all think that this is the mind of Christ. Much may be done to claim for more abstract and philosophic views, and especially for all views that profess to rise directly from the study of facts and promote rightness of conduct, a place within the recognised boundaries of the Christian Church.'

Then, after dwelling on the value of the discipline of established forms, he continues:—

' Why should we fail to recognise the fact that man ought to grow, and does grow, not only in stature and favour with God and man, but in wisdom also? No Church is honest which does not recognise that fact, and which is not anxious to secure a place of safety, nay, of honour, to those who have grown in goodness and wisdom and understanding, in the gifts of the Spirit, and have thus attained to a truer insight into the nature of religion than can, for the present at least, be reached by the majority of educated people. A Church which declines to recognise the right of the Few who are " fond of wisdom," not only to be tolerated, but to be respected, must become stagnant; and if it actually encourages the ignorant intolerance

of the multitude, if it identifies itself with the nar-
rowness and exclusiveness of the uneducated or half-
educated masses, it will drive its best champions into
silence, and many who under proper guidance might
have fought a good fight and done noble work for the
Church, into atheism, or what is still worse, into
hypocrisy. . . . When the Few cease to differ from the
Many, we may have uniformity and peace, but we
may also have dishonesty and death. When the Few
are respected by the Many, we may hope to have
again in the Church a true spiritual, that is, intellectual aristocracy—a small heart throbbing within, but
giving life and strength to the large body of Christian
people without.'

I have quoted this important passage, not only on
account of the authority which justly belongs to Mr.
James M. Wilson as a clergyman, but because of his
unrivalled experience as a schoolmaster. There is,
I believe, no argument that appeals so strongly to
every heart as the dangers that may arise, if the faith
of the young is undermined. Who does not remember the words of Christ: 'And whosoever shall offend
one of these little ones that believe in me, it is better
for him that a millstone were hanged about his neck
and he were cast into the sea.' I quote once more
from the Headmaster of Clifton (l. c., p. 164) :—

'I have spoken of the childhood of the individual
being like the childhood of the race, and said that,
therefore, the education of the one will follow the
lines of education of the other. And this is true, but
with some important qualifications. The child of the
present century is not in all respects like the man of
a bygone century. And the child may pass very

rapidly through the elementary stages; and we do him positive injury, we dispose him to reject religion, if we prolong these stages artificially, for in that case we make him identify religion with that which he will grow out of. Further: As education advances, this transition will inevitably become more rapid. It is more rapid now than most people think. . . . I feel quite sure that, as a rule, religious teachers postpone the higher teaching too long.'

Religious Education of Children.

Nothing, I believe, is so dangerous to the healthy growth of a child's mind as the impression that his parents and teachers withhold something, or are not quite honest when they speak of the Bible. The fact that children ask such perplexing questions about miracles in the Bible, shows that their minds are awake, and that everything is not exactly like what it ought to be. A child that had been stung by a wasp, asked the very natural question whether Noah in the ark was not stung by wasps. And what do you think the answer was? 'No, my child, the wasps were kept in glass bottles.' In these days, when boys see every day on the walls of their school collections of geological specimens, and maps representing the successive strata of the earth, we need not wonder at what Mr. James M. Wilson tells us of his own boy, when nine years old. He was reading the first chapter of Genesis to his mother, and she explained to him that the days were long periods of time. 'Why, mamma, I should think I knew that,' was his remark.

The human mind, and more particularly the child's mind, is so constituted, I believe, that it cannot take in more than what it is prepared for. If any one were to say to a little child, who had just repeated the Lord's Prayer, that Heaven was not the blue sky, the child would listen, but would turn up his hands and his eyes just the same to the clouds above.

I have often wondered what passes in the mind of a young man when he looks for the first time at his 'Articles of Religion,' and reads in the very first article that 'God is a being without body, without parts, and without passions.' Such a formula was intelligible when it was uttered for the first time by a philosopher in whose mind the Aryan thought of Greece and the Semitic thought of Judaea were closely blended. This is what Philo, the contemporary of Christ, says on the concept of God:—He is 'without body, parts, or passions; without feet, for whither should He walk who fills all things; without hands, for from whom should He receive anything who possesses all things; without eyes, for how should He need eyes who made the light.' But what meaning can all this convey to the unformed mind of a young boy? In its negative character, and as a warning against too human a conception of the deity this formula may be useful to him; but when he tries to realise it with all its positive consequences, he would shudder at the crippled image of the Godhead, thus brought before his mind. What would remain if he deducted from his early conceptions or rather imaginations of God everything that we call body or shape, everything that we call parts or distinguishable elements, everything that we call passions, not only wrath and indignation, which are so often ascribed to God, but likewise pity and love, which are passions in the true sense of the word, but which we can never separate from our human ideal of the Godhead.

Growth of the Mind.

My impression is that a boy's faith is not affected by any of these difficulties, till his understanding has grown strong enough to grapple with them. Though he would repeat the words that God was without body, parts, and passions, he would never think of Him as without those loving and pitying eyes without which God would be to him an eyeless and blind idol, not a living and loving God. The mind of a child, of a boy, and of grown-up men and women too, is protected against many dangers till the time comes when they are strong enough to face them, strong enough to reason and to say, that the words of the Article must be taken in a negative (*theologia negativa*), not in a positive sense (*theologia affirmativa*); and that, though we may deny that God has body, parts, and passions like human beings, we should never attempt to form any positive conception of Him according to this dangerous formula.

It may be quite right to guard against dangers, whether real or imaginary, so long as it is possible. But when it is no longer possible, I feel certain the right thing is to face an enemy bravely. Very often the enemy will turn out a friend in disguise. The use of Latin in all theological discussions would be a mere sham defence, and any restriction on free discussion would provoke a resistance ten times worse. We cannot be far wrong, if we are only quite honest, but if we are once not quite honest over a few things, we shall soon become dishonest over many things. As I said at the beginning of my lecture, I say once more at the end: In lecturing on religion, even on Natural Religion, we must look neither right nor left, but look all facts straight in the face, to see whether they are facts or not, and, if they are facts, to find out what they mean.

LECTURE II.

ON TOLERATION.

Bright Side of all Religions.

I HAVE often been told that in treating of the ancient religions of the world, I dwell too much on their bright side, and thus draw too favourable, that is, not quite correct a picture of them. I believe to a certain extent I must plead guilty to this indictment. One naturally feels more attracted by one bright jewel than by the heap of rubbish in which it is hidden; and, more than that, one is inclined to consider what is false and bad in any religion, whether our own or that of others, as a mere corruption, as something that ought not to be, and that will pass away; while what is good and true in all of them seems to constitute their true and permanent nature. You know the argument of the ancient Greek philosophers, when they were reminded of the often repulsive character of their gods. Nothing, they said, can be true of the gods that is not worthy of them.

However, I admit my weakness, and the only excuse I can plead is, that these same religions have so often been drawn from their dark and hideous side that there is less danger perhaps of people at large forming too favourable an opinion of them, if now and then I should have spoken too well of them. Perhaps I have given the Brâhmans too much credit for their tolerant spirit, and for allowing great latitude of philosophical speculation to the older and more enlightened members of their villages. They were able to solve a problem which to us seems insoluble, because they lived in a state of society totally different from our own. The Âranyakas or Forest-books, which contained the oldest Upanishads, the philosophical treatises of the Veda, were to be known by those only who had retired from active life into the forest, and the teaching contained in them was often called rahasya or secret. In ancient India there were no printed books, not even manuscripts, but all teaching was oral. Nothing was easier, therefore, for those who were the guardians or depositaries of the higher truth of religion than to keep it from all except those who were considered fit to receive it, men who had left the world, men living in the forest. So long as this was possible, it may have been right. What I doubt is whether in our time the few who, even while living in the world, have retired into their own forest, freed from many fetters which they had to wear in their youth and manhood, would be treated with the same forbearance, aye, reverence, with which the forest-sages, the Vânaprasthas, were treated by the students, the householders, and the very priests of ancient India.

Danger of keeping Truth secret.

But we shall see that even in India this device of keeping the highest truths carefully hidden, not only from younger students, but also from grown-up men, householders and fathers of families, broke down in the end, nay, proved one of the main causes of the downfall of Brâhmanism.

In a former course of lectures I explained to you how after a time Brâhmanism was supplanted by Buddhism, and how this Indian Buddhism was really the inevitable consequence of the old system of the four Âsramas or the successive stages in which the life of an orthodox Brâhman was supposed to be passed. Buddha, and those who followed him, seem simply to have asked the question why, if the real truth is reached in the third Âsrama only, should people spend their youth and their manhood in learning and practising a religion which was pre-liminary only to a higher and truer knowledge, and in performing sacrifices which were a snare and delusion rather than a means of grace[1]. Those who joined the Buddhist brotherhood looked upon the long apprenticeship spent in the study of the Veda, on the fulfilment of the duties of a householder, and on the performance of sacrifices, as mere waste. They left the world at once and listened to the highest truth, such as Buddha had discovered and taught it.

Antecedents of Buddhism.

The first signs of this rebellious spirit against the old system are already visible in the Brâhmanic literature. I shall read you an extract from the Mahâbhârata which has been well translated by my old friend, Dr. John Muir. It is a dialogue between

---

[1] *Hibbert Lectures*, p. 359.

a father and a son. The father exhorts his son to
keep to the old paths, to serve his apprenticeship,
then to marry and to perform the regular sacrifices,
and at the end of his life only to seek for the hidden
wisdom.   The son, however, does not see why he
should reach the highest goal on so circuitous a road,
and decides to leave the world at once, in order to
find rest where alone it can be found. The exact
date of the dialogue may be doubtful, but its spirit is
certainly pre-buddhistic.

Dialogue between Father and Son.

Son.

Since soon the days of mortals end,
How ought the wise their lives to spend ?
What course should I, to duty true,
My sire, from youth to age pursue ?

Father.

Begin thy course with study; store
The mind with holy Vedic lore.
That stage completed, seek a wife,
And gain the fruit of wedded life,
A race of sons, by rites to seal,
When thou art gone, thy spirit's weal.
Then light the sacred fires, and bring
The gods a fitting offering.
When age draws nigh, the world forsake,
Thy chosen home the forest make;
And there, a calm, ascetic sage,
A war against thy passions wage,
That, cleansed from every earthly stain,
Thou may'st supreme perfection gain.

SON.

And art thou then, my father, wise,
When thou dost such a life advise?
What wise or thoughtful man delights
In formal studies, empty rites?
Should such pursuits and thoughts engage
A mortal more than half his age?
The world is ever vexed, distressed;
The noiseless robbers never rest.

FATHER.

Tell how the world is vexed, distressed;
What noiseless robbers never rest?
What means thy dark, alarming speech?
In plainer words thy meaning teach.

SON.

The world is vexed by death; decay
The frames of mortals wears away.
Dost thou not note the circling flight
Of those still robbers, day and night,
With stealthy tread which hurrying past,
Steal all our lives away at last?
When well I know how death infests
This world of woe, and never rests,
How can I still, in thoughtless mood,
Confide in future earthly good?
Since life with every night that goes,
Still shorter, and yet shorter grows,
Must not the wise perceive how vain
Are all their days that yet remain?
We, whom life's narrow bounds confine,
Like fish in shallow water, pine.

No moment lose; in serious mood
Begin at once to practise good;

To-morrow's task to-day conclude ;
The evening's work complete at noon :—
No duty can be done too soon.
Who knows whom death may seize to-night,
And who shall see the morning light ?
And death will never stop to ask,
If thou hast done, or not, thy task.
While yet a youth, from folly cease ;
Through virtue seek for calm and peace.
So shalt thou here attain renown,
And future bliss thy lot shall crown.

As soon as men are born, decay
And death begin to haunt their way.
How can'st thou, thoughtless, careless, rest,
When endless woes thy life infest ;
When pains and pangs thy strength consume,—
Thy frame to dissolution doom ?

Forsake the busy haunts of men,
For there has death his favourite den.
In lonely forests seek thy home,
For there the gods delight to roam.

Fast bound by old attachment's spell,
Men love amid their kin to dwell.
This bond the sage asunder tears ;
The fool to rend it never cares.

Thou dost advise that I should please
With sacrifice the deities.
Such rites I disregard as vain ;
Through these can none perfection gain.
Why sate the gods, at cruel feasts,
With flesh and blood of slaughtered beasts ?
Far other sacrifices I
Will offer unremittingly ;
The sacrifice of calm, of truth,
The sacrifice of peace, of ruth,

Of life serenely, purely, spent,
Of thought profound on Brahma bent.
Who offers these, may death defy,
And hope for immortality.
   And then thou say'st that I should wed,
And sons should gain to tend me, dead,
By offering pious gifts, to seal,
When I am gone, my spirit's weal.
But I shall ask no pious zeal
Of sons to guard my future weal.
No child of mine shall ever boast
His rites have saved his father's ghost.
Of mine own bliss I'll pay the price,
And be myself my sacrifice.

Buddhism originally a Brâhmanic Sect.

Between this view of life and that of the Buddhists
the difference is very small. At first the followers
of Buddha seem to have been but one out of many
religious brotherhoods with which India has abounded
at all times. We only know a few of them, because
we know so little of ancient India, and all we know
is taken from two or three literatures, that of the
Brâhmans, that of the Buddhists, and that of the
Gainas. We must not imagine, however, that these
three literatures, or what remains of them, represented
at any time the whole intellectual and religious life
of India. India is as large as Europe, without Russia,
and its population is over 200 millions, most of them
scattered in villages. Many of these villages probably
never heard the name of the Veda, or the Tripitaka, or
the Aṅgas. We are told that even now there are
people in India who have never seen a white man.

India is swarming with innumerable sects, and has always been a very hotbed of religious ideas. It was Cousin, the great French philosopher, whose knowledge of the history of European philosophy was probably unrivalled, who declared that India contained the whole history of philosophy in a nut-shell. And yet philosophers will continue to write on philosophical questions, as if Kapila and Kanâda had never existed. And if India contains the history of philosophy in a nut-shell, it certainly is richer in material for the history of religion than any other country. No phase of religion, from the coarsest superstition to the most sublime enlightenment, is unrepresented in that country. And yet theologians will write on religious questions, as if the Vedas, the Pitakas, the Angas, the Purânas, and Tantras had never existed.

Religious Discussions.

It stands to reason that in a country swarming with religious sects like India, there must have been discussion and controversy on religious topics. And so there was from the earliest times. We read in the Upanishads of disputants who were ready to stake their heads, if they should be worsted by argument. Nor need we wonder that there should have been differences of opinion, represented by different schools. We saw how in the Veda there stand side by side the most transparent natural polytheism in the hymns, the most minute and unmeaning ritualism in the Brâhmanas, and the most subtle theosophy in the Upanishads. I do not doubt that these three strata represent originally three successive stages of historical growth; but so long as we know anything of India, we find hymns, Brâhma*n*as, and Upanishads co-existing, and united under the common name of Veda, the Veda being recognised, not only as the highest authority on all religious questions, but as divine revelation in the fullest sense of that word. Remember then that the Vedic hymns are addressed to a number of gods of whom sometimes one, sometimes another is represented as supreme; remember that in the Brâhma*n*as an enormous number of daily, monthly, quarterly, semestrial, and annual sacrifices are enjoined as the only means of salvation, whether they be offered to single gods or to Pra*g*âpati, the lord of creation; remember that the Upanishads, generally integral portions of these very Brâhma*n*as, teach in the clearest way that all the gods of the Veda are but names of one Supreme Being, whether we call it Brahman, or Âtman; that sacrificial acts, so far from helping man, are a snare and delusion, so long as he expects any reward for them, and that true salvation can be gained by knowledge only, by knowledge of the human self and its true relation to the Highest Self. All these opinions were upheld by certain teachers, and in their schools the minutest differences of opinion on religious ceremonial, and philosophical questions were discussed by the Brâhmans. Yet all this was done peacefully and quietly, and we hear of no persecutions on account of differences of opinion.

When Buddhism and *G*ainism arose, about 500 B.C. the Brâhmans had to defend their views against those of the new sects, the new sects criticised the old teaching of the Brâhmans, and very soon various teachers among Buddhists and *G*ainas began to differ one from another.

We read, for instance, in the Buddhist scriptures,
of several teachers, the contemporaries and rivals of
Buddha, the best known being the Niga*nth*a Nâtaputta, who has been recognised as the founder of the
*G*aina sect, Pûra*n*a Kassapa, Makkhali of the cattle-
pen (gosâla), A*g*ita with the garment of hair, Ka*kk*âyan
of the Pakudha tree, and Sa*ñg*aya, the son of the
Bela*tth*a, the slave-girl[1]. We hear of controversies
between them; and that even the imperturbable Buddha could use cutting words in these discussions, we
may gather from what on one occasion he said of
Makkhali of the cattle-pen : 'O ye disciples, as of all
woven garments a garment of hair is deemed the
worst, a garment of hair being cold in cold weather,
hot in heat, of a dirty colour, of a bad smell, and
rough to the touch, so, my disciples, of all doctrines
of other ascetics and Brâhmans the doctrine of
Makkhali is deemed the worst[2].' In the canonical
books of the *G*ainas also we read of Gosâla, the son
of Makkhali[3], being defeated in disputation by
Mahâvîra Nâtaputta.

But though during Buddha's life we hear of such
discussions, sometimes bitter discussions, between him
and his disciples and other teachers, we never hear of
persecutions on the side of the Brâhmans, nor of any
strong hostility on the side of the Buddhists. People
disputed, but they tolerated each other ; they agreed
to differ.

---

[1] See Mahâ-parinibbâna-sutta, V.60, as translated by Rhys Davids,
in *Sacred Books of the East*, vol. xi. p. 106. Others take Gosâla as a proper
name, the Sk. Gosâla.

[2] Oldenberg, Buddha, p. 69.

[3] *G*aina-sûtras, translated by Jacobi, *Sacred Books of the East*, vol.
xxii. Introd. p. xvi.

After a time, however, Buddhism seems to have spread very rapidly, and to have led to great social and political changes. The dynasty founded by *K*andragupta, at the time of Alexander the Great, was that of a pretender, a kind of Napoléon, not belonging by birth to the royal caste, and therefore bidding for popular support, wherever he could find it. It is possible that the Buddhists were more ready to recognise and support him than the orthodox Brâhmans. Anyhow, under the reign of his grandson, king Asoka (259–222 B. C.), we see the followers of Buddha not only recognised, but patronised by the king, and we hear of a great Council held under his auspices to settle the sacred canon of the Buddhists.

Toleration preached by Buddhism.

In some respects Buddhism may be called a kind of Protestantism directed against Brâhmanism, and we know that neither those who protest nor those who are protested against, are generally distinguished by mutual love and charity. The first authentic evidence of the political and social changes produced by the spreading of Buddhism in India, we have in those wonderful inscriptions of king Asoka, which are scattered over the whole of his dominions. They have suffered, no doubt, during the more than two thousand years that they have been exposed to the climate of India; but, as they exist in many copies, their text has been restored, they have been published and interpreted, and we can now read them exactly as they were read by the subjects of king Asoka, whether Buddhists or Brâhmans. Their decipherment is due to the combined labours of Prinsep,

Burnouf, Wilson, Norris, Bühler, and Senart. If then we remember that Asoka was a kind of Constantine, who owed much of his power to the support which he received from the new religion, or, if you like, a kind of Henry VIII, hated by all who suffered under the new reform, you will be surprised to see how much more of true Christian charity was shown by this Buddhist king in the third century B. C. than by Constantine in the fourth, or by Henry VIII in the sixteenth century.

The Edicts of Asoka.

It may be true that the idea of putting up public inscriptions struck the Indian mind for the first time when Greek ideas had reached India after Alexander's conquests. But when Asoka had his inscriptions engraved on rocks and pillars, it was not in order to perpetuate his name or the names of his ancestors, it was not to glorify his own origin; it was chiefly to preach toleration for all creeds. Thus he says in his Seventh Edict [1] :

' The king Piyadasi, dear to the gods, desires that all sects should dwell (in peace) everywhere; for they all desire the control of the senses and purity of mind. Men, however, have different wishes and different passions; they will perform the whole or a part only (of what they ought to do). But even he whose charity is not abundant, may surely always possess control of the senses, purity of mind, gratitude, and loyalty [2].'

---

[1] Senart, *Les inscriptions de Piyadasi*, Paris, 1881, vol. i. p. 174. Bühler, *Zeitschrift der D. M. G.*, xxxvii. p. 279.

[2] Bühler takes nîke, not for nityam, but for nîka, low, and

And again, in his Twelfth Edict (l. c., p. 251), he says: 'The king Piyadasi, dear to the gods, honours all sects, those of hermits and those of householders, he honours them by alms and by different kinds of worship. But the king, dear to the gods, does not value alms and worship as much as the increase of essentials. And[1] the increase of essentials does not differ much in different sects ; on the contrary, the true foundation of every one consists in the bridling of the tongue, so that neither should there be praising of one's own sect, nor disparagement of other sects, without a cause ; and whenever there is cause, it should be moderate[2]. The religions of others may even be praised for any given reason[3]. In this manner a man may much advantage his own sect, and at the same time benefit that of others ; while if he acts otherwise, he damages his own sect and injures that of others. For whosoever exalts his own sect and disparages all others from a strong devotion to his own sect, but, in truth, from a wish that it should be rendered pre-eminent, he will, in this wise, injure his own sect much more. Therefore a mutual understanding is best, that all should listen to the teaching of others, and wish to listen. This is indeed the wish of the king, dear to the gods, that all sects should listen much, and be possessed of pure doctrines. And all who belong to this or to that

translates : ' Even in a low person, to whom great liberality is not (possible), control of the senses, purification of the heart, gratitude, and loyalty are (something) beautiful.'

[1] Bühler translates : 'The increase of the kernel of all sects (happiness) in different ways ; but its root is prudence in speech.'

[2] Here I follow Bühler's translation.

[3] According to Bühler's conjecture, tena tena pakalanena.

sect, should have it said to them that the king, dear
to the gods, does not value alms and worship as much
as the increase of essentials, and that respect should
be shown to all sects [1].'

The Tolerant Spirit of Aṣoka.

The exact meaning of these edicts, which king
Asoka had engraved on rocks and pillars in different
parts of his kingdom, is not always easy to discover,
nor easy to express in our modern terminology. Still,
we cannot be mistaken in giving him credit for a
most tolerant spirit which finds but few parallels in
ancient or modern history. He had recognised what
many find so difficult to recognise even now, that we
must distinguish between what is essential in all
religions, what Asoka calls the sâra or sap, and what
is not. The number of religious and philosophical
sects prevalent in India during the third century
before our era must have been very considerable, and
on some points their differences were no doubt very
great. But Asoka gives them all credit for incul-
cating the same lesson, namely, control of the passions,
purity of mind, gratitude, and loyalty. And think
what would be gained, if these four points were really
gained by any religion! And when he comes to what
he calls the root or life-spring of religion, he finds
it in mutual forbearance, and more particularly in the
bridling of the tongue, as if anticipating the well-

---

[1] Bühler translates the last line by : 'as that there should be an
increase of the kernel with all sects, and a considerable one,' taking
bahukâ as an adjective referring to sâravadhi.

Professor Bühler has lately given a new translation of this twelfth
edict from the Shâhbhâzgari version, which differs in some passages
from the version given in the text.

known words : 'If any man among you seem to be religious, and bridleth not his tongue, but deceiveth his own heart, this man's religion is vain[1].'

I doubt whether any other religion could produce such royal edicts in favour of mutual toleration. They are one of the brightest pages in the history of India, and I thought it right to make you acquainted with them, because they show that a comparative study of religions has some important lessons to teach, even to us. If therefore I may sometimes seem to speak too favourably of some of these religions, may I not appeal to the words of king Asoka: 'For whosoever exalts his own faith and disparages all others from a strong devotion to his own, he will injure his own faith.' And again: 'The true foundation of every faith consists in bridling the tongue, so that there should be neither a praising of one's own religion, nor disparagement of others.'

Disappearance of Buddhism in India.

Whether these edicts of Asoka were always obeyed, is another question; but even as an aspiration, they deserve our respect. History, so far as we can speak of history in India, certainly seems to teach that the sentiments of forbearance and brotherly love, inculcated in these edicts, have not always been obeyed by the rulers and by the people of that country. The ruins of Buddhist monasteries, tombs, monuments, and pillars, scattered over the whole of India, tell a terrible tale. For some centuries the Buddhist religion must have ruled supreme in India. During the period covered by the travels of the Chinese pilgrims,

[1] Ep. St. James, i. 26.

from 400 to 700, though the kings still preached toleration, and encouraged peaceful congresses for the discussion of religious questions, we hear already of many Vihâras or monasteries being deserted, of many Stûpas, or pillars, lying prostrate. How Buddhism was exterminated in India, we shall never know. But the fact remains that Buddhism exists no longer as an Indian religion. It lives in Ceylon, from whence it has spread in its southern branch to Burma and Siam, and it lives in Nepal, from whence in its northern branch it spread to Tibet, Mongolia, China, and Japan. But in India proper Buddhism has ceased to exist, and the religious census returns no Buddhists except as strangers and pilgrims in their Holy Land, the birth-place of Buddha.

So much for king Asoka, the great ruler of India in the third century B.C. We have to remember so many kings for their intolerance. Let us give to king Asoka a niche in our memory for his tolerant spirit, for his benevolence, his large-heartedness,—for that broad and wide view of religion which in our days is so often stigmatised as latitudinarianism.

It seems often to be supposed that if we praise one religion, we tacitly blame others. That is not so. If I call Buddhism tolerant, I do not mean to imply that Christianity is intolerant. Some who call themselves Christians may be intolerant, but the spirit of Christianity itself is not so. Those who so often quote the words (Matth. xii. 30), ' He that is not with me, is against me,' forget the words (Mark ix. 40), ' For he that is not against us, is on our part.'

Toleration in the Jewish Religion.

The greatest minds, whatever their religion, have always been the most tolerant and charitable. We often see how the founders of new religions endeavoured to retain all that was good and true in the religions from which they seceded. They came to fulfil, not to destroy.

Even the Jewish religion, which is often represented as very intolerant, was not so from the first. The Mosaic Law commanded that the stranger should not be oppressed—'for you know the heart of a stranger, seeing you were strangers in the land of Egypt.' The Jews were told: ' Ye shall have one law as well for the stranger as for one of your own country.' Now in the eyes of a Jew a stranger was a man who worshipped false gods, and yet Moses claimed toleration and protection for him.

It was owing to political circumstances that the Jewish religion became in time so strongly national and exclusive, and it was the influence of the Rabbis that imparted to it in later times so narrow-minded and dogmatic a character.

Still, there were Rabbis and Rabbis, and some of them would, I believe, put the most enlightened of our Biblical critics to shame by the tolerant spirit in which they treat the most widely-differing interpretations of the Old Testament. Thus it is laid down in the Talmud [1] as a general principle of interpretation, ' that the Sacred Scriptures speak in a language that should be intelligible to men.' A living Rabbi, Dr. Fürst,

---

[1] Maccoth, 12 a ; Kiddushin, 17 b.

remarks on this that 'if the Bible speaks of the four ends of the earth, which rests on its pillars, or of the sky stretched out like a tent, or of the sun as running his course like a hero round the earth,' the Jews in ancient times were far from seeing in such expressions matters of fact which science was not allowed to question or to reject. People said that the Scripture used expressions which should be intelligible to men such as they were at the time[1]. No one was called a heretic because he did not believe in the pillars on which the earth was said to rest.

With us also, when children are taught to pray to their Father in heaven, the only idea which they, as children, can connect with heaven, is the blue sky. This is so during childhood, and it has been so during the childhood of the human race. The Romans called the gods *superi*, those above. They spoke of them naturally as descending from the clouds to the earth, and they spoke of the favourites of their gods as having been lifted up to heaven. Our own word heaven is derived from heaving, and meant originally what had been heaved on high. We know all this— we know it is inevitable, and we do not blame children when they retain for a time these childish ideas, inherited from the childhood of our race.

But, to judge from some recent theological controversies, the question seems no longer to be whether we can tolerate this language of children, but whether the children—children whether in age or in knowledge—will tolerate us.

---

[1] *Das peinliche Rechtsverfahren im jüdischen Alterthum*, Heidelberg, 1870, p. 38.

Jewish Interpretation of the Bible.

Let me explain more fully what I mean. I shall quote again a Jewish Rabbi, and you will see how much more enlightened some of these despised Rabbis were than some of our leading theologians.

Rabbi José says that ' the descent of God on Mount Sinai must not be taken in a literal sense,' and he continues, ' as little as the ascent of Moses and Elijah[1].'

Now, I ask, Do we always bear this in mind? Do we remember that the descent of Jehovah on Mount Sinai, as described in Exodus, and his carrying down the heavy tables of stone to hand them to Moses, must not, nay, cannot be taken, without irreverence, in a literal sense. Every educated, every serious-minded person knows it. The very Fathers of the Church, who have so often been appealed to in support of antiquated errors, protest against the literal interpretation of such passages in the Bible,—passages to which so many of our most troublesome miracles are due. May we no longer claim the same freedom of the spirit against the slavery of the letter, which even in the first half of the second century was boldly claimed by, and freely granted to, such a man as Justin Martyr! ' You are not to think,' he writes, ' that the unbegotten God came down from anywhere, or went up.' Thus by one stroke, this great Father of the Church, whom no orthodox theologian would venture to contradict, removes, or rather explains, a number of so-called miracles which we, in the nineteenth century, are told we must not touch, we must not venture to explain, we must not venture to try to

---

[1] Sukka, 5 a.

understand. Those who do so nevertheless, who study ancient language and ancient thought, are called Rationalists—a name meant, I believe, as a reproach, but in reality the proudest title in the eyes of every rational man, for it means a man who tries to use, to the best of his power, the best gift which God has given us, namely, our reason.

It is useless to fight against the truth—truth will conquer us all, even the most orthodox. I have often been told that I ought to have followed the example of my colleague at Edinburgh, Mr. Hutchinson Stirling, the only orthodox among the Gifford Lecturers. I grant that Mr. Hutchinson Stirling is most orthodox, but he is also a scholar and thoroughly honest. I doubt whether those who represent him as the champion of what they call orthodoxy have really read his lectures. When we read in the Bible that the walls of Jericho fell at the blast of the trumpet, or when the author of the Epistle to the Hebrews tells us that the walls of Jericho fell by faith, after they were compassed about some days, what does Mr. Hutchinson Stirling say? Does he accept this as a miracle? Far from it. He sees in it nothing but what he calls Oriental phantasy, expressing in a trope the signal speed of the event, as if we were to say, that the walls fell at the first blast of the trumpet. He goes still further and says, without any misgiving: 'He who would boggle at the wife of Cain (whose daughter she was) or stumble over the walls of Jericho, is not an adult: he is but a boy still.' This is quite true; the only question is whether the boys, because they are many, should rule the masters, or the masters the boys.

Should we then allow ourselves to be frightened

by another argument, namely that all this may be true, but that such facts and such interpretations are for the few, not for the many, and that more particularly the young would suffer shipwreck of their faith, if they were told that Jehovah did not reside in the blue sky, that He did not descend on Mount Sinai in fire, carrying in His arms the tables of the law to hand them to Moses?

Archdeacon Farrar has been a schoolmaster for many years, yet he did not hesitate to say, ' We do not suppose that heaven is a cubic city.' Is there really any danger in this, and, if there is, should it not be faced? I believe that so long as a child's mind is still unable to take in more than the idea of God dwelling in the clouds and descending on Mount Sinai in a bodily form, as working Himself with His own tools the tables of stone, as writing Himself with His own finger the ten commandments in Hebrew on the stone, nothing will disturb his childish thoughts. But if he has once learnt to conceive God as a spirit, whom no man can see and live, no authority will be strong enough to convince him that the account given in Exodus should be accepted in a literal and material sense.

The Ascent of Elijah.

And what applies to the descent of Jehovah applies equally, as Justin Martyr said, to all descents from heaven, and all ascents to heaven. If we understand the language of the time, we can well understand the true meaning of the ascent of Elijah, as told in the Old Testament. But I doubt whether any serious student of the Bible would bring himself to say that the passage, as we read it there (2 Kings ii. 11),

was meant to vouch for an historical event, namely
that there appeared a real chariot of fire, and real
horses of fire, and parted them both (Elijah and
Elisha) asunder; and that Elijah went up by a
whirlwind into heaven.

The Ascension of Christ.

If then their own learned Rabbis, who knew the
language of the Bible as their own, exhorted the Jews
to take Elijah's ascent to heaven in a spiritual, and
not simply in a material sense, why has so much intolerance been shown of late to clergymen of the
Church of England who claimed the same freedom
with regard to Christ's ascension, and tried to see in
it a spiritual truth, and not a merely material event?
The pictorial language is much stronger in the case of
the assumption of Elijah, and yet it was rightly interpreted. In the case of Christ the fact of His body
being lifted from the mountain and passing through
the clouds, as we see it in many well-known pictures,
and as it is impressed on the minds of many children,
is really never mentioned; and if it were, it ought to
be understood in its deep spiritual meaning, and not
as a merely miraculous event. The first Gospel is
altogether silent. In the Gospel of St. Mark the most
simple language is used, that 'He was received up
into heaven, and sat on the right hand of God.' Can
we doubt of the true meaning of these words? Does
any one really believe that the approach to God is
through the clouds? The third Gospel says, 'He was
parted from them, and carried up into heaven.' St.
John is reverently silent as to any bodily assumption,
though the expressions that Christ descended from

heaven and ascended up to heaven are most familiar
to him in their true spiritual meaning. (St. John
iii. 13; vi. 62; xx. 17.)

It is in the Acts of the Apostles that the ascension
seems to assume a more material character, though
even here the expressions of His being seen going up
to heaven, or taken up, and received by a cloud out
of their sight, must be taken in a spiritual sense.
The material fact was, that He was withdrawn from
their vision. The spiritual meaning was, that He was
raised up and exalted to the right hand of God (Acts
ii. 33), that He 'ascended on high and led captivity
captive' (Psalm lxviii. 18).

We can well understand that to some minds, and
more particularly to the minds of children, the
material miracle of a passage through our terrestrial
atmosphere is a necessity. It requires less effort, less
thought, it requires less of real faith. So long as
the blue sky is believed to be heaven, so long as the
lessons of astronomy do not open wider views of
God's universe, a mere passage through the clouds has
nothing to disturb a childlike imagination. Nor is
there any reason why this view should not be tolerated
for a time, during the days of childhood, as it is sure
to disclose its spiritual meaning in the end. It is the
discovery of that spiritual meaning which requires
real faith; while if we looked upon the ascension as
simply a material fact or an historical event, we should
simply have to submit the evidence, like the evidence
of any other historical event, to a critical examination,
and reject or accept it as we reject or accept the disappearance of Romulus on the authority of Livy, i. 16.

Spiritual *only*.

Some people say that they can derive no help, no comfort, from what they call spiritual *only*. Spiritual *only*—think what that *only* would mean, if it could have any meaning at all! We might as well say of light that it is light *only*, and that what we want is the shadow which we can grasp. So long as we know the shadow only, and not the light that throws it, the shadow only is real, and not the light. But when we have once turned our head and seen the light, the light only is real and substantial, and not the shadow.

All this is a matter of growth, of spiritual growth, and that growth, though it need not be hurried, ought never to be checked. There is a period in the history of the world, and there is a period in the life of every individual, during which the material shadows only seem to be real, while the light behind us seems a mere illusion, the result of a deduction. Nay, even when that deduction has been made, and has proved irresistible to human reason, the human heart often hesitates. There are many to whom the spirit seems something too shadowy, not half so real as the body, and the utmost they can grasp is what they call a spiritual body. If they can connect any definite meaning with such an expression, let them do so.

But why should others who have learnt to believe in the stern reality of the spirit, have to plead for toleration? Why should those to whom the material miracle would be no help at all, while the spiritual fact, the true ascension of Christ, is a necessity, why should they be deprived of that freedom which even

Jewish Rabbis and the Fathers of the Church enjoyed, of interpreting the Bible according to the language of the time? Why should not the two live peaceably together, remembering the edict of Asoka, 'that respect should be shown to all sects;' and if to all sects, why not to all ages of men, to all stages of thought? We want more faith, not less.

If there had been more of these Jewish Rabbis, think how many controversies might have been prevented.

The Solstice of Joshua.

Think of the long controversies carried on at the time of Galileo! At first so-called logical arguments were used to show that the earth could not possibly move. I shall give you a specimen or two:

'All animals which are able to move have members and muscles,
The Earth has no members and no muscles,
Therefore it does not move—*quod erat demonstrandum.*'

Or better still, to quote Chiaramonti:

'Angels cause Saturn, Jupiter, and the Sun to move, and
The Earth also, if it does move, must be moved by angels in its centre,
But in that centre of the Earth dwell devils,
Therefore devils would have to move the Earth —which is impossible.'

But when these neatly-contrived syllogisms produced no longer any effect, an irresistible appeal was made to the Bible. Ever so many passages were then quoted from the Bible to show that Copernicus and Galileo could not be right, because their view of the world was contradicted by the express language of the Bible. In the Bible the sun is spoken of as moving, and Joshua said to the sun, ' Sun, stand thou still.' Must we then surrender our faith in the Bible or shut our eyes to the facts of science? The Jewish Rabbis would have given a better answer than was given at the time by Popes or Councils: ' The Bible must be interpreted according to the language of the time.' Joshua spoke as many a hero or poet would speak even now, however convinced he might be that the sun never moved. We read in the Odyssey (xxiii. 243) that on the day when Odysseus and Penelope were reunited, Athene lengthened the night, and kept Eos, the dawn, back in the ocean, not allowing her to harness the quick-footed horses, Lampos and Phaeton, who bring light to men. But do we imagine that Athene really upset the course of nature? Does anybody with any sense of poetry doubt that all that Homer wished to say was that those who, like Odysseus and Penelope, believed in the protecting care of Athene, felt as if she had lengthened for them the happiness of their reunion?

Again, when we read in the Iliad (xviii. 239) that, after the death of Patroklos, Hera sent Helios against his will to dive into the waves of the ocean, can we doubt that what the poet really meant was no more than that the Trojans felt grateful to Hera, when the sun set sooner than they expected, and the revenge of Achilles was stayed for that day?

We lose nothing by accepting these true and

natural explanations. Even in the case of Joshua we lose nothing, we only gain. Joshua is represented to us as eager to destroy the Amorites, who had been defeated and were fleeing before him. Whatever we may think of his warfare, *he* believed that in destroying the Amorites, he was doing the work of God. When darkness seemed to come upon him and to prevent him from finishing his work, what was more natural than that he should exclaim: 'Sun, stand thou still upon Gibeon, and thou, Moon, in the valley of Ajalon.' He is not the only general who has uttered such a prayer[1]. And if the Israelites finished their slaughter before nightfall, their poets would have been very different from all other poets, if they had not sung that the Lord had delivered their enemies into their hands, and that 'the sun stood still in the midst of heaven, and hasted not to go down about a whole day.'

All this is natural and intelligible, and, what is most important, it does no violence to our sense of truth. For, however anxious people may be to accept every event recorded in the Old Testament as historical, it must require an effort to believe that such an event as stopping the sun and moon took place in the year 1520 B.C., without being observed anywhere except in the valley of Ajalon, and, let me add, without upsetting the whole order of the planetary system. These are what I mean by the so-called physical miracles which science has proved to be once for all impossible, not the true miracles of which Mohammed spoke, when he said, 'You want to see miracles— look at the sun.' And there is no necessity here for doing violence to our sense of truth, if only we

---

[1] See 'India, what can it teach us?' p. 182.

remember the ruling of the old Rabbis, that the Scripture speaks in language intelligible to men.

But now let me tell you what may happen, if we forget that ruling, and take this poetical language in its literal sense.

Fasti Temporis Catholici.

Many years ago, when I first came to Oxford, the University Press published a work in four large volumes, called *Fasti Temporis Catholici* and *Origines Kalendariae*, by the Rev. Edward Greswell, 1852. It is a work full of learning, full of ingenuity. But its principal object is to show that there is a perfect agreement between astronomical and historical chronology. The beginning of astronomical chronology is fixed most minutely in the year 4004, in the week between April 25 and May 2. Then by following the solar and lunar years, and by taking into consideration all eclipses of the sun and the moon, the dates of ancient and modern history are brought into perfect agreement with the recorded and calculated movements of the heavenly bodies. But when all is done, there remains a small discrepancy. There are twenty-four hours less of astronomical than of historical time. And how do you think this discrepancy is accounted for? By the time that the sun stood still at the command of Joshua, and by the time that the sun returned backward ten degrees on the dial of Ahaz in the time of Hezekiah, on the 31st of March, 710 B.C. (2 Kings xx. 11). You would be surprised at the learning that is expended in these four volumes in order to establish the fact that this addition of twenty-four hours was really made to what we call time, and how it agrees with the whole system of astronomical chronology, and forms in reality a most valuable confirmation of the historical truth of the Old Testament. It may be so in the eyes of some people, and if it is a plank which has saved them from drowning, who would interfere with them? Who would use against these learned arguments any weapons except those of unimpassioned verification? So long as the world remains what it is and always has been, so long as there are children and grandmothers, educated and uneducated, wise and foolish people, people who dare not speak the truth, even when they know it, and people who dare not not speak the truth, if once they know it, there will be difference in religious opinions as in everything else.

Diversity of Opinion inevitable.

However strong the desire for unity and uniformity in religion may be, it requires but a small knowledge of the history of religion, it requires no more than that we should look around, in order to feel convinced that this ideal will never be realised. One feels surprised when one reads how Mohammed, who is considered the most intolerant of prophets, exclaims in the Korân (X. 99): 'Had thy Lord pleased, all who are in the earth would have believed altogether: as for thee, wilt thou force men to become believers [1]?' And again: 'Follow what is revealed to you, and be patient until God judges, for He is the best of judges.' This was the language of Mohammed, though hardly his practice.

Look how Christianity is divided into three hostile

[1] Krehl, *Glauben*, p. 25.

camps, Roman Catholics, Greeks, and Protestants. Yet they are all Christians. Look at the divisions among Protestants, in Germany, Holland, England, and America. Yet they are all Christians. Look again in each division at the variety of opinions preached every Sunday from the same pulpits and listened to by the same congregations. Yet they are all Christians.

Why should we always dwell on the differences which divide the Roman Catholic, the Greek, and the Protestant Churches? Why should we be disheartened at the multiplicity of Protestant sects, and at the numberless shades of doctrine and ritual which we see in cathedrals, churches, chapels, and meeting-houses? Are not the beliefs which they all share in common infinitely more numerous and infinitely more essential than those on which they differ? And yet these differences, in some cases so small as almost to defy definition, are allowed to separate so-called Christian denominations, while the magnificent inheritance of truth which belongs to all of them is wilfully ignored. Christianity, which in the beginning was the most tolerant of all religions, seems to have become the most intolerant. We say, no longer, ' He who is not against us, is for us ; ' we always seem to say, ' He who is not with us, is against us.'

It is an easy excuse to say that this or that point is essential, and that whosoever will be saved must hold it. Many things seem essential to the young which are looked upon in a very different light by the old. To quote the words of one of the highest ecclesiastical dignitaries in this very city, ' Man judges more wisely of what is essential and what is indifferent in the quiet sunset of life, than during the heat and burden of the day[1].'

A Comparative Study of Religions teaches Tolerance.

And here I say once more, that a serious study of the great religions of the world may prove a great help and a most efficient remedy against intolerance. A story was told of Macaulay when, after his return from India, he stood as Member of Parliament for Edinburgh. He had been heckled by some ministers who wanted to find out whether he was quite sound on certain minute points of doctrine, which were too minute even for so acute an intellect as Macaulay's. 'Gentlemen,' he exclaimed at last, 'if you had lived for some years, as I have, in a country where people worship the cow, you would not waste your thoughts on such trifles.'

Macaulay was right. The essentials of religion may be found in almost every religion, even among those who have a superstitious feeling about a cow. When one sees the struggles through which mankind has to pass in order to establish the few fundamental principles of religion, and to gain a recognition for the simplest rules of morality, one learns to be very grateful to the founders of every religion for what they have achieved. Man can be a very wild beast, and to have induced him, not only to believe in a supreme government of the world, but to restrain his selfish passions in submission to a higher will, that is a real miracle. You remember what Asoka called

[1] Speech of the Bishop of Glasgow at the Church Congress ; see *Times*, Oct. 2, 1890.

the essentials, or the sap of religion—control of the
senses, purity of mind, gratitude, and loyalty. These
he finds inculcated by all the sects in India, however
different in other respects. We occupy a much higher
point of view than Asoka, and looking at the work
done by religion in all parts of the world, we may
learn that in these essentials all religions are really
one. There are differences, there are great differences,
between the great religions of the world, between their
sects, between their individual members. But there
is a unity which ought to comprehend them all—the
unity of toleration, the unity of love.

LECTURE III.

Outcome of Physical Religion.

BEFORE we proceed to an analysis of what is meant by Anthropological Religion, it will be useful to look back to see what has been the outcome of our last course of lectures. To put it as briefly as possible, it was this, that man, as soon as he began to observe, to name, and to know the movements and changes in the world around him, suspected that there was something behind what he saw, that there must be an agent for every action, a mover for every movement. Instead of saying and thinking, as we do at present, *the rain, the thunder, the moon*, he said, *the rainer, the thunderer, the measurer*. Instead of saying and thinking, as we do at present, *It rains, It thunders*, he said, *He rains, He thunders*, without caring as yet who that He might be.

Man could not help this. He was driven, as we saw, to speak in this way by a necessity inherent in language, that is, in thought. This necessity arose from the fact that his earliest concepts consisted in the consciousness of his own repeated acts, and that the only elements of conceptual speech which were at his disposal, the so-called roots, were all, or nearly all, expressive of his own actions. If this is true, and I do not know of any one who has seriously controverted it, it is clear that man in speaking of a rainer, a thunderer, a measurer, was unconsciously, or at least unintentionally, speaking and thinking in what Kant would call the category of causality. The rainer was not only a name for the rain, but a name for a rainer, the agent of the rain, whoever or whatever that agent might be. This category of causality which most philosophers consider as the *sine quâ non* of all rational thought, and as an indefeasible necessity of our understanding, thus manifests itself in the historical growth of the human mind as the *sine quâ non* of all rational speech, as an indefeasible necessity of our very language.

This is an unexpected coincidence, and therefore, if properly understood, all the more valuable and significant.

Origin of the Concept of Cause.

What is meant by philosophers when they speak of the category of causality as a form, and as a necessary form of pure reason, is simply this—that, whether we like it or not, we cannot help conceiving whatever we conceive, except as cause and effect. Our reason knows of nothing, and tolerates nothing that is not either cause or effect. We may not always dwell on this side of our experience, when we speak of rain or thunder, of sunshine or storm. But we always imply that every link in our experience is determined by a preceding link, and will in turn determine a succeding link. ' There is nothing in the world without a cause,' this is the fundamental article of all philosophical faith. Whether that faith is, as some philosophers maintain, the result of experience, is quite another question. I hold, of course, with Kant, that no experience could ever give to this article of philosophic faith the character of universality and necessity which it possesses, and without which it would cease to be what it is. Nay, I go further, and maintain that, if ever we were to find ourselves in a world not held together by causality, a mere chaos, we should still retain our belief in causality. The very name of chaos would prove our ingrained faith in causality, for it is a negation of causality, and we could not deny causality without first having conceived it.

But that is not the question at present. Our question is, how the human mind became possessed for the first time of that ineradicable faith in universal causality.

No one would venture to say that the human mind, though always under the sway of causality, was from the first conscious of it in its abstract form, as a law of thought. Historically and linguistically, what we now call cause, was first considered and named as an agent, nay as something like a human agent.

When I have used the argument that we are so made that whenever we see a movement, we require a mover, whenever we observe an action, we require an agent, I have been asked what I meant by ' we are so made.' Other philosophers, from Plato to Kant, have answered that question, each in his own, and yet all in the same way, so that I thought I need not repeat

their arguments. I preferred to give my own argument, namely, that our language is so made that from
the very first we cannot even speak of anything
except as a mover, an agent, a doer. This may to
some seem an illustration only. To those, however,
who know the true meaning of Logos, and who have
perceived once for all the inseparableness of language
and thought, it is a great deal more than an illustration,
and perhaps the strongest and most palpable argument
in support of the inevitable character of the concept
of causality that could be adduced.

But let us throw a glance at one of the earliest
arguments in support of our belief in movers in every
movement, and agents in every act.

Plato on the Gods.

Plato, in the Laws (p. 893), begins his induction in
proof of the existence of gods, by observing that all
things either move or are at rest. He then distinguishes
between what is able to move other things, but not to
move itself, and what is able to move itself as well as
other things; and he shows how self-motion is the
oldest and mightiest principle of change.

When that motion is seen in any earthy, watery,
or fiery substance, we should call it life, and likewise
when we observe in it what he calls psyche, and what
we translate by soul. He then proceeds to show that
what we mean by psyche is really the same as what
is able to move itself—what I call the agent—and
that soul is the first origin and moving power of all
that is, or has been, or will be, while body, or what is
moved, comes second and is born to obey the soul.

The soul, according to Plato, receives the divine mind and then controls heaven and earth and the whole world.

After these preliminary remarks, Plato proceeds to apply this reasoning to the heavens, the sun, moon, and stars. Every one, he says, sees the sun, but no one sees his soul. Yet there must be a soul, whether it is within the sun or without, and this soul of the sun should be deemed a god by every man who has the least particle of sense. And the same, he says, applies to all the other heavenly bodies, and to the months, and seasons, and years, so that we perceive that all things are full of gods [1].

You see that we have only to substitute for Plato's psyche, or soul, or what is able to move itself, what we call agents, and his argument for the existence of gods becomes the same as our own for the existence of agents, and, at last, of one agent behind all the phenomena of nature. And that we may do so, that Plato really means by psyche, soul, that which is able to move itself without being moved, he has told us himself in so many words.

What Plato called souls, what I call agents, others who speak a more poetical and legendary language have sometimes called angels. But we all mean the same thing. Thus Newman writes (*Apologia*, p. 28) : 'I considered the angels as the real causes of motion, light, and life, and of those elementary principles of the physical universe, which, when offered in their developments to our senses, suggest to us the notion of cause and effect, and of what are called the laws of nature.' This may sound very childish to our ears,

---

[1] A saying ascribed to Thales.

but it was a very common mode of expression in the early ages of Christianity.

Let us now return to our own argument.

First Consciousness of our Acts.

Psychologists tell us that the first manifestation of self-consciousness in man consists, not only as a fact, but by necessity, in the consciousness of our own acts. Even of our suffering, we are told, we become conscious only when we act, or react, against it, when we resist or try to escape from it. Mere sensuous impressions may come and go, unobserved, unnamed, unrecorded, but our own acts must always be accompanied by a consciousness that they are the acts of ourselves, the acts of a self different from other selves. I do not speak of purely mechanical or involuntary acts ; they would *ipso facto* cease to be what can properly be called acts.

If then we can well understand how our true consciousness begins with the consciousness of our own acts, whatever the impulse of these acts may have been, it would seem to follow that our true language also, as distinct from mere cries of joy or pain, should begin with signs of our own acts. And this, as we shall see, which at first was a mere postulate of the psychologist, has now received the most complete confirmation from the Science of Language.

Some philosophers try to go back even further. They observe that breathing of a certain sort is crying, and that children have no language but a cry. As the muscles of a child increase in strength, he begins to gesticulate, and his cries diminish in proportion to the increase of his gestures. His cries become also more differentiated, and they accompany certain of his acts and wishes with such regularity that a nurse can often understand the different meanings of these cries [1]. All this is true, and may throw some light on certain phases in the growth of the human mind and of human language. It may show the close connection between certain acts and certain sounds, but it does not touch the real problem, the historical origin and growth of language and thought, which must be studied first of all *a posteriori*, that is, by an analysis of language, such as we actually find it, not by a mere synthesis of possibilities.

Postulate of Psychology fulfilled by Language.

Now an analysis of language, and more particularly of the Aryan and Semitic languages, carried on without any preconceived psychological theories, has clearly shown that what we call roots, that is, the real elements of speech which defy further analysis, are all, with a few insignificant exceptions, expressive of the acts of man. They signify to go, to run, to strike, to push, to find, to bend, to join, to rub, to smoothe, and a number of similar acts of a more or less special character, such as would be most familiar to the members of an incipient society. Much may lie even beyond this stage when the acts of men received their simple expression. But these earlier stages concern the biologist, possibly the geologist. They do not concern the student of language and thought.

With a small number of radicals, such as we find at the end of our analysis of speech, more particularly of

---

[1] See an able article by Dr. J. M. Buckley, The Philosophy of Gesture, in Werner's *Voice Magazine*, Nov. 1890.

Aryan and Semitic speech, it was found possible to express all that was wanted in an early state of society; while looks, gestures, cries, accents would, no doubt, have helped to supply what in more developed languages is supplied by grammar.

How these radicals arose, why they had one sound and not another, we cannot tell. Not even the most careful observations of children in their cradles can help us here. What Bopp said in 1833 is quite as true to-day. We shall never know why the act of going was signified by the sound gâ, the act of standing by the sound sthâ. We can only accept the fact that they were felt to be natural expressions for the acts which they signified, or that they remained out of a number of cognate sounds which might have answered the same purpose. If I call, for instance, such a root as MAR, the *clamor concomitans* of the act of pounding or rubbing, I do not mean to say that this was the only possible sound that could have accompanied this special act, but simply that it was one out of many that did accompany that act, and that it survived in the struggle for existence in the Aryan family of speech.

I tried to explain how with such a root as MAR man might convey a command, asking his friends to pound or strike. He might also inform them that he was himself in the act of pounding and striking. Nay, he might point to a stone with which he pounded as a pounder, and to the pounded stones as the result of his pounding, as pounded or powder.

In this way the whole world of his experience would be divided into two spheres, what we call an active and a passive sphere. The result of an act, the pounded stones, for instance, would be passive, while whatever produces such results would be active. First of all, the man himself who pounded, then also his fellow-workers, would all be active. Even the instruments they used, whether of stone, or wood, or metal, would have to be named as active, as pounders, as borers, or cutters.

Naming of Objects.

It has been urged with an air of triumph that it might be quite possible with a given number of active roots to express all that is active, but that this theory would break down, when we try to account for the names of objects, such as a stone, or a tree, or a knife[1]. This, no doubt, is a difficulty, but when that difficulty has been fully discussed both by Professor Noiré and by myself, it is rather hard that we should be supposed never to have thought of it. It is true that we do not quite take the same view of the psychological process that led to the naming of objects. But we do not diffe as to the facts, and these facts are there to speak for themselves.

First of all, with regard to the naming of instruments, we find that even in our modern languages we still speak of scrapers, pincers, squeezers, borers, holders, etc., all conceived originally as active, though we are hardly conscious of it now. It was the same in Latin, Greek, and Sanskrit. Thus *vomer*, a plough-share, was really he who threw up; *securis*, an axe, was really she who cut; ζωστήρ was a girder, before it

---

[1] *Athenæum*, Dec. 6, 1890.

became a mere girdle. Even such words as ἐνδυτήρ, a
cloak, was at first he who helped to clothe, just as in
German, *ein Überzieher*, an overcoat, was originally
he who drew over or covered. All this may seem
strange to us, but it is still perfectly intelligible to
popular poets. There is a famous German Volkslied,
in which a soldier addresses his old cloak, and says :

> 'Thou art thirty years old
> And hast weathered many a storm—
> Thou hast guarded me, like a brother,
> And when the cannons thundered,
> We two have never trembled.'

In all these words, the masculine came first, then the
feminine, and lastly the neuter.

But how were mere objects named, it is asked.
Noiré has laboured very hard to show that, at
first, they too could only have been named and
conceived as our acts ; that a cave, for instance,
could only have become objective to us as our
subjective act, viz. as our excavating. This may
sound very unlikely, but here also language has
still preserved a few faint vestiges of its former
ways. Even now, how do people in a primitive state
of society call a newly-opened mine ? Our diggings,
they say. The French *maison*, house, meant originally a remaining, Lat. *mansio*, a mansion. The
venison which we eat was called *venatio*, our chase,
our sport, and all such words as *oration, invention,
pension, picture*, were names of acts, before they
became the names of objects. After a time, no doubt,
the human mind accustomed itself to look upon the
actions as independent of the agents, the *cutter*
became a ship, the *cutting* a slice, the *writing* a book.
But the chain from the active root to the passive

nouns was never broken, and every link is there to attest the continuous progress of human language and human thought.

The Agents in Nature.

If then we ask ourselves how, with such materials at their disposal as have been discovered by students in the lowest stratum of human speech, the ancient dwellers on earth could think and speak of the great phenomena of nature, say the storm-wind, the fire, the sun, the sky, we shall see that, at first, they could name and conceive them in no other way but as active or as agents, and not yet as mere causes. What we now call the category of causality is no doubt at the bottom of all this, but historically it manifested itself, first of all, not in a search for something like a cause, but in the assertion of something like an agent. The storm-wind, if it was to be singled out at all, if it was to be named with the materials supplied by the radical dictionary of that early period of thought, could be called in one way only, as the pounder, the striker, the smasher. And so it was as a matter of fact. From the root MAR, to smash, we found that the Âryas had formed the name Mar-ut, the smashers, the name of what we now call the gods of the storm-wind, while to them it was no more at first than a name of the agents of the storm-wind.

We saw that the same process of naming the most prominent phenomena of nature led in the end to the creation of a complete physical pantheon. Not only trees, mountains, and rivers were named as agents, but the sea and the earth, the fire and the wind, the sky, the stars, the sun, the dawn, the moon, day and night, all were represented under different names as agents.

Transition to Human Agents.

It might be said that with all this we had only explained why every object of experience had to be named and conceived at first as an agent, and that we have not explained why it should ever have been conceived as a human agent. This is quite true. But if we consider that all roots were originally the expressions of human actions, and that they were predicated at first of human agents, it becomes perfectly intelligible how, when nothing but human agents were known as yet, other agents, having the same names as human agents, should have been conceived as something *like* human agents. Suppose that a strong man had been called a *striker*, and that he had spoken of himself as *I strike*, of others as *thou strikest*, and *he strikes*, was it not almost inevitable that, if the lightning was called *a striker*, he should likewise be spoken of as something like a man who strikes, and that people should say of that lightning striker, *he strikes*, and not as yet, *it strikes*.

Difference between Human and Super-human Agents.

No doubt a difference was soon perceived between the ordinary human strikers, and that terrible and irresistible striker, the lightning. And what would be the inevitable result of this? The striker in the lightning would by necessity be called a non-human striker, and from a non-human striker to a super-human striker the steps are small and few.

So far, I hope, all is clear, for the process is really extremely simple. Whatever in nature had to be named, could at first be named as an agent only. Why? Because the roots of language were at first expressive of agency. Having been named as agents, and no other agents being known but human agents, the agents in nature were, if not necessarily, yet very naturally, spoken of as like human agents, then as more than human agents—and, at last, as superhuman agents.

The True Meaning of Animism.

Consider now how different this is from what is generally understood by Animism and Anthropomorphism. The facts are no doubt the same, but the explanation is totally different, theoretical in the one case, historical in the other; nay, irrational in the one case, rational in the other. I cannot help calling it irrational when we are asked to believe that at any time in the history of the world a human being could have been so dull as not to be able to distinguish between inanimate and animate beings, a distinction in which even the higher animals hardly ever go wrong; or again that man was pleased to ascribe life or a soul to the sun and the moon, to trees and rivers, though he was perfectly aware that they possessed neither one nor the other. Even Mr. Herbert Spencer protests against this insult to the human intellect.

A knowledge of the nature of language explains everything, not only as possible, but as necessary. Human language, being what we found it to be, could not help itself. If it wished to name sun or moon, tree or river, it could only name them as agents, simply as agents, without ascribing as yet life or soul to them.

Here, it seems to me, we often do great injustice to the ancients, when we translate their language literally, but after all not truly, into our own. Thus Epicharmos, no mean philosopher, who lived in the fifth century B.C., is often quoted as having declared that the gods of the Greeks were the winds, water, the earth, the sun, fire, and the stars [1]. The question is, were the winds and the water and the earth, the sun, fire, and the stars, to his mind mere things, dead material objects, or were they conceived, if not as masculine or feminine, at all events as active powers, possibly as something like what the so-called positivist philosophers would accept even now, when they speak of act and agent being one.

The transition from animate to man-like beings is much less violent, if we account for it not so much by the poetry, as by the poverty of language, which knew at first of no agents except human agents, and therefore had often to use the same word for natural agents and human agents, without thereby committing the speaker to the startling assertion that the sun and moon, the tree and river were, in the true sense of the word, anthropomorphous, or man-like. Later religious and mythological fancy, particularly when assisted by sculpture and painting, achieved this also, but that stage of thought was reached slowly and gradually, and not by the sudden impulses of what is vaguely called Animism and Anthropomorphism.

---

[1] Stobaeus, *Florilegium*, xci. 29 : Ὁ μὲν Ἐπίχαρμος τοὺς θεοὺς εἶναι λέγει Ἀνέμους, ὕδωρ, γῆν, ἥλιον, πῦρ, ἀστέρα.

General Names of the Agents in Nature.

There was one more step that had to be explained, namely, how these different agents, in or behind nature, came to be classed together and called by names which we, very glibly, translate by gods.

We saw how they came to be distinguished from merely human agents, as non-human, and super-human. And we also saw how from certain important features which all these superhuman agents shared in common, they were emphatically called d e v a, bright, v a s u, brilliant, a s u r a, breathing or living, and many other names. We saw how this word d e v a, meaning originally bright, was gradually divested of its purely physical meaning, and, instead of meaning brilliant agents, came to mean in the end great and good, or what we now mean by divine agents. The history of that one word d e v a in Sanskrit, and *deus* in Latin, disclosed, in fact, better than anything else, one of the most important channels of the historical evolution of the concept of deity, at least among our own Aryan ancestors.

Highest Generalisation or Monotheism.

When that concept of d e v a had been realised, it was at first a generic concept. It applied, not to one power, but to many. Even when the human mind tried to combine the idea of supremacy and therefore of oneness with that of deity, this was done at first by predicating supremacy of single d e v a s or gods only, each supreme in his own domain. After this stage in which we find a number of single gods, neither co-ordinate nor subordinate, there follows the next in

which all the single gods were combined into a kind
of organic whole, one god being supreme, the others
subject to him, but to him only, and standing among
themselves on a certain level of equality. After these
two stages, which I called *Henotheism* and *Polytheism*,
follows in the end that of real *Monotheism*, a belief in
one god, as excluding the very possibility of any other
gods. We saw that this highest stage was not only
reached by the most thoughtful and religious poets
in Greece and Rome, but even by some of the Vedic
poets in India.

These stages in the development of the idea of the
godhead are not therefore merely theoretical postulates. They are historical realities which we may
watch in many religions, if only we are enabled to
follow their history in literary documents. Nowhere,
however, can this be done more effectually than in
India, where some fortunate accident has preserved
to us in the Vedic hymns relics of the henotheistic
stage in wonderful completeness. Only we must not
imagine, as some scholars seem to do, that the whole
of the Veda belongs to the worship of single gods. On
the contrary, and this is what renders the Veda so
valuable, we see in it all the three stages together, the
henotheistic, the polytheistic, and the monotheistic,
representing the different levels of religious thought
that had been reached at that early time by different
classes of the same society.

The Biography of Agni representative only.

But though the regular development of religious
names and concepts can best be studied in ancient

India, every country and every sacred literature presents us with more or less complete portions of the same intellectual evolution. Not only among Aryan and Semitic races, but among Negroes, Polynesians, and Red Indians we find a belief in and a worship of the divine representatives of the principal phenomena of nature. If the Maruts or Storm-winds rose to the rank of supreme deities in India, the same process, as we saw, raised *Hurakan*, our hurricane, to the supreme rank among the gods among the Quichés in America, and left *Odin* or *Wodan* as supreme in the pantheon of the Teutonic nations. I placed before you a very complete analysis of the theogonic or god-producing process by which the Fire rose from the humblest beginnings to the rank of a supreme deity in India. I meant this one analysis to be representative only, and nothing could have been more remote from my mind than to imply that all religion took its beginning from fire-worship. Over and over again I pointed out that by the side of this one, and, no doubt, very important stream of religious development, there were many other streams and rivulets, all starting from the observation of natural phenomena, and all ending with the recognition of powers beyond nature, named by the names of these phenomena, and in the end by a recognition of one Power, of one God, the creator of Heaven and Earth.

The God of the Sky.

This may seem a long road, leading to a belief in gods and in God—but it was an inevitable road, and a road that it is even for us well to remember. The ancient philosophers never forgot it, and it would be difficult to sum up the results of Physical Religion, as treated in my last course of lectures, better than in the words of Maximus of Tyre: ' Let men know all that is divine, let them know it only! But whether the Greeks be roused to a remembrance of God by the art of Phidias, or the Egyptians by the worship of animals, and others by a river, and others by fire, I do not care for all these differences. Let men only know, let them only love, let them only remember the Divine [1].'

Principles of Comparative Mythology.

Having traced this process through the fire and other elements, through storm-wind and thunder, through rivers and mountain-peaks, I thought I could have dispensed with going once more over what are, no doubt, the two most important theogonic processes of the Aryan nations, one leading to the worship of the god of the sky, the other to the worship of the god of the sun, though the two are not always kept distinct. I thought that after all that has been written on that subject, no one would call in question the fact that by the same theogonic process which we examined in full detail in the case of fire or Agni, the sun and the sky have been raised to the rank of Devas or deities in India, Greece, and Italy, and in many other countries. I could not imagine that it was possible to doubt any longer the identity of the names of Dyaus, Zeus, Jupiter, and Týr [2]. But it seems that

[1] Maximus Tyrius, *Dissert.*, viii. 10. Εἰ δὲ ῞Ελληνας μὲν ἐπεγείρει πρὸς τὴν μνήμην τοῦ θεοῦ ἡ Φειδίου τέχνη, Αἰγυπτίους δὲ ἡ πρὸς τὰ ζῷα τιμή, καὶ ποταμὸς ἄλλους, καὶ πῦρ ἄλλους, οὐ νεμεσῶ τῆς διαφωνίας· ἵστωσαν μόνον, ἐράτωσαν μόνον, μνημονευέτωσαν μόνον.

[2] See *Science of Language*, vol. ii. p. 537 seq.

there is nothing that cannot be doubted, if only there is a sufficient amount of ignorance. Because etymologists have sometimes, or, if you like, have often been wrong, as astronomers have often been wrong, as chemists, geologists, and even anthropologists have often been wrong, therefore people seem to imagine that no etymology can ever be trustworthy, or, on the other hand, that any etymology is acceptable. They do not even know why one etymology is wrong, another right. They do not know where the seat of authority lies. They have no idea that there are phonetic rules which cannot be broken with impunity. So long as we recognise these phonetic rules, we may discuss certain etymologies and try to discover whether they are right or wrong. But if these rules are ignored or their authority questioned, all discussion becomes simply useless.

Brisaya and Brisêis.

Let me give you an instance. When, many years ago, I found in the Veda the expression Brisayasya séshah, the offspring of Brisaya, and when that offspring was said to have been conquered by the gods before they brought light to many (Rv. I. 93, 4; VI. 61, 3), I thought that we might possibly have here the same name which we know in Homer as *Brisêis*, the offspring of *Brisês*, who has likewise to be conquered before victory could be brought to the Achaeans. But unfortunately I had neglected a very simple phonetic rule, that in Greek an original s between two vowels always disappears. I did not at all like to surrender my identification of *Brisêis* and Brisayasya seshah, but there was no help for it. All I could

say in defence was that Brisêis might possibly stand
for Barseis, but even this was only an excuse; phonetically the equation was simply wrong, and had
therefore to be surrendered.   Here is a weapon for all
scoffers.

Dyaus and Zeus.

On the other hand, ask any student of Comparative
Philology what is the right form which such a word
as D y a u s in Sanskrit must assume, if it occurs at all
in Greek, and the unanimous answer will be *Zeus*.
No one doubts this, as little as we can doubt that the
sun, if it rises at all, will rise in the east.

No scholar ought to complain if men who are
eloquent in the pulpit or amusing in the press, attack
his conclusions or ridicule his facts. Only he should
not be accused of want of courtesy if he does not reply
when he is asked, why Jove should not be taken as
a corruption of Jehovah or Jahve, or why God should
not be derived from good, or from Wodan and Odin,
or from the Persian khodâ, or from Sk. dyut, to
shine.   There are statements which it is simply impossible to discuss, such as that Baga, the Persian
name for god, is derived from the Zend root vakhs, our
own 'to wax;' that the Persian Peri is found in our
fairy; and lastly that Jupiter is really a contraction
of ï ō Piter, i. e. O Father. Would any classical
scholar take notice of an antagonist who writes, 'We
now use the vocative *Jove* for the nominative, because
it was the form used when Jupiter was invoked, e. g.
Jov = O Jupiter!'

But while such outbursts may safely be ignored,
what shall we say, if an author like Dr. Lippert,

a man of considerable learning in his own subject, dares to write (p. 358): ' Whatever may be the meaning of the uncertain name of Zeus, I believe that it will more probably have to be looked for somewhere near Spirit or Lord than near the fetish-name of the sky. We must remember that the prevalent explanation of Zeus rests entirely on the by no means safe conjecture that a primitive word div means something bright, and must therefore signify the sky.'

That dyaus (fem.) means the sky in Sanskrit, every dictionary will prove. That Dyaus (masc.) was an ancient god of the sky, any dictionary of the Veda will prove. That *Zeus* in Greek corresponds regularly to Dyaus in Sanskrit, that dyaus must be traced back to a root *dyu, and that dyu and div are interchangeable forms, any manual of Comparative Philology will prove. In spite of that, we are told that Zeus may after all be derived from ζῆν, to live, and may have been originally a name for spirit.

I know that to many people a mere etymology may seem of little importance. But what is of immense importance in all scientific discussions is the spirit of truth. To make light of a fact that has been established, to ignore intentionally an argument which we cannot refute, to throw out guesses which we know we cannot prove, nay, which we do not even attempt to prove, is simply wrong, and poisons the air in which alone true science can breathe and live. No amount of downright blundering does half the mischief which is caused by an assumption of supreme indifference as to the truth of any statement, even of an etymology. And there are etymologies on the truth of which depend the most momentous issues.

The Lesson of Jupiter.

If I were asked what I consider the most important discovery which has been made during the nineteenth century with respect to the ancient history of mankind, I should say it was this simple etymological equation: Sanskrit DYAÚSH-PITÁR [1] = Greek ZEΥΣ ΠΑΤΕΡ [2] = Latin JUPITER [3] = Old Norse TÝR. Think what this equation implies! It implies not only that our own ancestors and the ancestors of Homer and Cicero spoke the same language as the people of India—this is a discovery which, however incredible it sounded at first, has long ceased to cause any surprise—but it implies and proves that they all had once the same faith, and worshipped for a time the same supreme deity under exactly the same name—a name which meant Heaven—Father.

This lesson cannot be taught too often, for no one who has not fully learnt, marked, and inwardly digested it, can form a true idea of the light which it sheds on the ancient history of the Aryan race. Ancient history has become as completely changed by that one discovery as astronomy was by the Copernican heresy.

And if we wish to realise to its fullest extent the unbroken continuity in the language, in the thoughts and words of the principal Aryan nations, let us look at the accents in the following list:

---

[1] Rv. IV. 1, 10.

[2] Ζεῦ πάτερ (Od. v. 7, etc.).

[3] Diespiter, Dispiter. As to the corresponding German names, see Grimm, *Teutonic Mythology*, i. p. 192. The Eddic name *Týr*, gen. *Týs*, corresponding to Sanskrit Dyaus, would be *Tius* in Gothic, *Tiw* in A. S., *Zio* in Old High-German.

Sanskrit.	Greek.	Latin.
Nom. Dyaús	Ζεύς	Ju-piter, or Jovis.
Gen. Divás	Διός	Jovis.
Loc. Diví	Διΐ	Jovi.
Acc. Dívam	Δία	Jovem.
Voc. Dyaŭs	Ζεῦ	Jupiter.

Here we see that at the time when the Greeks had become such thorough Greeks that they hardly knew of the existence of India, the people at Athens laid the accent in the oblique cases of Zeus on exactly the same syllable on which the Brâhmans laid it at Benares, with this difference only, that the Brâhmans knew the reason why, while the Athenians did not [1].

A scholar who ventures on the sea of ancient history, and more particularly of ancient religion and mythology, without having this short equation constantly before his eyes, is as helpless as an ancient mariner without a compass: he may weather many a storm, but he must be wrecked in the end.

But it is one thing to discover a truth, and quite another to make other people see that truth. Naturally, though perhaps unfortunately, the man who has discovered a truth, who sees it, knows it, and can no longer doubt it, is generally very indifferent as to whether other people can be made to see and to accept it. He knows it will conquer in the end, and he feels that he has more important work to do than to convert philological painim. Truth, he knows, is in no hurry. The Copernican theory was laughed at, it was anathematized, it was refuted by the highest authorities, but it lived on for all that; and, what is more wonderful still, it is at present accepted as

[1] *Selected Essays,* i. p. 220; *Lectures on the Science of Language,* ii. p. 468 seq.

gospel by millions, whereas the number of those who really understand it, and, if called upon, could defend it, might probably be counted by hundreds only.

But for all that, one cannot help feeling sorry, nay, even angry, when one sees scholars who in their own particular sphere deserve our respect and may claim considerable authority, speak of an etymology like that of Zeus and Dyaus as something that may or may not be.

Dr. Lippert.

It seems indeed as if his own conscience had smitten Dr. Lippert. After rejecting the only possible etymology of Zeus, and denying its connection with what he calls the sky-fetish—just imagine, if you can, what possible meaning can be conveyed by such a monstrosity as the compound sky-fetish—he seems to have remembered that, after all, *sub divo* in Latin means beneath the sky, and that if *divum* meant the sky, there might possibly have been some connection between *divum* and *dius*, and D y a u s and *Zeus*, and *Ju-piter*. Let us see now how he quiets his qualms of conscience. '*Divus*,' he writes (p. 422), 'is a concept of the widest extension, and so is *diva*. Whether this has any connection with the Greek διος-stem, does not concern us here. But no translation is so well adapted to all cases where it is used, as spirit, in the sense of soul, separated from the body. The German word *Geist* becomes inapplicable only because it has not, like the Latin word, both substantival and adjectival meaning. Whether the word goes back to the same root *dus*, from which the Slaves have derived their words for spirit, may be left to etymologists to settle. (No etymologist would for one moment even listen to this.) Certain it is from its use that of all synonyms it expresses more especially the concept of spirit, so that it can be prefixed to others as an attributive general name. Thus *Divus pater* means the father who continues to live as a spirit, *diva mater* the mother-spirit; and we also find *divi famuli*, and *divi manes....*'

'Latin does not distinguish in its usage between *dívus* and *dius*, as if both were dialectic forms of the same meaning. Particularly, and this is important, the *manes* are as often called *dii manes* as *divi manes....*'

And again, p. 441:

'The forms *divi*, *dîi*, and *dĕi* do not enable us to establish an essential difference between them. *Divus pater* and *Diespiter* (Jupiter) are so clearly synonymous that I cannot believe in any derivation of the former which would bring in the absolutely unconcerned sky. It would be extremely strange that beings dwelling on the earth or under the earth could directly or indirectly have been called, *divi*, and in the words of Livy (i. 32), *diique ... terrestres vosque inferni*, there would be an unaccountable contradiction.'

But after Dr. Lippert has thus far tried to persuade others, if not himself, that the root *div*, which means something bright, could never have yielded names for the bright sky, or for the bright god of the sky, his conscience awakes once more. There is that troublesome expression *sub divo*, which means beneath the sky. And that expression, as he himself remarks, must have been in use before Cato's time. There is evidently a momentary struggle in Dr. Lippert's mind; but at last, with a supreme effort, he waves his own objection aside. 'There are too many witnesses against it,' he says; 'and it probably arose at a time when Greek influence might have told on it.'

If this is not mere forensic pleading, I do not know what is. If Dr. Lippert knows that *sub divo* means beneath the sky, he surely knows likewise that *sub dio, sub diu,* and *sub Jove frigido* are used in the same sense. He knows that in Greek *diipétês* means swollen by rain, lit. fallen from the sky, and that *diosêmía* are portents in the sky. As dyaus in Sanskrit means not only sky and the god of the sky, but is used in the sense of day also, he knows that the Cretans used δία for ἡμέρα, and that *dium fulgur* was lightning by day which came from Jupiter. In fact, if by this time there still could be any reasonable doubt on the correctness of the common origin of Dyaus, Zeus, and Jupiter, the comparative study of languages might as well be banished from our Universities, the comparative study of mythology should be ostracised, and the comparative study of religions should take its place behind astrology and palmistry. Instead of forming the glory of the nineteenth century, these three sciences should be quoted in future, together with table-turning and spirit-rapping, as a disgrace to our generation.

Protest against Levity.

I am sorry that I should have had to use such strong language. I should gladly have remained silent, if it were a purely personal matter. I have

always held that it matters very little *who* is right,
but that it matters very much *what* is right. There
are many things in every branch of scientific research
which are doubtful. There are many questions in
the study of ancient language, mythology, and religion which at present, and possibly for ever, must be
left open questions. The exact spot, for instance, from
whence the Aryan languages—I do not speak of Aryan
people—started, cannot be determined with any approach to certainty, unless we can gain possession of
new facts. To speak on such a point, as if no difficulties existed, is unscholarly, and only shows that
those who rush in are ignorant of the dangers which
they ought to dread. But there are other questions
that have been solved once for all, and to re-open
them again and again, without a single scrap of new
evidence, is simply to impede the progress of knowledge. Nothing has been produced to weaken a
single link in the chain that unites the D y a u s of
the Veda with the *Zeus* of Homer. To say that Zeus
may be derived from ζῆν, to live, is simply to say
that which is not. And thus to trifle with an etymology is to trifle not only with what is true—that
is bad enough—but with what is sacred[1]. For the
history of the past is a sacred thing. The knowledge
that God has not left Himself without a witness in
India as well as anywhere else, is a sacred thing.
The evidence that the Âryas, before they separated,
had fixed on a name for god, and that a name, meaning the bright sky, is a sacred thing. In matters
of such import true science has a right to say, *Odi*

[1] See Appendix I.

profanum vulgus et arceo. A scholar who cannot grow indignant when he sees serious questions turned into ridicule[1] by mere trifling, does not deserve the name of a scholar, and to my mind the identity of these two divine names, Dyaus and *Zeus*, is with all its consequences as serious, as solemn, as sacred a matter as any article of our creed.

[1] Appendix II.

LECTURE IV.

THE HISTORICAL PROOF OF THE EXISTENCE OF GOD.

Securus Judicat Orbis Terrarum.

WE have lately been told that what finally determined Newman to leave the English Church and to join the communion of Rome, was a short sentence of St. Augustine, *Securus judicat orbis terrarum.* 'Cardinal Wiseman,' we are told [1], 'had written an article on the Donatist Schism, with an application to the Church of England. Newman read it, and did not see much in it. But one of his friends called his attention to St. Augustine's phrase, *Securus judicat orbis terrarum,* quoted in the article. The friend repeated these words again and again, says Newman; and when he was gone they kept running in my ears . . . "For a mere sentence," he says, "the words of St. Augustine struck me with a power which I never had felt from any words before. To take a familiar instance, they were like the 'Turn again, Whittington,' of the chime; or, to take a more serious one, they were like the '*Tolle, lege; tolle, lege*' of the child, which converted St. Augustine himself." *Securus judicat orbis terrarum*, by those great

---

[1] *Contemporary Review*, Jan. 1891, p. 141, Dean Church, by Canon Maccoll.

words of the ancient Father, interpreting and summing up the long and varied course of ecclesiastical history, the theory of the *Via Media* was absolutely pulverised.'

If we think how small and insignificant was the *orbis terrarum* to which St. Augustine could appeal, and yet how powerful the effect which that appeal produced at the time, and produced even in our own time on such a mind as Newman's, we are surely justified in appealing to the *orbis terrarum* in its widest sense, in support of the universal belief in God, whatever the images by which He was represented, whatever the names by which He was called [1]. And yet people ask what can be gained by a comprehensive study of religions, by showing that, as yet, no race has been discovered without some word for what is not-visible, not-finite, not-human, for something super-human, and divine.

It is curious that some theologians go even so far as to resent the discovery of the universality of such a belief. They are anxious to prove that human reason alone could never have arrived at a conception of God. They would much rather believe that God had left Himself without witness, than that a belief in something higher than the Finite could spring up in the human heart from gratitude to Him who gave us rain from heaven, and fruitful seasons, filling our hearts with food and gladness. At a recent Missionary Conference, held in London, it was gravely asserted by Dr. David Brown that the apostle Paul made a mistake at Athens, that he, when he appealed to the god whom the heathens ignorantly worship, meddled

---

[1] Τὸ δὲ βαρβαρικὸν, ὁμοίως μὲν ἅπαντες ξυνετοὶ τοῦ θεοῦ, κατεστήσαντο δὲ αὐτοῖς σημεῖα ἄλλοι ἄλλα. Maxim. Tyr., *Dissert.*, viii. 4.

with philosophy, and therefore had few converts [1]. And such irreverence is called Bible Christianity.

Universality of a Belief in God does not prove its Truth.

But there is another class of critics, far more difficult to deal with. Granted, they say, that a belief in gods, or even a belief in one Supreme God, can be discovered in every corner of the *orbis terrarum* as known to us—how does that prove that such a belief is true, and that either these different gods or a supreme deity really exist? In reply to the argument *securus judicat orbis terrarum*, 'the judgment of the whole world is safe,' it has been pointed out that the same *orbis terrarum* has been deceived again and again. We live in times of serious, nay, if you like, of honest atheism. People have not parted with their belief in the existence of a god, without a hard, a heart-breaking struggle. They declare that the old proofs for the existence of a divine Being, the *teleological*, the *ontological*, and the *cosmological*, have all failed them, and that a belief in revelation, without a previous belief in the existence of a divine Being, is impossible.

Let me remark that even if we admitted the truth of these objections, we might still claim for the history of religions the same right to a place among our academic studies which is conceded to other historical studies. If at our schools and universities we teach the history of literature, of art, and of the various branches of physical science, surely the history of religion ought to form a recognised department in the teaching of every university. Knowledge has a value of its

[1] *Madras Christian College Magazine*, Sept. 1889, p. 209.

own, even if it should not be of practical or marketable utility. Even if religion were nothing but hallucination, as we have lately been told, an accurate knowledge of the causes and the different phases of this universal disease might prove useful for its final cure.

But I claim a great deal more for an historical study of the religions of the world. To my mind the historical proof of the existence of God, which is supplied to us by the history of the religions of the world, has never been refuted, and cannot be refuted. It forms the foundation of all the other proofs, call them cosmological, ontological, or teleological; or rather, it absorbs them all, and makes them superfluous.

There are those who declare that they require no proof at all for the existence of a Supreme Being, or, if they did, that they would find it in revelation and nowhere else. Suppose they wanted no proof themselves, would they really not care at all to know how the human race, and how they themselves, came in possession of what, I suppose, they value as their most precious inheritance? Do they really think that in this case an examination of the ancient title-deeds might safely be dispensed with, while with regard to much less precious holdings it is considered a plain duty to guard these documents with the greatest care?

An appeal to revelation is of no avail in deciding questions of this kind, unless it is first explained what is really meant by revelation. The history of religions teaches us that the same appeal to a special revelation is made, not only by Christianity, but by the defenders of Brâhmanism, of Zoroastrianism, and of Mohammedanism, and where is the tribunal to adjudicate on the conflicting appeals of these and other claimants? The believer in the Vedas is as thoroughly convinced of the superhuman origin of his ancient hymns, as the Zoroastrian of that of the Gâthas, and the Mohammedan of that of the Sûrahs; and the subtle arguments by which each, but more particularly the Brâhman, supports his claims, would put some of our ablest casuists to shame. The followers of every one of these religions declare their belief in the revealed character of their own religion, never in that of any other religion. Many persons believe, and believe honestly, in visions they have had themselves, never in the visions claimed by other people. There is, no doubt, a revelation to which we may appeal in the court of our own conscience, but, before the court of universal appeal, we require different proofs for the faith that is in us.

Let our antagonists bear in mind that in what I call *Physical Religion*, the subject of my lectures of last year, we have proved not only the universality of a belief in something beyond the finite, in something infinite, in something divine. Even that would be something, considering the repeated attempts that have been made by students of great learning and research to prove the contrary. We have proved more than that. We have proved that, given man, such as he is, and given the world, such as it is, a belief in divine beings, and, at last, in one Divine Being, is not only a universal, but an *inevitable* fact.

Those who doubt the universality of the fact, have to take up the challenge, and produce their instances, or, at least one undoubted instance, of a really atheistic

race, I mean a race that *not yet* believes in superhuman
beings. The case of people who *no longer* believe in
gods is quite different, and has to be considered by
itself.

What we have to consider at present is, how it
follows that the universal belief in the Infinite, under
all its various disguises, is *true*.

Belief in God inevitable.

True is a strong word for any human being to use.
But suppose we could prove that universal dogma to
be inevitable, would not that suffice? Does it not
suffice us, for all geometrical calculations, to know
that, in this world at least, there are only three
dimensions, that the straight line is always the
shortest, and that two parallel lines can never meet?
Why then should it not suffice us to know that, in
this world at least, the belief in a Supreme Being is
inevitable for human beings, such as we are?

In former times it was the fashion to say that the
gods and all that was to be believed about them had
been invented by the priests, in order that they might
be better able to control the passions of men, and to
establish law and order on a firm basis. We saw, on
the contrary, that the gods were believed in long
before any priests were heard of, and that there was
no extraneous motive whatever for that belief. Unless
all historical evidence deceived us, that belief arose
everywhere naturally, irresistibly, and at first, we
might almost say, unconsciously. We may safely
say therefore that, as far as historical evidence goes,
man cannot escape from a belief in gods, whether
many or one. Philosophy may go so far as to teach

that the senses, the understanding, the whole intellect of man are all a fraud; but even philosophy will never teach us how to be anything but what we are, namely, human beings, and, in that sense, liable to human error. There may be truth beyond the reach of the human intellect, but that truth is not for us.

Philosophy has taught us to distinguish between what is phenomenal and what is real, but it stands to reason that we can know the real as phenomenal only. Everything we know, by the very fact that *we* know it, becomes phenomenal. To attempt to know what a thing is by itself, the *Noumenon*, *das Ding an sich*, is to attempt to know a thing as we do *not* know it, and this is a contradiction in itself. Nothing can be real to us, unless it submits to be phenomenal; nothing can be objective to us, except in the forms of our own subjective consciousness. It is strange that even philosophers should not see this,— at least some of them; and that they should attempt what even the ancient metaphysicians called a most troublesome athletic performance, namely, to stand on their own shoulders, to see beyond their own horizon.

Even physical science ought to have opened people's eyes. In music, for instance, we speak of tones, yet we know that by itself, that is, if not taken in by our ear, what we call A′, the A′ of our tuning-forks, consists really of 875 single vibrations in one second. If we speak of colours, we know that by itself, that is, if not taken in by our eye, what we call red is simply so many millions of vibrations of ether in one second. I use these, of course, as illustrations only, for even the number of these vibrations is phenomenal, or based on phenomenal experience.

But as illustrations they might teach us that whatever we perceive we must perceive by *our* senses, whatever we know we must know by *our own* mind, and call by *our own* language, that all our knowledge in fact must be phenomenal or relative, must be human knowledge.

All therefore that the historical student of religion maintains that he has proved is that man, being what he is, and simply using the instruments of knowledge which he possesses, cannot escape from a belief in an infinite Being, whatever forms it may assume in the historical development of the human race.

If then, from the standpoint of human reason, no flaw can be pointed out in that intellectual process which led to the admission of something within, behind, or beyond nature, call it the Infinite or any other name you like, it follows that the history of that process is really at the same time the best proof of the legitimacy and truth of the conclusions to which it has led.

History of the Belief in gods and God.

And here it is where our historical studies, which to some appear so far removed from the burning interests of the hour, touch the springs of our deepest religious convictions. Our own belief in God as the author of all that exists, whether we call Him father or creator or supporter of the world, has its deepest, its only living roots in that ancient, universal stratum of thought which postulated an agent in the sky, the sun, the fire, and the storm-wind; which was not satisfied with the mere play of appearances in nature, but yearned to know what it was that appeared; which felt the limits of the finite in all its sensuous perceptions, and in feeling the limits, felt at the same time the presence of something that was beyond those limits. This dissatisfaction with the finite, this struggle after the non-finite, this search for an agent for every act, of a mover for every movement, whatever shape it took, whatever name it claimed, forms the primitive and indestructible foundation of man's faith in God. If it is taken away, people may indeed have dogma and creeds, but they cannot have their own ineradicable conviction that there is and that there must be a God. Dogma can supply no argument against atheism. Dogma is what my excellent colleague at Edinburgh, Mr. Hutchinson Stirling (p. 12), has very truly called mere *Vorstellung*, which requires for its philosophical foundation the *Begriff*. But that *Begriff* has a history, and it is this history of the *Begriff* which to my mind is the true, because unanswerable, answer to all atheism. I should go so far as to say that the history of religion is the best proof of religion, just as the growth of the oak-tree is the best proof of the oak-tree. There may be excrescences, there may be dead leaves, there may be broken branches, but the oak-tree is there, once for all, whether in the sacred groves of Germany, or at Dodona, or in the Himalayan forests. It is there, not by our own will, but by itself, or by a Higher Will. There may be corruptions, there may be antiquated formulas, there may be sacred writings flung to the wind, but religion is there, once for all, in all its various representations. You can as little sweep away the oak-tree with its millions of seeds from the face of the earth, as you can eradicate religion, true religion, from the human heart.

(3)   H

Are all Religions True?

But it may be objected that, if everything at which man by his unassisted intellect arrives were true, then all religions would be true, and, as many of them contradict either themselves or one another, this cannot be.

This is the very objection which nothing, I believe, can meet and repel except an appeal to history.

History teaches us how all the predicates which were bestowed by man on the Transcendent, or what was beyond the finite, or what I 'call the Infinite, proved insufficient. One after another they were chosen as the best that the human mind possessed, but one after another they were rejected as inadequate for their highest purpose.

You remember how the Peruvian Inca, who had all his life looked upon the Sun as the true manifestation of the Divine, as the maker and ruler of the world, nay, as his father, and the father of his own royal race, was suddenly disturbed in his mind because the sun seemed to rise and set, to come and go, not of his own free will, but at the command of some one else. Hence he decided that the Sun could not be the true God, and that that name, however sacred, must be surrendered and replaced by another, a better, a higher name. But though he rejected the predicate, he did not reject the subject; on the contrary, the rejection of that predicate served only to raise the subject for which it had been intended, to a higher level.

Let us suppose that the same thoughtful Inca, after renouncing the name of Sun, had only retained the name of Father for that which he was searching for. That name might have satisfied him for a time. But

in moments of more serious reflection the same difficulties would have returned. Father could not have
remained for a long time a satisfactory predicate of
the godhead; for is not every father the son of
another father? Is not a father dependent on a
mother? Is not the son of the same substance as
the father? and if the son is mortal, is not the father
mortal also? All these and many more objections
might have troubled our conscientious Inca, and
might have led him after a time to discard the predicate father, as he had discarded before the predicate
sun. And if he had carried his speculations further,
he would probably in the end have arrived at the
conclusion at which the worshipper of the Vedic
deities arrived, that there is no predicate in human
language worthy of God, and that all we can say of
Him is what, as you may remember, the Upanishads
said of Him, No, no!

The Gradual Elimination of what is imperfect.

What does that mean? It meant that if God is
called all-powerful, we have to say No, because whatever we comprehend by powerful is nothing compared
with the power of God. If God is called all-wise, we
have again to say No, because what we call wisdom
cannot approach the wisdom of God. If God is called
holy, again we have to say No, for what can our conception of holiness be, compared with the holiness of
God! This is what the thinkers of the Upanishads
meant when they said that all we can say of God is
No, no.

Negative Definition in Greek Philosophy.

Nor were the philosophers of Greece behind the
philosophers of India in denying the possibility of

naming or predicating anything rightly of the Deity. We know the protests of Xenophon, of Plato, and of Aristotle against all attempts of applying human names and concepts to the Supreme Being. But even in later times, in the second century A.D., we find philosophers, such as Maximus Tyrius, for instance, still repeating the same protest. 'God,' he writes (Dissert. viii. 10), 'the father and maker of all things, who is older than the sun, older than the sky, who is beyond time and age and all changing nature, is without a name given Him by legislators, inexpressible by language, invisible to the eyes. And as we cannot grasp His essence, we try to approach Him through words, names, pictures, images of gold, ivory, and silver, through plants, rivers, mountains, and lakes, yearning to know Him, but from our weakness predicating all that we know as most beautiful of His nature [1].'

In all this we can still clearly perceive the spirit of Plato. In fact, Maximus Tyrius quotes Plato in his seventeenth Dissertation, when he says: 'Thus this messenger from the Academy places before us the father and creator of the universe. He does not tell his name, for he knew it not; he does not tell his colour, for he saw it not; he does not tell his size, for he touched it not. These natural qualities are the perceptions of the flesh and the eyes, but the Divine itself is not seen by the eyes, nor spoken by the voice, nor touched by the flesh, nor heard by the ear. Only by what is most beautiful, most pure, most clear-sighted, most swift, and most ancient in the soul is it seen through likeness, and heard through kinship,

[1] See Hatch, *Hibbert Lectures*, p. 242.

taken in whole and complete by complete perception.'

Negative Definition in Christian Theology.

The early Christians also, many of whom, as the late Dr. Hatch has clearly shown in his Hibbert Lectures, were Greek rather than Jewish, who had been brought up in the schools of Plato and Aristotle, and were perfectly familiar with the metaphysical terminology of these powerful thinkers, spoke of the Deity in the same abstract language, in the same negative terms. To them God was no longer simply Jehovah, the God of Abraham, Isaac, and Jacob, the God who walked in the garden of Eden in the cool of the day, not even the God who maketh the clouds His chariot, who walketh upon the wings of the wind. 'Listen, my friend,' writes Theophilus, when asked by a heathen opponent to describe the form of the Christian God : 'the form of God is unutterable and indescribable, nor can it be seen with fleshly eyes : for His glory is uncontained, His size is incomprehensible, His loftiness is inconceivable, His strength is incomparable, His wisdom is unrivalled, His goodness beyond imitation, His beneficence beyond description. If I speak of Him as light, I mention His handiwork : if I speak of Him as reason, I mention His government : if I speak of Him as spirit, I mention His breath : if I speak of Him as wisdom, I mention His offspring : if I speak of Him as strength, I mention His might : if I speak of Him as providence, I mention His goodness : if I speak of His Kingdom, I mention His glory' (Hatch, l. c., p. 253). Clement of Alexandria (Strom. v. 12) asserts still more strongly that there is no name that can properly be named of Him,—'neither the One, nor the Good, nor Mind, nor Absolute Being, nor Father, nor Creator, nor Lord' (Hatch, l. c., p. 255).

True Agnosticism.

Would not many of these early Christians be condemned for such utterances as Agnostics by our modern theologians—at least by some of them? And yet, it was not pride of intellect, it was, on the contrary, intellectual humility that made them silent before the majesty of an infinite Being.

True Agnosticism, so far from being a negation of all true religion, seems to me the only safe foundation of it. How can we be said to know what we cannot name, and who is there that would maintain that God can be named? Let us hear what Philo says on this point:

'God is invisible,' he writes, 'for how can eyes that are too weak to gaze upon the sun be strong enough to gaze upon its Maker? He is incomprehensible; not even the whole universe, much less the human mind, can contain the conception of Him. We know that He is, we cannot know what He is. We may see the manifestation of Him in His works, but it were monstrous folly to go behind His works and inquire into His essence. Hence He is unnamed, for names are the symbols of created things, whereas His only attribute is to be [1].'

And if Philo is not considered as an authority, perhaps Cardinal Newman may be with some at least

---

[1] Hatch, *Hibbert Lectures*, p. 245.

of my hearers. Yet he expresses exactly the same conviction when he says: 'God is incommunicable in all His attributes.'

If people would only define what they mean by knowing, they would shrink from the very idea that God could ever be known by us in the same sense in which everything else is known, or that with regard to Him we could ever be anything but Agnostics. All human knowledge begins with the senses, and goes on from sensations to percepts, from percepts to concepts and names. And yet the same people who insist that they know God, will declare in the same breath that no one can see God and live, and that no flesh that hath heard the voice of the living God speaking out of the midst of fire, can live (Deuter. v. 26). Let us only define the meaning of knowing, and keep the different senses in which this word has been used carefully apart, and I doubt whether any one would venture to say that, in the true sense of the word, he is not an Agnostic as regards the true nature of God. If any one doubts, let him read the almost-forgotten works of Cusanus, particularly his *Docta Ignorantia*, and let him remember that before the Reformation such true Agnosticism was not only tolerated, but that Cusanus who held it and taught it died as a Cardinal and as a friend of Pope Nicolaus V.

This silence before a nameless Being does not exclude a true belief in God, nor devotion, nor love of a Being beyond our senses, beyond our understanding, beyond our reason, and therefore beyond all names.

All Names well meant.

On the contrary, every one of the names given to

this infinite Being by finite beings marks a stage in the evolution of religious truth. If only we try to understand these names, we shall find that they were all well meant, that, for the time being, they were probably the only possible names. Dyaus, Zeus, whether it was meant for light or for sky, was originally a well-meant name. It did not mean at first the material sky only, as an object, but it meant, as we saw, the agent postulated behind or within the sky, what Plato meant by the soul of the sky. If the agent or the sky was often mistaken for the sky itself, and many things that could be truly predicated of the material sky only were predicated of Dyaus or Zeus or Jupiter, history teaches us how this confusion arose, and thus warns us against similar errors.

In China also the name of the supreme deity is *Tien* or sky. And not only Chinese scholars in Europe, but scholars in China also have been disputing for centuries whether what is meant by Tien is the real sky or the Supreme Being, supposed to be residing in the sky, or invoked by the name of the sky. We ourselves should never be in doubt, if we heard any one say, 'Heaven knows.' We should know at once that he did not mean the visible heaven, but much the same as if he were to say 'God knows.' When the prodigal son says, 'I have sinned against Heaven and in Thy sight,' we know that against Heaven means against God.

But most missionaries will assure us that, when the Chinese address their prayers to Tien, when they say, 'Tien knows,' when they say, 'I have sinned before Tien,' they mean the blue sky and nothing else. It is quite possible that thousands of uneducated

Chinese would give the same answer. But when the once famous Commissioner Yeh was asked to give an account of what an educated Chinese meant by Tien, he said that Tien meant, no doubt, the material heaven, but that it also meant Shang-te, the supreme ruler or God. It is not lawful, he added, to use the name of Shang-te lightly, and therefore we name him by his residence, which is *tien* [1].

Let it be clearly understood, therefore, that the Historical School does not look upon all the names that were given to divine powers as simply true or simply false. We look upon all of them as well meant and true for the time being, as steps on the ladder on which the angels of God ascend and descend. There was no harm in the ancient people, when they were thirsting for rain, invoking the sky and saying, 'O dear sky, send us rain.' There was no harm when they saw their stable struck by lightning, in their imploring the thunderer to spare their home and their children. There was no harm when they were dying of cold, in their greeting the rising sun as a dear friend and protector. And when after a time they used more and more general words, when they addressed these powers as bright, or rich, or mighty, as kings and lords, as friends and fathers, all these were meant for something else, for something they were seeking for, if haply they might feel after Him and find Him. This is St. Paul's view of the growth of religion, this is the view defended and supported by new evidence by the Historical School,—and this is the view condemned as heretical and blasphemous by men who call themselves Christian Divines.

[1] See Hilderic Friend, in *Folk Lore Record*, vol. iv. p. 6.

Names of the Infinite.

When I said that all these names had been from the beginning names of the Infinite, I hardly expected that I could have been so far misunderstood as if I supposed that the name and concept of the Infinite had been fully elaborated, before it was called Sky and Earth, Sun and Moon, Day and Night, Lord, Maker, Ruler, Friend, and Father. I have actually been told, as something I ought to have known, that when the prehistoric Semite built altars to and called on the name of Shaddai, Jehovah, or Baal, the object of his worship was not at first conceived as Infinite, but as very local and limited and finite indeed. The Himalayan mountain range has different names in different dialects and in different parts of its long extent. We who know its unbroken continuity from east to west, speak of the whole as the Himalayan range; but the inhabitants of every small valley, by whatever name they call their own hills, *mean* likewise the Himalayan range, though they have as yet no name for it. It is in that sense that the people who spoke of their own gods as Zeus, or Apollo, or Athene, meant the Infinite that was behind or in these names, though as yet they had no name for it. When I speak of the Infinite, I simply use the widest generalisation within my reach, wider even than what is comprehended by the name of the Unknowable. To suppose that such generalisations had been realised in the minds of the earliest observers of thunder and lightning, would be to invert the whole historical growth of the human mind. But as soon as an altar was built to Shaddai, as the giver of rain, as soon as such a name was formed, something more was meant than the visible cloud or the finite sky, something which by the most general term I shall continue to call the Non-Finite and the Infinite.

There are indeed misapprehensions against which it is almost degrading to defend oneself.

I Am that I Am.

When we find in the old Testament such names as Elohim, Adonai, Jehovah or Jah, we never doubt that they were all meant for the same Being. But when, as we are told in the book of Exodus, iii. 14, Moses asked the God of his fathers what was His true name, is it not wonderful that that name contains no predicate whatever, 'no manner of similitude,' but is simply, 'I Am that I Am'?

To a student of the history of religion such unexpected rays of light are quite dazzling. I call them unexpected, because the language in which Jehovah is spoken of in the Old Testament is often, as you know, not very different from the language applied to the deity in other ancient religions. It is human language, full of metaphor; it is, what is called, anthropomorphic; and what else could it be?

It is true that in India also we meet with the same or a very similar name. We read in one of the Upanishads[1], 'He, looking round, saw nothing but himself. He first said: "This is I;" and therefore he became "I" by name.'

But in India we can see how the way was slowly

[1] Brihad-âranyaka Upanishad, I. 4, 1, *Sacred Books of the East*, vol. xv. p. 85.

prepared for so abstract, so unmetaphorical, and in no
sense anthropomorphic a name as ' I am I.' We can
see there a class of philosophic theologians, working
hard to free their thoughts from the inevitable
leading-strings of language. But among the Jews at
the time of Moses (placing ourselves on the ordinary
standpoint of readers of the Old Testament), so sudden
a burst of the purest light, so transcendent a name of
the deity, as ' *I am*,' comes upon us indeed like a
revelation, in the truest sense of the word.

And what is more marvellous still, we find joined
with this, the most abstract conception of the deity,
that truly human feeling for God which is expressed
in such words as: ' Hear, O Israel: the Lord our God
is one Lord: And thou shalt *love* the Lord thy God
with all thine heart, and with all thy soul, and with
all thy might' (Deuter. vi. 4). I doubt whether we
can find anything like this anywhere else. When
God has once been conceived without 'any manner of
similitude,' He may be meditated on, revered, and
adored, but that fervent passion of the human breast,
that love with all our heart, and all our soul, and all our
might, seems to become hushed before that solemn
presence. We may love our father and mother with
all our heart, we may cling to our children with all
our soul, we may be devoted to our wives and husbands and friends with all our might, but to throw all
these feelings in their concentrated force and truth on
the deity, has been given to very few elect souls only,
the true Saints of the world. Others must rest con-
tent with the hope that true love shown to any human
being, to father and mother, to husband and wife, to
sons and daughters, aye to the stranger also, if there

is a stranger, may take the place of that love of God which Moses demanded, and that 'what ye have done unto one of the least of these My brethren, ye have done it unto Me' (Matth. xxv. 40).

The Three Vedânta Predicates.

But while in some places the ancient philosophers of India would go so far as to protest against all predicates of the deity, even against that of existence, lest it might be mistaken as identical with the transient existence of human or any other beings, we find that even in the Vedânta philosophy, these Indian metaphysicians condescended to recognise a somewhat more human view of the Supreme Being, and allowed at least three predicates. They were *to be, to know,* and *to rejoice,* or, possibly, *to love,* and I doubt whether the most rigid metaphysician could rightly object to any one of them. When in the historical process of name-giving and name-removing, the Infinite has been freed again of all names that proved inadequate, no philosophy, and no religion need give up these three predicates. What is meant by the Infinite, or the Unknown, or the Divine, for all these names have the same intention, must be allowed *to be,* must be allowed *to know,* and must be allowed *to rejoice,* or, as others will have it, *to love,* to be blessed in itself, to be satisfied. The opposite of these three propositions is unthinkable, and this must suffice for us, as long as we are what we are. We cannot conceive the Infinite, or the Unknown, or the Divine, and conceive it as not being. This is the purely human side of the ontological argument. Nor

can we conceive it as not-knowing, however different
its knowledge may be from human knowledge. *Esse*
with the Infinite, is in reality *percipi,* and who
should be the percipient, if not the Infinite itself?
We may be more doubtful about the third predicate,
that of bliss or love, because it seems to have too
much of a human character, too much of a πάθος,
about it. But again the absence of bliss, satisfaction,
and love would be a defect, I mean from a human
point of view.

It is well known that even the Epicureans who
predicated so little of their gods, predicated of them
perfect blessedness. 'Eternal existence and perfect
happiness are, according to Epicurus, the two fundamental elements which, in all ages and nations, constitute the true idea of godhead—an idea which is as
widespread as the human race [1].'

We may therefore grant the Hindu triad of divine
predicates, and say, if there is an Infinite, an undefin-
able and unnameable Being, if there is an Agent
behind all acts, we cannot deny its perfect bliss, its
perfect knowledge, and its everlasting existence.

Masculine or Neuter.

You may have observed how difficult it is when
speaking of that infinite Being, to know whether we
ought to speak of it as He or It. With us that
distinction always implies something human. *He*
implies masculine gender and excludes feminine
gender, and from either point of view it is inapplicable to God, while *It*, implying neither, seems
preferable. But on the other hand *He* implies agency,

[1] W. Wallace, *Epicureanism*, p. 207.

activity, not to say life, while *It* implies mere objectivity, passivity, not to say lifelessness. In languages which distinguish no gender this difficulty does not exist. In languages again which distinguish two classes only, one of animate, the other of inanimate beings, the choice is much easier. But being what we are, speaking an Aryan language and thinking Aryan thoughts, there can be no doubt that we must speak of the Infinite as *He*, though with certain reservations, and not as either *She* or *It*.

Here then is the last point at which we arrive by a continuous progress from the lowest perception of the unknown Infinite, to the highest expression that poor human nature can find for it. The predicates become wider and wider, purer and purer, truer, we hope, and truer, and yet their subject is always beyond their reach. The last result of Physical Religion will always remain, that there is something within or behind the finite world which, by a most comprehensive, but from one point of view, no doubt, by a very empty name, we may call the Infinite. But the history of religion, and a knowledge of our own human nature, teaches us likewise that so vague and so cold a name ceases to be religious, and cannot satisfy the deepest yearnings of the human heart.

Return to the Old Names.

In times of trouble and despair, and in moments of intensest happiness too, the heart falls back on the old names, and utters once more the language of the childhood of the world and of its own childhood. It does not call for help on the Infinite, but though feeling the overwhelming presence of the Infinite, it says Lord, it says my God, it says Our Father. And what harm is there ? If we have understood the lessons of the history of religion, we know that all these names, and even much less perfect names, were well meant, were all meant for the same, and that He who is beyond all names, understands them all. I have often quoted the words placed in the mouth of K*rishna*, 'Even those who worship idols, worship me.' Whatever we do, however pure and abstract our language may be, in one sense we are all idolators, we idolise the deity in the imperfect ideas which we have formed of it, and under the ever-varying names which we have given to it.

The Minimum.

What, however, we may say with a good conscience, both as philosophers and as historians, is this, that how high so ever above all our ideas, and all our names and concepts, the Infinite may be, that Infinite is *at least* the source of light that beams from heaven, it is *at least* the giver of the fire that warms and cheers us, it is *at least* in the storm-wind, it is *at least* the Lord, it is *at least* the Father, whatever else He may be. We still use the name of Jehovah, though we know how many things have been predicated of Jehovah which are incompatible with our reverence for the Deity. We shrink from using the names of *Zeus* and *Jupiter*, but the early Christians had no such fears. Thus Tertullian (ad Scap. 4) speaks of 'the people shouting to the God of gods who alone is powerful, as bearing witness to our God by the name of Jupiter,' while in another passage he actually appeals to 'Jovem Christianum.' Dante also still uses Giove in the sense of God, when he says (Purg. vi. 118):

'O sommo Giove, che foste in terra per noi crucifisso.'

And Petrarca does not hesitate to say (Son. 133):

'Se l'eterno Giove della sua grazia sovra me non piovi.'

Nor are we ourselves afraid to speak of God as the *Deus Optimus Maximus*, though the word *deus* also is of heathen workmanship, and was meant originally for the bright powers of the sky, the sun, the moon, the dawn, and the spring; though *maximus* meant probably no more, at first, than the greatest among such gods as Mars, Janus, Quirinus, and Bellona (Liv. viii. 6, 9; 10; x. 28; 29), while *optimus* conveyed at first the idea of the richest rather than of the best.

I could hardly have believed it, if I had not seen it black on white, that there are some classical scholars left who seem to look upon Jupiter as a real person, and who have asked me whether I really mean that Jupiter is the same individual as the God of the Jews and the Christians. What meaning can they connect with such words? Do they really imagine that Jupiter was some kind of potentate who lived on Mount Olympus, and, then, after changing his name and clothing, emigrated to Mount Zion? If they do not mean that, what do they mean?

The Names and what is named.

Surely, if the study of the history of religion has taught us anything, it has taught us to distinguish between the names and what is named. The names

may change, they may become more and more perfect,
and as they become more perfect, our concepts of the
deity may become more perfect also, but the deity itself
is not affected by our names. However much the
names may differ and change, there remains as the
last result of the study of religion, the everlasting
conviction that behind all the names there is a something named, that there is an agent behind all acts,
that there is an Infinite behind the Finite, that there
is a God in Nature. That God is the abiding goal of
many names, all well meant and well aimed, and yet
all, far, far away from the goal which no man can
see—and live. Convince the human understanding
that there can be acts without agents, that there can
be a limit without something beyond, that there can
be a Finite without a Non-Finite, and you have
proved that there is no God. But let it be shown
that the universality of that belief rests on that
without which sense would not be sense, reason
would not be reason, man would not be man, and we
may say that for man as he is, for reason as it is, nay,
even for the perceptions of the senses as they are,
belief in something infinite, in an agent, in a God, is
irresistible. All names that human language has invented may be imperfect. But the name, ' I Am that
I Am,' will remain for those who think Semitic
thought, while to those who speak Aryan languages
it will be difficult to invent a better name than that
of the Vedânta, Sa*k*-*k*id-ânanda, He who is, who
knows, and who is blessed.

LECTURE V.

ABOUT THE TRUE CHARACTER OF ANCESTOR-WORSHIP.

The Name of Anthropological Religion.

IT was not easy to find a satisfactory name for that branch of Natural Religion of which I mean to treat in this course of Lectures. The discovery of the Infinite in nature, traced from its first poor beginnings to its culminating point, the belief in One God, as manifested in the whole of nature, could be called by one name only, namely *Physical Religion*. By a proper definition, this Physical Religion might easily be kept distinct from *Natural Religion*, of which it forms one branch.

But what name is there for the second branch of Natural Religion, which is to comprehend the history of the various attempts at discovering something infinite and divine in man or mankind, beginning with the first surmises of the existence of something different from the body, and culminating in a belief in the divine sonship of man, the true key-note of the religion of Christ? Perhaps the proper title would have been *Anthropic* Religion. But I shrink from forming new words, if it can be avoided. And, as for the third branch of Natural Religion, which deals with the true nature of the soul or the self, the most intelligible name seemed to be *Psychological Religion*, I determined to use *Anthropological* for the second branch, only guarding against the supposition that Anthropological Religion is in any way more closely connected with what is now called Anthropology, the Science of Man and Civilisation, as Dr. Tylor defines it, than the other branches of Natural Religion. It may be true that the languages of uncivilised races throw more light on the problems of Anthropological Religion than on those of Physical and Psychological Religion ; and it is for that reason that we shall have to examine the true value of this kind of testimony more carefully now than we were called upon to do when tracing the development of the universal belief in the gods of nature. But otherwise Anthropological Religion has nothing to do with Anthropology. It is called anthropological, simply and solely in order to comprehend under that name all the attempts which have been made to discover something not merely human, then superhuman, then divine and immortal in man. The most interesting parts of this process are the beginning and the end, the first discovery of something different from the body, and the final identification of that something with the Divine. To these two parts we shall have to devote most of our attention, leaving the intermediate steps, which are better known, to the historian of religion and of philosophy.

Former Opinions on the Sources of Religion.

It is unfortunate that in tracing this second development of religious thought, the *anthropological*, we shall have to defend almost every step we take, against certain philosophers who have traversed the same ground, but who have done so without an accurate knowledge of the facts that have to be interpreted, and, what is still worse, with certain preconceived ideas of their own, which they have applied to the interpretation of these facts,—I mean, more particularly, Comte in France, Mr. Herbert Spencer in England, and Lippert, Gruppe, and several other scholars in Germany. The fatal mistake which, according to my opinion, vitiates all their researches is their not seeing, or not being willing to see, that religion has had many sources, and that any attempt to trace all phases of religion back to one source must lead to the most forced and unnatural theories. If anything is all-embracing, it is what we call religion. We might as well derive the ocean from one river as religion from one source.

Fetishism.

The theory first broached by De Brosses, and afterwards adopted by Comte, that all religion arose from Fetishism, need not be slain again. It broke down, because it tried to make one small and very late tributary the main source of all religion.

De Brosses himself, however, still kept within certain bounds[1]. He claimed for fetishism a share in the early growth of religious ideas; he did not make it the only source of all religion. It was Bastholm who, in his famous work on Anthropology, published

---

[1] Bastholm, *Historische Nachrichten zur Kenntniss der Menschen*, aus dem Dänischen übersetzt von H. E. Wolf, Altona, xi. 1818, vol. iv. p. 168.

in 1805, claimed 'everything produced by nature or art, which receives divine honour, including sun, moon, earth, air, fire, water, mountains, rivers, trees, stones, images, and animals, if considered as objects of divine worship, as fetish.' Of late another step has been made, and Lippert[1] now defines fetishism 'as a belief in the souls of the departed coming to dwell in anything that is tangible or visible in heaven or earth.'

But while anthropologists mostly contented themselves with collecting facts, more or less carefully observed and comprehended under the ill-defined name of fetishism, Comte went further still, and claimed fetishism as a necessary plan in the universal growth of religion. This of course was a mere theory, unsupported by facts, and called by a misleading name. But it took a long time before that theory was completely annihilated. The ease with which it explained everything, recommended it to many who dislike the trouble of vigorous thought. If it was asked why people worshipped the sun, the answer was always ready, because they took the sun for a fetish. The same answer was supposed to account for tree-worship, serpent-worship, idol-worship, stone- and shell-worship, in fact for everything. I do not mean to say that the ghost of fetishism has been entirely laid, but it only haunts deserted places now. Mr. Herbert Spencer himself has formally surrendered that theory, and has set an excellent example in doing this. How much rubbish that now stops the way of further advance might be removed, if all who have dis-

---

[1] *Die Religionen der Europäischen Culturvölker*, 1881, p. 10.

covered a theory which they once held, to be untenable, would follow his excellent example, and say so openly. This is what Mr. Spencer writes in his *Principles of Sociology* (1877), p. 343:

'How untenable is the idea that fetishism comes first among superstitions will now be manifest. Suppose the facts reversed. Suppose that by Juángs, Andamanese, Fuegians, Australians, Tasmanians, and Bushmen, worship of inanimate objects was carried to the greatest extent; that among tribes a little advanced in intelligence and social state it was somewhat restricted; that it went on decreasing as knowledge and civilisation increased; and that in highly-developed societies, such as those of ancient Peru and modern India, it became inconspicuous. Should we not say that the statement was conclusively proved? Clearly, then, as the facts happen to be exactly the opposite, the statement is conclusively disproved.'

Mr. Herbert Spencer explains very truly how this extraordinary superstition—I do not mean fetishism, but a belief in fetishism as a primordial religion—arose (p. 344):

'Made,' he writes, 'on the strength of evidence furnished by early travellers, whose contact was chiefly with races partially advanced and even semi-civilised, the assertion that fetishism is primordial gained possession of men's minds; and prepossession being nine points of belief, it has held its ground with scarcely a question. I had myself accepted it; though, as I remember, with some vague dissatisfaction, probably arising from inability to see how so strange an interpretation arose. This vague dissatisfaction passed into scepticism on becoming better acquainted with the ideas of savages. Tabulated evidence presented by the lowest races, changed scepticism into disbelief ; and thought has made it manifest that the statement, disproved *à posteriori*, is contrary to *à priori* probability.'

It was indeed high time that this spurious fetishism should have been exterminated, for it had almost been introduced into the very country from which it had at first been carried away by those Portuguese sailors whom De Brosses followed as his authorities. Lander, as quoted by Mr. Spencer (*Sociology*, p. 134), when narrating his voyage down the Niger, says : ' From time to time, as we came to a turn in the creek, the captain of the canoe—a Negro, I suppose—halloed to the fetish, and where an echo was returned, half a glass of rum and a piece of yam and fish were thrown into the water. When asked why, he said—" Did you not hear the fetish ? " '

It must be clear that, whatever the facts of the case may have been, the form in which it is told is simply impossible. First of all, the fetishes of De Brosses were never supposed to speak through the echo. Secondly, the name fetish, assigned by Portuguese priests to the Negro amulets and talismans, is of course utterly unknown to the natives themselves. To ask a Negro, as has often been done, whether he believes in a fetish, is much the same as to ask him whether he believes in Satan or the Devil. How is he to know what we mean by Satan or the Devil ?[1]

---

[1] It is curious, however, that in conversation with Europeans, some African tribes actually use now the word fetish. W. J. Müller, in his *Die Africanische Landschaft Fetu*, Nüremberg, 1675, says : 'When they talk to whites, they call their idolatry *Fitiseken*, I believe because the Portuguese call *Zauberei fitiso*.'

We might as well ask him whether he believes in Constitutional Government or in the Law of Gravitation.

Fetishism, however, need not be banished altogether from the history of religious thought. On the contrary, it has its place, as I tried to show in my Hibbert Lectures, as a very late phase of superstition, during which, with or without reason, some peculiar charm is ascribed to the most casual objects. Our peasants still believe in the efficacy of a horse-shoe, and many of us, I suspect, carry a halfpenny with a hole for luck. I am not ashamed to say I have myself done so for years. This is what is called a survival. The world is still full of such survivals, but it does not always follow that they are the rudiments of a primordial faith. There is old rubbish, but there is new rubbish also—a point which we may have to discuss more fully hereafter.

Totemism.

And what applies to Fetishism, applies to Totemism also. Totemism is, no doubt, a most curious phase in the evolution of religious thought. But we want an accurate definition of it. Everything almost that is considered sacred in any religion, has by some writer or other been called a *totem*. But why should the original and true meaning of totem be so diluted and destroyed ? *Totem* became known to us first of all through missionaries among the Indian tribes of Canada. They tell us that in the language of the Indians it meant ' clan mark,' or, rather, ' my clan mark.' Father Cuoq (see *Academy*, Sept. 20, 1884) states that the word is properly *ote*, meaning ' clan mark.' The possessive form is *otem*, and with the personal pronoun *nind otem*, ' my clan mark,' *kit otem*, 'thy clan mark, &c.' These clan marks still exist, and an Ottawa Indian has told us that the people to whom he belonged were divided into tribes, sections, and families, according to their clan marks or *ododams*. All people belonging to the same *ododam* or sign-post were required to dwell in their own section of the village. At the principal entrance of their enclosure there was often a sign set up. Those who had a bear for their sign were called the Bears; others, the Gulls, the Hawks, the Finches, the Hares, and so on.

After a time every family had to adopt some kind of *totem*, which became more and more important as signs of recognition in war, and in migrations from one place to another. What would be more natural under these circumstances than that those who called themselves Bears should be supposed to be descended from a bear, that they should feel a certain reverence for their ursine ancestor, should look upon real bears as some distant relations, and abstain from killing and eating the animal?

All this is perfectly intelligible, and it is equally intelligible that similar, though not identical, customs and ideas should have sprung up in many parts of the world. Nor was there any harm if, at first, all such customs should have been comprehended under the name of Totemism. But Anthropology has left that early stage, and its best representatives are now engaged, not so much in comparing as in discriminating. Comparative Philology also began with comparing; it is now almost entirely occupied with discovering what is peculiar to each family of languages, to each language, to each dialect. To treat all animal worship as due to totemism is a mistake. Animal worship has many different sources. Nor is totemism the only reason why people abstain from eating certain animals. Surely the Jews did not abstain from eating pork because they were totemists, and believed themselves descended from a pig. It does not follow that because savage tribes in different parts of the world do the same thing, they do it for the same reason. For the purposes of clear thought we must, as much as possible, keep one name for one thing, and endeavour to prevent its definition from becoming blurred by promiscuous usage. Comparison and generalisation are interesting and useful, as a first step; but real knowledge is based on discrimination.

If we once knew what is meant by fetishism, what by totemism, and what by worship of ancestors, we can follow the course of these three independent streams of religious thought in different parts of the world, and derive many useful lessons from what they share in common and what is peculiar to each. But when we are told by Long (*Academy*, Sept. 20, 1884) that totem designates the protecting animals or other worshipful objects of each sept, or by Schoolcraft that totems are the mother-class of the Algonquins, or by Lippert (l. c., p. 12) that 'a totem is the same as a fetish in which the soul of some departed ancestor has taken up its abode,' we have a right to protest, and to say, 'Define what you mean by fetish, by totem, and by ancestral spirits, and do not mix up three things which, as has been shown again and again, have had three distinct and totally independent beginnings.'

In many cases what are called *totems* are nothing of the kind. For instance, the same Indians who have their totems, which may well be translated by family crests, have also charms in the shape of animals. But these charms have a totally different origin. For instance [1], when a young man intends to become a medicine-man, he fasts and prays, until in a vision there is revealed to him his god, in the shape of a bird or animal, 'which he seeks, and carries with him as his protector and guide. Every young man must seek such a god to protect him. The representation of this god he carries at all times as a charm. . . . The skins of animals and birds seen in visions are stuffed and worn on the person. Sometimes deer-skins and cow-hide are cut into strips and made into snakes, toads, and various reptiles, ornamented with beads, and carried about on the person or in the medicine bag.'

Now these charms are quite different from the totems. Men belonging to the same totem may each have his own charm, some one of these animals or birds seen in a vision. And while there is no secret about totems, these charms were often kept secret, or displayed on sacred festivals only.

If a man among the Santec Indians should dream of a buffalo, he takes the head of the buffalo which he has killed, removes the skin, restores it to its natural shape, and allows it to cure. He then removes the rods from a few square feet of earth behind a lodge, works the exposed earth very fine, takes a new blanket or robe, which must not have belonged to a woman, and places it over this prepared soil, which was called the *Umane*. The skin of the buffalo head,

---

[1] McLean, *The Indians*, p. 70.

having retained its natural shape, was painted blue on one side and red on the other, and then placed in the centre of the blanket. Upon the blue side tufts of white swan's down or small eagle feathers were tied to the hair, and upon the red side tufts of down painted red were tied. When this part of the ceremony was completed, a pipe was filled, the feast-kettle hung over the fire, and after presenting the pipe to the head, the dreamer addressed the head as follows : ' Grandfather, Venerable Man! Your children have made this feast for you, may the food thus taken cause them to live, and bring them good fortune [1].'

What has this to do with the idea embodied in the totems or sign-posts of Indian tribes ?

Again, 'there are war-charms borne upon poles and standards, and these were held to be sacred in war. Such was the faith of the Red Indians in the potency of these charms that, when the standard-bearer was slain, their courage departed, and they were easily defeated by the enemy.' These standards were by no means identical with totems.

Sir George Grey, in his Journals of two expeditions of discovery in Western Australia (vol. ii. p. 228), was the first to point out among Australians something very like, and yet, as we shall see from his own description, something very different from, the totem of the Red Indians, namely the *kobong*.

This is what he writes :

' But as each family adopts some animal or vegetable as their crest or sign, or kobong, as they call it, I

---

[1] Loc. cit., p. 121.

imagine it more likely that these have been named after their families than that the families have been named after them. A certain mysterious connection exists between a family and its kobong, so that a member of the family will never kill an animal of the species to which his kobong belongs, should he find it asleep; indeed, he always kills it reluctantly, and never without affording it a chance of escape[1].'

Here, then, if Sir George Grey's description is right, we have the very opposite of totemism, the kobong or crest derived from the name of the family, not the name of the family derived from the kobong. I do not say that the explanation of Sir George Grey is right, but it is surely right to distinguish kobongs and totems, and not to mix them up all together under a vague name.

The custom of totems, of dream-signs, of standards, of kobongs, may each and all become sources of religious ideas. But in order to understand these various ideas, we must carefully distinguish their sources, and not mix them all together and then label them Totemism [2].

Hallucination.

If then we can recognise neither Fetishism nor Totemism as the exclusive source of religion, we are not likely to allow ourselves to be persuaded by Dr. Gruppe that the only source of religion all over the world was—hallucination. No one who has studied the annals of religion would deny that hallucination has played a very prominent part in religion, and does so still. But to say that all religion is hallucination

---

[1] See also *Journal of American Folk Lore*, April–June, 1890.
[2] Appendix III.

is—I say so with all respect for Professor Gruppe's great learning — not very far from hallucination itself.

Ancestor-worship.

We now come to Mr. Herbert Spencer's own favourite theory of the origin of religion. According to him the root of every religion is *ancestor-worship*. Here again, who would deny that ancestor-worship is an important ingredient of ancient and modern religion? But to say that it is the root of every religion, is a thoroughly one-sided view. Why should religion, one of the most comprehensive terms in our language, be supposed to have had one beginning only? Lest I should be suspected of misrepresenting Mr. Herbert Spencer's theory, I must quote his own words (p. 440): 'Anything,' he writes, 'which transcends the ordinary, a savage thinks of as supernatural or divine : the remarkable man among the rest.'

We may admit that the savage considers what is outside the ordinary as extra-ordinary, and, if he has the concept of order in nature, as extra-natural or supernatural. But let us reflect for a moment. How could he call it divine, unless he had already elaborated the concept of divinity or divinities? We saw what labour it took before the crude metal supplied by the senses, such as the fire, the sky, the sun, could be hammered into a coin equivalent to deity. Are we to suppose that the same coin was handed to the savage out of mere charity?

But let us go on with Mr. Herbert Spencer's definition. 'The remarkable man,' he continues, 'may be simply the remotest ancestor remembered as the founder of the tribe; he may be a chief famed for strength and bravery; he may be a medicine-man of great repute; he may be an inventor of something new; and then, instead of being a member of the tribe, he may be a superior stranger bringing arts and knowledge; or he may be one of a superior race gaining predominance by conquest. Being at first one or other of those, regarded with awe during his life, he is regarded with increased awe after his death; and the propitiation of his ghost, becoming greater than the propitiation of ghosts which are less feared, develops into an established worship. There is no exception then. Using the phrase ancestor-worship in its broadest sense as comprehending all worship of the dead, be they of the same blood or not, we conclude that *ancestor-worship is the root of every religion.*'

Ancestor-worship presupposes a Belief in Gods.

That ancestor-worship is more fertile in religious thought than fetishism or totemism, will be denied by no one who is acquainted with any of the ancient religions of the world, with those of Rome and Greece, and, more especially, of India. But any scholar acquainted with the literature of these countries, knows at the same time how in every one of these religions ancestor-worship presupposes nature-worship, or, more correctly, a worship of the gods of nature.

We constantly hear that the Departed, the Fathers, the Ancestors, the Heroes are *admitted* to the society of the gods, they are often called half-gods, they may at times claim even a certain equality with the gods. But the gods are always there before them, and even when their individual names are forgotten, there is the general concept of deity to which the ancestral spirits aspire.

Thus we read in the golden words ascribed to Pythagoras, whoever their author may have been:

'First to the immortal gods pay reverence due,
Honour thy oath, and give the Heroes praise,
And those beneath the earth by actions just;
Reverence thy parents, and thy nearest kin:
And count him friend whose virtue brightest shines,
To gentle words incline and useful deeds.'

'Αθανάτους μὲν πρῶτα θεούς, νόμῳ ὡς διάκεινται,
τίμα καὶ σέβου ὅρκον, ἔπειθ' ἥρωας ἀγανούς,
τούς τε καταχθονίους σέβε δαίμονας, ἔννομα ῥέζων·
τούς τε γονεῖς τίμα, τούς τ' ἄγχιστ' ἐκγεγαῶτας;
τῶν δ' ἄλλων ἀρετῇ ποιεῖ φίλον ὅστις ἄριστος [1].

Again, when Plato speaks of the divine powers that ought to be reverenced by obeying their laws and wishes, he says (Laws, xi. 927): 'But if these things are really so, in the first place men should have a fear of the gods above, who regard the loneliness of orphans; and in the second place of the souls of the departed, who by nature incline to take an especial care of their own children; and they are friendly to those who honour them, and unfriendly to those who do not.'

There are exceptions where the spirits of the departed are mentioned before the Olympian gods, but they are intelligible. When Epaminondas exhorted his Greeks to fight and die for 'their country, for the graves of their fathers, and for the altars of the gods,' he placed the graves of the fathers even before the altars of the gods. But why? Because he knew

---

[1] *Fragmenta Philosophorum Graecorum*, Mullach, vol. i. p. 193; translated by W. Marsham Adams, in *The Drama of Empire*, p. 76.

the human heart, and what would most powerfully stir it for noble deeds at such a moment.

But we may appeal to the very passages quoted by Mr. Herbert Spencer himself in illustration of the worship of ancestors among civilised and uncivilised peoples, in order to show that these ancestral spirits are again and again represented as *admitted* to the society of the gods, or seated *by the side* of the gods. On p. 418 he tells us of a Maori chief who scornfully repudiated an earthly origin, and looked forward to rejoining his ancestors, the gods.

Williams says of the Fijians, that they admit very little difference between a chief of high rank and one of the second order of deities.

Bastian tells us that the king of the Benin in Africa is not only the representative of God upon earth, but God himself.

Battel states that the king of Loango is respected like a deity.

In America. F. de Xeres relates that Huayana Ceapac was so feared and obeyed that they almost looked upon him as their god.

In Peru, according to Acosta, a dead king was immediately regarded as a god.

According to Thomson, the New Zealanders believed that several high chiefs after death became deified.

I could go on quoting such passages from page after page, all showing not that the gods became ancestors, but that the ancestors became gods, or, at all events, approached to the status of a second order of deities. How this deification or apotheosis could have taken place, unless people had formed beforehand a name and concept of gods, Mr. Herbert Spencer seems never to have asked himself. Anyhow, it has never been explained by him, and I am afraid, it never will be.

China and Egypt.

China is the country in which ancestor-worship is most widely spread, and where it may be studied in the largest number of ancient literary documents. But no ancestor in China has ever become a god. Dr. Victor von Strauss, to whom we owe so many learned works on Chinese religion, says [1]: 'It can be proved that in China ancestor-worship has enjoyed the highest respect for four thousand years, probably even for longer. It is practised most conscientiously by the emperor and by the common people. But it has been, and has always remained, a concern of the house or the clan only, and even for them the spirit of an ancestor has never become a god.'

The same scholar, when treating of Egyptian religion, writes: 'In Egypt divine honours were paid to kings even during their life-time, divine qualities were ascribed to them, and for many of them there existed during thousands of years sanctuaries, priests, and sacrificial services. But even the best and mightiest among them have never become popular deities. If in the oldest times the spirits of the departed had been changed into gods, the same process would have been repeated afterwards, and it would at all events remain inexplicable, why these deities, if their origin had been what it is pretended, should ever have been metamorphosed into natural phenomena.'

Among uncivilised races of whose religion we possess only a fragmentary, and often a very doubtful

---

[1] *Entstehung und Geschichte des altägyptischen Götterglaubens*, p. 9.

knowledge, the worship of nature-gods may sometimes seem to be entirely absent.

How easily might it happen, if a traveller were to question a Neapolitan lazzaroni about his religion, that he might take him for a mere worshipper of saints, if not for a fetish-worshipper.

It may happen also, as in the case of Buddhism, that the old nature-gods have been completely used up, and, if not entirely discarded, are tolerated only in a subordinate capacity, chiefly for the satisfaction of the populace. Buddhism has outgrown the old Devas. It may be called *adevistic*, though not atheistic, for the place, formerly occupied by the Devas of nature, was not left entirely vacant. Buddha himself, the man who had obtained enlightenment, took. that place, and though he could not be called divine in the old sense, he was at all events conceived as eternal, at least in some of the sects of the Mahâyâna division of Buddhism, or of what I call Bodhism.

However, granting even that there are races whose religion consists of ancestor-worship only, though, as at present informed, I know of none, would that prove that the worship of nature-gods must everywhere be traced back to ancestor-worship?

No one, so far as I know, has ever maintained that, because there are countries where religion consists of the worship of nature-gods only, therefore all ancestor-worship must be traced back to nature-worship. Why then should the worship of nature-gods, nay, according to Mr. H. Spencer, of all religion, be traced back to the worship of ancestors? The one conclusion would be as absurd as the other.

What is the result of this one-sidedness in the

study of religion, may best be seen in Mr. Herbert
Spencer's *Sociology*. I always wish to speak with
respect and courtesy of a man who in his own sphere
is justly regarded as a very high authority. I have
no doubt that Mr. Herbert Spencer's knowledge in
physical science is very great. In expressing my
strong difference of opinion with regard to the facts
and the theories in his *Principles of Sociology*, I can
clearly see that the responsibility lies less with him
than with the 'tabulated evidence' on which he
founded his theories. Some years ago, for instance,
when I doubted the evidence which was to prove that
'reverence for stones is in some cases accompanied by
the belief that they were once men and will eventually
revive as men' (l. c., p. 335), I did not question the
good faith of the upholders of that theory. I simply
doubted the facts on which they relied. And my
doubts proved to be well-founded. If a pleader may
tell a judge that he has been misinformed as to facts,
surely we may claim the same privilege, without
being guilty of any want of respect towards a man
who, in his own sphere, has done such excellent work.
I make no secret that I consider the results of Mr. H.
Spencer's onesided explanation of the origin of religion
as worthy of the strongest condemnation which a love
of truth can dictate; but to show that a scholar has
been led and almost driven to certain false conclusions,
by trusting to evidence which is untrustworthy, or by
attending to one kind of evidence only, is no more than
what every student of history is constantly doing, and
what every real lover of truth is bound to do. Mr.
H. Spencer has always been so courteous in the criti-
cisms which he has addressed to me, that in stating

that I mistrust his evidence, and that I differ from his conclusions *toto coelo*, I hope I may not say anything that could be considered as personally offensive.

I wish I could have followed the example of other scholars who pass his theory by in silence. But would that have been more respectful? Thus Erwin Rohde, who has just published a learned work, *Psyche, Seelen-cult und Unsterblichkeitsglaube*, 1890, and whose very object is to prove the existence of this cult of souls in Greece, writes: 'I have taken no notice of the attempts to derive the whole of Greek religion from ancestor-worship, which at first existed alone,— attempts made not only by De Coulanges, but by several savants in England and Germany' (p. 157). And yet this writer is on many points a follower of Mr. Herbert Spencer, and cannot be suspected of any prejudice against him. But in England these theories cannot be simply ignored, and I only hope that I may succeed in criticising them without seeming discourteous to their author.

The Euhemeristic Explanation of Zeus.

As I am addressing those who are familiar with Greek and Latin literature, I shall confine my remarks to some of the explanations which Mr. Herbert Spencer has given us of classical deities; and first of all of *Jupiter* or *Zeus*.

We are told (l.c., p. 230) that Rajah Brooke, in describing a prolonged contest with a mountain-chief in Borneo, shows us what would be likely to happen when a stronghold was in possession of a superior race. His antagonist had fortified an almost inaccessible crag on the top of Sadok—a mountain about

5000 feet high, surrounded by lower mountains. Described by Rajah Brooke as 'grim and grand,' it figures in Dayak legends and songs as 'the grand Mount, towards which no enemy dare venture.' The first attempt to take this fastness failed utterly ; the second, in which a small mortar was used, also failed ; and only by the help of a howitzer dragged up by the joint strength of a hundred yelling Dayaks, did the third attempt succeed. Their chieftain, driven out only by the appliance of a civilised race, was naturally held in dread by surrounding tribes.

'Grandfather Rentap,' as he was commonly called, was dangerously violent ; occasionally killed his own men ; was regardless of established customs ; and, among other feats, took a second wife from a people averse to the match, carried her off to his eyrie, and, discarding the old one, made the young one Ranee of Sadok. With his followers and subordinate chiefs, Layang, Nanang, and Loyish, holding secondary forts serving as outposts, he was unconquerable by any of the native powers. Already there were superstitions about him. Snakes were supposed to possess some mysterious connection with Rentap's forefathers, or the souls of the latter resided in these loathsome creatures.'

' Now if, instead of a native ruler thus living up in the clouds (which hindered the last attack), occasionally coming down to fulfil a threat of vengeance, keeping the country around in fear, and giving origin to stories already growing into superstitions, we suppose a ruler belonging to an invading race, which bringing knowledge, skill, arts, and implements unknown to the nations, were regarded as beings of

superior kind, just as civilised men now are by
savages; we shall see that there would inevitably
arise legends concerning this superior race seated in
the sky. Considering that among the very Dyaks,
divine beings are conceived as differing so little from
men, that the supreme god and creator, Tapa, is
supposed to dwell "in a house like that of a Malay
. . . himself being clothed like a Dyak," we shall see
that the ascription of a divine character to a conqueror
thus placed would be certain. And if the country
was one in which droughts had fostered the faith in
rain-makers and "heaven-herds"—if, as among the
Zulus, there was a belief in weather-doctors, able to
"contend with the lightning and hail," and to "send
the lightning to another doctor to try him;" this ruler,
living on a peak round which the clouds formed and
whence the storms came, would, without hesitation,
be regarded as the causer of these changes—as a
thunderer holding the lightnings in his hand. Joined
with which ascribed powers, there would nevertheless
be stories of his descents from this place up in the
heavens, appearances among men, and amours with
their daughters. Grant but a little time for such
legends and interpretations to be exaggerated and
idealised—let the facts be magnified as was the feat
of Samson with the ass's jawbone, or the prowess of
Achilles making "the earth flow with blood," or the
triumphant achievement of Ramses II in slaying
100,000 foes single-handed;—and we reach the idea
that heaven is the abode of superhuman beings com-
manding the powers of nature and punishing men.'

I had to give you the whole of this long passage in
order to enable you to form an independent judgment of

Mr. H. Spencer's theory of the origin of religion.   The story which you have just heard is meant to account for the genesis of Zeus, the gatherer of the clouds (νεφεληγερέτα), the wielder of the thunderbolt (τερψικέραυνος), the ruler of gods and men (ἄναξ πάντων τε θεῶν πάντων τ' ἀνθρώπων), and at the same time, no doubt, the lover of Leto and other heroines.   This Zeus, and let it not be forgotten, this Dyaus also in India, was, according to Mr. Herbert Spencer, originally no more than a ' Grandfather Rentap.'   How a divine character could have been ascribed to this Grandfather Rentap by people who had as yet no knowledge of divine beings, has never been explained.   Who was Tapa, whom the Dayaks considered the supreme god and creator ?   Whence did he come ?   Mr. H. Spencer seems to think that he also was originally a robber, and why?—because he was supposed to dwell in a house like that of a Malay, and to be clothed like a Dayak.   How else, I ask, could he have been housed or clothed ?   How was Zeus himself housed or clothed by the imagination of the early Greek poets ?   But granting all this, granting that Tapa, the supreme god and creator, was originally a mere Dayak—where is this retrogression to end, and whence came the first god to whom these deified men could be assimilated ?

All I can say at present is that, if Mr. H. Spencer can find a single classical scholar to accept this view of the origin of Zeus in Greece, and of Dyaus in Sanskrit, I shall not write another word on mythology or religion.

The Euhemeristic Explanation of other Gods.

Other gods share the same fate as Jupiter, when

arraigned before Mr. Herbert Spencer. He thinks he has proved that savage tribes often ascribe ordinary and extraordinary events to ghosts, and these ghosts, he maintains, were always originally the ghosts of dead people. I doubt whether he has proved the latter point. For instance, when Major Harris tells (l. c., p. 237) us that no whirlwind ever sweeps across the path without being pursued by a dozen savages with drawn creeses, who stab into the centre of the dusty column in order to drive away the evil spirit that is believed to be riding in the blast, how does this prove that the Danâkils believed they were stabbing the ghosts of their own ancestors, or of any ancestors at all? When certain tribes shoot their arrows into the sky to bring down rain, we have no reason to suppose that they were trying to kill their deceased ancestors once more.

Again (p. 238), it may be quite true that, 'if an eddy in the river, where floating sticks are whirled round and engulfed, is not far from the place where one of the tribe was drowned and never seen again,' there should be stories told that 'the double of this drowned man, malicious as the unburied ever are, dwells thereabouts, and pulls these things under the surface, nay, in revenge, seizes and drags down persons who venture near.' But are we to suppose that all over the world, whenever we hear of watersprites, or Naiads, or Nickers, some person must have been drowned before people could speak of streams and torrents as *doing* mischief, or of springs and rivulets as *conferring* blessings?

Expressions such as 'possessed by a spirit,' particularly by an unclean spirit, or again, filled by a good spirit or by the spirit of prophecy, occur in many parts of the world, and in languages quite unrelated to each other. But where is the evidence that in all these cases the spirits meant were, as Mr. Herbert Spencer asserts, originally the ancestral spirits? It is well known that the spirits of the departed were dreaded, because they had power to return, and to cause disease and death in other members of the family. Many of the funeral ceremonies were intended to prevent the return of the dead and to pacify their anger. In special cases the spirits of the departed, particularly of a father or a mother, may seem to call for vengeance, and may be believed to drive a criminal into madness. It is quite true also, as Mr. H. Spencer says, that sneezing, yawning, and even hiccup are often ascribed to a devil who has entered the body of the afflicted. But nowhere do I remember that sneezing, yawning, and hiccup were ascribed to the spirits of a father, grandfather, or great-grandfather.

Even the idea of Death, as an agent or as a power that cannot be resisted, or what Mr. Herbert Spencer called 'personalised Death,' is supposed by him to have begun everywhere in the tradition of some unusually ferocious foe, whose directly seen acts of vengeance were multitudinous, and to whom, afterwards, unseen acts of vengeance were more and more ascribed.

It is the disregard of the simplest facts of language which makes Mr. H. Spencer look here as elsewhere for what must seem to all students of language an almost incredible solution of self-made difficulty. If death was to be named at all, it could only be named like hunger, thirst, illness, sleep, and all the rest, as an agent. The Sanskrit mrityu, death, comes from the root mri or mar, to grind down, to destroy, and means originally no more than the agent of destruction. Who that agent was, the early speakers and thinkers knew as little as they knew the agents of rain and sunshine, of cold and heat, when they formed these names. But having once framed a name for death, and having called him the destroyer or killer, there was nothing to prevent them from imagining him as something like a human agent, and picturing him according to the flights of their poetical fancy, whether as a skeleton, or as a reaper, or even as a kind friend. The process was in fact the very opposite of what Mr. H. Spencer would wish it to have been. When they saw an unusually ferocious foe approaching, they might say that it was Death himself. But they would not wait till they saw an unusually ferocious foe, before they conceived and named the extinction of life, which they witnessed every day, and ascribed, not to a known, but to an unknown agent.

If therefore Mr. Herbert Spencer (p. 239) sees in the gods who ward off death from Hector, in Minerva who assists Menelaos, in Venus who saves Paris, in Vulcan who snatches away Idaeus, as well as in the Jew's ministering angel and in the Catholic's patron saint, the ghosts of the dead changed into supernatural agents, I can only say, once more, let him get a single classical scholar to second his bill, and I shall vote for it myself.

But though I differ from Mr. Herbert Spencer when he thinks that ancestor-worship is the only source of all religion, I readily acknowledge the useful service he has rendered in showing how important an influence a belief in worship of ancestors has exercised on the development of religious thought.

And here I must call attention once more to a strange misapprehension under which Mr. Herbert Spencer seems still to labour.

Did Ancestor-worship exist among the Aryan Nations?

Mr. H. Spencer, who has been so diligent a collector of every kind of information from the most distant parts of the world on the worship of the departed and of ancestors, seems to think that some serious doubt has been entertained as to the existence of that worship in Greece and in Italy. On p. 313 of his *Principles of Sociology* he writes: ' It is said that ancestor-worship is peculiar to inferior races. I have seen it implied, I have heard it in conversation, and I have now before me in print the statement that " no Indo-European or Semitic nation, so far as we know, seems to have made a religion of worship of the dead." And the intended conclusion appears to be that these superior races, who in their earliest recorded times had higher forms of worship, were not, even in their earlier times, ancestor-worshippers.'

Mr. H. Spencer returns once more to the same subject. In his Appendix, p. 1, he writes: ' The more I have looked into the evidence, the more I have marvelled at those who, in the interests of the mythological theory, assert that the Aryans have been distinguished from inferior races by not being ancestor-worshippers, and who ascribe such ancestor-worship as cannot be overlooked, to imitation of inferior races.'

Nay, he appeals to Mr. A. C. Lyall as one who had unusual opportunities of studying Aryan superstitions as even now being generated, and who says in a letter: 'I do not know who may be the author of the statement which you quote at p. 313, that "No Indo-European nation seems to have made a religion of the worship of the dead;" but it is a generalisation entirely untenable. Here in Rajputâna, among the purest Aryan tribes, the worship of famous ancestors is most prevalent; and all their heroes are more or less deified.'

Considering the importance ascribed to this statement, that 'No Indo-European or Semitic nation seems to have made a religion of the worship of the dead,' what reason could there have been for withholding the name of its author? I do not doubt that Mr. H. Spencer saw it implied, heard it in conversation, and at last had it before him in print—for what is more patient than paper? But why withhold the name? Nay, I should say, why quote it at all? For either the author of that statement was simply not acquainted with Latin, Greek, and Sanskrit, or he may possibly have laid down so narrow a definition of religion that the worship of the dead would have fallen with him under the head of superstition rather than of religion. Would any one quote a statement, by whomsoever it might have been made, that no Indo-European nation ever made a religion of the worship of the powers of nature? We might as well say that we had seen it implied, heard it in conversation, and seen it in print, that there was no such place as Rome in Italy, or Benares in India, and then invoke high authority to say that these two towns did really exist.

Whoever has only read the Antigone knows how deep roots reverence for the departed had struck in the Greek heart. In Rome we can see the three stages of that worship in full detail, while in India it may be studied more fully even than in Rome and Greece. The facts which Mr., now Sir Charles, Lyall mentions from Rajputâna belong to quite a different phase, to the very last period, I should say, of religious development. First of all, the unmixed Aryan blood in the Rajputâna of the nineteenth century is more or less problematical. Secondly, the unmixed Aryan thought of that country, centuries after Greek, Mongolian, and Mohammedan and English conquests, is very problematical. But granting all this, it is not the worship of some famous ancestors or of some more or less deified heroes that forms our problem, but the worship of ancestors, and afterwards of All Souls, and All Saints, and this worship not as a curious psychological phenomenon by itself, but as the supposed source of all religion. Does Sir Charles Lyall really think that his experience in Rajputâna will support such a theory?

So far from admitting that ancestor-worship is peculiar to inferior races, it will be the chief object óf this course of Lectures to show you from authentic sources how a belief in the existence of departed spirits and a worship of ancestors arose among the Aryan nations, how it was combined with the áncient belief in gods, and how it pervaded not only their religious cult, but the whole of their social, civil, and political life. What I protest against is the attempt to make ancestor-worship the only source of all religion. It is one source of religious sentiment—

nay, it is a very important source, but it is second in importance, and second in origin, as compared with the worship of the powers of nature. It is only as following after *Physical Religion* that what I call *Anthropological Religion,* or the discovery of something divine in man, and more particularly in the departed or in our ancestors, can be properly treated and rightly understood.

LECTURE VI.

THE UNTRUSTWORTHINESS OF THE MATERIALS FOR THE STUDY OF RELIGION.

Literary Documents of Aryan and Semitic Religions.

BEFORE I began to give you an outline of Physical Religion, I felt it incumbent on me to describe the materials which are accessible to us for studying the origin and growth of the gods of nature. The most important among them was the Veda, and so it is again for our present purpose. For information, therefore, of what the Veda is, I must refer you to the description of Vedic literature which I gave in the second volume of my Gifford Lectures.

Besides the Veda, our chief authorities were then the Avesta, the sacred book of the followers of Zoroaster, the Homeric poems, and the religious and mythological traditions preserved to us in the later literatures of Rome and Germany. I touched but rarely on Celtic and Slavonic traditions, partly, because they have not yet been so carefully collected and sifted; partly, or I should say, chiefly, because I felt unable to control as strictly as they ought to be controlled, the statements on which I should have had to rely.

Considering how ample the materials are with which the literature of the Aryan nations supplies the students of the Science of Religion, it is but natural, nay, it seems most desirable, that they should devote their principal attention to this wide field of research, and not attempt to glance at other fields, till they have gained a firm footing on their own. Still, the time must come when they have to look beyond the limits of the Aryan world, in order to compare their results with the results obtained by other explorers, and thus either to modify or to confirm the convictions at which they have arrived by their more special studies.

The same applies to the study of the Semitic religions, and we can see in a recent work by Professor Robertson Smith, how wide and accurate a survey of extraneous religions may be commanded by a scholar, if he has once gained a firm footing on his own special vantage-ground.

Literary Documents of other Religions.

But even from this higher point of view the instinct, or, it may be, the prejudice, of the scholar would naturally lead him to approach, first of all, the study of those non-Aryan religions which are represented by a real literature. Wherever I allowed myself to survey the wider fields of religious thought, I dwelt chiefly on what may be called the historical religions of the world, the Semitic in Babylon, Nineveh, and Judæa, the Hamitic in Egypt, and the national religion of China, as restored by Confucius.

All these may be called the religions of civilised or

historical races, and, what is more important still, they can all be studied in literary documents.

The Religions of Illiterate Races.

But it has been said very truly that religion is not confined to civilised races, nor is civilisation essential to religion. On the contrary, the lowest savage has his religion, and that religion, for all we know, may be far more primitive, far more simple, nay even far more true, than the religions of many civilised races.

Now I have not one word to say against all this. On the contrary, there was a time when I thought myself that a study of the religions of uncivilised races would help us to reach a lower, that is, a more ancient and more primitive stratum of religious thought than we could reach in the sacred books of the most highly civilised races of the world.

Comparative Study of Languages.

I was led to this opinion chiefly through the study of Comparative Philology.   After exploring the most important languages of the Aryan and the Semitic families of speech, I devoted, as a young man, several years to a study of other languages, in order to see how far they agreed and how far they differed from the Aryan and the Semitic types.   I examined for that purpose, not only literary languages, such as the Dravidian languages of India, Chinese and Mandshu, Turkish and Finnish, but likewise some of the Malay and Polynesian dialects, some representatives of American speech, of one of which, the Mohawk, I wrote a grammatical analysis, and some of the more important linguistic specimens from Africa, and even from Australia. You must not imagine that I studied these languages as we study Greek and Latin. The age of Methuselah would not suffice for that. I studied chiefly the grammars, I made myself acquainted with the general structure of each language, and I was thus enabled to compare, not only the materials of these languages, but their grammatical expedients also with those of the Aryan and Semitic languages. I consider this more comprehensive study of languages extremely useful as a preparation for more special studies. It frees us from many prejudices, it enables us in many cases to go behind the grammars of Sanskrit and Hebrew, not genealogically, but psychologically, and it helps us to recognise beneath a great variety of grammatical formations one and the same fundamental purpose.

I am quite aware that the results of these researches, which I collected in a letter to Baron Bunsen, *On the Turanian Languages*, published in 1854, have been to a great extent corrected and superseded by subsequent labours. Some of the classifications which I then proposed have had to be surrendered, and the very comprehensive name of Turanian, under which I included a large number of languages neither Aryan nor Semitic, has very properly been banished for a time from linguistic science. But with all that, I do not regret the time devoted to these studies, and I still hold that for gaining a firm grasp on the general principles of human speech, nay for fully appreciating the distinctive character of the Aryan and Semitic languages, nothing is so useful as to be able to contrast them even with such imperfect attempts at embodying human thought as we find in the jargons of the Australian Blacks.

Comparative Study of non-Aryan and non-Semitic Religions.

When in later years I was led from a study of languages to a study of mythologies and religions, it was but natural that I should have felt strongly drawn towards the same sources from which I had already derived so much useful information. Undeterred by the dark looks of classical scholars, I endeavoured to show how some of the best-known mythological and religious traditions of Greece and Rome found their analogy and explanation in the Veda. I went even further, and did not shrink from pointing out striking parallels between the gods and heroes of Homer and the gods and heroes of Polynesian, African, and American savages. Here again, I do not deny that later information has shown in several cases that some of these parallelisms were no parallelisms at all, that what seemed like was essentially unlike, and that the chapter of accidental coincidences was larger than we expected. But the principle that there was, quite apart from any historical borrowing, a common fund of thought in all the mythologies and religions of the world, has remained untouched, and must continue to inspire all serious students of the ancient history of man.

New Epoch in the Study of Uncivilised Races.

But there has been of late a strong reaction. First of all, it has been shown that it was certainly a mistake to look upon the manners and customs, the legends and religious ideas of uncivilised tribes as representing an image of what the primitive state of mankind must have been thousands of years ago, or what it actually was long before the beginning of the earliest civilisation, as known to us from historical documents. The more savage a tribe, the more accurately was it supposed to reflect the primitive state of mankind. This was, no doubt, a very natural mistake, before more careful researches had shown that the customs of savage races were often far more artificial and complicated than they appeared at first, and that there had been as much progression and retrogression in their historical development as in that of more civilised races. We know now that savage and primitive are very far indeed from meaning the same thing.

But another and even more important change has come over the study of anthropology, so far as it deals with illiterate tribes. Formerly the chief object of students of anthropology was to collect as much information as was available. Whatever a sailor or a trader or a missionary had noted down about out-of-the-way people, was copied out, classified and tabulated, without any attempt at testing the credibility of these witnesses. This was particularly the case whenever the evidence seemed to tally with the expectations of the philosopher, or furnished amusing material to the essayist. At last, however, the contradictions became so glaring, the confusion so complete, that serious students declined altogether to listen to this kind of evidence.

The Two New Principles.

This, no doubt, was going too far. It was what the Germans call pouring out the child with the bath-water. But it has left at least two principles firmly established and recognised by all conscientious students of anthropology:

1. That no one is in future to be quoted as an authority on savage races who has not been an eye-witness, and has proved himself free from the prejudices of race and religion. But even to have been an eye-witness does not suffice. Let us suppose that a traveller had passed through a desert, and seen there a race of savages, perfectly naked, and dancing round a graven image which they called their god. Suppose that after a time these savages had quarrelled among themselves, and the traveller had witnessed at the end of their orgies a massacre of about three thousand men, the corpses weltering in their blood. What account would he have given of that race? Would he not have described them as worse than the negroes of Dahomey? Yet these savages were the people of God, the image was the golden calf, the priest was Aaron, and the chief who ordered the massacre was Moses. We, no doubt, read the 32nd chapter of Exodus in a very different sense. But the casual traveller, unless he could have conversed with Moses and Aaron, could only have described what he saw, and the ethnologist, knowing his authority to be trustworthy, would naturally have ranged the Israelites among the lowest of savage races.

2. It was necessary therefore to lay down a second principle, namely that no one is in future to

be quoted as an authority on the customs, traditions, and, more particularly, on the religious ideas of uncivilised races, who has not acquired an acquaintance with their language, sufficient to enable him to converse with them freely on these difficult subjects.

No true scholar requires any proof in support of these two demands. He knows how difficult it often is for the best informed Greek, Latin, or Sanskrit scholars to gain a correct view of the religious opinions of ancient writers. He knows how much depends very often on a single various reading in the text of Homer or Pindar. He knows how often he has himself changed his opinion as to the actual import of a verse in Homer or in the Veda. If, therefore, he has simply to rely on authority, he knows that he must first examine the claims to authority possessed by special students, and he would never dream of relying on the statements of casual travellers in Italy, Greece, or India, ignorant of the languages spoken in these countries, for information either on the modern or the ancient religions of their inhabitants.

Anthropologists can no longer ignore the fact that the languages of Africa, America, Polynesia, and even Australia are now being studied as formerly Greek, Latin, and Hebrew only were studied. You have only to compare, for instance, the promiscuous descriptions of the traditions of the Hottentots, in the works of the best ethnologists, with the researches of a real Hottentot scholar, like Dr. Hahn, to see the advance that has been made. When we read the books of Dr. Callaway on the Zulus, of the Revs. William Wyatt Gill and Edward Tregear on the Polynesians, of Dr. Codrington on the Melanesians, of Horatio Hale on some of the North American races, we feel at once that we are in safe hands, in the hands of real scholars. Even then we must, of course, remember that their knowledge of the languages cannot compare with that of Bentley, or Hermann, or Burnouf, or Ewald. Yet we feel that we cannot go altogether wrong in trusting to their guidance.

A Third Principle for the Future.

I go even a step further, and I believe the time will come when no student will venture to write on any religion, unless he has acquired some knowledge of the language of its sacred writings, or of the people who believe in it. I think, of course, of serious students only, of men who wish to assist in the discovery of truth and in the real advancement of knowledge, not of that class of anthropologists, so well described by Professor Tiele as, 'Ces braves gens qui, pour peu qu'ils aient lu un ou deux récits de voyages, ne manqueront pas de se mettre à comparer à tort et à travers, et pour tout resultat produiront la confusion' (*Le Mythe de Kronos*, p. 17).

This may seem to be exacting too much, but you have only to look, for instance, at the description given of the religion, the mythology, the manners, customs, and laws of the Brâhmans about a hundred years ago, and before Sanskrit began to be studied, and you will be amazed at the utter caricature that is often given of the intellectual state of the inhabitants of India, compared with the true picture reflected in their literature. Yet there was plenty of evidence, from Greek and Roman, from Arabic and

Persian writers, and from many intelligent travellers and missionaries, which seemed perfectly trustworthy and was accepted as such without any misgivings.

This question of the trustworthiness of writers on religion who are ignorant of the language in which religion lives and moves and has its being, has of late become the object of so keen a controversy that it seems best to argue it out, once for all. I do not wonder that those who depend for their information on the tabulated extracts published by Mr. Herbert Spencer, should be unwilling to surrender these convenient 'Aids to Faith' without a struggle. The best I can do, therefore, is to give some of the results of my own experience, and to show, in some critical cases, on how broken a reed I myself and others with me have been resting, when we thought that mere outside observers, ignorant of the language of the people, could ever be qualified to give us trustworthy information as to the real religion of uncivilised or even of civilised races.

Testing of Evidence, (I) with regard to Civilised Races.

I suppose we may reckon the Hindus of the present day among civilised races, and we might suppose that, as many of them speak English, they were quite capable of giving an accurate and intelligible account of their religion. I have tried the experiment again and again with educated Indians staying at Oxford, and I have been startled at their ignorance of their own religion. Many of them have never heard the names of their own sacred books. I do not mean of the Vedas only, but even of the more modern Purânas. They have learned a few prayers from their mothers, they have watched the priest coming to their houses to receive gifts, and they remember some festivals, though often for their secular rather than for their religious character. If you ask them what their religious convictions are, they will say that they are followers of Vish*n*u or *S*iva or some other popular deity, but what they have to believe and not to believe about these gods or any gods, they are unable to say. In fact, they hardly understand what we mean by religion. Religion, as a mere belief, apart from ceremonies and customs, is to them but one, and by no means the most important, concern of life, and they often wonder why we should take so deep an interest in mere dogma, or, as they express it, make such a fuss about religion.

However, we must not be too hard on these young gentlemen who come from India to study in England. Consider what answer an English boy would give, if he were suddenly asked to give an account of the Christian religion. No doubt he would have seen and read the Old Testament and the New Testament, and acquit himself well to a certain extent. Still, I know what answers are sometimes given in the examinations in the Rudiments of Religion by undergraduates at Oxford, and knowing it, I can make allowance for the answers which I sometimes receive from my young Indian friends. I shall give you two specimens only. In the questions on the Old Testament there was one, 'State what you know about Jezebel.' The answer was short and pithy: 'Jehu ate him.' In the viva voce examination on the New Testament, a candidate was asked: 'Who was Salome?' The answer came quick, 'The father of the sons of

Zebedee.' The examiner paused and said: 'Do you really mean that, Sir?' He thought for a moment, and then said, 'Oh no, Sir, a pool.'

After this we must not be too much scandalised, if we do not always get the most trustworthy information about the Indian religion even from highly educated young Hindus, preparing for the Indian Civil Service examinations.

Different Accounts of the Religious Beliefs of the Hindus.

But while these natives themselves are generally very reticent on their religion, and unable or unwilling to give an account of the faith that is in them, England possesses a large class of persons who have spent their life in India in various pursuits, and who might safely be supposed to know everything about what is called the religion of the natives. These men were formerly quoted as the highest authorities, and it would have seemed an unwarrantable scepticism to question their statements. There are, no doubt, very able, learned, and thoughtful men among these Anglo-Indians. These generally speak with great caution. But there are others who are most positive in their statements, whether favourable or unfavourable, about the manners, the customs, and the religious opinions of the natives, and who think it the height of presumption for a student who has never been in India to differ from their opinions. Fortunately the number of Anglo-Indians is large, and as they often contradict each other flatly, it is open to us to appeal from one to the other, and in the end to form our own opinion from recognised authorities in the ancient and modern literature of the country.

I shall mention a few only of the dangers which beset the inquiries into the religious opinions of the natives of India, as carried on by gentlemen residing for a number of years at Calcutta, Bombay, or Madras.

First of all, there is no such thing as a general religion of the natives. There are probably a hundred different forms of religious belief and worship in that enormous country, but there is no general standard of belief, no pope, no councils, no confession of faith, to guide the masses of the people. The sacred books are read and understood by the few only. There are many educated Hindus who have never seen a copy of a Purâna, still less of the Veda. No wonder, therefore, that observations made in one part of India should not always agree with observations made in another locality and among a totally different population.

Secondly, in the great towns the whole atmosphere is now pervaded by European ideas. Schools, newspapers, and books have introduced words and ideas into the native languages of India which are quite foreign to the native mind.

Thirdly, some natives, particularly those who have been brought in contact with Europeans, are very apt to give the answers which they are expected to give, even if they do not go quite so far as Wilford's and Jacolliot's friends.

Like Roman Catholic theologians who, when they are charged with tolerating idolatry, have recourse to a distinction between objects of adoration and objects of veneration, the educated Hindu repels indignantly the charge of idol-worship, and shows that sacred

images are only meant as memorials or as temporary
abodes of the deity. This may be quite true for the
educated classes, but it is not so for the mass of the
people.

To illustrate what I mean I shall give here a
description by a missionary who has had long and
intimate relations with the Hindus, both the educated
and the peasantry, as to the way in which an idol is
made and unmade in India, and an account of what
the Hindus themselves think of the indwelling spirit
of the deity.

The Goddess Durgâ or Kâlî.

Durgâ or Kâlî is the most popular goddess in
Calcutta, and in the whole of Bengal. Her temple at
Kalighat is the most sacred in the country. The
image-maker, preparing for the great Durgâ-Pûgâ
festival, buys bamboos, straw, clay, paint, &c. He
then fastens the bamboos together so as to form, as it
were, the bones or framework of the future image.
Having twisted the straw into ropes, he gives the
bamboos their required thickness by twisting these
ropes round them, and lastly, he gives the outward
form of limb and feature by plastering the whole
with clay, which, when dry, is painted, and set up in
his shop for sale. But it is as yet no more a goddess
than an earthern pot is. A day or two before the
Pûgâ, the worshipper visits the shop of the image-
maker, and selects an image, larger or smaller, according to his means. Having paid for it, he hands it to
a coolie, or to three or four coolies—if large—to carry
home. Meanwhile he himself goes to another shop,

and buys Durgâ's hair, in a third her sari, in a fourth gorgeous jewellery made of *mica* or *talc*, in a fifth the tin weapons, &c., with which her hands are armed. Laden with these purchases he arrives at home, and commences to tie on the hair, and to array the image in gorgeous apparel.   Still, when all this is done, and the image is enshrined in the Pûgâ house, she is yet no goddess.   Durgâ must be entreated to leave her beloved husband, and to descend and dwell in the image ; and it is only when she has done this, that the image is to be bowed before, and offerings of money, &c., presented at the shrine.   She condescends to dwell on earth for three days.   On the afternoon of the third day, the image is borne aloft on men's shoulders, to the deafening sound of gongs and tom-toms.   Baboos, often men who never put a foot to the ground on any other day of the year, follow through the dusty and not very odorous streets of Calcutta.   When the banks of the Hooghly are reached, the image is put on board a boat, which is rowed to the middle of the stream ; and, just as the sun is setting, it is allowed to sink below the water, while a Nîlkanth (the beautiful Indian jay, also a name of *S*iva) is released from a cage in which he has been carried, to fly away to *S*iva, to tell him that his beloved Durgâ is coming back to him.   The image was not sacred till animated—so to speak—by Durgâ, nor are the frameworks of the images, which in a day or two plentifully strew the shore, sacred.   Durgâ has gone away, and they are again but bamboo and straw.

This is one account of the goddess Durgâ, the most popular deity of Bengal.

If we asked an educated native, he would probably say that all these festivals with their processions and shoutings and images were meant for the people who could not understand anything else. Educated people in England say the same of the corybantic processions of the Salvation Army. They say that they appeal to minds to whom nothing else would appeal. But to the Kuli and his wife and children the very question, what the image of Durgâ was, would be hardly intelligible. To him it is Durgâ, the wife of Śiva, who has to be propitiated, and whose festival is to them one of the happiest days in the whole year.

We should find but few, if any, among the learned natives who could tell us the real character, the origin and history of this goddess. They see, no doubt, more in her than a mere idol, and look upon the hideous accessories of her worship as things that must be tolerated, though they cannot be approved. But her real antecedents and her historical origin would be as great a puzzle to them as it is to us.

The Higher Conception of Durgâ.

I had a correspondence not long ago with a learned and thoughtful native of India, a real believer in Durgâ, in order to find out how he reconciled his own exalted ideas of the godhead with the popular conception of this deity. 'Behind the popular conception,' he writes, 'there is, as many of us believe, a beautiful and grand idea of godhead. Durgâ represents to us universal Śakti or power, i. e. every force, spiritual and physical, of Nature in every form. This may be seen from the famous hymn addressed to her as *Kandî* (in the Devîmâhâtmya of the Mârkaṇḍeya

Purâna), beginning with the words, yâ devî sarva-
bhûteshu, "she who is the goddess in all things,"
occurring in every verse. The Vedic deities represent
separate forces or manifestations of Nature. Agni is
fire, Varuna is water, Indra is the firmament or clouds
or rain. But Durgâ includes in herself every deity,
being universal power. She is all the Vedic deities
and all the Paurânic ones combined in a grand unity.
The teachers of the Âdi Samâg (Devendranâth Tagore,
&c.) have already familiarised the people with the
idea of God being either Father or Mother. Durgâ is
Mother-God. Divested of personality and sex, Durgâ
is universal power, almighty, irresistible power. What
Krishna says of himself to Arjuna in the Bhagavadgîtâ, about his being everything, would apply to this
conception of Durgâ equally. For Krishna in the
Bhagavadgîtâ read Durgâ, and you will readily understand who and what Durgâ is in the estimation of all
genuine and educated Sâktas.

'How a deity of Paurânic origin could come to
supplant all the earlier Vedic deities, and to be iden-
fied with the idea of supreme Godhead, is, perhaps,
not very difficult to understand. The manner in
which the Mârkandeya Purâna has described her
(notwithstanding the late origin ascribed to her) has
naturally led to this development. No Christian can
compose a hymn to the Godhead (without reference to
Christ, of course, and to the Holy Ghost) that would
not apply to Durgâ. Indeed, if a personal God,
almighty and all-perfect, is to be believed in, it
makes very little difference whether that God is called
Father or Mother.

'I have only to add what the meaning of the word
(3)   M

Durgâ is. Etymologically the word means, She who is approached with difficulty. Of course, in this sense, she is the unapproachable supreme godhead ; one, that is, who cannot be approached without years upon years of the austerest of penances and meditations. It may also mean, one who can cross every difficulty, and hence ward off all difficulties from her devotees. You know that Râma worshipped Durgâ, and it was on the fourth day (i. e. the first day after the worship had been over) that Râvana was slain. No Hindu rises from his bed in the morning without repeating the following :—

Prabhâte yah smaren nityam Durgâ-Durgâkshara-
    dvayam,
Âpadas tasya nasyanti tamas sûryodaye yathâ.

"He who recollects every morning the two syllables Durgâ, Durgâ, his calamities vanish like darkness at the rising of the sun."'

Who would deny that there are true religious elements in this view of Durgâ, so different from the image made of bamboos, straw, clay, and paint ? Who would deny that motherhood has as much right as fatherhood as one of the many forms under which man may conceive the godhead ? Durgâ, as conceived by my friend, seems a kind of deified Nature, or an image of Divine Omnipotence, such as we find most frequently elsewhere, particularly in Semitic religions.

The Origin of Durgâ.

But there is one difficulty that remains. My correspondent says that the manner in which the Mârkandeya Purâna has described Durgâ has naturally led to this development. No doubt it has. But the question is, How did that late Purâna come to describe her thus? Are there any historical antecedents of such a goddess as the Durgâ described in the Mâr-kandeya Purâna? If the study of religion has taught us anything, it has taught us that no goddess springs suddenly from the brain of man, like Athene from the head of Zeus. Now it is well known that female deities act a rather subordinate part in the Vedic mythology of India, and even those who, like the Dawn, receive the warmest homage, never attain to the dignity of the female deities in Semitic mythology who represent the active power (sakti) of their male companions.

Some scholars, such as Weber, Muir[1], and others, endeavoured, many years ago, to show that the Paurânic Durgâ was the continuation of the Vedic Kâlî, the dark flame, also the wife of Agni, and of Ambikâ, the sister, later the wife of Rudra. There is some truth in this, as there is also in the other theory that Siva, the husband of Durgâ, may be looked upon as connected with Rudra and Agni.

But I cannot bring myself to believe that this modern god and goddess represent really a continuous development of the older Vedic gods and goddesses. There is such a decidedly non-Vedic spirit in the conception of Durgâ and her consort Siva that I feel inclined to trace it to some independent source. A goddess with four arms, or ten arms, with flowing hair, riding on a lion, followed by hideous attendants, could hardly have

---

[1] See Muir, *Original Sanskrit Texts*, vol. iv. pp. 420-437. Nearly all the important passages, bearing on Durgâ, have been carefully collected here. I have quoted some of his translations also, with but few alterations.

been the natural outcome either of Rodasî, the wife of
Rudra, and of the Maruts, or even of the terrible flames
of Agni, Kâlî, and Karâlî. The process to which
Durgâ and Śiva owe their present character must, I
believe, be explained in a different way. It was
probably the same process with which Sir Alfred
Lyall and others have made us acquainted as going
on in India even at the present time. When some
outlying, half-savage tribes are admitted to a certain
status in the social system of the Brâhmans, they
are often told that their own gods are really the
same as certain Brâhmanic gods, so that the two
coalesce and form a new incongruous mixture. Many
years ago I suspected something like this in the
curious process by which even in Vedic times the
ancient gods, the Ribhus, had been assigned to the
Rathakaras, literally the chariot-makers, a not quite
Brâhmanic class, under a chief called Bribu. If we
suppose that some half-barbarous race brought their
own god and goddess with them, while settling in the
Brâhmanised parts of India, and that after a time they
forced their way into the Brâhmanical society, we
could then more easily understand that the Brâhmanic
priests, in admitting them to certain social privileges
and offering them their partial services, would at the
same time have grafted their deities on some of the
minor Vedic deities.

Traces of a foreign, possibly of a Northern or North-
eastern Durgâ, may still be discovered in some of her
names, such as Haimavatî, coming from the snow-
mountains; Pârvatî, the mountaineer; Kirâtî, belonging to the Kirâtas, a race living in the mountains east
of Hindustan. One of her best-known names, *Kandî*,

explained as violent, savage, belongs to an indigenous vernacular rather than to Sanskrit. *Kanda* and Mu*nda*, the latter possibly meant for the Mu*nda* tribes, are represented as demons conquered by the goddess, and she is said to have received, from her victory over them, the name of *K*a-mu*nd*â. Possibly *K*and*â*la, the name of one of the lowest castes, may be connected with *Kanda*, supposing that, like Mu*nda*, it was originally the name of a half-savage race. Even in so late a work as the Hariva*m*sa, v. 3274, we read that Durgâ was worshipped by wild races, such as *S*abaras, Varvaras, and Pulindas. Nay even *S*arva, another name of *S*iva, and *S*arvâ and *S*arvânî, names of Durgâ, may be interpreted as names of a low caste (see *S*arvarî, a low-caste woman, a devotee of Râma).

If then *K*and*î* was originally the goddess of some savage mountaineers who had invaded central India, the Brâhmans might easily have grafted her on Durgâ, an epithet of Râtrî, the night, or on Durgâ, as a possible feminine of Agni (havyavâhanî), who carries men across all obstacles (durga), or on Kâlî and Karâlî, names of Agni's flames, or Rodasî, the wife of the Maruts or Rudra. This goddess is called vishita-stukâ, with dishevelled locks, and *K*and*î* also is famous for her wild hair (ke*s*inî).

In the same way her consort, whatever his original name might have been, would, as a lord of mountaineers, have readily been identified with Rudra, the father of the Maruts, or storm-winds, dwelling in the mountains (giristhâ, Rv. VIII. 94, 12, &c.), or with Agni, whether in one of his terrible, or in one of his kind or friendly forms (*s*ivâ tanû*h*, *S*atarudriya, 3). In his case, no doubt, the character of the prototypes on which he

was grafted, whether Rudra or Agni, was more
strongly marked, and absorbed therefore more of his
native complexion, than in the case of Durgâ, his
wife. But the nature of *S*iva's exploits and the
savage features of his worship can hardly leave any
doubt that he too was of foreign origin. It should
be remembered also that Rudra and Agni, though
they were identified by later Brâhma*n*ic authors, were
in their origin two quite distinct concepts [1].

I hold therefore that neither Durgâ nor *S*iva can
be looked upon as natural developments, not even as
mere corruptions, of Vedic deities. They seem inexplicable except as importations from non-Brâhmanic
neighbours, possibly conquerors, or as adaptations of
popular and vulgar deities by proselytising Brâhmans.

But even this would not suffice to account for all
the elements which went towards forming such a
goddess as we see Durgâ to be in the epic and
Paurâ*n*ic literature of India.

If she was originally the goddess of mountaineers,
and grafted on such Vedic deities as Râtrî, Kâlî,
Rodasî, Nir*r*iti, one does not see yet how she would
have become the representative of the highest divine
wisdom. The North, no doubt, was often looked upon
as the home of the ancient sages, and, as early as
the time of the Kena-upanishad, the knowledge of the
true Brahma is embodied in a being called Umâ Hai-

---

[1] As early as the time of the *S*atapatha-brâhma*n*a, Agni was
identified with Rudra (VI. 1, 3, 10), and among his other names
we find Sarva (sic), Pa*s*upati, Ugra (Vâyu), A*s*ani (lightning),
Bhava (Par*j*anya), Mahân Deva (moon), Îsâna (sun), Kumâra (boy).
In the same Brâhma*n*a (I. 7, 3, 8) Agni's names are given as Sarva
(among the eastern people), Bhava (among the Bâhîkas), Pa*s*ûnâm
pati, and Rudra.

mavatî. She is also called Ambikâ, mother, Pârvatî, living in the mountains, and her husband Umâ-pati is identified with Rudra (Taitt.-Âr. 18). Some authorities (Râm. I. 36, 13) speak of Umâ and Gaṅgâ as two daughters of Himavat, which might lead us to suppose that Umâ was the name of a Northern river, possibly, like the Sarasvatî, a river protecting the settlement of some Vedic sages. But whoever this Umâ or Ambikâ was, she too, as representing the highest wisdom, was sometimes embodied in the goddess Durgâ, who thus became the incarnation of wisdom quite as much as the terrible goddess, the destroyer of thousands of evil demons. Nor is she only the representative of that Brahma-vidyâ (Mahâ-bh., Bhîshmaparva, v. 803), or of that Vedântic philosophy which discovers the true Brahma behind the veil of Mâyâ; but in the Devî-mâhâtmya she is represented also as Mahâmâyâ herself, or the cause of all phenomenal existence. We read there (V. 56): 'By thee the universe is upheld, by thee this world is created, by thee it is preserved, O goddess; and thou always devourest it in the end.' And again (V. 63): 'Thou art the power of whatever substance, existent or non-existent, anywhere is, O thou soul of all things; why art thou praised then? Who is able to magnify thee, by whom the creator of the world, the possessor of the world, and he who devours the world, have been made subject to sleep?'

Here then we see to a certain extent the justi-fication of the opinion expressed by my Indian correspondent, as to the true nature of Durgâ. What he says of her, is exactly what the gods, headed by Indra, said to her, after she had vanquished the demon

Mahisha: 'We bow down with devotion before the goddess Ambikâ, who stretched out this world by her own power, in whom are impersonated the various energies (saktis) of all the gods; she is to be adored by all the deities and *Ri*shis.'

But the steps by which Durgâ became what she is now will never be laid bare from beginning to end, unless we can gain much fuller information of the religious life of the people at large than has hitherto been accessible to us in Sanskrit literature [1].

This may give some faint idea of the difficulties which confront the student of religion, even under the most favourable circumstances. They could hardly anywhere be more favourable than in India. We have the advantage there of a large number of witnesses, whose observations can be compared and checked one by the other. We have natives who speak English, and missionaries and others who speak Hindustani, and yet we see how they not only contradict one another, but how what they relate is hardly ever the whole truth. There are more varieties, dialects, patois, and jargons of religion than of language, and to construct out of all of them a classical grammar, a rule of faith accepted by all, is one of the most difficult tasks [2]. Some people would consider it almost impossible. Every one, they say, has a right to his own religion. Religion lives only in the heart, and no one has any right to touch or to correct it. Such a view, though I do not deny that there is some truth in it, would, of course, put an end to all

---

[1] See Appendix IV.

[2] See some very pertinent remarks on this subject in the *Pioneer Mail* of April 9, 1891.

historical study and religion. It would be the same as if in the study of language we were to say that every one has a right to his own dialect; that language lives only as it is spoken, and no one has any right to touch or to correct it.

Authoritative Books.

Among most nations this difficulty has been solved, for religion by sacred books and creeds, for language by classical literature and grammar. But among races who have neither the one nor the other, you will see now why the task of discovering the general outlines of their religion is so difficult a task, quite as difficult as that of discovering the general outlines of their grammar, nay even more difficult.

Testing of Evidence, (II) with regard to Illiterate Races.

I tried once to collect from the mouth of a Mohawk a grammar of his language. The circumstances were most advantageous. My Mohawk friend knew English and a little Latin. He had been educated at a Missionary school, and he was ready to answer all questions which I addressed to him. Besides, the Mohawk being one of the North-American polysynthetic languages, I knew on the whole what to expect.

It was most curious, however, that this young Mohawk, who knew what grammar meant, insisted from the first, that Mohawk was really no language, like English, that it had no real grammar, and that it was useless to attempt to construct a grammar of it.

This is exactly what some Negro converts say, when examined about their former religion. It is really no religion at all, they say; their old gods are quite different from their new God, and yet, when they are in trouble, they will pray to their old gods to avert dangers, while they shrink from troubling their new God with their petitions.

I soon discovered that Mohawk, as spoken by my friend, was a most systematic, most regular, most transparent language. The roots stood out clearly by themselves, and the most minute grammatical modifications were expressed by a number of short suffixes which left no doubt as to their original pronominal character. After I once knew the character of these suffixes, there was little difficulty in telling how to conjugate a new verb, even though my friend had not repeated to me the actual forms. This surprised him very much, and I remember one occasion when he was almost frightened by my knowledge of the Mohawk grammar. In Mohawk there are different forms not only for singular and plural, but also for a dual. Now if we want to say, 'I love my children,' we must say, 'I them love my children.' The suffix for *them* is really what is called an infix, and seems to form part of the verb. I then asked my teacher to give me the Mohawk for 'I love my parents,' which was 'I them love my parents.' Here I stopped him, and asked whether it should not be 'I them two love my parents,' substituting the dual for the plural infix. He stared at me when he heard my grammatical compound, as if it were not quite canny. 'Why,' he said, 'that is how my grandmother used to say. How came you to know it?' I explained to him how I came to know it. The fact was that in Mohawk, as in other languages, the old dual forms were dying out. His grandmother still used them— he himself found the plural sufficient.

If this correcting and reconstructing process is necessary for a knowledge of the languages, how much more is it for the religions of uncivilised people. As I have spoken of my Mohawk friend, I may give you another curious case that arose in my conversations with him, and which shows how the peculiar character of a language may influence even religious expressions. In Mohawk we cannot say father, mother, child, nor the father, the mother, the child. We must always say, my father, or thy mother, or his child. Once when I had asked him to translate the Apostles' Creed for me, he translated, 'I believe in our God, our father, and his son,' all right. But when he came to the Holy Ghost, he asked, is it *their* or *his* Holy Ghost ? I told him that there was a difference of opinion on that point between two great divisions of the Christian Church, and he then shook his head and declared that he could not translate the Creed till that point had been settled.

Of course, my friend, the Mohawk, having been educated at a Missionary school in Canada, knew nothing of the old religion of his tribe. He was a Christian, and if he had known anything of the religious beliefs and customs of his ancestors, he would probably have said that they really had no religion like the English religion, just as he thought that their language had no grammar like the English language. Such an answer has very often been given to inquisitive travellers, and some of them have told us in consequence that certain races had really no religion at all.

This belief, however, that there are savage races without any trace of religion, has now, I believe, been completely surrendered by those who have made the history of religion a subject of scholarlike study. Tribes without religion have been hunted for in the most remote and inaccessible corners of the globe, but in every case, so far as I am aware, the statement that a whole race was ever without any religion, has been controverted by ocular observation.

I cannot here go through every case where a more or less savage race has been described to us first, as entirely without religious ideas, and afterwards, not only as religious, but as superstitious, pious, and even priest-ridden. It might seem as if there had been on one side a wish to establish the fact that man could exist without religion, and, on the other side, that he could not. There certainly was for a time a tendency to discover men standing on so low a level as to form a bridge between animal and man. All such tendencies are much to be deprecated, as hindrances to the progress of science. But in most cases, I believe, the conflict of evidence is due to misconception rather than to prejudice.

We all know from our own experience within a smaller sphere, what contorted and distorted images our own peculiar angle of vision, our own religious, moral, national, or political spectacles may produce, what we can bring ourselves to believe, and, as we call it, honestly to believe, if there is nothing to make us hesitate.

Read the descriptions of Mohammed by his disciples and by his enemies, read the enthusiastic panegyrics of Socrates by Plato and his condemnation as a corruptor of the Athenian youth, read the account of Napoléon by Thiers and by Lanfrey or by Mad. de

Remusat, read in our daily papers the representations of the same person as a pattern of unselfish patriotism and as a reckless political gambler, and you will learn to make allowance for the strange opinions expressed by travellers and missionaries of races of men whom they are pleased to call savages or brutes.

The Andaman Islanders.

I shall only mention one more case, which seems more flagrant than all the rest, that of the Mincopies, or the inhabitants of the Andaman islands. It is a case of taking away not only their religious character, but their character altogether. Owing to the exaggerated accounts of travellers, the inhabitants of these islands had acquired such a bad reputation for ferocity and brutality that for centuries no ships passing there, on the very high road of commerce, would go near these islands. An Arab writer [1] of the ninth century states that their complexion is frightful, their hair frizzled, their countenance and eyes terrible, their feet very large, and almost a cubit in length, and that they go quite naked. Marco Polo (about 1285) declared that the inhabitants are no better than wild beasts, and he goes on to say: 'I assure you all the men of this island of Angamanain have heads like dogs, and teeth and eyes likewise; in fact, in the face they are just like big mastiff dogs.'

In 1857, after the Sepoy mutiny, it was necessary to find a habitation for a large number of convict prisoners. The Andaman Islands were then selected for a penal colony. The havoc that was wrought by this sudden contact between the Andaman islanders and these Indian convicts was terrible, and the end

[1] Flower, *On the Pygmy Races of Men*, p. 6.

will probably be the same as in Tasmania,—the native population will be extirpated. If these natives had really been like what Marco Polo describes them, their disappearance would not have been a cause of regret. But let us hear what Mr. Edward Horace Man, the Assistant-Superintendent of the islands, and specially in charge of the natives, has to tell of them. He is a careful observer, a student of language, and perfectly trustworthy. According to him the Andamanese are certainly a very small race, their average height being 4 feet $10\frac{3}{4}$ inches. The tallest woman was 4 feet $4\frac{1}{2}$ inches, the smallest 4 feet 2 inches. Their hair is fine, very closely curled and frizzly. Their colour is dark, not absolutely black. The features possess little of the most marked and coarser peculiarities of the negro type. The projecting jaws, the prominent thick lips, the broad and flattened nose of the genuine negro are so softened down in the Andamanese as scarcely to be recognised.

Before the introduction into the islands of what is called European civilisation, the inhabitants lived in small villages, their dwellings built of branches and leaves of trees. They were ignorant of agriculture, and kept no poultry or domestic animals. Their pottery was hand-made, their clothing very scanty. They were expert swimmers and divers, and able to manufacture well-made dug-out canoes and outriggers. They were ignorant of metals, ignorant, we are told, of producing fire, though they kept a constant supply of burning or smouldering wood. They made use of shells for their tools, had stone hammers and anvils, bows and arrows, harpoons for killing turtle and fish.

Such is the fertility of the islands that they have abundance and variety of food all the year round. Their food was invariably cooked, they drank nothing but water, and they did not smoke.

People may call this a savage life,—I know many a starving labourer who would gladly exchange the benefits of European civilisation for the blessings of such savagery.

But this is not all. It has been the custom of a certain class of anthropologists to illustrate their theories of the growth of civilisation by descriptions of savage life, such as it was supposed to exist in Africa, Australia, and America. In these descriptions the Andaman islanders have generally been made to serve as specimens of the very lowest stratum of humanity, and it is fortunate that before they have been altogether improved off the face of the earth, they should have found one advocate at least to redeem their character. This is what Mr. Man, who witnessed their last struggle with civilisation, says of them :

' It has been asserted that the " communal marriage " system prevails among them, and that " marriage is nothing more than taking a female slave ; " but so far from the contract being regarded as a merely temporary arrangement, to be set aside at the will of either party, no incompatibility of temper or other cause is allowed to dissolve the union ; and while bigamy, polygamy, polyandry, and divorce are unknown, conjugal fidelity till death is not the exception, but the rule ; and matrimonial differences, which, however, occur but rarely, are easily settled with or without the intervention of friends.' ' One of the most striking features of their social relations is the marked equality and affection which exists between husband and wife,' and the 'consideration and respect with which women are treated might with advantage be emulated by certain classes in our own land.' 'As to cannibalism or infanticide, they are never practised by the Andamanese.'

But this is not all. These little fellows who inhabit these beautiful islands have lately found another defender in the person of Colonel Cadell, the Chief Commissioner of the Andaman Islands. As to the scenery, he describes it like fairyland. 'The water deep and clear as a crystal; on either side, within a stone's throw, magnificent forest trees, reaching to a height of 200 feet, the stems of some straight and white, like gigantic silver rods, with umbrella-like tops; others clothed from foot to summit with creepers in beautiful festoons; palms, rattans, and canes of many varieties interspersed among the forest trees, creating striking contrasts of form and colouring, while beneath the vessel were inconceivably beautiful coral gardens.' 'But year after year,' he continues, 'in his cruises among the islands, he saw a perceptible diminution in the number of people. It was undoubtedly a moribund race, and probably none of them would be found alive twenty-five or thirty years hence, except perhaps in Little Andaman, where the inhabitants had been kept free from the dire effects of contact with civilisation.'

I have said before that I cannot share the feeling of regret that certain races are dying out, particularly when they are succeeded by a stronger and better race. If the Celtic race were effete, why should it not be replaced by the Saxon race? If the Saxon race were effete, why should it not make room for a better race? Nothing would be lost so long as we have on earth sound minds in sound bodies. But I must protest when I see certain races represented as unworthy to cover the face of the earth, simply in order to have an excuse for removing them from the face of the earth. Now think of all that has been alleged against the poor Mincopies. They had feet a cubit long —and yet we know now that they are hardly five feet in height. They had faces like dogs, they were like big mastiffs; but Mr. Man tells us that the coarse features of the Negro type were softened down in them so as scarcely to be recognised. And now let us hear Colonel Cadell once more. He is a Victoria Cross, and not likely to be given to excessive sentimentality. Well, this is what he says of these fierce mastiffs: 'They are merry little people. One cannot imagine how taking they are. Every one who had to do with them fell in love with them. Contact with civilisation had not improved the morality of the natives. In their natural state they were truthful and honest, generous and self-denying. He had watched them sitting over their fires cooking their evening meal, and it was quite pleasant to notice the absence of greed and the politeness with which they picked off the tit-bits and thrust them into each other's mouths. The forest and sea abundantly supplied their wants, and it was therefore not surprising that the attempts to induce them to take to cultivation had been quite unsuccessful, highly though they appreciated the rice and Indian corn which were occasionally supplied to them. All was grist that came to their mill in the shape of food. The forest

(3)   N

supplied them with edible roots and fruits. Bats, rats, flying foxes, iguanas, sea-snakes, molluscs, wild pig, fish, turtle, and last, though not least, the larvae of beetles, formed welcome additions to their larder. He remembered one morning landing by chance at an encampment of theirs under the shade of a gigantic forest tree. On one fire was the shell of a turtle, acting as its own pot, in which was simmering the green fat delicious to more educated palates; on another its flesh was being broiled together with some splendid fish; on a third a wild pig was being roasted, its drippings falling on wild yams, and a jar of honey stood close by—all delicacies fit for an alderman's table.'

According to strict anthropological terminology these men are savages, nay, the very lowest among savages, because we are told they have no knowledge of kindling a fire, they do not cultivate the soil, and they do not domesticate any animals. How they can boil a turtle and roast a pig without a fire is difficult to understand. It may be true that they sow not, neither do they reap, nor gather into barns, but the reason which they give for it would prove satisfactory even to an alderman. They need not toil, and they need not spin, and yet they have enough to eat.

However, I do not want to defend these merry, lazy islanders, or to maintain that Solomon in all his glory was not arrayed like one of them in their almost complete nakedness. All I wished to point out was the insecurity of the evidence on which so many theories have been erected, and the necessity of trusting to no witnesses except those who have lived among so-called savages for many years, and who have acquired a practical knowledge of their language.

And now let us consider their religion. According to some authorities they were quite guiltless of any religion, whether good or bad. This opinion received the support of Sir John Lubbock, and has been often repeated without ever having been re-examined. As soon, however, as these Mincopies began to be studied more carefully, more particularly as soon as some persons, resident among them, acquired a knowledge of their language, and thereby a means of communication with them, their religion came out as clear as daylight. According to Mr. E. H. Man, they have a name for God, *Púluga* ; and how can a race be said to be without a knowledge of God, if they have a name for God ? *Púluga* has a very mythological character. He has a stone-house in the sky. He has a wife whom he created himself, and from whom he has a large family, all, except the eldest, being girls. The mother is supposed to be green (the earth ?), the daughters black. They are the spirits, called *Mórowin*. His son is called *Píjchor*. He alone is permitted to live with his father, and to convey his orders to the *Mórowin*. But *Púluga* has a moral character also. His appearance is like fire, though now-a-days he has become invisible. He was never born, and is immortal. The whole world was created by him, except only the powers of evil. He is omniscient, knowing even the thoughts of the heart. He is angered by the commission of certain sins, some very trivial, but he is pitiful also to all who are in distress. He is the judge from whom each soul receives its sentence after death.

According to other authorities, some of the Mincopies look on the sun as the fountain of all that is good, on the moon as a minor power, and they believe in a number of inferior spirits, the spirits of the forest, the water, and the mountain, as agents of the two higher powers. They believe in an evil spirit also, who seems to have been originally the spirit of the storm. Him they try to pacify by songs, or to frighten away with their arrows.

All this has been known for years, and yet the old story is repeated again and again that the Andaman islanders are devoid of all religious sentiments. Is that right [1]?

Negative and Positive Evidence.

It can easily be seen that there is in these matters an essential difference between negative and positive evidence. If travellers tell us they have never discovered any signs of religion among certain races, this may or may not be a proof that these races are without religion. But if a traveller tells us that he has seen people believing in God or gods, showing reverence to the spirits of the forest, the water, and the mountains, and trying to pacify an evil spirit, we can hardly ignore all this and ascribe it either to imagination or wilful untruth. It is quite possible that a traveller or missionary may misapprehend and misunderstand what he sees and hears, but there are few cases where downright falsehood as to facts has been proved against any of them. I fear, however, that, unless the students of religion acquire themselves a certain knowledge of the languages in which religious ideas have taken their origin and their shape, Comparative Theology will never hold its place by the side of Comparative Philology, and will never assume a truly scientific character [2].

[1] See Appendix V.
[2] See my address as President of the Anthropological Section at the Meeting of the British Association at Cardiff in 1891.

LECTURE VII.

THE DISCOVERY OF THE SOUL.

Physical Religion Incomplete.

PHYSICAL religion, beginning with a belief in agents behind the great phenomena of nature, reached its highest point when it had led the human mind to a belief in one Supreme Agent or God, whatever his name might be, whether Jehovah or Allah, whether Jupiter, Dyaus, or Zeus. Homer calls Zeus the father, the most glorious, the greatest, who rules over all, mortals and immortals. Xenophanes[1] goes even further: 'There is one god,' he says, 'the greatest among gods and men, neither in form nor in thought like unto mortals.' What more could we require from Physical Religion?

It was supposed that this God could be implored by prayers and pleased by sacrifices. He was called the father of gods and men. Yet even in his highest conception he was no more than what, as we saw, Cardinal Newman defined God to be. 'I mean by the Supreme Being,' he wrote, 'one who is simply self-dependent, and the only being who is such. I mean

---

[1] Εἷς θεὸς ἔν τε θεοῖσι καὶ ἀνθρώποισι μέγιστος, οὔ τι δέμας θνητοῖσι ὁμοίϊος οὐδὲ νόημα. (*Clem. Alex. Strom.* v. p. 601, C.)

that he created all things out of nothing, and could destroy them as easily as he made them, and that, in consequence, he is separated from them by an abyss, and incommunicable in all his attributes [1].'

This abyss separating God from man remains at the end of Physical Religion. It constitutes its inherent weakness. But this very weakness becomes in time a source of strength, for from it sprang a yearning for better things. Gods like those of the Epicureans, who exist, indeed, but never meddle with the affairs of men, could not satisfy the soul of man for any length of time. Even the God of the Jews, in His unapproachable majesty, though He might be revered and loved by man during His life on earth, could receive, as it were, a temporary allegiance only, for 'the dead cannot praise God, neither any that go down into darkness.'

The Soul of Man.

God was immortal, man was mortal; and Physical Religion, such as we found it and defined it, could not throw a bridge over the abyss that separated the two. Real religion, however, requires more than a belief in God, it requires a belief in man also, and in an intimate relation between God and man, at all events in a life to come. There is in man an irrepressible desire for continued existence. It shows itself during life in what we may call self-defence. It shows itself at the end of life and at the approach of death, in the hope of immortality.

You may remember how it was the chief object of my Lectures on Physical Religion to discover the faint

[1] *Open Court*, p. 977.

vestiges of that intellectual progress which led the human mind to the formation of a name and concept of God. We saw how that progress began with the simplest perceptions of the great phenomena of nature, and then advanced step by step from what was seen to what was not seen, from what was finite to what was not finite, till at last all that was merely phenomenal in the ancient names was dropped, and there remained in the end the one infinite Agent, still called by the old names, but purified from all material dross.

As in treating of Physical Religion it was our chief object to watch this genesis of the name and concept of God in the various religions and languages of the ancient world, we shall now have to do the same for what forms the necessary counterpart of God in every religion, namely the human soul, or whatever other name has been given to the infinite, and therefore the immortal element in man. The name of that immortal element also was not given to man as a gratuitous gift. It had to be gained, like the name of God, in the sweat of his face. Before man could say that he believed his soul to be immortal, he had to discover that there was a soul in man. He had to shape its name and concept from such materials as were within his grasp, till at last, by a process of abstraction which we found to be inherent in language, certain names became more and more freed from their material elements, and more and more fitted to express something entirely immaterial, invisible, infinite, and divine. It required as great an effort to form such a word as *anima*, breath, and to make it signify the infinite in man, as to form such a

word as de va, bright, and to make it signify the
infinite in nature.

Animism.

You may remember the arguments which I produced against admitting Animism of any kind as a
primitive form of religious thought. You cannot
have animism unless you first have an *anima*. In
order to ascribe an anima, a soul, to anything, be it
a stone, or a rag (Fetishism), a sign-post (Totemism), a
tree, or a mountain (Animism), man must first have
gained the name and concept of anima. If, as we are
told, trust in a fetish arose always from ' the doctrine
of spirits embodied in, or attached to, or conveying
influence through certain material objects,' how can it
longer be doubted that fetishism, under all its forms,
presupposes a belief in spirits, and that what has
really to be accounted for, is how for the first time
a spirit was named, conceived, and believed in, not
how a spirit was attributed to a stone, a sign-post,
or a tree?

The problem therefore with which we have to deal
at first, is not how man came to believe in the immortality of the soul, but how such a thing as a soul was
ever spoken of, how man was supposed to be anything but what he was seen to be, how here also
behind the finite, something not-finite, or infinite, was
perceived or postulated and believed in.

Primitive Man.

When we try to trace human thought, such as we
find it in early language, back to its first beginnings,
we ought to make it quite clear to ourselves, that
these first beginnings are entirely beyond the reach of

what we mean by history. We shall never know what primitive man, or what the first man on earth, may have been. When we speak, nevertheless, of primitive man, we mean, and can only mean, man as he is represented to us in his earliest works.

We do not mean man while he was emerging from brutality to humanity, 'while he was losing his fur and gaining his intellect.' We leave that to the few biologists who, undeterred by the absence of facts, still profess a belief in the descent of man from some known or unknown animal species [1].

Nor do we mean man as known to us by skulls and skeletons only. Here, no doubt, we have to deal with real and most important facts. But the historian leaves these to the ethnologist, not because, as Socrates said of the leaves of trees, they cannot teach him anything, but because the lessons which they teach would only be spoiled, if mixed up with the lessons which concern him more immediately. Even the earliest works of art, the flints and bones and stones, which display clear traces of human handiwork, and

[1] Virchow, no mean authority on this question, writes to Haeckel : 'Vous savez que c'est précisément à l'anthropologie que je travaille maintenant avec une prédilection tout particulière. Je dois cependant le déclarer, chacun des progrès positifs que nous avons faits dans l'anthropologie préhistorique nous a particulièrement, et de plus en plus, éloignés de la preuve de cette parenté. . . . Nous devons réellement reconnaître qu'aucun des types fossiles ne présente le caractère marqué d'un développement inférieur. Et même, si nous comparons la somme des fossils humains connus jusqu'ici avec ce que nous offre l'époque actuelle, nous pouvons hardiment prétendre que parmi les hommes actuellement vivants il existe un beaucoup plus grand nombre d'individus relativement inférieurs que parmi les fossils en question. . . . Nous ne pouvons pas considerer comme un fait acquis à la science que l'homme descend du singe ou de tout autre animal.' (*Revue scientifique*, 1877, p. 542.) Compare with this Mr. Clodd's article in the *New Review*, July, 1891, p. 19. Surely a challenge from Virchow cannot be ignored ; why then has it never been taken up ?

therefore of human intellect, are outside his special domain, and are better dealt with by the anthropologist.

The documents from which we study primitive man are contained in language. Whether language was older than anything else, whether the Neanderthal skull was the abode of a speechless man, whether the rudest palaeolithic flints were fashioned by mute workmen, we cannot tell. All we know is that in the world of intellectual beings there can be nothing older than language. With us primitive man means therefore speaking man, and if speaking man, then rational and intelligent man.

Materials for our Studies.

The historical materials for studying the earliest phases in the growth of man are found in one store only, namely in language, and yet they are enormous, enormous in number, and enormous in age. Remember that English alone contains 250,000 words, and that every one of these words is an ancient chronicle. Remember that English is but one dialect of one branch of one great stem of human speech, and you will see that the students of the history of man will not lack for materials for some time to come.

But though there is nothing more ancient than the chronicles contained in every word, let us guard against the absurd idea that even words or roots can ever bring us to the beginning of human thought. All beginnings are by their very nature and by our nature, beyond our ken. But when we come to a stratum of thought and language that is still intelligible to us, when we are able to enter into ancient words and concepts, as if we had formed them ourselves, when there is nothing left in them that is irrational and unintelligible, then we may speak of primitive, using the word in the sense of something that, whatever its chronological date may be, requires no antecedents, but has its own beginnings in itself.

Poor primitive man has had many things to suffer at the hands of the ethnologist, the linguist, the psychologist. He has been represented on one side as no better than an ape, on the other as a primeval and divinely inspired prophet. We must try to look upon him and to understand him as essentially the same as ourselves, only as moving in different surroundings.

If from this point of view we ask, how primitive man, or how man in a primitive state of life, came to invent a soul, came to discover that he had, or, that he was a soul, our answer is, look at his language, and try to find out what he called the soul.

Names for Soul.

To us the two words 'body and soul' are so familiar that it seems almost childish to ask the question how man at first came to speak of body and soul. It is true also, and, I believe, it has never been contested, that even the lowest savages now living possess words for body and soul. If we take the Tasmanians, a recently extinct race of savages, we find that however much different observers may contradict each other as to their intellectual faculties and acquirements, they all agree that they have names for soul and souls, nay, that they all believe in the immortality of the soul.

We saw how long it took to frame a name for God.
We also saw that man could never have framed such
a name, unless nature had taken him by her hand,
and made him see something beyond what he saw, in
the fire, in the wind, in the sun, and in the sky. The
first steps were thus made easy for him. He spoke of
the fire that warmed him, of the wind that refreshed
him, of the sun that gave him light, and of the sky
that was above all things, and by thus simply speaking of what they all *did* for him, he spoke of agents
behind them all, and, at last, of an Agent behind and
above all the agencies of nature.

We shall find that the process which led to the discovery of the soul and the framing of names for soul
was much the same. There was no conclave of sages
who tried to find out whether man had a soul, and
what should be its name. If we follow the vestiges
of language, the only true vestiges of all intellectual
creations, we shall find that here also man began
by naming the simplest and most palpable things,
and that here also, by simply dropping what was
purely external, he found himself by slow degrees in
possession of names which told him of the existence of a soul.

What was meant by Soul?

But what did he mean by soul? What do we
ourselves mean by soul? Here, you see, our difficulties begin, and they are due, as in nearly all philosophical questions, to the indiscriminate use of our
words.

Think of the many meanings which are contained
in our word soul, as used in ordinary conversa-

tion, and even in philosophical works. Our soul may mean the living soul; it may mean the sentient soul; it may mean the soul as the seat of the passions, whether good or bad; it may mean the soul as the organ of thought; and lastly, the immortal element in man.

It is quite clear that no name could ever have been framed to embrace all these meanings, though in the end all these meanings may cluster round one and the same name.

The question, therefore, which we have to ask, is not, how man arrived at a name for soul, but how he came for the first time to think and speak of something different from the body. To a question rightly put, we may expect a right answer.

We saw how man was startled, was made to wonder at the wonders of nature, the true miracles presented to him on every side, and how he was led on by the irresistible laws of his mind to look for the workers of these wonders, the agents in these miracles.

The Problem of Man.

Next to nature, the most startling problem for man was man himself, man seen as coming into the world, living his short life, and then departing.

The Lessons of Death.

When we say departing, we adopt already a conclusion which may be quite natural to us, but which was anything but natural to early thinkers. When we speak of the departed, we assume something for which there is no material evidence. What was seen was simply death, cessation of life and activity, a horrible corruption of the body, and, at last, a mere handful of dust.

If anything could frighten man, could force him to meditate, it was surely death, and we shall see how some of the most important and most permanent ingredients of the intellectual life of the world were supplied, the first time, by the aspect of death.

When a friend who in every respect had been exactly like themselves, was suddenly seen by those who knew and loved him, prostrate, without motion, without sight, without speech, the simplest process of reasoning, a mere adding and subtracting of perceptions, would teach the bystanders that something that was formerly there was there no longer. Something had gone.

Blood as Life.

What then was that which had departed? If a man had been killed, and the blood was seen pouring away from his wound, it was the most natural conclusion that the blood had left him, and, with it, life. Hence the well-known expression, 'the blood is the life,' which we find not only in Hebrew and in the Bible (Deut. xii. 23), but in other languages also, and which became the source of ever so many religious and superstitious acts. Homer uses the two expressions, the blood ran down from the wound (Il. xvii. 86), and the life ($\psi v \chi \acute{\eta}$) ran down from the wound (Il. xiv. 518), almost synonymously. Kritias, a Greek philosopher quoted by Aristotle (De Anima, i. 2, 19), declared that the soul was the blood. The Arabic expression, 'The soul flows (from his wound),' instead of 'he dies,' shows that the Arab also believed the blood to be the life or soul of man.

We have no time to enter on the question whether people who said the blood is the life, meant also that the life is the blood, so that the two words would be entirely synonymous ; or whether they had formed an independent idea of life, and meant simply to say that life was in the blood and depended on it. The difference is considerable, but it hardly affects the superstitions which arose from that ancient belief.

The Jews were forbidden to eat or drink the blood, and they gave a reason for it which is of a religious character. The blood, they said, was the life, and the life belonged to God. Hence the blood was to be poured out upon the altar of the Lord, but not to be eaten. Among savage nations, on the contrary, the idea is very prevalent that in drinking the blood of an enemy, his life, his strength, and his courage were absorbed by the living.

Another widely-spread custom is the drinking of blood, as the highest sanction of a promise or a treaty. Herodotus (iii. 8) alludes to this custom as existing in Arabia, and how long it prevailed and how firmly it was established we may gather from the fact that Mohammed had to forbid it as one of the heavy sins,—idolatry, neglect of duties towards parents, murder, and the blood-oath [1]. Stanley found the old custom still prevailing in Central Africa. 'After making marks,' he writes, 'in each other's arms and exchanging blood, there was a treaty of peace as firm, I thought, as any treaty of peace made in Europe.'

[1] Kremer, *Studien zur vergleichenden Culturgeschichte*, p. 35.

I feel convinced, however, whatever anthropologists may say to the contrary, that the evidence of the senses was as stróng with ancient people as it is with ourselves. When they saw how after a time blood became putrid and offensive, they could hardly continue to believe that what had departed at death was simply the blood.

The Heart.

What applies to the blood, applies to a certain extent to the heart also. As the heart ceased to beat at death, we find in many languages that heart is used in the sense of life and soul. The eating of the heart of an enemy[1], nay even of his eyes, was sometimes supposed to produce the same effect as the drinking of an enemy's blood[2]. Some languages[3] use the same word for the beating of the heart, for the pulse, and for the soul. But they can distinguish perfectly well between the actual heart, and heart as a name of the soul.

We must keep this distinction in mind, if we wish, for instance, to understand the answers given by the Indians of Nicaragua to Bobadilla[4]. They stated

[1] 'Among certain of the mountain tribes (of South Africa) there is a curious custom regarding an enemy who falls after displaying considerable bravery. They immediately cut out his heart and eat it. This is supposed to give them his courage and strength in battle.' (Rev. J. Macdonald, *Journal of the Anthropological Institute*, vol. xx, p. 137.)

[2] 'Some writers have fancied that the idea prevails among the Blacks of Australia that the man who partakes of such food acquires the strength of the deceased in addition to his own; but I have never been able to verify this statement, nor do I believe it.' (Curr, *The Australian Race*, vol. i. p. 77.)

[3] Kremer, l. c., p. 40.

[4] Tylor, *Primitive Culture*, i. p. 390. Oviedo, *Hist. du Nicaragua*, pp. 21–51. Spencer, l. c., p. 190. I must confess to some misgivings as to the trustworthiness of Bobadilla.

that 'when they die, there comes out of their mouth something that resembles a person, and is called *julio* (Aztec *yuli* means 'to live'). This being goes to a place where the man and the woman are. It is like a person, but does not die, and the body remains here.'

The following dialogue took place between a Christian and a native of Nicaragua:

Question: 'Do those who go up on high keep the same body, the same face, and the same limbs, as here below?'

Answer: 'No; there is only the heart.'

Question: 'But since they tear out their hearts (i.e. when a captive was sacrificed), what happens then?'

Answer: 'It is not precisely the heart, but that in them which makes them live, and that quits the body when they die.' And again: 'It is not their heart that goes up above, but what makes them live, that is to say, the breath that issues from their mouth and is called *julio.*'

We can understand that the blood and the heart should have been supposed to have something to do with the living soul during life. But after death that which had lived could hardly have been sought there, as little as in the flesh or in the bones.

Other nations placed the seat of life or the living soul in other organs, such as the liver, the kidneys, or in the chest, and in the diaphragm which surrounded the most important internal organs. But all these were perishable, and it was difficult to believe that what had departed at death, and what by its departure had produced the tremendous change from life to death, could be identified with these decaying organs.

It is curious that the brain, which in modern languages is so frequently used as the seat of the thinking soul, should have played so insignificant a part in the intellectual nomenclature of the ancient world. It is hardly ever mentioned as a name of the soul.

Breath.

We enter into quite a different stage of language and thought when we come to deal with breath as a name of soul, or, more correctly, as a name which, by a very natural development, or divestment, came to mean soul in its various applications. Breath vanished at death, but it did not perish before the eyes of people, like the blood, or the heart. No doubt, the actual breathing, the most certain sign of life, ceased at death. With the breath life was seen to have departed. To *expire*, to breathe out (uz-anan) became in many languages one of the most common expressions for to die.

But in the case of breath a question arose very naturally, namely, what had become of the breath which was formerly in the body;—where it was, and what it was. Breath did not putrefy before their eyes, and nothing led to the conclusion that it had actually perished. Another great advantage was that language could distinguish between the act of breathing and that which breathed, the former the life, as an act, the latter the soul, as an agent, or a living subject. This distinction was most important, as we shall see, in all its consequences.

Here, then, we may discover the first and very natural suggestion arising in men's minds, that the breath which had departed at the moment of death was something different from the dead body, different from the putrid blood, different from the decaying heart, and from the dissolving brain.

We must remember, however, that with the breath, not only life, but all that constituted the man himself, his thoughts, his feelings, his language, had departed, and that therefore the conclusion was not unnatural that the breath had carried away with itself all that constituted the very being of man. When people said, his breath has departed, they could not help saying at the same time that his thoughts, his feelings, in fact, all that belonged to the individual man, had departed. We can thus understand how the words which originally meant breath, real, tangible breath, supplied the first material that was shaped in time into words meaning soul in its widest sense.

Soul after Death.

And here we can watch at once another step. If it is true that the discovery of the soul was made, not so much during life, when body and soul were almost indistinguishable, but at the time of death, when the breath, and all that was implied by that word, had departed from the body, the question could hardly be avoided, whither that breath had gone.

To us the idea of annihilation, though it is really an idea inconceivable to any human mind, has become quite familiar. Not only among a certain class of philosophers, but even among uneducated people, the thought of man being utterly destroyed or annihilated by death is by no means uncommon. But to unsophisticated minds the thought that a man who but yesterday was, like ourselves, eating, drinking, working, fighting, should have utterly perished, was almost impossible to grasp. It was far more natural to suppose that he continued to exist somewhere and somehow, though the where and the how were unknown, and had to be left to the imagination. Imagination, however, was more busy in ages of comparative ignorance than in our days, and if the expression had once been used, 'our father's breath has fled,' that would soon grow into the expression that his spirit had fled, that he himself had departed from his house, and had gone where all spirits had gone before him, to a world of spirits.

This is a very general outline of a process which, under varying forms, we can trace almost everywhere, among uncivilised and among civilised people, and which has led to a belief, first, in something in man different from his body, call it breath, or spirit, or soul; and secondly, to a belief in the existence of disembodied spirits, to a belief in immortality, and to a large number of acts intended to keep up the memory of the departed, to secure their favour, to escape their anger, till in the end they were raised to an exalted position, second only to that of the immortal gods.

Words for Soul.

The principal, if not the only evidence which we can produce in support of the theory just propounded, is naturally taken from language. But the ancient archives of language are often very difficult to decipher. It is particularly difficult to watch the growth of meaning in the ancient words for soul, because most of them become known to us at a time when they had passed already through various stages, and had been more or less arbitrarily restricted in their meanings. They generally convey at the same time the ideas of mere breath, of vital breath, and of understanding. Whether they are used by certain writers in one sense or the other is often a question of idiomatic usage only, while in the end there generally arise learned discussions as to the exact meaning in which each term ought or ought not to be used.

Words for Soul in Hebrew.

Let us look at some of the words for soul in Hebrew. The distinction between the body and a something that gives life to it was familiar to the Jews from the earliest times[1]. Body was the flesh, בָּשָׂר, bâsâr. Hence 'all flesh' meant everybody, every living being, and 'my flesh' was used for I myself. The flesh, as active and living, was opposed on one side to what is without life, stones or bones; on the other side, as being mortal, weak, and perishing, it was distinguished from what is eternal and imperishable, God and the soul.

The question then arises, how did the Jews call that which was not the body? They called it by different names, and these names had at first a very vague and undefined meaning, so that they are often used one in place of the other. To attempt to define

---

[1] See H. Schultz, *Alttestamentliche Theologie*, p. 622.

these words strictly is a mistake, though at a later time the Jews themselves tried to define their old vague terms.

One of these words is רוּחַ, rûach, which means originally what moves, either the wind or the breath. As thunder was called the voice of God, the storm was conceived as His breath. This rûach in man is life, given by God and returning to God. It is used for man's breath, but not for breath only, but likewise for what we mean by soul, for we read of the rûach being embittered, cast down, and grieved, or being revived and glad.

Another word, נְשָׁמָה, neshâmâh, has nearly the same meaning. It is used for the vital breath which every creature has received from God, and likewise for the creature that breathes and lives. Thus, when we read in Genesis ii. 7, that 'the Lord God formed man of the dust of the ground, and breathed into his nostrils the breath of life: and man became a living soul,' the word neshâmâh is clearly conceived as breath coming from God, and as giving not only life, but also what we mean by soul, the latter being impossible without the former.

A third word also, נֶפֶשׁ, nephesh, does not seem from the beginning to have had a very different meaning. But it soon came to be used for the individual soul rather than for life and spirit in general. Nephesh is the living soul, the self-conscious soul. Hence it is the nephesh that loves and hates, that is glad and sorrowful, and 'my nephesh' is a very common expression for I myself. We meet with such expressions as 'my soul lives,' 'my soul dies,' and even the dead is still called a nephesh. But to say in every passage where

nephesh occurs, whether it was meant for breath or
life or soul is impossible. When Elijah prayed over
the dead child, he said: ' O Lord my God, I pray thee,
let this child's soul come into his inward parts again.'
'And the Lord heard the voice of Elijah, and the soul of
the child came unto him again, and he revived.' Here
(1 Kings xvii. 21) the soul may be meant for mere
breath, the actual breath, just as we say that a
drowned person has been reanimated by breathing
into his lungs. But it may also mean the soul as
given by God and returning to God at the time of
death.

We saw that this soul is sometimes said to be in the
blood, or to be the blood. And like the blood, the
heart also, lêb, is conceived as the seat of the soul, or
is used synonymously with soul. Not only feelings
and passions, but the conscience also, nay reason and
understanding, dwell in the heart. Hence we read of
a pure heart, of a new heart. We read (Hos. vii. 11)
of Ephraim being 'like a silly dove without heart,'
that is, without understanding.

We see here the same wealth of expression which
we generally meet with in ancient languages. The
same thing is called by different names, according to
some characteristic mark that strikes the speaker.
These names, being at first almost synonymous, become
gradually differentiated by usage, till the time comes
when they are defined more or less arbitrarily by
grammarians, philosophers, or theologians[1].

---

[1] In later times the Jewish Rabbis defined the different names
of soul more accurately, but also more arbitrarily. They tell us
(Midrash Genes. Rabba, cap. 14 ad fin.) that there are in man
five spiritual potentiae, each having its own name. They are (1)
נפש, the vital power ; (2) רוח, the vital spirit ; (3) נשמה, conscious-

What is important for us to observe is the fact that the original meaning of all these words was material. The idea of life was borrowed from blood, from heart, from breath, and that idea included in time not only physical life, but feeling, sensuous perception, and understanding, nay soul itself, as a self-conscious and personal, if not immortal, being. There are other expressions in Hebrew which start from even more material beginnings, and end by meaning the soul or the self. Thus when the Psalmist (vi. 3 seq., xvi. 9) speaks of 'my bones,' 'my body,' he means, not his bones or his body only, but his soul, his self, and he has entirely forgotten the material meaning of the words which he is using.

Words for Soul in Sanskrit.

It is curious that the ancient language of India which generally allows us so clear an insight into the earliest history of words, should tell us so little by its names for soul or spirit.

The best known word for soul is âtman. But unfortunately its etymology is doubtful. It has been derived from AN, to breathe, a root which has yielded many words for wind, breath, soul, and mind. Thus we find in Sanskrit an-ila, wind, also an-ala, fire; in Greek ἄν-εμος, wind; in Latin an-ima, air, wind, breath, but also life, soul, and even mind, and animus, soul and mind. But an + man would not give âtman, nor should it be forgotten that in the Veda we find tman also for âtman. Others have thought of the

ness; (4) יחידה, and (5) חיה, the two last being in the Bible epithets only of the soul. See an important article by Kohut, in *Zeitschrift d. D. M. G.*, xxi. p. 563. Kohut ascribes this fivefold division to Persian influences.

root AV = VÂ, to blow, and have connected it with
ἀϋτμήν. The original meaning, however, of âtman was
certainly breath. Thus the wind (vâta) is called, Rv.
V. 168, 4, âtmấ devấnâm, the breath of the gods. In
Rv. X. 16, 3, where the dead is addressed, we read:
sŭryam kấkshuh gakkhatu vấtam âtmấ, let the eye go
to the sun, the breath to the wind.

In other places âtmâ can best be translated by life.
To be separated from the âtman (âtmanâ viyukta)
means to be dead. From meaning the vital principle, it came to be used for what we call the essence
or substance. Thus in I. 164, 4, 'Who has seen
him who was born first, when he who has no bones
(form) bore him that has bones (form)? Where
was the breath (asu), the blood (asrig), the essence
(âtmâ) of the world? Who went to one who knew it,
to ask him?' Here we see how âtmâ is employed
with the same metaphorical meaning as asu, breath,
and asrig, blood. In another place, I. 115, 1, the sun is
called âtmấ gấgatah tasthúshah ka, the soul of all that
moves and stands. In later times âtmâ meets us as the
recognised name for soul, and the more abstract the
conception of soul becomes, the more abstract the
meaning conveyed by âtmâ, till at last we cannot
translate it any longer by soul, but must render it by
self. Such has been the reaction of thought on language, that âtmân has become a recognised pronoun,
corresponding to the Lat. ipse, the Greek αὐτός. In
some passages it can even be translated by body, as
when we read in the Katha-upanishad IV. 12, the
person (purusha), of the size of a thumb, stands in the
midst of the âtman, the body [1]. Having passed through

---

[1] See also Taittirîya-upanishad I. 7; II. 1.

all these stages, âtman was at last used by philosophers as the best name for the soul of the world, the Supreme Being.

While the derivation of âtman is doubtful, it is clear that ana, breath, is derived from AN, to breathe, and likewise the more common prâna, breath. Prâna, however, does not only mean the breathing in its various modifications, or the life, but likewise what are called the five senses, viz. the nose, the tongue (speech), the eye, the ear, and the mind (manas), with their respective functions.

Other words for soul in Sanskrit are equally uninteresting. Pudgala means beautiful, then body, then soul, but why it has any of these meanings we cannot even guess. If we are told that ka also may be used for soul, this is evidently a merely philosophical name. It means Who, and was used at a very early time as a name of the deity as well as of the soul.

Words for Soul in Tamil.

Before we proceed to examine the words for soul in Greek, we have still time to glance at some other languages in India, I mean the Dravidian. You know that, before the Âryas migrated into India, the country was occupied by people speaking a totally different language, a language which still lives all over the South of India, as Tamil, Telugu, Canarese, and in several local dialects.

In an able article on the study of Tamil, lately published in the *Madras Christian College Magazine*, Dec., 1890, p. 15, the Rev. G. Mackenzie Cobban informs us that uyir is the Tamil word for life, and that where in English we should use the word soul, the Tamil man would use uẏir. This uyir comes from a verb û-thu, which means to blow, or from u-yi, which means to breathe, and to exist. As, too, in Sanskrit, meant to breathe, though as a verb it means simply *to be*, as-mi, I am. But ú-yir means more than breath and life. It means the soul. Another curious name for soul is kûttan, and this means a dancer, or a leaper, thus recalling the Greek θύμος, which originally meant shaker or shaking or commotion, and the Gothic saivala, soul, which likewise seems to have had the original meaning of violent movement. There are other expressions for soul, or for mind, which simply mean what is within, like the Sk. anta*h*karana, the working within.

Polynesian Words for Soul, &c.

We have only to consult the dictionaries of any language, whether spoken by civilised or uncivilised people, and we shall find everywhere the same process, that is to say, words meaning originally blood, heart, chest, breath, becoming in time the recognised terms for life, feeling, thinking, and soul. Mr. Edward Tregear has lately published a most excellent Comparative Dictionary of Maori and other Polynesian languages, particularly Samoan, Tahitian, Hawaian, Tongan, Rarotongan, Marquesan, Mangarevan, Paumotan, and Moriori. When we look for words for mind, we find, for instance, *manawa*. This *manawa* means in Maori the belly, the heart, the lungs, breath, but also the seat of the affections. In Samoan *mânawa* means to breathe, to rest; *manatu,* a thought. In Tahitian *manava* is the stomach, the interior man, and *manavanava* is to think, to pónder; *manao*, thought or idea; *dumanava*, affection of the heart. In Hawaian *manawa* stands for affection, but likewise for spirit, and even for a spirit, as an apparition; *mana* is intelligence, *manao* to think, *mananao*, thought, opinion.

In Tongan *manava* is breath, life; to throb, to pulsate, and also to be careful of.

In Mangaian *manava* is mind, spirit; in Marquesan *menava* is breath, life, soul; in Mangarevan soul and conscience.

Another word for bowels and heart in Maori is *ngakau*, but it is also used for heart as the seat of the affections and of sorrow. In Tahitian, the same word appears regularly as *aau*, and means heart, mind, courage, spirit, and conscience. In Hawaian *naau* still signifies the small intestines of men and animals, but it is likewise used for the seat of the affections and of thought, for memory, conscience, learning, and wisdom.

A third word, *hinengaro*, is used in Maori for a certain portion of the intestines, but likewise for heart and affections; in Samoan for will and desire; in Tahitian for love, desire, will, choice, pleasure; in Tongan, as *finengalo*, for the mind, but applied to a king only.

Material Beginnings.

We have learnt so far that the discovery of the soul, the first attempts at naming the soul, started everywhere from the simplest observations of material facts. It was the running away of the blood, the beating of the heart, the breathing, and more particularly the cessation of breathing at the time of death, which suggested the idea that there was something different from the decaying body, and at the same time supplied the first names for that something. In fact the lesson cannot be inculcated too often that the whole wealth of our most abstract and spiritual words comes from a small number of material or concrete terms.

Only we must guard against two very common mistakes.

We constantly meet with such statements as that ancient and uncivilised people used metaphorical language when they spoke of the soul as breath, or as air, or as a bird, that at first they knew these names to be merely poetical expressions, but that afterwards they forgot and mistook the simile for the reality. There is no sense in this. If metaphor means transference, how can transference take place, when as yet there is only a word that can be transferred, but nothing it can be transferred to? This kind of poetical transference is very familiar to ourselves. A poet who knows what he means by soul, may metaphorically call the soul half angel and half bird, but until he has two concepts and two words, he cannot transfer one to the other. When people spoke of breath, they at first meant breath, and it was only by what I call the process of divestment inherent in language, that breath came in the end to mean something from which all the material characteristics of breath had vanished, the postulated agent of breath, the living soul, the spirit, the mind.

But it is as great a mistake to say that *spirit*, because it originally stood for exhalation, means and can never mean more than exhalation, or material breath. Spirit, as it became developed from age to age, meant less than breath, but by meaning less, it also meant more. It meant less than breath, because it became divested of many of the material qualities which *spiritus* originally implied. It meant more, because, by being freed from its material limitations, it came to stand for something less limited, and in the end for something unlimited or infinite, for the immortal, the eternal, the divine agent within man.

This process, which has hitherto been treated as a mere psychological postulate, stands before us as a simple fact in the history of all the languages of the world. Take whatever dictionary you like, and you will find how the words for soul, if they can be analysed at all, invariably point back to a material origin, and invariably disclose the process by which they were freed from their material fetters.

It may sound very strange to us when we are told that the word which in Tamil is used for soul has the original meaning of dancer. Yet it is but another attempt to name and grasp that which moved within, that which even the greatest philosophers could not define better than as something moving itself, without being moved, that is, as dancing.

We are not aware how often in our own language, which has grown so rich in abstract terms, we still use the old material words. We say that a man's blood is up, meaning half that he is flushed, half that he is angry. We speak of taking things to heart, knowing things by heart, without thinking of the heart that actually beats within our breast. The human mind, as led by human language, starts from different beginnings, and follows different roads in climbing up to the highest summits which it can reach. Nothing can be more instructive than to watch these patient toilers, and nothing can more strongly confirm our belief that they were following a right direction than when we see them in the end arrive at the same summit, at the same religious hopes, nay, at the same philosophical convictions.

LECTURE VIII.

DISCOVERY OF THE SOUL IN MAN AND IN NATURE.

The Three Stages of Early Psychology.

WE saw in our last Lecture how man came first to speak about a *soul*, or, more correctly, about a *breath*. We saw that there was nothing altogether unreasonable in such a name. In fact, whenever we examine that autobiography which man has left us in his language, we shall always find some good sense, something reasonable, even in what seems at first sight most unreasonable or foolish.

If we only bear in mind, what is now a fact doubted by no one, that every word in every language had originally a material meaning, we shall easily understand why that which at the dissolution of the body seemed to have departed and which we consider the most immaterial of all things, should have been called at first by the name of something material, viz. the airy breath. This was the first step in human psychology.

The next step was to use that word breath, not only for the breath which had left the body, but likewise for all that formerly existed in the breathing body, the feelings, the perceptions, the conceptions, and that wonderful network of intellectual threads which constituted the man such as he was in life. All this depended on the breath. It certainly was seen to have departed at the same time as the breath.

The third step was equally natural, though it soon led into a wilderness of imaginations. If the breath, with all that belonged to it, had departed, then it must exist somewhere after its departure, and that somewhere, though utterly unknown and unknowable, was soon painted in all the colours that love, fear, and hope could supply.

These three consecutive steps are not mere theory ; they have left their foot-prints in language, and even in our own language these foot-prints are not yet altogether effaced.

Let us look at Greek, as we find it in the Homeric poems. At present, I do not mean to speak of what the poet himself may have thought about the soul, about its work during life, and its fate after death. We shall have to speak of that hereafter. What we are now concerned with is what the language which Homer had inherited had to say to him on this subject.

The Original Meaning of Psyche.

The most common word for soul in Greek is psyche (ψυχή). This psyche meant originally breath. When a man dies, his psyche, his very breath, is said to have passed through the bar of his teeth, the ἕρκος ὀδόντων. Here we see the first step. This word ψυχή, as you know, assumed afterwards every possible kind of meaning. Even in this passage we might translate it by life, or by soul, without destroying the sense. But we can clearly see that what passed through the

(3) P

ἕρκος ὀδόντων was originally meant for the actual breath.

The Psychological Terminology of Homer.

Much has been written by Greek scholars about the exact meaning of psyche in every passage where that word occurs in Homer. I am not going to enter on that subject beyond stating my conviction that it is a mistake in poems, such as the Iliad and Odyssey, to look for a consistent use of words. It would be difficult even in modern poetry to find out what Shakespeare, for instance, thought about the soul, by collecting and comparing all the passages in his plays in which that word occurs. Poets are not bound by logical definitions, and if they used all their words with well-defined meanings, I doubt whether they could have written any poetry at all. They use the living language in which the most heterogeneous thoughts lie imbedded, and whatever word serves best for the moment to convey their thoughts and feelings, is welcome.

In the Homeric poems this difficulty is increased tenfold. Whatever may be thought about the final arrangement of these poems, no one can now hold that they were all originally the outcome of one mind. Nor must we forget that in epic poems different characters may be made to speak very different thoughts, and use the same words in very different meanings, as they best suit the circumstances in which they are uttered.

The Meaning of αὐτός.

I shall give you one instance only to show what happens, if we try to interpret Homer as we should interpret Aristotle's treatise on the soul. You remember how it is said in the beginning of the Iliad, that Achilles sent the souls of the heroes to Hades, but he gave themselves, αὐτούς, a prey to the dogs. It has been inferred from this and similar passages that Homer looked upon the body as constituting the true self of man. But this is to forget the requirements of poetry. Homer here wanted to bring out the contrast between the souls that went to Hades, and the corpses suffering the indignity of being devoured by dogs. 'They themselves' means here no more than 'they themselves, as we used to know them in life.'

How free Homer feels in the use of such words, we can see from another passage. In the Odyssey, xi. 601, we read that Odysseus saw Herakles, or his eidôlon, that is, his psyche, in Hades, but he himself, αὐτός, he adds, rejoices among the immortal gods.

In one passage, therefore, αὐτός means the body, or even the corpse, in another, the soul, and to attempt to reconcile the two by any theory except a poet's freedom of expression, would lead, and has led, to mere confusion of thought.

I shall attempt no more than to give you the general impression which a study of the Homeric poems has left on my mind, as to what was thought about the soul, if not by Homer himself, at least by those whose language he used.

Psyche and Menos.

What strikes me as most characteristic of *psyche* in the Homeric Greek, is that, whether it means breath, or life, or soul, it is never localised in any organ of the body. It is not in the heart, or in the breast, or in the phrenes, where thought resides. It is in the whole body (σῶμα), yet different from the body.

The Homeric language clearly distinguishes between psyche and menos, including under the latter name all that we should call mind.

But the most important distinction between psyche and menos, or any other name for mind, seems to me this, that the psyche is something subjective, while all other names express originally rather acts or qualities.

Thymos.

Take, for instance, thymos (θυμός). Of course, the Greeks had no recollection of the etymological meaning of that word, as little as we have of our own word soul. But there can be no doubt that thymós is derived from thýein, to move violently, from which we have also thýella, storm. In Sanskrit we have exactly corresponding to thymós, dhûma; but this has retained the material meaning of smoke, literally what moves about quickly. Dhûli, also, the Sanskrit word for dust, meant originally what is whirled about.

The Greek thymos, therefore, meant originally inward commotion,—you remember how in Tamil the soul was called the dancer—and we find in consequence that it is chiefly used with reference to the passions. But though originally thymos meant simply what moves within us, it afterwards comprehended both feelings and thoughts, and has often to be translated by mind in general. It seems to me that it was only *after* it had assumed this meaning, that it could also be used in the sense of life. For if it was said that one man had torn out or destroyed another man's thymos, that was tantamount to his having taken his life [1]. Or when it is said that the thymós left the bones (λίπε ὀστέα θυμός), we know that what is meant is that his mind, and therefore his breath, or his life, had left his body. But it is important to remember that we never hear of a thymos continuing by itself after death, like the psyche, which shows, as I said, that originally the thymos was really an activity, and not, like psyche, a something active.

Phrenes.

Another important word which Homer had to use is phrenes. It means literally the midriff or diaphragm, which holds the heart and lungs, and separates them from the lower viscera. It is therefore much the same as stêthos (στῆθος), the chest, as the abode of the heart. We find it used of animals as well as of men, as when the lion is said to have a stout heart in his chest, ἐν φρεσί, Il. xvii. 111. But it soon drops its material meaning, and is considered as the seat of all inward acts, both of feeling and of thought. The work of the menos, mind, of noûs, thought, and boulê, will, takes place within the phrenes, just as much as it takes place within the thymos. The Homeric Greek rejoiced, perceived, remembered, reasoned, ἐνὶ φρεσίν, as we should say, in the breast or in the heart. When we meet with such expressions as κατὰ φρένα καὶ κατὰ θυμόν, we should not try to distinguish between the two, as thought and feeling, but translate ' in the heart and in the thought,' the heart being the

---

[1] The same process of thought accounts for such expressions as ἀπὸ γὰρ μένος εἵλετο χαλκός, Il. iii. 294.

locality, the thought the activity.   We find a similar
juxtaposition in κραδίη καὶ θυμός.

But it is important to observe that the psyche, the
soul, is never spoken of as dwelling within the phrenes,
the breast, or within the heart (ἦτορ), nor is the psyche
ever spoken of by Homer as the abode of the mind.

It has been pointed out that while phrenes in the
plural is often used in its purely physical meaning, as
we use the words breast and heart, the singular phrên
has always reference to the mind or the intellect.

The derivation of phrên and phrénes is not clear in
Greek, but there can be little doubt that its meaning,
like that of all words, was originally material.   It
meant the actual diaphragm ; then, what was enclosed
in the diaphragm, particularly the heart, and lastly
what took place within the breast or the heart.   To
suppose that it was derived from phroneîn, to think,
and meant originally thought, and afterwards only
the seat of thought, the chest or the heart, is to invert
altogether the natural order of things.   It was only
after phrenes had become familiar in the sense of mind
in general, that we can account for a large number of
derivatives in Greek, such as ἄφρων, πολύφρων, φρονεῖν,
and all the rest.

Soul and Ghost.

It would be easy to follow the same process in other
languages, but the result would always be the same[1].

It is unfortunate that our own words, soul and
ghost, are not quite clear in their etymology.   It is
most likely, however, that soul, the German *Seele*,
the Gothic *saivala*, meant originally, like the Greek

---

[1] Tylor, *Primitive Culture*, ii. p. 388 ; *Hibbert Lectures*, pp. 89 seq.

θυμός, commotion, and that it is connected with the names for sea, the Gothic *saiv-s*[1]. And I feel inclined now to trace the English *ghost*, the German *Geist*, which, following an idea of Plato's[2], I formerly thought connected with *yas*, to boil, with *yeast*, and German *Gischt*, back to the Sanskrit hî*d*, to be angry, he*d*a, anger, so that it meant originally heat or commotion.

Differentiation of Meaning.

This linguistic process which led to the formation of words for the different phases of the intellectual life of man is full of interest, and deserves a far more careful treatment than it has hitherto received, particularly at the hands of the professed psychologist. What is quite clear is that all these words begin as names of material objects and processes, such as heart, chest, breath, and commotion, just as the names of the gods began with the storm-wind, the fire, the sun, and the sky. At first every one of these words was capable of the widest application. But very soon there began a process of mutual friction and determination, one word being restricted idiomatically to the vital breath or the life, shared in common by man and beast, other words being assigned to the passions or the will, to memory, to knowledge, understanding, and reasoning. This process of widening and narrowing the meaning of words goes on for ever; it goes on even now, and can only be stopped by that dictatorial definition of terms which is so offensive to the majority of mankind, and yet is the *sine quâ non* of all accurate thought. Our own language is over-

---

[1] *Science of Language*, i. p. 522.
[2] Θύσις καὶ ξέσις τῆς ψυχῆς, Kratylos.

burdened with an abundance of undefined names, such as soul, mind, understanding, intellect, reason, thought, to say nothing of breast, and heart, and brain, of passion, desire, and will. Who is to define all these words, and to keep one distinct from the other? There is here a real Augean stable to be cleared out, and until it is cleared out by a new Hercules, all philosophy will be in vain.

The Agent.

For the purposes of Anthropological Religion we wanted to know how man, for the first time, came to speak and think about a soul as different from the body. We have now seen that the way which led to the discovery of a soul was pointed out to man as clearly as was the way which led him to the discovery of the gods. It was chiefly the breath, which almost visibly left the body at the time of death, that suggested the name of breath, and afterwards the thought of something breathing, living, perceiving, willing, remembering, and thinking within us. The name came first, the name of the material breath. By dropping what seemed material even in this airy breath, there remained the first vague and imperfect concept of what we call the soul.

This something breathing, living, perceiving, and thinking, or, as we may now say again, this postulated agent of the acts of breathing, living, perceiving, and thinking, was recognised as within the body during life, and as without the body after death. It went by the same name, being called psyche in Greek, while inside the living body, and likewise psyche, after having departed from the dead body.

In all this there is nothing strange, nothing which we cannot follow and understand, nothing, or almost nothing, that we cannot make our own. There is one step, no doubt, which we find it difficult to take. We may admit the agent within, we may admit the persistence of that agent after it has left the body, but we should probably consider its identification 'with the breath as too material. We stand here before the old problem whether the human mind can ever conceive anything, entirely divested of all material attributes. Certain it is, that language cannot express anything except with names taken from material objects. This is a fact to be pondered on by all philosophers, aye even by those who do not claim that proud title. Language, no doubt, can go on and negative all that is material. One of the poets of the Veda, when speaking of the Supreme Being, says ' that it breathed without air' (Rv. X. 129, 2), ânît avâtám ; and, if we want to follow his example, we may say of the soul after death, that it is a breath without air. Language will perform wonderful feats in that way. But the ancients evidently thought they had gone as far as they could, when they spoke of the soul after death as a breath, that is, as a breathing and as a breather, and with all due respect for modern metaphysical phraseology, I doubt whether, if we keep to positive terms, we shall ever find a better word for the agent within us than breath or psyché.

Different Origin of other Names for Soul.

But even though the process which led the ancients to a belief in a soul and in souls may not be quite perfect in the eyes of modern metaphysicians, to study it

in the annals of language has one great advantage.
It teaches us again and again that the first framers of
our language and our thoughts, even though they were
not philosophers by profession, were on the whole
reasonable beings, men not very different from ourselves, though living in a very different atmosphere.
We cannot protest too strongly against what used to
be a very general habit among anthropologists, namely
to charge primitive man with all kinds of stupidities
in his early views about the soul, whether in this life
or in the next.

Shadow.

When we are told, for instance, that there was
another road also on which man was led to his first
discovery of the soul, by recognising it in his own
shadow, we simply cannot follow. When man had once
realised the idea of a soul and found a name for it, he
might liken that soul to many things, and we shall see
that he did liken it to many things, such as a bird, a
butterfly, a cloud of smoke, and also a shadow. But
all this is poetical metaphor, and carefully to be distinguished from that process which we have hitherto
examined. There we saw that breath, the actual
breath, was identified with life, the individual breath
with the living individual, and the departed breath
with the departed individual. But to suppose that
any human being should ever have mistaken the
shadow of his body on the wall as the true agent
within, and as that which would remain after his body
had been burnt, or buried, or devoured, is more than
we can father even on the most primitive savage. It
is said that a savage does not know what a shadow is,

and how it arises. I doubt it. He might fell a tree, he would never try to fell the shadow of a tree. Anyhow the very word, shade or shadow, shows that the primitive Aryan savage at least knew, even before the Aryas separated, that shade was simply a covering, whether the covering from the sun-light, given by the branches of a tree, or a covering of any light by an opaque body. The name is derived from a root meaning to cover. We can understand how the name of breath became the name of many things dependent on breath, from the breathing of the living man to the soul of the departed. But that any person should ever have looked on his outside shadow which came and went, and could be produced at a moment's notice, as something by which he lived in this life, or something by which he would live in the next, is more than we can take in and digest, more than we ought to charge even against the most primitive savage.

The name of shade did not help the birth of the concept of soul, but the soul, having been conceived as breath flown from the body, was afterwards, for one of its qualities, its thinness or impalpableness, likened to a shadow. So long as the soul was in the body, no likeness was required, and shadow would have been the very last to answer the purpose. After death, however, such a simile became quite natural. The soul was supposed to be like the body, hence it was often called an eidôlon or likeness, and what likeness was so like as the shadow which bore the very outlines of the human body, and seemed always to be doing exactly what the man himself was doing? If, as we are told, shadows on a wall suggested to the early artist the first idea of a portrait, what better

name could poetical imagination suggest for a disembodied soul than shadow?

We can watch this process in many languages. Thus
ata, which in Maori means spirit and soul, is clearly
identical with *ata*, shadow, image, with the Tahitian
ata, cloud, with the Marquesan *ata*, likeness. In
Mangaian *ata* has actually come to signify the essence
of a thing, a concept which many people would consider
far beyond the reach of these uncivilised people.

The Maori *wairua* also, which means a spirit, and
the human soul, is clearly connected with *wairua*, a
shadow, a reflection. In Hawaian *waitua* is a ghost
or spirit of a person seen before or after death, separate
from the body.

This will show how important the distinction
between *radical* and *poetical* metaphor [1] really is for
a right appreciation of the thoughts of primitive man
in their historical development. He, poor primitive
man, can no longer defend himself, but his descendants
ought all the more to stand up for his good name. If
Mr. Herbert Spencer is right that our common ancestor
could never have mistaken a dead for a living thing,
how can he believe that a mere shadow was mistaken
by him for his own living soul, whether before or after
death?

And here language comes again to our help. Though
shadow becomes at a very early time a recognised
name for the souls after death, its original character
as a poetical metaphor· is not yet quite forgotten, for
instance, by Homer. No doubt, the dead are to him
skiaí (σκιαί) shades, quite as much as psychaí, souls.
But in certain passages we can still discover traces of

---

[1] *Science of Language*, vol. ii. pp. 456, 479.

the poetical metaphor. When Odysseus tried to lay hold on the psyché of his dead mother, then thrice it flew away from his hand, 'like unto a shadow or even a dream' (σκιῇ εἴκελον ἢ καὶ ὀνείρῳ). And when she explains to him that this is the state of mortals after death, 'that their nerves no longer hold the flesh and bones, for these the strong force of fire has consumed, what time their thymos first left the white bones,' she adds, 'but their psyche flying flits about, *like a dream.*'

All these were originally poetical comparisons. The souls were like shades, like dreams, like smoke (ἠΰτε καπνός); but we never hear of shades, dreams, or smoke leaving the body[1]. That applies to breath only, to psyche, and these two processes must therefore be kept carefully distinct, if we wish to gain a true insight into the working and growing of the human mind in its earliest phases[2].

Dreams.

I have still to say a few words with regard to another theory, according to which the idea of a soul in man is supposed to have been suggested for the first time by dreams and apparitions. What I said with regard to the theory that the soul was originally conceived as a shadow, applies with even greater force to this theory. Before primitive man could bring himself to imagine that his soul was like a dream or like an apparition, it is clear that he must have already framed to himself some name and concept of soul. All the illustrations which have been collected

---

[1] See on this subject an interesting paper by Mr. C. F. Keary, 'The Homeric Words for Soul,' in *Mind*, XXIV, Oct. 1881. Though I differ from his conclusion, the facts collected by him have proved very useful.

[2] See Dr. Codrington, as quoted in *Hibbert Lectures*, p. 91.

in order to prove that man's first conception of a soul was derived from what he saw in dreams and apparitions, leave no doubt on that point. They all presuppose some knowledge of the soul. When Mr. St. John [1] tells us that the Dayaks think that in sleep the soul sometimes remains in the body, and sometimes leaves it and travels far away, it is clear that they must have elaborated their concept of soul, quite independently of its travels in sleep. They might indeed have likened it to a dream, but they could not have received the first intimation of a soul from hypnotic apparitions.

It is quite true that the separation of subjective and objective impressions is much less fully carried out by uncivilised than by civilised nations, by uneducated than by educated persons. But with regard to dreams the first impression, whether with civilised or uncivilised people, is that they are not like ordinary objective impressions. As soon as a man wakes even from the most vivid dream, he knows that it was *only* a dream. When, as Sir George Grey describes it, a savage jumps up to get rid of a nightmare, catches a lighted brand from the fire and flings it with many imprecations in the direction where the apparition was seen, he knows, as soon as he is fully awake and has quite shaken off his dream, that the spirit he saw in his dream is not like a real person whom he can lay hold of, punish, and kill. As soon as he is awake, he feels relieved. It was only a dream, he says, it was a nightmare, or whatever name suggests itself; and he comforts himself in his fright by saying: 'the fellow only came for a light, and having

[1] Tylor, *Early History of Mankind*, p. 7.

got it, having been hit by the lighted brand, he will go away.'

If people once possess the idea of something within themselves different from the body, even though they call it as yet a commotion or a mover or a dancer only, and if they have once brought themselves to believe that after death, though the body may perish, that which was in the body has not perished, then visions, whether by day or by night, will no doubt help to strengthen their belief in departed spirits, though alas! that belief would soon vanish like a dream, if it had nothing but dreams to depend on.

Once given the name and concept of soul, and of departed souls, there would be no limit to poetical metaphor. They might be likened to birds flying away, to smoke vanishing in the air, to shadows that can be seen, but cannot be touched, to dreams that come when least expected, but can never be called back. How far this popular poetry may be carried, may be seen from many popular sayings current among uncivilised and civilised people.

Superstitious Sayings about Shadows.

Thus Bastian states that the Benin-negroes regard men's shadows as their souls, that is to say, that they speak of the souls as shadows. Nothing can be more natural. But if he adds that the Wanika are actually afraid of their own shadows, that depends very much on the authority of the interpreter. In the presence of white people, the Wanika may have seemed afraid of many things, even of their own shadows. The reason given that 'possibly they think, as some other negroes do, that their shadows watch all their actions and bear witness against them,' shows that the explanation was a mere surmise, and all depends on who 'the other negroes' were meant to be. If Crantz tells us that the Greenlanders believe a man's shadow to be one of his two souls, is it not clear that they must previously have possessed an independent idea at least of one or the other of the two souls?

Most likely, however, the fact that bodies threw no shadows in the dark, was quite sufficient to suggest the expression, that during sleep and in the darkness of the night a man's soul left his body, just as the shadow did. When speaking of inseparable friends, we may say even now, one follows the other like his shadow, or that one never leaves the other, like his shadow. Even when their relations are less friendly, we speak of one man being shadowed by another. Why then should not the same simile have suggested itself to early thinkers, that in sleep the soul left the body as the shadow leaves the body during night?

There is another popular saying among the Zulus [1], that a corpse throws no shadow. Is this really to be taken as a myth of observation, as Mr. Tylor would call it? Did any human being ever persuade himself that a corpse, when carried on the bier, threw no shadow, while the bier and those who carried it were followed by their shadows? Mr. Herbert Spencer, in spite of his repeated warnings against taking savages for fools, thinks it was so. I can see in it nothing but a perfectly intelligible process of language. People who had adopted *shades* as one of many idiomatic names for the souls of the departed, might very naturally say that the shade had left the corpse, or

---

[1] Callaway, *Religious System of the Amazulus*, p. 91.

that the corpse was without its shade. Fond of riddles as ancient people are, they might even ask, ' What is there in the world without a shadow,' and the answer would be, ' a corpse.' When Eastern nations say now, ' May thy shadow never grow less,' they know perfectly well that a shadow never grows less by itself. What they mean is perfectly under-stood, namely, ' Mayest thou thyself never grow less.'

There are many things which half-educated people repeat and which they pride themselves on believing, though they would often laugh at others for believing that they believe them. Think with how serious and almost solemn a face young ladies will tell ghost-stories in these days. Even though they have never seen a ghost themselves, they are fully convinced that their friends have, and it would amount almost to rudeness to doubt their good faith. However, I ought not to restrict these remarks to young ladies, for I see in the newspapers that the young men at Oxford have just carried a resolution in their Debating Society that they believe in ghosts. And yet they do not really believe in ghosts. They do not even believe that they believe in ghosts, unless they use ' to believe' in a very peculiar sense. They like to make believe that they believe in ghosts. To believe is always supposed to be more proper than not to believe. But ask them to bet one shilling on the due apparition of a ghost, and, if I know them well enough, they will decline. It is exactly the same with savages. They also are proud to believe or to profess to believe what ordinary people are not able to believe. The Zulus, for instance, not only profess to believe that a corpse throws no shadow, they look equally serious when they assure their European questioners that ' as a man approaches his end, his shadow shortens, and contracts into a very little thing [1].' However, when Bishop Callaway spoke to his Zulu friend seriously, and asked him whether he really believed that the shadow thrown by his body, when walking, was his spirit, he soon collapsed, and falling back on his popular idiom, declared, ' No, it is not your *itongo* or spirit (evidently understanding me to mean by my spirit an ancestral guardian spirit watching over me, and not my own spirit), but it will be the itongo or ancestral spirit for your children when you are dead.' This is hardly more than if we were to say that after death a man's spirit would be to his children a mere shadow, or like a shadow.

Unless we study the wonderful ways of language, we shall never understand the wonderful sayings of men, particularly during the earlier phases of human speech. Here Mr. Herbert Spencer has deprived himself of a microscope that would have disclosed to him again and again perfectly organic thought, while he can see nothing but incoherent specks.

The Ci-près in Language.

He often accuses savages of what he calls erroneous classing. He wonders that the Esquimaux should have taken *glass* for *ice*, and quotes this as an instance of their erroneous classing. I do not believe it for a moment. Do we not ourselves call glass *crystal*, and κρύσταλλος meant ice, before it came to mean rock-crystal. This is not a case of erroneous classing; it is simply and solely a necessity of

[1] Callaway, l. c., p. 126.

language. When we become acquainted with a new subject, such as glass, we have either to invent an entirely new name, and that, particularly in the later periods of language, becomes almost an impossibility, or we must be satisfied with what lawyers call a *ci-près*, and in the case of glass the most natural *ci-près*, or the nearest likeness, seemed to be ice.

Thus again, when we say, ' the wall sweats,' it is not because we really assume that water comes out of the wall, after a frost, as perspiration comes out of our skin. It is simply a case of poetical metaphor, without which half of our language would become impossible.

I do not believe that because the Orinoco Indians call the dew 'the spittle of the stars,' they believe that the stars spit during the night. We speak ourselves of cuckoo-spittle, even though we know perfectly well that it is no more than a small grub enclosed in a slimy substance. Nor is it more than a poetical metaphor when we say, it spits with rain.

The Infinite in Man.

A student of language knows that all these expressions are not only perfectly natural, but simply inevitable. And the same applies to the words for soul. The soul was discovered in the breath, and hence it was called breath, or psyché, by people who at first really believed that that which left the body at death and continued to exist was the breath. This something, called breath, or psyche, was afterwards likened to many things, if they possessed certain attributes

which seemed compatible with the nature of the
psyche or soul. As the souls after death were supposed to fly away, they were called winged, or even
birds, not because they were really taken for birds,
or birds for them, but simply and solely because they
were supposed to pass through the air, like winged
creatures. Even biologists may sometimes speak of
angels' wings, but do they believe that vertebrate
beings can have wings as well as arms?

The souls were called shades, not because they were
ever supposed to be nothing but images thrown on
the wall, but because they shared one attribute in
common with the shadows, namely, that of being
without a body, and almost unsubstantial. Another
name, eidôla, meant really not much more than
shadow. It meant likeness, such as the outline of
a man's shadow, or his image reflected in the water.
And if the souls were called dreams, this was again
because they shared in common with the visions of
dreams their unsubstantial nature, their withdrawing
themselves from the touch and the embraces of their
friends.

When mythology steps in with its irrepressible
vagaries, or, what is even more serious, when art
invests these unsubstantial similitudes with a substantial form, no doubt the souls often become in
the popular mind actual shadows and dreams, birds
and winged angels. But though such expressions
may satisfy the human heart in moments of grief
or hope, though they may inspire the poet with his
happiest strains, the serious thinker knows that they
are no more than relics of ancient poetry. The soul
is not a bird, the soul is not a shadow, the soul is not

a dream, not even the shadow of a dream.   Here we have the same No, no, which in the Upanishads we saw applied to God.   But when the ancients called the soul breath, they really meant what they said ; at least, they meant it as much as when they spoke of Dyaus or the sky, meaning not the material sky, but the agent in the sky.   No doubt, as the sky was recognised afterwards as only a vesture of God, the breath also was conceived, as early as the time of the Vedic poets, as ' breathing without air.'   On this point we are not wiser than the most primitive savage.   We retain his words, however knocked and battered during ages of intellectual toil and moil, and we shall have to retain, whether we like it or not, some of his thoughts also.   If breath sounds too material to our ears, we may like the Latin word better, and translate breath by spirit.   But so long as we think in human language, we shall never arrive at a truer expression than breath or spirit, unless we rise to a higher octave of thought altogether, and agree to call it the Infinite in Man, as we recognised in the gods of nature the ancient names for the Infinite in Nature.

Why a Belief in a Soul is necessary.

It has been asked what our belief in a soul can have to do with religion and with a belief in God, and what room there is for anthropological by the side of physical religion.   To judge from many works on religion, and, more particularly, on the origin of religion, it might seem indeed as if man could have a religion, could believe in gods and in One God, without believing in his own soul, without having even a name or concept of soul.   It is true also that our creeds seldom enjoin a belief in a soul as they enjoin a belief in God; and yet, what can be the object, nay, what can be the meaning of our saying, 'I believe in God,' unless we can say at the same time, 'I believe in my soul.'

This belief in a soul, however, exactly like the belief in gods, and, at last, in One God, can only be understood as the outcome of a long historical growth. It must be studied in the annals of language, in those ancient words which, meaning originally something quite tangible and visible, came in time to mean something semi-tangible, something intangible, something invisible, nay, something infinite in man. The soul is to man what God is to the universe, and as it was the object of my last course of Lectures to follow in the ancient languages and religions of the world the indications of man's progress towards a knowledge of or a faith in God, it is my object now to discover, if possible, in the same historical archives, some evidence that may be left there of man's progress towards a knowledge of or a faith in his own soul. The search for that evidence may often prove tedious, and its interpretation by no means so satisfactory as when we had to deal with the history of man's belief in God. Yet the subject itself is so important that we must not allow ourselves to be discouraged. It is a first attempt, and first attempts, even though they fail, encourage others to try again.

The Soul in Man and the Soul in Nature.

The problem which we have to face in trying to discover how the agent within us was first discovered, was first named and conceived, is really in many respects the same as the problem the solution of which we had to study when treating of Physical Religion. There we saw how the agent without, or, at first, the many agents behind the phenomena of nature, had to be named by the names of visible outward phenomena. There, too, if you remember, the question arose whether what had been called Dyaus, the sky, or in Chinese, *Tien*, the sky, was the actual, visible, blue sky, or something else, the Agent in the sky. That postulated Agent was actually called in later times the *psyche*, the soul of the sky.

In exactly the same way, we find that the question was asked whether what had been called prâna in Sanskrit, or *psyche* in Greek, or *spirit* in Latin, was the actual, visible, warm breath, or something else, the agent in the breath.

We, at our time in the history of the world, may smile at such questions. We know that if we speak of heaven, we do not mean the blue sky. We know that when we speak of our Father in heaven, we do not mean our Father in the clouds. We know that if we speak of the dead as ascending into heaven, as dwelling in heaven, we mean more than a mere ascension into the higher strata of our terrestrial atmosphere. We live in post-Copernican times. Still we must remember that what was once the language of the childhood of the world, will remain for ever the language of the childhood of every generation. A child will always look to the blue sky as the abode of his Father in heaven. A child will always lift his hands and his eyes upward, when praying to God. And no child could conceive the return of the spirit to God who gave it, the return of the Son to the

Father, except under the image of an ascent through
the clouds. Some bear these fetters of language
longer than others. Some bear them all their life,
without even being aware of them. Who would
blame them, if only they would not grudge to others
the freedom for which they have often paid a very
heavy price!

In the same way, the soul or the spirit will with
many people always remain a breath, an airy breath,
for this is the least material image of the soul which
they can conceive, just as the sky was the least
material image of the deity which many of the
ancient nations could conceive.

If we only remember this, we shall better understand how old age is able to use, and, from an historical point of view, to use honestly, the language of
childhood, though with a deeper and truer meaning.
An old man who prays, 'Our Father which art in
heaven,' is not necessarily a hypocrite. It is a study
of the ancient religions of the world that best enables
us to see behind the imagery of their language, and
the outward show of their sacred customs and ceremonies, something which we can at least understand,
something with which to a certain extent we can
even sympathise, something that is true, though
expressed in helpless and childish words.

But there is another lesson also which an historical
study of the origin and growth of the words for soul
and for God may help to impress upon our mind. In
teaching us how the concept of God arises of necessity
in the human mind, it teaches us at the same time
that nothing can satisfy the human mind but what we
mean by an agent, that is, a real, self-conscious, agent,

or, as we express it, in more anthropomorphic language, a personal soul and a personal God.

We have to guard here against two misunderstandings. There are theologians, even Christian theologians, who hold that the concept of God was the result of a special disclosure, and made to Jews and Christians only. Such assertions can only be silenced by facts, such as I gave in great abundance in my Lectures on Physical Religion, though one would have thought that some of these orthodox sceptics would on this point have yielded more ready submission to the express teaching of St. Paul.

But there are other philosophers who hold that the concept of God, though, like the concept of soul, it may be the result of a long-continued historical development which can be traced in all languages and all religions, is nevertheless a name only, which we may retain for old association's sake, but which denotes merely the unity of nature and no more.

This has been repeated again and again, and yet a little reflection would have shown that this whole argument rests simply on a mistake in language and thought. If people prefer to call the agent of their own acts and the agent of the acts of nature a mere unity, modern languages allow such a licence. But we must remember that unity is an abstract term, and that we can never have abstract terms without concrete objects from which they are abstracted. Unity is nothing, if it is not a predicate.

We may predicate unity either when what is substantially one has become differentiated, or when what is substantially different has become combined. The latter is clearly impossible in our case when, if we

may trust our reason at all, our reason postulates a
self-conscious agent for everything that deserves to
be called an act. To speak of an act that acts itself,
or of an agent not different from his act, is not to
speak, but only to use words. In the former acceptation of unity, we may predicate it of that which is
one and the same in different acts, whether the soul
in man, or God in nature; but in predicating unity
we cannot predicate it except of a unit. We cannot
define that *unit*, whether in ourselves or in nature,
beyond saying what we mean by it, namely, a self-
conscious agent, such as we know our self to be, apart
from all other qualifications, and such as we require
the self of nature to be, apart from all phenomenal
attributes.

Now then we see clearly how closely what I call
Anthropological and Physical Religion hang together.
The former teaches us how we have come to discover
an agent within, and to call that agent soul or person,
or ego or self, but not simply a cause, still less a mere
unity. The latter shows us how we have come to
discover an agent without, and to call that agent soul
or person or ego or self, but not simply a cause, still
less a mere unity. If in religious language we prefer
the name of God, we may do so, but we must not leave
out any of the elements of which it is composed. If
soul is nothing except it be a self, a self-conscious
agent, or a person, God would be nothing, unless He
was at least a self, at least a self-conscious agent, or a
person, in the highest sense which that word conveys
to ourselves.

LECTURE IX.

The Import of Customs.

WE have hitherto examined the evidence which lies imbedded in the very words for life, soul, and mind, such as we find them in some of the more important languages of the world. Every one, as we saw, tells the same story. Man began by naming what he could perceive; and by simply ignoring what was purely material in his words, he gained possession of a large array of expressions to convey to himself and to others what could not be perceived, but had to be conceived, something more abstract, yet by no means less real than what was perceived. Heart, for instance, though no longer meant for a mere muscle, was still meant for something that could account for real feelings, for real passions, for real thoughts. Breath, though being divested of its visible attributes, remained in man's language as the sure sign of something or of some one that breathed and lived. This simple process of slow and almost unconscious divestment revealed behind the perceptible world a new world which, though invisible, became to man the necessary substratum of the visible world. We saw that the discovery of the soul was not a mere accident, but that it was the necessary consequence of the progress of human language from the singular to the general, from the concrete to the abstract, from the phenomenal to the noumenal, from what seems to be to what is.

After having explored this lowest stratum of language, in order to discover, if possible, some of man's earliest thoughts about the soul, we shall now have to carry on our search for new evidence to a new stratum, the stratum of ancient customs. Ancient customs contain, no doubt, a less articulate expression of man's thoughts and feelings than ancient words, or what we shall have to examine afterwards, ancient poetry and ancient philosophy. But, for that very reason, they are important to us when we wish to discover the earliest impressions of the human mind, when brought face to face with the great problems of life, and more particularly the greatest of all, namely, the problem of death.

Motives of Customs.

The feelings roused by death are naturally of a religious character. The sight of death brings man, whether he likes it or not, face to face with what is beyond, with what transcends the limits of our senses, with what may be called once more the Infinite. If anything was solemn and sacred, if anything could stir even the hardest heart, it was the sight of a sudden and violent death, or the watching of the slow ebbing away of a beloved life. Whatever mode of disposing of the dead was adopted, we can perfectly understand that the place where the body, the bones,

or the ashes were deposited, was regarded as different
from other places, was entered with a certain awe,
and soon acquired a sacred character. So far scholars,
such as Stackelberg for instance, were right when
they imagined that much of the worship of the gods of
Greece had been derived from the custom of addressing prayers to the dead, or offering gifts to them on
their graves. In some countries, particularly in China,
the room of the ancestors became really a temple, but
that was not the case in Greece. In the eyes of the
Greeks the care bestowed on the graves was considered
the truest measure of the real culture of a people.
It may seem a mere superstition when we find how
the Greeks from the earliest times thought that the
departed found no rest till they had received a proper
funeral, or till their bones had at least been covered with
a handful of earth. But the concatenation of ideas
which led to this belief was likewise perfectly natural.
At first came the impulse to treat the body with respect
and kindness. This surely requires no explanation,
though it is well known that there are what seem to
us startling exceptions [1]. Then followed the thought
that what was done for the dead was for their good,
and would be appreciated by them; and at last came
the conclusion that the souls would be displeased
or would find no rest, unless and until these acts
of kindness had been rendered to them. Homer,
though he touches but seldom on the state of the
departed after death, was evidently familiar with
these ideas. You remember how the soul of Elpenor
is the first to meet Odysseus in the Nekyia (Od. xi.
51). Elpenor had broken his neck in the house of

[1] Grimm, *Das Verbrennen der Leichen*, p. 4.

Circe, but had been forgotten and left behind, unburnt
and unhonoured. He therefore could not join the
other departed, and could find no rest till Odysseus
should have performed the proper funeral rites for
him.

In the case of Patroklos, we see that the departed
may appear to his friends. Achilles saw the soul
of his friend, he recognised his eyes and his voice, but
he could not touch him. We must remember, however,
that the soul of Patroklos had at that time not yet
entered the gates of Hades. After the bones had
once been consumed by fire, the departed were not
supposed by the Greeks to reappear to the living.

Again, if Odysseus gives the shades blood to drink,
we must recollect that blood was looked upon as the
condition of life. As the word had become almost
synonymous with life, it was but a natural conclusion
that the departed in the house of Hades were without
blood, that is, without life, and that they had to
drink blood, before they could live, and hear, and
speak again.

Still, this need not have been a general belief, nor
is this process of reviving the departed with blood,
I believe, mentioned anywhere else. We must not
expect consistency, where so much had to be left
to the fancy of the poet or the poets. In the Iliad, for
instance, the abode of Hades is supposed to be beneath
the earth, in the Odyssey it is placed in the West,
behind the island of Circe. We speak of Hades as a
place, and so did the later Greeks. In Homer, however,
there is no passage where Hades need be taken as
anything but the name of the god.

But though Homer may differ from himself, and

though other Greek poets may differ from Homer, on one point all Greek testimonies agree, namely, that some funeral obsequies are essential to the repose of the dead. This belief prevails in Homeric as well as in post-Homeric times. Antigone, as represented by Sophocles (v. 1322), looks upon them as ordained by a divine law, a law before which all human laws must give way. Euripides goes so far as to call the graves 'the sacred temples of the dead[1].' They became places of solemn meetings, the natural centres of a family, of a clan, and in time of a whole neighbourhood.

The great national festivals in Greece were mostly games, instituted at first in honour of some departed hero or benefactor. They began like the games celebrated by Achilles and his companions in honour of Patroklos, and when repeated grew into national institutions.

The earliest account of an Aryan funeral is found in the Âranyaka of the Taittirîya-veda. Here, however, we find only a large collection of the hymns and verses, which are to be recited at different parts of a funeral. The description of the funeral itself we must take from the Sûtras, which are later than the Âranyakas.

I place the Âranyakas at the end of the Brâhmana period, about 600 B.C. This is, of course, hypothetical, like all dates in India, previous to the rise of Buddhism. But a welcome confirmation of that date has been supplied by the editor of the Taittirîya-âranyaka, Rajendralal Mitra. I had pointed out that nowhere in Vedic literature is there any mention of the burning

---

[1] Troades, 96, ναούς τε τύμβους θ', ἱερὰ τῶν κεκμηκότων.

of widows at the funeral of their husbands. On the
contrary, there is clear evidence that they were not
burnt. Rajendralal Mitra, however, calls our attention
to the fact that nevertheless, according to Diodorus
Siculus, xix. 33, this custom was fully recognised in
India in 316 B.C. Diodorus, the contemporary of
Caesar and Augustus, gives a full description how the
two wives of Keteus were both anxious to be burnt
with him. One of them, however, being with child,
could not be burnt, but the other, the younger one,
was burnt in the sight of the Greek army, rejoicing in
her victory, and offering no resistance, when lying on
the funeral pile by the side of the dead husband. This
shows that a custom, not yet recognised in the Veda,
was recognised in the fourth century B.C. Nay, Dr.
Rajendralal Mitra might have added that Diodorus
states that this cruel custom was then sanctioned by
an ancient law (ὄντος δὲ παλαιοῦ νόμου), which would
push the date of the Âranyaka still further back.
However, though there is some force in this argument,
we must not forget that India is a large country, and
that an old law may have existed in the North-West
and among the martial nobility, which was unknown
among the Brâhmans of Âryâvarta at a much later
date. We are told, for instance, in the Khândogya-
upanishad, VIII. 8, 5, that the so-called Âsuras had
their own form of burial, that they 'decked out the
body of the dead with perfumes, flowers, and fine
raiment by way of ornament, and thought thus to
conquer the next world.'

We find a more detailed description of a Vedic
funeral in the Sûtras of Âsvalâyana. Without claiming for this description a very primitive character or

an extravagant age, we must remember that, even if it presents to us what a funeral was at about 600 B.C., we have nothing more ancient in any other Aryan literature.

It was in the year 1855 that I published in the journal of the German Oriental Society, the text and translation of the Sûtras of Âsvalâyana. I shall here give you an abstract of them.

If it was death that made man conscious for the first time of life, we have a right to expect that the acts of men in the presence of death will disclose to us something of what passed through his mind at that solemn moment. It is true that when these acts become known to us they have almost ceased to be real acts, and have become mere customs, half-understood traditions, nay often, misunderstood ceremonial. Still, we may discover in them some relics of what is ancient, for there is in customs, as in language, an unbroken continuity. Much may be changed, but little is entirely thrown away.

Funeral Ceremonies in India.

I shall begin with a description of the funeral ceremonies in India, as preserved to us in the Âranyakas and Sûtras, both still belonging to the Vedic period of literature.

Âsvalâyana-sûtras IV. 1:

'If some one who has set up the sacred fires (in his own house) begins to ail, he should depart (with his fires) towards the east, the north, or the north-east. People say, the fires love the village, and hence it is understood that longing and desirous to return (to the village), they will make him whole. If he is well again, he should sacrifice with Soma or with an animal, and settle down again in his house, or also without such a sacrifice.'

Here you have an old piece of folk-lore. First of all, a proverb—'the fires love the village.' Here we need hardly think of the fires as divine beings, though such sayings contain, no doubt, the germs of mythology. We ourselves might say just the same, without being in any sense fire-worshippers, or even believers in Agni. Secondly, the proverb leads to a superstition. Because the fires love their village, therefore, if you take them away with you, they will try to make you return to their home and to their hearth, and in order to induce a sick person to return home, they will make him whole.

Then the Sûtra continues:

' If he dies, let some one have a piece of land dug up, south-east or south-west (of the village), inclining towards the south or the south-east; others say, towards the south-west. It should be as long as a man with outstretched arms, one fathom (vyâma) in breadth, and one span (vitasti) in depth.'

Here there is nothing to remark, except the names of the ancient measures. What Protagoras said in a philosophical sense, is true in a material sense also. Man was the measure of all things. One measure is the man with his arms lifted up, the other a vyâma, as much as a man can embrace with his two arms, five aratnis or ells [1], as the commentator explains it. The

---

[1] *Ell*, Germ. *Elle*, O. H. G. *elina*, ὠλένη, *ulna*, all point to a common source, probably to the root AR, from which we have ἄρ-θρον, *ar-tus*, joint, literally, what moves. Sk. ar-atni, fore-arm, and Goth. *arm-s* may come from the same root. Five aratnis make a vyâma, Germ. *Klafter*.

next is vitasti[1], the outstretched hand, or twelve fingers.

' The place (smasâna) should be free on all sides and rich in plants. If they should be thorny and milky, let it be as said before. One requirement of a burning ground (smasâna) is that the water should run down from it on all sides.'

The place is the cemetery, but it is the place both for burning and afterwards for burying also. Smasâna is one of those old words in Sanskrit, the origin and formation of which we cannot explain. They must have been formed of materials which exist no longer in the language, such as we know it.

Why thorny and milky plants should be removed, is not explained. In a former passage (II. 7, 5) it had been said that in building a house a man should clear the ground of thorny and milky plants. This is intelligible, but for burning purposes thorny plants would have been useful, and they were often preferred for constructing a pile[2].

' What has to be done with the hair of the head, the beard, and the hair of the body, has been explained before (Srauta-sûtra VI. 10, 2). There should be a full supply of sacrificial grass and of butter. Then they pour clarified butter into curds, which makes the sprinkled butter for the Fathers.'

Certain rules as to how the dead body should be treated before it is taken to the place of burning had been given in the Srauta-sûtras, the rules for the Srauta or great sacrifices. Burial does not properly

---

[1] Vitasti is explained as the measure from the joint of the hand to the top of the fingers, and as equal to twelve fingers, or angulas, the angula again being defined as equal to eight barley-corns.

[2] Grimm, Das Verbrennen der Leichen, p. 21, &c.

fall under the *S*rauta, but under the G*ri*hya or domestic sacrifices. But it may happen that a man dies while offering one of these great sacrifices. This is considered as an accident, just as the breaking of a sacrificial vessel, and has to be remedied. Certain rules had therefore to be inserted in order to explain what should be done with the dead body of the sacrificer, if he should die before the sacrifice is finished.

'When he dies they take him out on the sacrificial path (or, according to others, *not* on the sacrificial path), and perform the adornments of the dead in the place where the sacrificial vessels are cleaned. They shave the hair of the head, the beard, and the hair of the body. They anoint him with spikenard and put on him a wreath of spikenard. Some clear the body of its contents and fill it with sprinkled butter. They then cut off the seam of a new piece of cloth, and cover the body so that the other seam is turned towards the west, and the feet remain uncovered. The sons should keep the piece that has been cut off.'

All these rules should be observed at the time of an ordinary funeral also, but as they had been learnt by heart before, they need not be repeated here [1].

The ceremony now proceeds, IV. 2:

'They now carry his fires and his sacrificial vessels to the same place. The old people follow with the dead, in odd numbers, and not in couples (i. e. not men and women together). Some say (that the dead should be carried) on a car drawn by cows. Some lead an animal behind (the anustara*nî*, that is to be burnt with the dead), a cow, or a she-goat, of one

---

[1] See Appendix VI, Note 1.

colour, or, according to some, a black one, after having tied a rope to its left fore-foot (bâhû for bâhau). Then follow the relatives (amâtya), wearing their sacrificial thread below (round the body), with their hair-locks untied, the old men first, the young ones last [1].

'When they have thus reached the place, the performer walks three times round the spot with his left side turned towards it, sprinkles water on it with a Samî branch, and says :

> 'Go away, disperse, remove from hence,
> The Fathers have made this place for him.
> Yama grants him this resting-place,
> Sprinkled with water day and night.'

This is a verse which is found in the Rig-veda, X. 14, 9. It is supposed to be addressed to spirits hovering round the place of burial. Yama, as we shall see, is the god of the fathers, and he is supposed to have assigned this place to the dead person as his final resting-place. When it is said that the place is sprinkled with water day and night, this implies that it ought to be thus honoured by the relations of the dead.

' He then places the fires on an elevated corner, the Âhavanîya-fire to the south-east, the Gârhapatya-fire to the north-west, and the Dakshina-fire to the south-west.

' Thereupon a person who understands it, piles up between the fires a pile of fuel for him. After the sacrificial grass and the skin of a black antelope with the hair outside have been spread over this, they place the dead on it, taking him north of the Gârhapatya-fire, and with his head turned towards the Âhavanîya-fire. North of him (they place) his wife, and for a

---

[1] See Appendix VI, Note 2.

Kshatriya the bow. Then her brother-in-law, standing in the place of her husband, or a pupil, or an
old servant, should make her rise, reciting the verse
(Rv. X. 18, 8):

'Rise, O woman; come to the world of the living; thou liest by
him whose breath is gone, come back! Thou hast fulfilled this
thy wifehood to him who took thy hand and made thee a mother [1].'

'If an old servant (a Sûdra) makes her rise, the
performer should repeat this verse. He then removes
the bow, saying (Rv. X. 18, 9):

'I take the bow from the hand (of the dead), to be to us protection, glory, and strength. Thou art there, we are here with good
men; let us overcome all the wiles of the enemy.'

'If it is a Sûdra, the same applies as before. After
he has stringed the bow, he should walk round the
pile, break it, and throw it (on the pile).'

These rules are full of interest, but also of difficulty.
What is quite clear is that in Vedic times the widow,
though she was placed for a time near her husband
on the pile, was not burnt with him. Nothing can
be clearer than the words of the verse when she is
asked to return to the world of the living. Yet, with
all their regard for the divine authority of the Veda,
the Brâhmans tried to explain it away, and to
change the world of the living into the world of the
dead.

That the old servant is not allowed to recite the
Vedic verses, shows that these rules date from a time
when the Brâhmans had secured already the exclusive
privilege of the three upper classes, so that no

---

[1] Rajendralal Mitra translates the second half of the verse by :
'become the wife of him who holds thy hand and is willing to
marry thee.'

*S*ûdra was allowed to learn the Veda by heart. The word used, however, in the text is not *S*ûdra, but V*ri*shala.

The second half of the verse is not quite clear, but I believe my translation is the right one.

We should observe that the bow given to the dead, if he is a Kshatriya, is broken before it is burnt. It was, therefore, a mere gift, and the idea, that he might have to use it in the next world, seems not to have presented itself to the Indian mind.

Then follow special regulations (IV. 3) as to how the various sacrificial implements should be placed on the different parts of the dead body. These again show a considerable development of the Brâhmanic ceremonial, but are otherwise of little interest. That the Vedic Indians with all their devotion to the dead were thrifty, may perhaps be gathered from the fact that the two mill-stones, and all that is made of copper, iron, and earthenware is kept by the son, who is here mentioned for the first time. There may, however, have been another reason, namely, the fact that these things were not combustible.

Then follow rules as to how the animal should be dissected and how again different portions of it should be placed on different parts of the dead body.

'After cutting out the omentum of the Anustaranî, (the animal that had been brought to the pile) he should cover the head and mouth with it, saying (Rv. X. 16, 7):

'Put on this armour against Agni (fire), (taken) from the cows; cover thyself with their fat and marrow, that the fierce Agni, rejoicing in his glare, the bold one, may not, when he flares up, injure thee.'

'Having taken out the kidneys, he should lay them into his hands, saying (Rv. X. 14, 10):

'On the good path run past the two dogs, the brood of Saramâ, the four-eyed, the grey; then go towards the wise Pitris who are happily rejoicing with Yama.'

Here we enter on mythological ground. It is quite clear that the dead is supposed to proceed on a good or right path till he reaches the Pitris, the fathers, who have died before him. On that path he has to run past two dogs. These dogs are called sârameya, according to the Brâhmans, the sons of Saramâ, four-eyed, and grey or dark.

Now it is well known that the Greeks also believed that the entrance of the realm of Hades was guarded by a dog, a dog with several heads, called *Kerberos* by Hesiod. The idea itself is natural enough. Their houses were probably guarded by a dog or dogs, therefore why not the house of the Pitris? Still we should remember that this watch-dog has a name in Greece, *Kerberos*, and that the Greek language supplies no etymology and no meaning of that word. If then it can be proved that sarvarî is a name of the night, can there be any possible doubt that the Greek word κερβερος is the same as the Sanskrit sarvara. I hold the original meaning of sarvara to have been dark, like the night, not speckled, and as sarvara has become savara in certain words, I hold that sabala, the adjective applied to the two dogs of Yama, meant originally dark or grey, like the night.

This identification is so perfectly simple and clear and unobjectionable that it has been accepted by the severest critics[1]. But a small acquaintance with

[1] Aufrecht, *Indische Studien*, iv. p. 342.

phonetic rules is certainly required in order to see the force of the argument, and we must not be surprised if writers, ignorant of the Sanskrit alphabet and of the invariable correspondence between Sk. palatal *s* and Greek *κ*, express a learned doubt as to the identity of *sarvara* and *kerberos*. Every letter is simply the same in the two words, and if we are to doubt this equation, we may as well doubt the equation of Sk. mâtar and Lat. *mater*.

Âsvalâyana then continues, IV. 4:

'The heart of the animal is placed on the heart of the dead, and two rice-cakes, according to some; according to others, only when the kidneys are absent.

'Having thus distributed the whole animal, limb by limb, and having covered it with its hide, he recites, while the Pranîtâ water is carried forward, the following verse (X. 16, 8):

'Agni, do not hurt this cup, which is dear to the gods and to the Somyas (the Fathers). It is that which the gods drink, and in which the immortal gods delight.'

'Bending his left knee he should sacrifice âgya-oblations (clarified butter) in the Dakshina fire, saying: "Svâhâ to Agni! Svâhâ to Kâma (love)! Svâhâ to the world! Svâhâ to Anumati!"

'A fifth oblation (is to be poured) on the chest of the deceased, with the verse:

'Thou (Agni) hast verily been born from him, may he (N. N.) now be born from thee. Svâhâ to the heaven-world[1]!'

'He now gives the word of command, "Light the fires together!" If the Âhavanîya-fire reaches him

---

[1] This verse is not in the Rig-veda, and is therefore given in full in the Sûtra. See Vâg. Samh. XXXV. 22; Satap.-Brâhm. II. 3, 3, 5; XII. 5, 2, 15.

first, he should know that it has brought him to the Svarga-world (heaven). He will prosper there, and this, his son, here on earth.

' If the Gârhapatya-fire reaches him first, he should know that it has brought him to the Antariksha-world (air). He will prosper there, and this, his son, here on earth.

' If the Dakshina-fire reaches him first, he should know that it has brought him to the Manushya world (the world of men). He will prosper there, and this, his son, here on earth.

' If the three fires reach him at the same moment, they call it the highest luck.

' While the body is being burnt, he recites the following verses in the same way as described before [1]:

' Rig-veda X. 14, 7 ; 8 ; 10 ; 11.

' Go forth, go forth on those ancient paths on which our fore-fathers departed. Thou shalt see the two kings delighting in Svadhâ, Yama and the god Varuna.

' Come together with the Pitris, and with Yama in the highest heaven, as the fulfilment of all desires. Having left all that is un-speakable (sin), go home again, and radiant in thy body come together with them.

' On the good path run past the two dogs, the brood of Saramâ, the four-eyed, the grey ; then go towards the wise Pitris, who are happily rejoicing with Yama.

' Protect him, O king, from those two dogs, which are thy watchers, O Yama, the four-eyed guardians of the road, spying for men. Grant him happiness and health !'

' Rig-veda X. 16, 1–6.

' Do not burn him altogether, O Agni, do not scorch him, do not confound his skin and his body ; when thou shalt have cooked him, O Gâtavedas, then send him forth to the Pitris.

' As soon as thou cookest him, O Gâtavedas, thou shouldst hand him over to the Pitris. As soon as he enters that life, he will become the servant of the gods.

' May the eye go to the sun, the breath to the wind ; go to the sky

[1] As described in Srauta-sûtras VI. 10, 19; see note in Z.D.M.G.

and the earth, as is right, or go to the waters, if it is good for thee there, rest in the plants.

'The unborn part[1], warm it with thy warmth, may thy heat warm it and thy flame! O *G*âtavedas, carry him in thy kindliest shape to the world of those who have done well.

'O Agni, send him back to the Pit*ri*s, he who comes sacrificed with offering to thee! When clothed with life, may what remains[2] come back, may he be joined with a body, O *G*âtavedas!

'Whatever the black bird injured, the ant, the snake, or a wild beast, may Agni make that whole from all (mischief), and Soma who has entered into the Brâhmans!'

' Rig-veda X. 17, 3–6.

'May Pûshan carry thee hence. the provident shepherd of the world, who never lost an animal; may he deliver thee to those Pit*ri*s, and Agni to the wise gods!

'Âyu (life), the all-enlivening, will guard thee; may Pûshan guard thee in front at the outset. May the god Savi*tri* place thee where the good people dwell and whither they have gone.

'Pûshan knows all those places; may he lead us on the safest path! May he, the knowing, walk in front without faltering, he who gives blessings, the brilliant, the great hero!

'Pûshan was born at the outset of the roads, at the outset of the sky, at the outset of the earth; he, the wise, walks to and fro to the two best homesteads.'

' Rig-veda X. 18, 10–13.

'Creep close to the mother, that earth there, the broad, the all-embracing, the blissful! She is like a maiden, soft like wool to the pious; may she guard thee from the lap of Nir*ri*ti (destruction).

'O Earth, open wide, do not press him, be kind in admitting and in embracing him! Cover him, O Earth, as a mother covers her son with her cloth.

'May the opened earth stand firm, and may a thousand supports stand near; may these dwellings be running with gh*ri*ta-offerings, and may there always be safety for him there!

---

[1] I retain my translation of a*g*ó bhâgás, the immortal part, because, after the poet has said how the material portions of the body go to the sun, the wind, the earth, the water, and the trees, he now speaks of what survives. The translation, 'the he-goat is (thy) portion,' is impossible, first, because it is a she-goat, not a he-goat, that may be offered as anustara*nî*; secondly, because, if one portion is especially assigned to Agni, the pronoun cannot be left out. There is no doubt, however, that from a very early date, a*g*o bhâga*h* was taken in the sense of : 'the goat is thy share.'

[2] I take sésha as a masculine, the rest, what remains of him. The word does not occur again as a masculine in the Rig-veda, but all other translations are impossible.

'I raise up the earth all around thee, may I not hurt thee in putting down this slab; may the Pit*ris* hold this cairn of thine; may Yama there make seats for thee.'

'Rig-veda X. 154, 1–5.

'For some (Pit*ris*) Soma is clarified, some sit down to cream (gh*rita*); those also for whom honey runs,—may he go to them indeed!

'They who are unapproachable by their penance, they who went to heaven by penance, they who performed penance mightily, to those also may he go indeed!

'They who fight in battle, the heroes who lost their life, or they who gave a thousand gifts, to those also may he go!

'And they who formerly followed the right, who did the right, and increased the right, to the Pit*ris* rich in penance, to those also may he go, O Yama, to the Pit*ris* rich in penance!

'The poets of a thousand lays, they who guard the sun, the *Ri*shis rich in penance, O Yama, may he go to them, the sons of penance!'

'Rig-veda X. 14, 12.

'The two messengers of Yama, broad-nosed, blood-thirsty, and tawny, go about among men; may they grant us again happy life here, so that we may see the sun!'

'If a man is burnt by some one who knows all this, it is understood (from the *S*ruti) that together with the smoke he goes to the Svarga-world.

'North-east of the Âhavanîya-fire he should dig a pit, knee-deep, and deposit in it an Avakâ, that is, a water-plant, called *S*îpâla. For it is understood from the *S*ruti that the deceased, when he comes out thence, will go with the smoke to the world of Svarga.'

It would take a long time to bring out all that is contained in these verses. Unfortunately, we do not know whether they originally succeeded each other as we now read them. It seems as if they had been taken from different hymns as they suited certain portions of the funeral ceremony. But other scholars would probably say that they were written originally for the funeral, and afterwards worked up into hymns. The decision is difficult, perhaps impossible, but I incline towards regarding the succession of the verses, as they stand in the hymns of the Rig-veda as more original than their order in the Sûtras.

What we learn from the verses as I have just translated them, is that the departed, the Pitris, the Fathers, have gone to a realm of Yama and Varuna, in the highest heaven. Nothing is said of their going to a lower world. The dead in being burnt, is supposed to follow the old path of the Pitris, to be guided by Pûshan, Savitri, and Agni, to pass the two watchdogs, to escape from the lap of Nirriti, and to arrive in the world of the pious, to become the servant of the gods.

The process of burning is not supposed to destroy the body altogether, but only to warm or to cook it, and thus prepare it for a new life with a new body. The elements are supposed to return to the elements, the eye to the sun, the breath to the wind. But, if my translation is right, an unborn or eternal part is mentioned, and this part Agni is asked to carry gently to the world of the good.

So far there is a thread that may be followed. But immediately after, the earth is invoked to receive the dead, as a mother receives her child, and to keep him from the lap of Nirriti or destruction. The grave is spoken of as the resting-place of the dead, and Yama is said to have prepared a seat for him there.

It is the same everywhere. There can be no consistency where everybody has a right to express his own imaginations, as if they were real, and his wishes, as if they had been fulfilled.

We now proceed to consider the ceremonies which follow the actual burning of the corpse. The corpse is as yet left on the pile, but the idea evidently is, not that it should be completely reduced to ashes, but that it should be warmed, roasted, and made ready for a new life, and that any injury it may have suffered should be made good by Agni.

'They now turn to the left, and go away without looking back, reciting the verse (Rv. X. 18, 3):

'These living people have turned away from the dead, the sacrifice of the gods was auspicious for us to-day. We went forth to dance and laughter, we who continue a longer life.'

'When they have come to a place where there is standing water, they dive once, throw up one handful of water, pronounce the name of the deceased and his family (gotra), go out from the water, put on new garments, wring the others once, spread them out towards the north, and then sit down till they see the stars, or the sun.

'When the sun has been seen [1], they may return home; the young should go first, the old last [2].

'When they have come to their dwelling, they touch a stone, the fire, cow-dung, fried barley-corns, oil, and water.

'They should not cook food during that night. They should live on what has been bought or what is there. For three nights they should not eat anything pungent and salt. They may also for twelve nights

---

[1] I have followed Dr. Winternitz in referring âdityasya vâ to â nakshatradarsanât. The option of waiting for the appearance of the Nakshatras, or waiting the whole night till the sun is seen, is confirmed by Pâraskara, III. 10, 35. Rajendralal Mitra translates: They sit down till the stars are seen; according to others, they do not go home before sunrise.

[2] See Appendix VI, Note 3.

omit almsgiving and study (of the Veda), if one of their great Gurus (father, mother, or teacher) has died; or for ten nights, if one of their near relations (Sapindas) has died, or the guru, if unrelated, or unmarried female relatives, or a child that has no teeth, or a deadborn child; or for one day, if a fellow-pupil has died, or any learned Brâhman of the same village.'

We now come to a new ceremony, namely, the gathering of the bones. The corpse is supposed to have been left on the pile, covered with the sacrificial implements of the deceased.

' The collection of the bones takes place after the tenth day (after death), on odd days of the dark fortnight, and under a single Nakshatra [1].' ·

This would mean that ten days must have passed, first of all, after the day on which the death took place, and that then they must wait for the dark fortnight and for an odd day in it [2].

' A man is placed into an urn (kumbha, masc.) without any marks, a woman into an urn (kumbhî, fem., an urn with a spout, according to Rajendralal Mitra) without any marks. It is done by old people of an odd number, and without their wives.

' Then the performer walks three times round the place turning his left to it, and with a Samî branch

---

[1] A Nakshatra with one name, not therefore under the Ashâdhâs, Phalgunîs, or Proshthapadâs.

[2] There has evidently been much difference of opinion on this point among the Brâhmans. Some, such as Vishnu, XIX. 10–12, fix the gathering of the bones on the fourth day, and prescribe that they should be thrown into the Ganges. This seems a later rule. Nârâyana explains the Sûtra so that it should mean, ' on any odd day after the tenth day of the dark fortnight,' i.e. on the 11th, 13th, or 15th day of the waning moon. Bodhâyana enjoins the 3rd, 5th, or 7th from the day of cremation.

sprinkles milk and water on it, reciting a verse, Rv. X. 16, 4.

'They should put each bone (into the urn) with the thumb and the fourth finger, without rattling them, the feet first, the head last. Having well gathered them, and swept them together with a broom, they should put (the urn) into the pit, where the water does not run together from all sides except in the rainy season, and recite the verse, Rv. X. 18, 10:

'Creep close to the mother, that earth there, the broad, the all-embracing, the blissful! She is like a maiden, soft like wool to the pious; may she guard thee from the lap of Nirṛti (destruction).'

'With the following verse, Rv. X. 18, 11, he should throw earth (into the pit):

'O Earth, open wide, do not press him, be kind in admitting, and in embracing him, cover him, O Earth, as a mother covers her son with her cloth.'

'After he has thrown the earth, he should recite the next verse, Rv. X. 18, 12:

'May the opened earth stand firm, and may a thousand supports stand near: may these dwellings be running with ghṛita offerings, and may there always be safety for him there.'

'He then covers (the urn) with a lid, saying, Rv. X. 18, 13:

'I raise up the earth all around thee, may I not hurt thee in putting down this slab. May the Pitṛis hold this cairn of thine, may Yama there make seats for thee.'

'Then returning without looking back, and after bathing, they should give him the Śrâddha offering[1].'

The actual burial is now finished, and it is clear that the Vedic Indians both burnt and buried their dead. The urn into which the bones were deposited

[1] See Appendix VI, Note 4.

must have been large, and it is strange that none of them, so far as I know, should ever have been discovered.

The honours to be paid to the dead do not cease, however, with the burial. We saw that at the end of it a Srâddha offering was to be made. These offerings, meant for the deceased, are continued afterwards during a whole year. After that time they cease to be addressed to him individually, he having taken his place among the three ancestors, father, grandfather, and great-grandfather, and receiving the common Srâddhas at the times appointed [1].

Before, however, we proceed to consider this important branch of the Indian religion, the Srâddha, we have still to follow the mourners to a kind of expiatory service, which was meant to pacify death, and to guard the survivors against every evil.

'They who have lost a Guru (father, mother, or teacher), or have been afflicted in any other way, should on the day of the new moon perform an expiatory service. Other authorities fix on the ninth day after death, i.e. on the tenth day, for this ceremony. Before sunrise they should carry the fire and ashes in a receptacle southward, saying, Rv. X. 16, 9 :

'Agni, the flesh-eater, I send away far; may he, the evil-bringer, go to those who own Yama as their king.'

'They then throw the fire away where four roads meet, or somewhere else, and walk three times round it, turning their left to it, and striking their left thighs with their left hands. They then return home without looking back, wash, have their hair, their

---

[1] On the Srâddhas, see *India, What can it teach us?* pp. 234–242, 374–376.

beard, the hair of the body, and their nails cut, and
procure for themselves new jars, pots, and vessels
for rinsing, adorned with wreaths of *S*amî flowers,
fuel of *S*amî wood, two pieces for kindling fire and
(fifteen) for laying round it, also dung of bulls, a hide,
fresh butter, a stone, and as many bunches of Kusa
grass as there are young women (in the house). Then
at the time of the Agnihotra (in the afternoon) he
(the oldest person present) should kindle the fire,
saying, Rv. X. 16, 9:

' But here may this other (Agni) *G*âtavedas, carry the sacrifice to
the gods, knowing (how to do it).'

' Keeping that fire burning they sit until the still
night, repeating the tales of the old, and having sacred
stories, such as Itihâsas and Purâ*n*as, recited to them.

' When all sounds have ceased, and when (others)
have gone to their house or resting-place, he (the performer), stepping from the south side of the door to
the north, should pour out a continuous stream of
water, reciting a verse (Rv. X. 16, 9).

' Having then lit a fire (aupâsana), he spreads west
of it the hide of a bull, its neck turned to the east,
and the hair outside, and asks the people of the house
(amâtya), to step on it, saying, Rv. X. 18, 6:

'Mount up the life, choosing old age, striving forward, as many
as you are, one after the other. Tvash*tri* who grants good offspring
may graciously yield you here a long life to live.'

' He should then place logs round the fire, the first
with the words, Rv. X. 18, 4:

'This fence I place for the living, may no other of these here go
to that place ; may they live through full a hundred harvests,
hiding death with this stone.'

' While he says, " hiding death with this stone," he

places a stone north of the fire. He then recites four verses, and sacrifices with each, Rv. X. 18, 1:

'O Death, go off on another path, that is thy own, and different from the way of the gods. I speak to thee who hast eyes to see and ears to hear, do not hurt our offspring, or our men!'

'Be pure and clean, ye who are partakers in the sacrifice, so that, effacing the track of death, ye may continue a longer life, abounding in offspring and wealth.'

'Then follow two verses, translated before. He should then look at his people (amâtya) and recite, Rv. X. 18, 5:

'As days follow one another, as seasons go rightly with seasons, so shape our lives, O Creator, that the young may not leave the old behind.'

'The young women should then with some young Darbha-blades take fresh butter, and anoint their eyes with the thumbs and fore-fingers of both hands (at the same time); and after that turn round and throw (the blades) away. While they are anointing themselves, the performer should look at them and say, Rv. X. 18, 7:

'These women, not widows, but having good husbands, may anoint themselves with collyrium and butter. Without tears, without ailments, and well adorned, may the wives go first to the house[1].'

This has indeed proved a fatal verse to thousands of women who have been burnt on the pile with their husbands, on the strength of a spurious reading. 'They should go first to the house' is in the text yonim agre. By changing agre into agneh, the line would mean, 'They should go into the house, or into the lap of Agni (fire).' This reading was foisted into the Veda, and after that, widow-burning was represented as having a sacred authority in the Veda.

[1] For other readings of this verse, see Rajendralal Mitra, l. c., p. 52. The Taitt. Âr., VI. 10, 8, reads âṅganena sarpíshâ sam mrisantâm, which Rajendralal Mitra translates, 'let the women smear themselves with collyrious butter.'

'Then the performer should first touch the stone, (the others after him), saying, Rv. X. 53, 8:

'The river full of stones flows on; hold together, rise up, and move on, O friends! Let us leave here those who are luckless; we shall turn out on lucky raids.'

'Then, while the others walk round with the fire, with the dung of the bull, and with an uninterrupted stream of water, the performer, stationing himself to the north-east, should recite the verse, Rv. X. 155, 5:

'They have led the cow round, they have taken the fire round, they have given praise to the gods,—who then will defy them?'

'While they pour out the stream of water, they recite three verses, Rv. X. 9, 1:

'You are truly the blissful waters, give us strength, that we may see great rejoicing,' &c.
'Whatever is your best sap, let us here share in it, like loving mothers,' &c.

'A brown bull should be led round, thus they say.

'Then they sit down where they like, covering themselves with a new garment, and they sit till sunrise without sleeping.

'When the sun has risen they repeat the hymns sacred to the sun and benedictions, prepare food, and offer libations with every verse, while reciting the hymn, Rv. I. 97, "May he by his light drive evil away from us," &c.

'After having fed the Brâhmans, he should make them repeat a benediction.

'A cow, a metal jar, and a new garment form the priestly fee.'

I have given you this description of an ancient Indian funeral in full, because it is less known than the funeral ceremonies of Greeks and Romans, and may serve as a typical instance of an ancient Aryan funeral.

Funeral Ceremonies in Greece.

We do not possess the same minute accounts of the funeral among Greeks and Romans. There was probably more local variety with regard to funeral rites in different parts of Greece and Italy than there was in India, if indeed we may judge of the whole of India by the literature preserved by the Brâhmans. Still, making allowance for the greater spirit of independence and the more restricted influence of a priestly caste among Greeks and Romans, we can gain some general idea at least of what their funeral was, and we can discover in their customs also some indications of the thoughts which they had formed about the dead [1].

The Greek language has preserved a curious relic which testifies to the ancient and wide-spread custom of burning as antecedent to burying. The verb θάπτω, which means to bury, must originally have meant to burn. All scholars agree that θάπ-τω and τάφος are connected with the Sanskrit root dah, which means to burn and to burn only. It is a root common to several of the Aryan languages, and wherever it occurs, it means to burn. It must therefore have had the same meaning in Greek also (as we see in the name Daphne) [2], and have lost it when burying took the place of burning. A similar transition of meaning

---

[1] Fuller information on funerals in Greece may be found in Manuals of Greek Antiquities, such as K. T. Hermann, *Lehrbuch der Griech. Antiquitäten*, vol. iv, Privatalterthümer. See also Rohde's treatise, *Psyche, Seelencult und Unsterblichkeitsglaube*, 1890.

[2] *Science of Language*, vol. ii. p. 621, n.

has been pointed out by Schott in some of the words for burying in the Ural-Altaic languages.

In Greece it was primarily the duty of the son to bury his father. This was a duty from which nothing could release him. A son might under certain circumstances be released from his obligation to support his father during life, but after death the law of Solon, as quoted by Aeschines (Timarch. 13), made it incumbent on him to bury his father and to perform all that was considered right (ἀποθανόντα δ' αὐτὸν θαπτέτω καὶ τἄλλα ποιείτω τὰ νομιζόμενα). If, however, there was no son and no relative to perform the last sacred rites, the whole community or the Demos was held responsible for the proper disposal of the dead body, or, during war, the General. The vengeance of the gods was believed to fall on all who left a corpse unburied. It was not only a crime, it was felt to be an ἄγος, a sin, probably because there was the old belief among the Greeks that the dead found no rest or could not enter Hades till their body had been burnt or buried, and that they would haunt the abode of their relatives and friends till this last duty had been performed. There is a meaning in most customs, and even mere superstitions have generally a foundation of truth.

It was the custom in Greece that the nearest relative should close the eyes and the mouth of the departed, that the women should wash and anoint the body, clothe it in clean garments, as in India, and then leave it on a couch in the interior of the house. Here people might come to see it, and it was usual at Athens to place a vessel full of water near the door, so that those who had become impure by entering the house, might purify themselves. The purifying by touching

water was mentioned in India also. The house with
the dead in it was considered impure, though that is
hardly the right translation for μιαρός in Greek, or for
asauḱa in Sanskrit, both conveying the feeling of awe,
with which the Greek felt inspired by death, rather
than the sense of actual impurity. Even the water, in
order to be pure, had to be fetched from another house.

While the dead body was exposed in the house,
various marks of affection were bestowed on it. If
we may judge from legal enactments, forbidding the
killing of sacrificial animals and restraining the
excessive wailing of women, before the body was
carried away (ἐκφορά, udvâha), these marks of love and
outbursts of grief must at times have been carried to
excess in Greece as in other countries. After a time,
however, a reaction set in in Greece as elsewhere, particularly in Germany [1], and a new popular belief arose
that the dead could find no rest till the violent grief
of their friends had been appeased [2].

On the morning of the third day [3], before sunrise, the
couch with the body on it was carried out of the
house. Here again there must have been at times
much extravagance, for the law had to interfere and
limit vain display. Though the prevalent custom was
to burn the dead, yet it was never forbidden in Greece
to bury without burning. We must remember also
that burning did not mean a complete reduction of
the body to ashes, but that often, after it had been

---

[1] Rochholz, *Deutscher Glaube und Brauch*, i. 207.

[2] Plato, Menex. 248 E, δεόμεθα πατέρων καὶ μητέρων εἰδέναι ὅτι οὐ
θρηνοῦντες οὐδὲ ὀλοφυρόμενοι ἡμᾶς ἡμῖν μάλιστα χαριοῦνται. Lucian, De
luctu 24, μέχρι τίνος ὀδυρόμεθα; ἔασον ἀναπαύσασθαι τοὺς τοῦ μακαρίου
δαίμονας.

[3] Plato, Laws, xii. 959.

for some time on the funeral pile, the bones were collected without having been entirely destroyed or
reduced to ashes, and then deposited in a tomb.
Traces of these different kinds of burial are found in
Greece. There are urns holding ashes, containing
corpses, there are tombs in which skeletons, more or
less perfect, are placed on the ground, and there are
graves in which the bodies have simply been deposited
in the earth. There are coffins also of wood or earthenware, but this is supposed to be a custom of foreign
origin. Even the embalming of dead bodies was not
unknown in Greece, as, for instance, in the case of the
kings of Sparta.

As many tombs have been found to contain various
articles that had been dear or useful to the living, it
has been supposed that the Greeks also believed that
the dead remained, for some time at least, in or near
their tombs. But although such a belief may have
existed, for even Plato alludes to it, the custom itself
admits, as we shall see, of a different explanation.

The general idea among the Greeks seems to have
been that, after the body had been properly disposed
of, the soul, the ψυχή, would join the better ones
(βελτίονες καὶ κρείττονες). It is supposed that in
ancient times the Greeks deposited the remains of the
dead in their own houses, near the hearth, which was
the primitive altar of the family. Here the memory
of the departed was kept alive by various observances.
In later times also, when the bodies were deposited
outside the town, each family liked to keep its tombs
separate, and as a sacred spot for family gatherings.
These places were enclosed, marked by monuments,
ornamented with trees and flowers, and often covered

with gifts which by a kind of unreasoning love were intended for the dead. Many of these customs, whether reasonable or unreasonable, were apt to be repeated by others without any clear motive beyond that very common motive of doing what others had done before. After a time they became fixed, and were regarded as proper, as necessary, nay as sacred. These offerings began even at the time of the funeral, and consisted of wine, oil, honey, sometimes of sacrificial animals also.

When the relatives and friends of the departed had returned from the funeral, they were expected to purify themselves, and then, adorned with wreaths, to proceed to a common meal in honour of the dead. While this meal was sometimes considered as given by the departed, the departed himself was honoured with a meal on the third (τὰ τρίτα) and on the ninth day (τὰ ἔνατα) after the funeral. After that the proper mourning was supposed to be at an end. Sometimes, however, we hear of eleven days of mourning, and at Athens a funeral meal was celebrated also on the thirtieth day. After that, sacrificial offerings (ἐναγίζειν) were due to the departed on certain days, such as the thirtieth day of the month, and his birthday.

On great occasions, when the members of a family were gathered to celebrate the birth of a new child or a wedding or some other joyful event, the souls of the departed were seldom forgotten, particularly those of the Tritopátores, probably the three generations of ancestors who in India also received on joyful occasions [1] regular offerings (srâddha), and who represent

---

[1] *India, What can it teach us?* p. 374.

the whole body of ancestors, and, in a certain sense, the family heroes and gods.

There were also certain days set apart on which the souls of all departed had to be honoured or pacified. In Athens this All Souls celebration took place in spring, at the end of the Anthesteria. When it was over, the souls were asked to depart again, with the words : θύραζε Κῆρες, οὐκ ἔτ' 'Ανθεστήρια, 'Away, ye Kêres, the Anthesteria are over.'

In all these customs we must distinguish between their first impulse and their later interpretation. At first the idea of impurity attaching to the house and the relations of the departed, need not have meant more than a wish to be left alone, not to be spoken to, and not to be disturbed. After a time, the awe that was inspired by a death would have caused people to regard the family that was 'in mourning' as sacred for a time, possibly as afflicted and disgraced, and thus as impure. This so-called impurity seems, in fact, to be something like the *taboo* which by other tribes is placed for a time on all the relations of the dead. It is not restricted to the days of mourning, for a family may be placed under the same kind of taboo at the birth of a child also, otherwise one of the most joyful events. In the law-book of Vishnu, 20, this kind of impurity is clearly distinguished from being in mourning. We read : 'As both his good and his bad actions follow a man after his death like companions, what does it profit a man whether his relations mourn for him or not? But so long as they remain impure, the departed guest finds no rest, and returns to visit his relatives.'

Again, the mere fact that offerings were made to the dead near their tombs would impress the popular mind with the idea that the souls in some form or other were hovering round their tombs [1]. The next step would be that the souls were believed to rejoice in these offerings, and if to rejoice, then actually to eat and to drink what was offered to them. There is no evidence to show that the educated classes in Greece believed that the souls actually devoured the offerings of honey mixed with milk (μελίκρητον) which were poured on the grave, yet the offerings were made, and we can easily understand that it did their hearts good to give up something, whatever it was, for those who had been the object of love and reverence, though they were no longer present in the body. That feeling exists to the present day in spite of all so-called enlightenment.

The Theory of Survivals.

I know it is the custom to call such things survivals. But that name should, I think, be reserved for customs which have no longer any intelligible object, and can be made intelligible only when traced back to times and circumstances in which their origin can be shown to have been perfectly natural. A survival means what has no longer any life in it, 'was sich überlebt hat.' There are many customs, however, which may seem to us irrational or unintelligible, but which need not therefore be traced back to the childhood of the human race. They seem to me to receive a far easier explanation in that never-ceasing childhood of the human heart, which breaks out in different

---

[1] Plato, Phaedo 81, ψυχή . . . ὥσπερ λέγεται, περὶ τὰ μνήματά τε καὶ τοὺς τάφους κυλινδουμένη· περὶ ἃ δὴ καὶ ὤφθη ἄττα ψυχῶν σκιοειδῆ φαντάσματα. . . .

strata of our own society as it did thousands of years ago.

I remember, when Lord Palmerston was buried in Westminster Abbey, a friend, a member of Parliament, was seen to take off some valuable rings and throw them into the grave. Some people called it foolishness, others fondness. It might, no doubt, be called a survival, for the habit of throwing what seemed most precious upon the funeral pile or into the grave, was certainly more common in former times than it is with us. But the true sense in which it may be called a survival[1] is that the same sentiment which prompted the ancients, whether civilised or uncivilised, to give up something to the dead, to make some kind of sacrifice, has survived in our hearts also. There was but a small step from throwing a ring into the grave to saying, 'He would have liked it, let him have it, let him enjoy it.'

There is a similar case, so well known that I suppose it may be mentioned without indiscretion. An eminent English poet insisted on placing the MS. of his own unpublished poems—probably the most valued treasure which he possessed—in his wife's coffin. We need not try to analyse all his feelings, but we should probably be not very far wrong, if we recognised here too a real survival, that is, a permanent manifestation of that profound human impulse which prompted the ancient mourners to sacrifice what they valued most, on the funeral pile of their dearest friends.

[1] See Appendix VII.

Gifts produced a Belief that they would be used by the Dead.

It is generally said that because among many people the dead were supposed to carry on the work of which they had been most fond in this life, therefore a bow and arrow were placed in the grave of the hunter, a sword and shield were buried with the soldier, and even horses and wives were burnt with the body of their master. Psychologically, I believe, the process was exactly the reverse. Bow and arrow were thrown on the grave because it seemed natural. In India, as we saw, the bow was actually broken. Sword and shield were essential almost to the complete dress of a soldier; and wives at first were certainly prompted by fondness to follow their husbands into death. But when people were pressed for an answer, what could they say? Some might say, it was all mere foolishness. But the early rationalists would soon discover a reason. What could be the use of the bow and arrow, unless there was in the other world also a hunting-ground? Why waste a valuable sword and shield, unless the departed really wanted them for their defence? And why should a wife wish to be burnt with her husband, if the dead rise not, if there is not another world in which husband and wife will be united again? What seems the effect may here, as in so many cases, have really been the cause. Anyhow, the cause and effect of customs are here as elsewhere inseparably united. Because honey mixed with milk was poured on the graves, the dead were believed to be fond of milk and honey. The real cause having been forgotten, another was soon supplied, just as the old negro woman, when pressed about the medicine bottles thrown on the tombs of children, replied that people thought they would help the children after their burial. The human heart has many chambers, and we must be on our guard against supposing that we know and can count all its pulses and impulses.

And what gave rise in every family to these simple gifts of milk and honey offered to their deceased parents, led afterwards to a more elaborate worship of ancestors, and likewise to the worship of national heroes. When we are told that the Lokrians always left a place empty for Ajax Oileus in their battle array, did they believe that this national hero was actually present in the flesh during the fight, that they saw him, touched him, or spoke to him? No doubt there were many who said so, for there are many things that we can say, many things that we can say we believe, many things that we can believe we believe, and which nevertheless are but metaphorical and poetical expressions, and at first not meant to be anything else. And yet this belief soon became a reality, nay more than a reality. The presence of Ajax during the battle was a real presence, nay more than a real presence. Those who held the place of honour as fighting on each side of the half-divine hero, would probably fight with greater bravery than if he himself had been present. When the excitement of the fight was over, they would declare that they had felt his presence, that they had been inspirited by him, very soon, that they had seen and heard him. And when they celebrated their victory, was it so very strange that they should have poured out the first drops of wine to Ajax, that they should have expressed their gratitude for his help, or celebrated his valorous deeds in song? From such thoroughly natural beginnings arose the worship of heroes, belonging no longer to one family only, or receiving honour from their own descendants only, but claimed as their own by a whole village, or a town, or a state, or, at last, by the whole of Greece.

We can thus distinguish in Greece four stages in the worship of ancestral spirits, (1) mourning for relatives and friends (*Trauer*), (2) honour paid to one's own ancestors (*Ahnen-cult*), (3) memorial services of national heroes (*Heroen-cult*), (4) worship paid to departed souls in general (*Seelen-cult*).

These four forms of ancestral worship often co-exist, but it is sometimes useful to distinguish between them.

Funeral Ceremonies in Rome.

The funeral ceremonies of the Romans have been very carefully studied by classical scholars. The well-known work by Kirchmann, *De Funeribus Romanorum*, 1672, contains all the evidence most carefully collected, and has formed the chief foundation for all subsequent treatises on this subject.

It seems to have been the custom at Rome, after the dead body had been washed, anointed, and clothed, to keep it for seven days in the vestibule of the house. Possibly this was done to prevent the possibility of a person being buried while in a trance. During that time the house itself and all that belonged to it were considered impure, and passers-by were warned by a cypress tree placed before the door. On the eighth day the corpse was carried out and burnt. Afterwards the remains were collected, sprinkled with wine and milk, placed in an urn, and deposited in the sepulchre. The relations on returning home stepped over a fire and were sprinkled with water.

The departed was now believed to be a kind of divine being, and on the eighth day after the funeral the *sacrificium novendiale* or the *feriae denicales* were celebrated in his honour. The offering consisted in a swine or a sheep, dedicated to Ceres, and was followed by a feast, called the *silicernium*, during which much was said and sung in honour of the departed, libations were made for him, and incense was burnt. But though the body was burnt, it was always considered essential that some earth should be thrown on it. Sometimes, particularly in war, a single bone was taken and covered with holy earth. No Roman would pass a dead body anywhere without throwing some earth on it. This looks like a survival of the more ancient custom of burying, and it is well known that in certain Roman families, for instance, in that of the Cornelii, the bodies were not burnt, but buried. It may also contain a remnant of the old feeling for the Earth, as the mother of all living beings [1].

When all had been done that was required (*justa facere*), the soul of the departed was supposed to be at rest. It had become one of the Manes. Once every year, on the 19th of February, there was a commemoration festival, called *Feralia* or *Parentalia*, on which certain offerings were made to the Manes. This was called *parentare*. Similar offerings, however, had to be made on certain days, such as the calendae, nonae, and idus, and other occasions also,

[1] See Liv. viii. 6, 9, Diis manibus matrique Terrae.

whenever some important event brought the members of a family together, such as the investiture with the toga virilis, the arrival of the bride, &c. We also hear of funeral games at Rome, like those described by Homer at the funeral of Patroklos. In Rome they were chiefly gladiatorial contests, lasting sometimes for several days. Some scholars have seen in these bloody combats survivals of an original human sacrifice in honour of the dead, but this can hardly be proved.

The Manes were supposed to dwell in the lower world (*mundus* and *orcus*), though little is said about their receiving either rewards or punishments. A distinction, however, was made. As kind beings, they were called *lares*; as unkind, *larvae*. They were called *dii manes* also, or simply *dii*, though they were not supposed to live in company with the great gods. The Romans swore by the Manes as well as by their gods, and how near the Manes were sometimes brought to the gods, we may gather from the scoffing words of Pliny (vii. 56), that 'those who had ceased to be men were worshipped as manes and exalted into gods.' Tertullian also (Apol. 13) inveighs against these superstitions, though from a different point of view: 'What honour do you show to the gods,' he says, 'which you do not show to the dead? What difference is there between a funeral feast and a feast of Jupiter; between the *obba*, goblet, with which you sacrifice to the dead, and the *simpulum* used at sacrifices; between a *pollinctor* (who washes the corpse) and a *haruspex*? You employ a *haruspex* even for the service of the dead.'

All this shows how near in the thoughts of the

Romans the dead were to the gods. That this was not a late idea, influenced by Greek thought, we may gather from Cicero, who says (Leg. ii. 22) in so many words, that the days kept sacred for the dead, would not, like the days kept sacred for the gods, have been called *feriae*, had not our ancestors wished that the departed should be considered as gods. We are told even of a treatise ascribed to Labeo, a Roman lawyer, *De diis quibus origo animalis est* (Servius, ad Aen. iii. 168), and these gods who derive their origin from human souls are the *lares*. Apuleius ('De deo Sacr.' p. 688), who may have known Labeo's work, tells us that 'Every departed spirit is called a *lemur*. If he abides in the house peaceful and beneficent, and confers security and bliss on his descendants, he is called a *lar*. If, tormented by the consciousness of his evil deeds, he roams about restlessly, distracting the good and terrifying the bad, he is called *larva*. If he is indifferent, he is simply counted as one of the *manes*.'

There are private and public lares. The former are also called *penates*. The latter, such as Romulus, Remus, Acca Larentia, &c., come nearest to the Greek heroes. Then there are lares of the town, of the field, of the high roads, and of the sea, to all of whom some kind of worship has to be paid on certain occasions.

Funeral Ceremonies among Savages.

The funeral ceremonies of Indians, Greeks, and Romans which we have hitherto examined, though they are old, do not claim to be considered as the customs of primitive men. They cannot even be considered as primitive, in the sense in which I sometimes use that word, namely as requiring no antecedent, and as being perfectly natural and intelligible. There are features in all these ceremonies which are no longer quite intelligible, and the origin of which can only be discovered by conjecture, sometimes not even by that. How the so-called primitive savages disposed of their dead, we shall never know. There has been considerable discussion whether cremation or interment was the more primitive form of burial. By those who believe that modern savages represent to us the customs of primitive humanity, an appeal has been made to the lowest of savages, such as the Australians, and whatever their mode of burial is, has been supposed to have been the first and most natural.

I have taken some pains to examine the accounts which eye-witnesses have given us of the manner in which the Australians disposed of their dead. This evidence, however, so far as I can judge, leaves the question as to the priority of cremation or burial quite undecided. There is hardly any kind of burial that is not practised by the Australians. They inter, but they also cremate[1]. They take little trouble about the corpses of women and children, but men are interred with a good deal of ceremony. The corpse is firmly tied together, enveloped in a rug or in strips of bark, and placed in soft ground or sand, at the depth of three or four feet. Above the grave a mound, generally a foot or two high, but sometimes rising to five feet, is erected and covered with logs to prevent wild dogs from disturbing the corpse. Some tribes erect a hut over the grave. Not unfrequently some

[1] Curr, l. c., p. 87.

T 2

trees close at hand are marked with rude cuttings
in memory of the deceased, and curved paths made
round the grave, which is visited from time to time
and kept in order for several years.

When the corpse is burnt, the few bones which
remain are likewise deposited in the earth. But that
is not all. Some Australian tribes make a sort of
mummy of a dead body by drying it before the fire.
Others, again, erect a stage either on posts or among
the branches of trees, and there leave the corpse,
between sheets of bark, until the flesh has decayed.
The bones are then cleaned, made into a parcel, and
carried about for many months, till at last they are
either dropped into a hollow tree or interred.

Among the most savage tribes the flesh of the
deceased is cut off the bones, the skulls are used as
drinking vessels, and in some cases the dead are
actually eaten by the aborigines of Australia.

What then is the most primitive form of burial?
Is it the devouring of the dead bodies? I doubt it;
for I feel convinced that what are called the lowest
savages, are quite as often the result of centuries
of corruption and degeneracy as the survivals of a
primitive and unadulterated state of human life on
earth.

Polynesian Funerals.

Among the Polynesians also, who stand no doubt
on a higher level among savages than the Australians,
we find nothing that seems more primitive than the
funeral customs of Hindus, Greeks, and Romans.

The Rev. W. Wyatt Gill, to whom we owe so much
of really trustworthy information about the Poly-

nesians, has lately given us the following description
of a funeral in Mangaia (Hervey Islands)[1]:—

'The bodies of deceased friends were anointed with
scented oil, carefully wrapped up in a number of
pieces of cloth, and the same day committed to their
last resting-place. A few were buried in the earth
within the sacred precincts of the appropriate *marae*;
but by far the greater number were hidden in caves
regarded as the special property of certain families.

'If a body were buried in the earth, the face was
invariably laid downwards, chin and knees meeting,
and the limbs well secured with strongest sinnet cord.
A thin covering of earth was laid over the corpse, and
large heavy stones piled over the grave. The intention was to render it impossible for the dead to rise
up and injure the living! The head of the buried
corpse was always turned to the rising sun, in accordance with their ancient solar worship.

'It was customary to bury with the dead some
article of value—a female would have a cloth-mallet
laid by her side; whilst her husband would enjoin
his friends to bury with him a favourite stone adze,
or a beautiful white shell (*Ovula ovum*, Linn.) worn
by him in the dance. Such articles were never
touched afterwards by the living.

'Numbers were buried in caves easily accessible, to
enable the relatives to visit the remains of the dearly-
loved lost ones from time to time. The corpse was
occasionally exposed to the sun, re-anointed with oil,
and then wrapped in fresh *tikoru* (white native cloth).
The dead were never disembowelled for the purpose

[1] *Transactions of the Australian Association for the Advancement of Science*,
Melbourne Meeting, 1890, p. 343.

of embalming. The corpse was simply desiccated, and daily anointed with cocoa-nut oil. A month would suffice for this.

'Warriors were in general carefully hidden by their surviving friends, through fear of their being disinterred and burnt in revenge.

'The people of the entire district where the deceased lived take up "taro" and prepare a feast in honour of the dead. A grand interchange of presents is usual on these occasions; but, excepting the near relatives of the deceased, no one is really the worse for it, as it is etiquette to see that distant relatives get back similar articles to what they brought.

'Whatever is laid upon the corpse is buried with it and no further notice taken of it; but whatever is placed by the side, *without touching it*, is repaid.

'The moment the sick died, the bodies of near relatives were cut with sharks' teeth, so that the blood might stream down the bodies; their faces were blackened, and the hair cut off. At Rarotonga it was usual to knock out some of the front teeth in token of sorrow. Everywhere the moment of death was the signal for the death-wail to commence. The most affecting things are said on such occasions, but always in a set form, commencing thus:—

> "*Aue tou e! Aue! Aue!*
> Alas for us! Alas! Alas!" &c.

The wailers usually lose their voices for several days, and their eyes are frightfully swollen with crying.

'As soon as the corpse was committed to its last resting-place, the mourners selected five old cocoanuts, which were successively opened, and the water poured out upon the ground. These nuts were then wrapped up in leaves and native cloth, and thrown towards the grave; or, if the corpse were let down with cords into the deep chasm of "Auraka," the nuts and other food would be successively thrown down upon it. Calling loudly each time the name of the departed, they said, "Here is thy food; eat it." When the fifth nut and the accompanying "raroi," or pudding, were thrown down, the mourners said, "Farewell! we come back no more to thee."

' A death in the family is the signal for a change of names amongst the near relatives of the deceased.

' Chiefs and priests occasionally received the honour of a "spirit-burial," the corpse being borne to the most renowned *marae* of his tribe on the island, and allowed to remain within the sacred enclosure for some hours, but the same day hidden away in the tribal cave. In such cases the depositing of the body in the *marae* was "the burial," or the committal of the spirit to the care of the god worshipped in life, whilst the letting down of the corpse into the deep chasm was designated "the throwing away of the bones" (*tiringa ivi*), the well-wrapped-up body being regarded as a mere bundle of bones after the exit of the spirit.

' In the olden times, relatives of the deceased wore only "pakoko," or native-cloth, dyed red in the sap of the candle-nut tree, and then dipped in the black mud of a taro-patch. The very offensive smell of this mourning garment was symbolical of the putrescent state of the dead. Their heads were encircled with chaplets of mountain fern, singed with fire to give it a red appearance.

' The *eva*, or dirge, and the mourning dance suc-

ceeded. Of this dirge, four varieties are known.
They invariably took place by day, occupying from
ten to fifteen days, according to the rank of the
deceased. Sometimes a "death-talk" was preferred,
consisting of sixty songs in honour of the dead,
mournfully chanted at night in a large house built
for the purpose, and well lighted with torches. Each
adult male relative recited a song. A feast was the
inevitable *finale*.

'Each island of the Hervey Group had some variety
of custom in relation to the dead. Perhaps the chiefs
of Atiu were the most outrageous in mourning. I
knew one to mourn for seven years for an only child
(a woman), living all that time in a hut in the vicinity
of the grave, and allowing his hair and nails to grow,
and his body to remain unwashed. This was the
wonder of all the islanders. In general, all mourning
ceremonies were over in a year.'

It seems to me that in spite of some savage ingredients, these funeral customs of Australians and
Polynesians differ but little from those of the civilised nations of the ancient world. Those of the
Polynesians, in particular, are full of indications of
deep sentiment and even of exalted thoughts about
death and life after death. In fact, when brought
face to face with the great problems of life and death,
when welcoming the rising of a new life at birth, or
standing by the grave of a beloved child, men differ
far less than we imagine. They all have tears of joy
and tears of sorrow, and in the end there is for all of
them the same silence.

LECTURE X.

The Soul *minus* the Body.

WE saw in a former Lecture how the name and concept of soul arose. It was a perfectly simple process ; what may almost be called a mere process of subtraction. There was man, a living body, acting, feeling, perceiving, thinking, and speaking. Suddenly, after receiving one blow with a club, that living body collapses, dies, putrefies, falls to dust. The body, therefore, is seen to be destroyed. But there is nothing to prove that the agent within that body, who felt, who perceived, who thought and spoke, had likewise been destroyed, had died, putrefied, and fallen to dust. Hence the very natural conclusion that, though that agent had departed, it continued to exist somewhere, even though there was no evidence to show *how* it existed and *where* it existed.

Continuance of Feelings towards the Dead.

We next examined the different ways in which some of the principal nations of antiquity treated the dead bodies of their friends, and we could clearly perceive that they were all suggested by feelings of either love or fear, not directed towards the material remains which had either been destroyed by fire or hidden in the earth, but directed towards something else which they called the souls, or the spirits, or the shades.

If a father had been loved and revered while living among his children, it would have been against all the tendencies of the human heart, if those sentiments had suddenly ceased at death. And if an enemy had died or had actually been killed, it seemed by no means unnatural that feelings of hatred and fear should be entertained against him, even after his death.

However, whether it was due to the fact that among uncivilised races the sentiment of love was less prevalent, or whether the terrible appearances which often accompanied death told on the survivors, certain it is that in ancient times the feelings towards the departed consisted more largely of fear or awe than of tenderness and love.

The Zulus, however, when giving an account of their ancestral worship to Bishop Callaway, laid great stress on their feelings of love and gratitude towards the deceased. Their father whom they knew is the head by whom they begin and end in their prayer, for they know him best, and his love for his children; they remember his kindness to them whilst he was living; they compare his treatment of them whilst he was living, support themselves by it, and say: 'he will still treat us in the same way now he is dead.'

It was this feeling of love that led to a continuance of acts of kindness towards the departed. Not only was their body carefully disposed of, but their memory was cherished, and at the ordinary meals of the family and at festive gatherings some share of food and drink was often thrown into the fire of the hearth, as a gift to them.   This led to what I believe to have been a subsequent belief, namely, that, in some way or other, the souls were really able to enjoy these gifts, nay, that they had a right to them, and would resent their withdrawal.

The feelings of fear would dictate almost the same acts, though the motive would be rather a wish to propitiate than a desire to benefit the departed.   The thought that the souls of the dead had the power of injuring the survivors seems to have been very common, and the great attention paid to a proper disposal of the dead bodies, was due in no small degree to a desire to pacify the departed spirits, and to give them what was considered their due ($\tau\grave{a}$ $\nu\acute{o}\mu\iota\mu\alpha$).

I hardly think, however, that, as has lately been suggested, we can ascribe the wide-spread custom of burning the dead, to an apprehension lest, if only buried, their ghosts might return.   There are many much more natural motives that would have suggested cremation rather than burial.   Nor do I know of any evidence that people who burnt the dead bodies thought that they were safe thereby against the mischievous power of the ghosts of the departed, or that they were freed from the obligation of honouring and appeasing the ancestral spirits by commemorations and sacrificial offerings.

The Germs of Ancestral Religion.

Two results would almost inevitably follow.   The honours paid to the dead at the time of the funeral, would assume a solemn and sacred character, and their continuance at certain times and seasons would become part and parcel of the religious life of the people. Secondly, the souls themselves, to whom these honours were paid, would soon assume a more and more exalted character, and occupy in the minds of their worshippers a place second only to that which had been assigned to the gods.

This process would naturally assume different forms among different people, but its general character would be the same. A second religion would arise, a second class of no longer human, and soon of half-divine beings would be believed in, and the powers ascribed to them and the worship paid to them would become almost, if not entirely, identical with those of the gods.

The First Ancestor.

It has been asserted that in some cases this worship of the departed formed all that can be called religion among certain tribes. Religion has sometimes been called a *retrogressio in infinitum*, and by a very simple *retrogressio in infinitum* certain tribes were supposed to have argued that as they had known a father, a grandfather, and a great-grandfather, there must have been earlier fathers, and fathers of fathers, all to be honoured and to be feared, all in their way powerful, able to punish and able to reward, till at last human reason wanted a rest, and postulated at the beginning of all things one father, the father of all fathers, and, very soon, the maker of all things. You see that this process of reasoning is perfectly natural, however startling its result may seem to us. When a missionary tells us for the first time that a savage believes that the world was made by his grandfather, we find it difficult to believe such a statement. Nevertheless the train of thought that leads from a real father to a father of all fathers, is not so very different from that which leads our own minds from the conception of one cause to the conception of a cause of all causes. The Zulus, for instance, believe in *Unkulunkulu*, the great-grand-father, and this great-grandfather is regarded by some of the Zulu tribes as the creator and ruler of the world.

Were there Races without Physical Religion ?

Some students assure us that there are· races whose religion consists entirely of ancestral worship. This question, whether there are and whether there have been races whose whole religion consists in worship of ancestors, can only be solved by a careful examina-tion of those very troublesome accounts of travellers of which I had to speak before. As far as my own studies go, I have not succeeded in discovering one single race believing in ancestral souls only, and not in gods. Among civilised and literary nations, whose history must always form the starting-point and the foundation of any truly scientific research, there is no trace of such a state of things. That does not prove its entire impossibility, by no means. But it will certainly make the true historian very careful, before he draws his general conclusions from the fragmentary accounts of travellers among Zulus and Australians, rather than from the sacred literature of the great nations of the world.

Are there Races whose Religion is exclusively Ancestor-worship ?

I have been looking out for many years, wherever there was any likelihood of meeting with a religion that consisted entirely of ancestor-worship. There is no *à priori* reason why races should not exist now who, even in the eyes of careful observers, might seem to worship nothing but their ancestors. Even where a worship of nature-gods existed, it is quite possible that it might have vanished and have been superseded by a worship of ancestral spirits.

Religion of Zulus.

The best-known of the races who were formerly considered as having no religion except ancestor-worship are the Zulus, and the other so-called Bântu tribes of South Africa. I do not wonder that this mistake should have arisen. These tribes are migratory, they are not held together by a common priesthood, and, like most savages, they are very unwilling to allow themselves to be examined on religious topics. It was quite natural therefore that some missionaries, when they were told that these Kafirs worshipped *Unkulunkulu*, the great-grandfather, should have stated that the whole religion of these natives consisted in worship of grandfathers and ancestors. When at a later time some missionaries, such as Dr. Colenso or Dr. Callaway, acquired a more accurate knowledge of the dialects spoken by the Bântu tribes, and were able to carry on rational discussions with some old chiefs and priests, they were able to give a much better account. But they also

were under the impression for a long time that the
Zulu religion was exclusively ancestral.

We owe the best description of the Zulu religion
to Bishop Callaway, in his *Religious System of the
Amazulus*, a book which certainly leaves us under
the impression that, at present, the Zulu religion
consists almost exclusively of worship of ancestors.
Their ancestral spirits are called *Amatongo*[1], and at
their head stands *Unkulunkulu*.

This Unkulunkulu, their great primal ancestor, has
come to be regarded as the Creator, though other
authorities deny that the Zulus have any idea of creation. The Rev. J. Macdonald[2], for instance, assures us
that 'they hold that the earth and the heavenly bodies
have always been as we see them now, and that they
will thus always continue, unless some terrestrial
catastrophe should set the whole on fire, or, in some
other way, disperse everything.' But even when
Unkulunkulu is regarded as the Creator, he is not
exactly an object of worship, awe, or reverence with
the Zulus. He is often supposed to have given place
to newer men of more recent times. The great objects
of fear and reverence to which they pray and sacrifice are the spirits of dead ancestors for the last few
generations.

'Ancestor-worship,' as the same intelligent observer,
the Rev. J. Macdonald, remarks[3], 'is not only professed by them, but they actually regulate their
conduct by it. If a man has a narrow escape from
accident and death, he says, " My father's soul saved

---

[1] *Amatongo* is the plural of *itongo*.
[2] *Journal of the Anthropol. Institute*, Nov. 1890, p. 128.
[3] *Ibid.* p. 122.

me," and he offers a sacrifice of thanksgiving accordingly. In cases of sickness, propitiatory sacrifices are offered to remove the displeasure of the ancestors, and secure a return of their favour. Should any one neglect a national custom in the conduct of his affairs, he must offer sacrifice to avert calamity as the consequence of his neglect. When offering propitiatory sacrifices, the form of prayer used by the priest is: "Ye who are above, accept our offering and remove our trouble." In free-will offerings, as in escape from danger or at the ripening of crops, the prayer takes the following form: "Ye who are above, accept the food we have provided for you; smell our offering now burning, and grant us prosperity and peace." '

Many missionaries who did not consider that ancestor-worship could be considered as religion, declared in consequence that the South African tribes had no religion at all, and no belief in God. Even Dr. Callaway, though fully aware of the religious character of ancestral worship, seems to have been doubtful for a time whether the Bântu tribes had any knowledge of divine beings, apart from their ancestral spirits.

All observers[1], however, agree now that these tribes believe in other spirits also, besides those of men. They speak of water or river spirits, whom they describe as dwarfs or fairies. These are called *Incanti*, and are always mischievous.

They have also a number of superstitions about thunder, lightning, rain, the rainbow, eclipses of sun and moon, and other physical phenomena. But all this would not yet prove that they believed in any

[1] Macdonald, l. c., p. 124.

of the gods of physical religion, or in a Supreme
Being above the ancestral spirits.

However, in his last paper, 'On the Religious
Sentiment amongst the Tribes of South Africa,' Dr.
Callaway reports the statement made to him by an
intelligent Gqika chief. 'We used not to say,' he
told the bishop, ' *Utikxo* for God, but *Ukqamata*.
When men feared anything they used to say, "May
Ukqamata help us."' 'Here then,' the bishop writes,
'we have hidden in the language of the people a word
which shows that long ago, before the word Utikxo
was introduced amongst them for God, they had a
name representative to them of the Supreme—a being
not like Unkulunkula amongst the Zulus, who is
sometimes represented as having begun, died, and
passed away ; but one who is seen now with them,
and to whom they constantly appeal in time of
necessity, much in the same way as the devout
amongst ourselves appeal to God.'

Other people whom the bishop asked, told him that
Ukqamata is a living spirit, but that they knew not
where it dwells ; and if asked where it dwells, they
would answer, 'It goes beside me, and yet I see it
not.' And they said, ' Spirits go out of men to go
to Ukqamata, to the place where they dwell with
him. The corpse does not go to Ukqamata, it is the
spirit only which goes to him ; the corpse remains
in the earth.'

Dr. Callaway then continues : 'I have been long
aware that apparently apart from, above, and beyond
their mere ancestral worship, . . . the Kafir races . . .
universally speak of a Great *Itongo*, and appeal to it,
pretty much in the same way as these frontier Kafir

(3)   U

tribes are said to appeal to Ukqamata.' The bishop also states that the Kafirs seem quite aware that the various names applied to the Supreme Spirit are but various names of the same Being. They admitted that they had borrowed Utikxo as the name of the Supreme Spirit from their neighbours, the Hottentots.

In spite of much confusion in these statements, one thing is clear, that the Kafir races of South Africa are not exclusively worshippers of ancestral spirits, but that they recognise or remember a Supreme Spirit, standing above their ancestors, and exercising a personal power over nature [1].

Religion of the Niassans.

Another race which quite recently revived my hopes of finding a religion consisting exclusively of ancestor-worship are the ·Niassans. An interesting description of the religion of the Niassans was published lately by Kramer in the *Tijdschrift vor Indische Taal-, Land-, en Volkenkunde,* deel xxxii, 1890.

These Niassans, who live in a solitary island west of Sumatra, have more than a hundred idols. Formerly they had less, now they go on adding to their number. Priests and priestesses make a living by serving these idols.

Their really important and permanent idols are the images of ancestors and house-idols. The ancestors are represented as human figures, about six to eight inches high, and carefully carved. Poor people, how-

---

[1] Callaway, *Religious System of the Amazulus,* p. 117, 'The Lord of Heaven.'

ever, have to be satisfied with a piece of wood, with holes for eyes and mouth.

The house-idols are in the shape of children, and in the houses of rich chiefs these also are carefully executed.

After a man has been buried, the priest covers his grave with a mat, and seeks till he find a six-legged spider under it. That is taken as the soul of the departed, deposited in a reed, and placed by the side of the image.

Such images, however, are made of those only who have left male descendants. They occasionally borrow them from one another.

The Niassans expect all blessings from their ancestors, who likewise protect them against all dangers. But for that purpose it is necessary that they should receive constant offerings. No event of any importance takes place without some communication being made or some honour shown to the ancestral images. On some occasions their names have to be repeated. In fact their whole life seems to be under the sway of their ancestors. It is true they believe in evil spirits also (Bechus), and even in a devil (Bela). But these might be traced back to a belief in hostile ancestors, or ancestors of hostile tribes. At all events, they would not prove the existence of anything like a belief in nature-gods. What are called their *hazimas* (p. 492), and what many people would call fetishes, are really nothing but amulets, stones, teeth, pieces of lead, &c., which they wear as a protection against evil spirits. They are often supposed to have fallen from the sky, to have been the head of a serpent, or to consist of condensed stormwind.

However, within and above all this chaos of ancestral spirits, ghosts, and fetishes, there suddenly appears our old friend, the sun. Yes, solar worship even among the Niassans! The owner, the lord and master of all men is Lature, and he dwells in the sun. As we are the possessors of our pigs, the Niassans say, Lature is the possessor of all men. Nay, they are proud to call themselves the pigs of the sun. Sacrifices are offered to the sun-god that he may grant a long life to his pigs.

But though we look in vain for a religion consisting of ancestor-worship only, we often find that in the same religion the worship of ancestral spirits and the worship of the gods of nature exist side by side, and, what is important, we find that they are never confounded, but kept carefully distinct even in the terminology that is applied to them (pp. 478, 490).

Worship of Gods and Worship of Ancestors kept distinct.

Professor Ch. de la Saussaye, in his *Manual of the Science of Religion* (p. 113), has pointed out that in Greece, for instance, 'other names are applied to the altars, sacrifices, and offerings connected with the dead than those used in the worship of the Olympian gods. The altar is called ἐσχάρα, not βωμός; the offering of the sacrifice ἐναγίζειν, ἐντέμνειν, not θύειν; the libations themselves χοαί, not σπονδαί.' This is the rule, but there are exceptions.

Dr. Rohde also, in his *Psyche*, p. 140, remarks that 'the Greeks sacrificed to the gods by day, to the heroes in the evening or by night, not on high altars, but on a low sacrificial hearth, which was close to the ground, and sometimes hollow. Black-coloured animals of the male sex were killed for them, and their heads were not, as in the case of victims intended for the gods, turned towards the sky, but pressed down to the ground. The blood was allowed to run on the ground or on the sacrificial hearth, as a blood-feast (αἱμακουρία) to the heroes; their body was burnt entire, so that no man might eat of it. Sometimes cooked viands were offered to the heroes, and they were invited to partake of them.'

Much the same applies to Sanskrit. When offerings are made to the gods, the Brâhmanic thread has to hang from the left shoulder, under the right arm (upavîtin). When the offering is intended for the departed spirits, the same thread has to be hung on the right shoulder, and under the left arm (prâkîna-vîtin)[1].

The departed spirits are called Pitris, fathers, the gods, Devas, the bright.

The exclamation used in sacrificing to the gods is svâhâ; in sacrifices to the departed it is svadhâ.

This shows among two nations, so widely separated as Greeks and Hindus, but whose language is known to us accurately, a clear recollection of the different meaning with which from the very first, gods and ancestors were worshipped by the Âryas.

Let us now see more in detail what some of the Aryan nations thought on this subject, and what place in their religion they assigned respectively to the worship of the gods and to the worship of ancestral spirits.

---

[1] Âpastamba Paribhâshâ-sûtras, Sûtras 58 and 59 ; *Zeitschrift der D. M. G.* 1850, p. lv.

It is easy to see that when we speak of worship of ancestors and worship of gods, the meaning of worship must be different according to the different nature of those to whom it is addressed. The worship of the dead began with acts of kindness shown to the departed from the day of their death to the day of their funeral; the worship of gods was inspired by a feeling of awe, and arose from a sense of what was due to higher powers. In the end these two kinds of worship may have become almost identical, but in their first motives they stand wide apart.

Before we proceed further, however, we must first try to find out by what process of reasoning, or, it may be, unreasoning, people came to believe anything about the dead beyond their mere existence. The fact of their existence, as we saw, was proved, if it required any proof at all, by an argument as irresistible to-day as it was thousands of years ago. In the absence of all proof to the contrary, the agent in man was believed to exist on the same ground on which the agents in nature were believed to exist. There can be no action without an agent. Agni, the agent of fire, was not believed to be destroyed and annihilated, although the individual fire in which he appeared might be extinguished. And the soul, the agent in man, could not be believed to be destroyed and annihilated, although the individual body in which it appeared had fallen to dust and ashes.

But the human mind, and more especially the human heart, is not satisfied with this general belief in the mere existence of souls. It wants to know, what it cannot possibly know, *where* and *how* the soul exists after the body has left it, or rather, after it has left the body. Here we enter into the domain of mythology as different from that of religion. A study of the imaginations of ancient people with regard to the state of the soul after death may be useful for a knowledge of the character of different nations, possibly for a knowledge of human character in general. But it can no longer influence our own convictions. What Plato says in support of his belief in one God 'who holds in His hands the beginning, middle, and end of all that is, and moves according to His nature in a straight line,' is said for us quite as much as for the ancient Greeks, and even the name of Zeus, if we but know its true meaning, need not offend us. But the mythological stories told of Zeus and the other Olympian gods, are nothing to us. They were very little even to Plato.

It is the same with the mythology concerning the souls of the departed. That these souls exist is as true for us as it was for Plato. But where they exist and how they exist is a question the various answers to which may form an important subject of study to the historian, but can hardly, if at all, influence our own conviction that here, as in so many other things, we must learn to wait, and for a while to remain ignorant.

Such ignorance, however, was difficult to brook, and we find, I believe, among all nations some attempts, however futile, at lifting the veil and catching a few glimpses of the life of the souls after death.

Where do the Departed exist?

With people who burn their dead, there can be little doubt that the body, as such, has come to an end, when there is nothing left of it but dust and ashes. Their views about the abode of the departed souls are therefore generally less coarse and material than the views of people who bury their dead near their own abodes, sometimes beneath their own houses; or of the Egyptians and other races who mummify the bodies and keep them daily before their eyes.

When the Greeks say that the likenesses of men, the eidôla, mere shadows, went to the realm of *Hades*, we have only to restore the meaning of *Hades*, namely *Aides*, the Invisible, and we could ourselves use their language, that the likenesses of the departed go to the realm of the Invisible. It is only a more poetical expression for what we express in more homely terms, when we say that the soul has departed and has become invisible. You know, however, how very soon this invisible world, this house of the Invisible, becomes a Hades, with terrible rivers to be crossed in Charon's boat [1]; with a three-headed watch-dog, with judges judging the souls, and punishments and tortures inflicted on the wicked.

All this is mythology, and cannot affect us.

With people who buried their dead new ideas sprang up, as we see, for instance, among the Jews, who placed the abode of the dead below the earth. Their Sheol was indeed a lower world, and the same idea gained ground among other nations also. So long as the souls of the departed were supposed to exist in a place separated from the seats of the gods, they were naturally considered as *Inferi*, living

---

[1] Charon, and the obolos to be put into the mouth of the departed, are later. See Hermann, *Griechische Privatalterthümer*, p. 368.

below, in opposition to *Superi*, the gods, living
above. From this simple distinction have sprung
in time all the horrors of the infernal regions, which
are supposed to have influenced the lives of men
more powerfully than any other article of religious
faith.

Before this definite localisation of the departed
took place, we find another very general impression
prevailing among civilised and uncivilised nations,
that the departed went to the West. The Hervey
islanders believed that when a man died his spirit
returned to *Avaiki*, the original home of their ancestors in the region of sunset. Sometimes this
region is called *te-po*, the night, i. e. the place where
the sun hides itself at night, or, in other words, the
West. Dr. William Wyatt Gill[1] thinks that this is
due to the fact that the Eastern Polynesians came
originally from the West, from Avaiki (=Hawaiki,
Hawai'i, Savaiki, Savai'i, all forms of the same name).
This may be so. But Avaiki is conceived also as a
vast hollow beneath the earth. In it there are many
regions, bearing separate names, but all to be regarded
as parts of spirit-land. And in this sense Avaiki is
clearly the West, as the land of departed spirits.

It required but little poetical imagination to speak
of the sun as dying every day and vanishing in the
west, and no expression seemed more natural than
to speak of man's day having closed, of his life
having set, of his soul following the path of the sun
to the abode of the Blessed. The sun was even conceived as the first who found the way to a realm

[1] *Transactions of the Australian Association for the Advancement of
Science*, Melbourne, 1890, p. 636.

beyond, and under various names he soon assumed the character of the Lord of the Departed, and then, by a natural reaction, was claimed as a man, as the first of men who had lived and died [1]. Sometimes, however, as in the Veda, that realm of Yama, the first of the departed, and the Pit*ris*, the Fathers, is placed in the highest heaven, an expression which almost ceases to be local, and assumes something of an ethical character.

Nor is this more exalted view as to the abode of the departed confined to civilised races. Though the Zulus, for instance, localise some of their spirits in caverns, on the roofs of houses, and other places, yet their general idea seems to be that at death the spirit goes upwards to the spirit-land. This is best shown by their own usual form of prayer, which is: ' Ye who are above, ye who have gone before [2].'

So much with regard to the ideas as to *where* the departed existed after death.

How do the Departed exist?

The answer to the question *how* they existed was suggested, in the first place, by moral sentiments. We know of several nations who, though they believed in the existence of the departed after death, did not believe that they were liable to punishments or rewards for what they had done in this life.

Belief in Punishments and Rewards.

But suppose a crime had been discovered after the death of the man who had committed it, how could

---

[1] Rv. X. 14, 2 ; Ath. XVIII. 3, 13. Kaegi, pp. 69, 159.
[2] Macdonald, l. c., p. 121.

the thought be suppressed that he would be punished in the next world? And if people stood at the funeral pile of a father or a mother or a friend whose kindness they had not been able to requite during life, what was more natural for them than to hope and to believe that their love would be rewarded in the next world? And this did not remain a fond hope. It was soon looked upon as a necessity and a certainty, for without it there would be no justice in the world, and that there is justice in the world is an ineradicable belief of the human heart.

I know that this expression, 'an ineradicable belief of the human heart,' gives great offence to certain philosophers. They either deny the existence of such beliefs *in toto*, or they try to account for them as the result of repeated experience. But in our case, how could it be said that a belief in universal justice arises from repeated experience? Surely, no one would say that our experience teaches us again and again that the good are rewarded and the bad punished in this life. One might even go so far as to say that it is the repeated experience of the very contrary, namely, of the misfortunes of the good and the triumphs of the bad, that provokes an appeal to and a belief in a higher justice.

Plato.

Plato, in a famous passage in the Laws, p. 959, says: 'Now we must believe the legislator when he tells us that the soul is in all respects superior to the body, and that even in life what makes each one of us to be what we are is only the soul; and that the body follows us about in the likeness of each of us.

and therefore, when we are dead, the bodies of the dead are rightly said to be our shades or images ; for the true and immortal being of each one of us, which is called the soul, goes on her way to other gods, that before them she may give an account—an inspiring hope to the good, but very terrible to the bad, *as the law of our fathers tells us.*'

I quote this passage, not because it is Plato's, but because we see from it how even Plato submits to the authority of this νόμος πάτριος, this law of our fathers, which without vouchsafing any proof, declares that justice will prevail.

The Law of Cause and Effect.

But though I call this an ineradicable belief of the human heart, I do not mean to say that no proof can be produced for it. I only mean that no proof is required, until doubt has first been thrown on it. When this belief in justice has been challenged, it requires but little reflection to see that it is but another form of the old law of causality which under-lies the whole of our thoughts, nay, without which no thought whatever would be possible. It may be said that this law of causality is an abstraction, which must of necessity belong to a much later phase in the history of the human mind. So it does. But it exists, nevertheless, even in the most ancient times, and in the laws of our fathers ; nay, it exercises its influence on the thoughts of men, even though they have as yet no name for it.

We saw in our last course of Lectures how the same hidden law of causality necessitated a belief in agents. behind the acts of nature. In its most general form this belief might be called the inevitable result of the simple and universal proposition, *Ex nihilo nihil fit*. Applied to the phenomena of nature, it would mean, 'Nothing can be done without a doer.'

Now the ancient belief in justice is likewise but another version of the same rule, namely, *Ex aliquo fit aliquid*. If we call the former the law of causality, we may call the latter the law of effect, which denies in the most absolute way that anything can be annihilated, can be without an effect.

Karma na kshîyate.

There is a saying among the old laws of our fathers in India, which as applied to our moral actions expresses this truth in the simplest and strongest words, karma na kshîyate [1], 'a deed does not perish,' that is to say, whatever guilt or merit there is in a human action, man will not come out of it till he has paid or received the uttermost farthing.

This idea of karma, which forms the foundation of the system of Buddhist morality, does not belong to the Buddhists only. In the Upanishads, karma has become already a technical term, and its power and influence must help to account for many things that otherwise seem unaccountable. Thus in a dialogue between Yâgñavalkya and Gâratkârava Ârtabhâga (Brih.-Âr. Up. III. 2), the latter asks: 'When the speech of this dead person enters into the fire, breath into the air, the eye into the sun, the mind into the moon, the hearing into space, into the earth

---

[1] It occurs in Vasishtha XXII. 4, in Gautama XIX. 5, in Baudhâyana III. 10, 4.

the body, into the ether the self, into the shrubs the
hairs of the body, into the trees the hairs of the head,
when the blood and the seed are deposited in the
water, where is the man himself?'

'Yâgñavalkya answers: "Give me thy hand, O
friend. We two alone shall know of this; let this
question of ours not be (discussed) in public." Then
these two went out and argued, and what they said
was karma, what they proclaimed was karma, viz.
that man becomes good by good karma, and evil by
evil karma.'

In the ancient codes of law the same idea occurs
again and again. In the Code of Vishnu, for instance, it
is fully placed before us among the words of comfort
to be addressed to the mourners at funeral ceremonies.
Here we read (XX. 28 seq.): 'Every creature is seized
by Kâla (time) and carried into the other world. It
is the slave of its actions. Wherefore then should you
wail?' (28.)   'As both his good and bad actions will
follow him like associates, what does it matter to
a man whether his relatives mourn over him or
no?' (31.)

You see that here again there is no doubt in the
mind of the old lawgiver on this subject. It is simply
stated as a fact, that his good and his bad actions
follow a man into the next world, and that he is the
slave of his acts, that is, that he has to bear their
consequences.

The same idea meets us again, though in a more
mythological dress, in the Kaushîtaki Upanishad (I. 4),
where the good and evil deeds are represented as following the departed till he approaches the hall Vibhu
and the glory of Brahma reaches him. Then he

shakes them all off, and his good deeds go to his beloved, his evil deeds to his unbeloved relatives.

Still more mythological is the account given of the soul after death in the Avesta (Vîstâsp Yast, 56). Here the soul is represented as being met by a beautiful maiden, white-armed, tall, and noble, as if in her fifteenth year, and when he asks her who she is, she replies : ' O thou youth, of good thoughts, good words, and good deeds, of good religion ! I am thy own conscience.'

If, then, I call this belief in rewards and punishments ' an ineradicable belief of the human heart,' I mean that, if divested of its many mythological disguises, it is but one of the many paraphrases of the law of cause and effect, a law which for beings, such as we are, is irresistible, which requires no proof, nay, which admits of no proof, because it is self-evident.

Are the Departed conscious of what passes on Earth?

These two beliefs, the belief in the continued existence of the soul after death, and that in its liability to rewards and punishments, seem to me as irresistible to-day as they were in the days of Plato. We cannot say that a belief in rewards and punishments is universal. We look for it in vain, for instance, in the Old Testament or in Homer. But when that belief has once presented itself to the human mind, it holds its own against all objections. It is possible, no doubt, to object to the purely human distinction between rewards and punishments, because, from a higher point of view, punishment itself may be called a reward. Even eternal punishment, as Charles Kingsley used to say, is but another name for eternal love, and the very fire of hell may be taken as a childish expression only for the constant purification of the soul. All this may be conceded, if only the continuity of cause and effect, between this life and the next, is preserved.

But when we come to the next question, whether the Departed, as has been fondly supposed, are able to feel, not only what concerns them, but likewise what concerns their friends on earth, we may call this a very natural deduction, a very intelligible hope, we may even admit that no evidence can be brought forward against it, but beyond that we cannot go.

Still, if we have followed the thoughts of the early Greeks so far, that they did not, like Homer, believe the departed souls to be simply senseless, ἀφραδέεις, or, like the Jews, simply to sleep and be at rest, but capable of suffering from punishments, and rejoicing in rewards, we can understand at least, even though we cannot follow them, when they go a step beyond and hold that the departed souls could be cognisant of and take pleasure in the honours rendered to them by their relatives and friends on earth. It is curious to find that Plato (Laws xi. 927) admits that the souls of the dead have the power after their death of taking an interest in human affairs. It is true he does not attempt any proof of this belief, but he appeals to ancient tales and traditions, and to lawgivers who tell us that these things are true, nay, he actually condescends to use the old, though by no means extinct argument, that these ancient lawgivers would have been utter fools, if they had said such things, without knowing them to be true.

Sometimes we meet with a still lower, though

likewise quite intelligible view, that the Departed
could actually be pleased by food and drink and such
other things as they enjoyed during their life on
earth. Here, no doubt, the evidence of the senses
would soon lead to a wholesome scepticism. Gifts
thrown into the fire and burnt in it, might be
supposed to reach the Departed, as the smoke of
sacrifices was believed to reach the nostrils of the
gods. But other gifts, left untouched on the graves,
could hardly be supposed to have benefitted the
Departed. However, even the savages of Rarotonga
have found a way out of these difficulties. It is true,
they say, that the visible part of the food is eaten by
the rats, but the gods come at dusk and feed on the
essence of these offerings. This is not bad for a
Rarotongan casuist.

We have thus seen how the psyché, the breath, the
anima, had in the eyes of the ancients, whether
civilised or uncivilised, become endowed with all that
was implied by the *thymós* or *animus*, the mind, and
man's fancy was thenceforth set free to finish the
picture with such colours, and such light and shade,
as best suited the taste of poets, artists, philosophers,
and last, not least, of priests.

The poets would speak of the souls flitting about
in the air like birds, or hiding beneath the earth like
serpents. This was purely symbolical language. But
as soon as artists began to speak the same language,
we find in sculpture and paintings the souls of the
departed represented as small winged beings, others
also as serpents, dwelling near their graves. Such
symbolical representations are apt to become myths
and to be believed in their literal sense by a portion

(3)   X

at least of the people. But we must take care not to
see in them proofs of a former serpent-worship, as
little as of bird-worship. Their true explanation is
much more simple and natural.

Even philosophers remain poets. The Emperor
Hadrian, though initiated in Greek philosophy and in
the Greek mysteries, addressed his soul, when dying,
in words half-childish, half-poetical:

> Animula, vagula, blandula,
> Hospes comesque corporis,
> Quae nunc abibis in loca?
> Pallidula, rigida, nudula,
> Nec ut soles dabis jocos.

> 'Whither—thou wandering, fondling sprite,
>   The body's mate and guest—
>   Soon must thou fly?
> Wan, robeless, homeless, formless mite!
>   Thy mirth and wonted jest
>   With thee shall die.'

> (Translated by the Hon. Lionel A.
> Tollemache, in *Safe Studies*, p. 396.)

Influence of Priests.

Lastly, we must not forget, when we sometimes
wonder at the elaborate and extravagant offerings
made to the Departed, that there was somebody else
to be fed besides the spirits. The profession of a
priest is a very old one, and we find it almost everywhere. Now it stands to reason that if people want
to have priests, they must feed them, or, as we call it
by a slightly changed term, they must fee them. I
mean that *fee* is the same word as the Latin *pecus*,
and meant originally an animal, given by way of
payment. What is called a sacrifice to the gods and
to ancestral spirits was almost always an offering to

the priest also. And if it did not mean a fee, it always meant a feast, more particularly in the case of funeral functions. A single case will serve to make this clearer than any general theories.

The Rev. J. Macdonald [1] tells us that 'should a Zulu dream the same dream more than once, he consults the magicians, who profess to have much of their own revelations through dreams. . . . If a dreamer sees a departed relative, the magician says oracularly, "He is hungry." A beast is then killed as a quasi-sacrifice. The blood is carefully collected and placed in a vessel at the side of the hut, farthest from the door. The liver is hung up in the hut and must not be eaten, until all the flesh of the animal has been used. During the night the spirit is regaled and refreshed by the food thus provided, and eats or withdraws the *essence* that goes to feed and sustain spirits. After a specified time all may be eaten except the portions the magician orders to be burned; generally bones and fat.'

Is not all this simple human nature? The man is disturbed by a repeated dream. He asks the priest. The priest says, 'the spirit is hungry,' the fact being that he himself is hungry. He advises the killing of an animal. The essence of the animal goes to the spirit, the fat and bones are burnt, and the rest is eaten by the hungry priest and his friend, who, after a good feast, has probably another terrible dream, and thus provides fresh employment to the priest.

It is easy to see how rapidly a stone will roll downhill after the first impulse has been given. It is that first impulse which interests the psychologist,

[1] *Journal of the Anthropological Institute*, Nov. 1890, p. 121.

and that must, if possible, be accounted for. To discover the secret springs of the first movements of the human mind, when brought face to face with the problems of nature and the problems of its own existence, has been my chief object throughout all these lectures. Our progress, I know, has sometimes been slow and tedious. But it seems to me that to discover the sources of religion in the darkest antiquity is a task worthy at least of the same devotion and the same perseverance as to discover the sources of the Nile in darkest Africa.

LECTURE XI.

SOUL AFTER DEATH.

Greek Epic Poetry.

IF we wished to know what the ancient Greeks thought about the departed, we should naturally turn to the Homeric poems, and therein more particularly to the eleventh book of the Odyssey, or the visit of Odysseus to the shades in Hades, the Nekyia.

We have no doubt a perfect right to take Homer as expressing the earliest thoughts of the Greeks on any subject. And this is the case all the more, if we look upon his poetry, not simply as the work of one individual, but as the result of the same growth of popular poetry which we meet with everywhere, but particularly in ancient times, and before the invention of writing. To suppose that a single line of poetry has ever grown up by itself, or by the combined labour of a large number of poets, is of course absolutely absurd. Every metrical line, every couple of lines that rhymes or scans, is a work of art, and must have been originally the work of one individual poet. But during times when memory is the only guardian of poetry, those for whom poetry is intended, I mean the public, whether large or small, have a much

greater influence on the life of poetry than in our
times.

If the work of a poet does not take the fancy of
others, it comes and goes, and is forgotten. It may
be an excellent poem, but unless it rouses the sym-
pathy of the hearers, it cannot live, or survive the
poet that made it. In that sense, therefore, the
people at large had a share and a very important
share in its poetry. Poetry had to be composed to
please the people, and poetry could not survive unless
it pleased the people. It was not exactly a survival of
the fittest or the best, but it was always a survival of
what best fitted the taste of the many. Think what
would be the effect on modern literature, if all books
of which the newspapers disapprove, were *ipso facto*
to vanish. Life would be lighter, no doubt, but it
would prove poorer also. The popular poetry of
England would be without its Wordsworth, its
Tennyson, and certainly without its Browning.

But the verdict of the many did not only determine
whether the children of the Muses should live at all,
by either taking them up or rejecting them, but it
likewise exercised the strongest influence on their
later life. Those who had to preserve in their
memory the songs which had become popular, felt
themselves at liberty to leave out any lines that
fell flat, to add lines which might suit the views of
different audiences, nay to combine portions of poetry
which belonged to the same cycle, and this often
regardless of contradictions, such as have been de-
tected in the Homeric and other popular poems by
modern scholars. All this, if you think about it,
is so natural that it could hardly have been other-

wise. Memory and oral tradition are indeed wonderful keepers of popular poetry, and when once certain productions of that popular poetry have been recognised and invested with a sacred authority, I do not hesitate to say that poems are safer in the memory than in manuscripts. But there are certain influences in the first gathering and in the later adaptation of popular poetry to changing popular tastes, which justify us in saying that in one sense the poetry of the people is not the work of one poet, but the result of the combined labour of many popular poets and many popular critics.

It might seem as if this were mere theory, plausible, no doubt, as accounting for the peculiar character of popular poetry such as we find it, not only in Greece, but among many other nations. Nor have there been wanting objections. We are so little aware of the powers of the human memory, before it was systematically ruined by the invention of writing and reading, as Plato knew, and by the invention of printing, as we all know, that many a scholar has declared it absurd to suppose that the Homeric poems could have been preserved by oral tradition, and many a poet has added his testimony that no man could write,—I mean, could compose, so long a poem as the Iliad and the Odyssey, without pen, paper, and ink. Facts, however, are stronger than arguments. I have seen Hindus who knew the Veda by heart, and who could detect by ear any misprint, any false accent, in my edition of the Rigveda. As to the possibility of composing long poems without writing them, I shall not argue like a lawyer and point out that Homer, if he was blind, could not possibly have written the Iliad and the Odyssey, but could only have dictated them, always supposing that writing had been known at his time. But here, too, it is better to appeal to facts, and to facts coming from a quarter where we should least have expected them.

Finnish Epic Poetry.

You remember the Fins, of whom I spoke to you in my first course of Lectures. They belong neither to the Aryan nor to the Semitic stock. They speak one of the Ural-Altaic group of languages. They now live partly in Sweden, partly in Russia. You may remember how Mr. Gladstone [1], when lately in Scotland, stood up for them as one of the oppressed nationalities of the world. Whether they are fit for Home-rule, and whether Mr. Gladstone's advocacy [2] is likely to secure to them the benefits of Home-rule, and at the same time seats in the Imperial Parliament at St. Petersburg—whenever there is such a Parliament—are matters that do not concern us. But what concerns us is, that among the peasants of Finland, among people ignorant of reading and writing, large fragments of epic poetry have been discovered during the first half of our century, entirely preserved by oral tradition, never written before, either by the poet or by his admirers, and yet easily fitted together into one epic poem. I wish I had time to explain to you the process by which these poems had been preserved, and at last have been collected, printed, critically edited, and translated [2]. But I think you

---

[1] See *Times*, Oct. 29, 1890.   [2] See Appendix VIII.

will have seen, even from these short remarks, in what sense popular poetry, such as the Homeric poems, for instance, may be said to reflect not only the thoughts of one poetic mind, but at the same time the thoughts of many people, who would not have listened to, that is to say, who would not have allowed any poetry to survive, except what they themselves approved of.

The Nekyia does *not* represent the popular Belief.

The question now arises, May we take what Homer says or implies about the dead, may we, more particularly, take his Nekyia, as reflecting the general ideas of the Greeks at his time? I doubt it.

First of all, what do people mean by his time? That there may have been epic poetry, or Homeric poetry, about 1000 B.C., among Asiatic and European Greeks, need not be questioned. But that the Homeric poems, as we now possess them, were reduced to writing much before 700 B.C., has never been proved, for the simple reason that the use of alphabetic writing for literary purposes, in the full sense of that word, before that date, has never been established, whether in Greece, or anywhere else.

But whether we place these poems in the form in which we now possess them, 1000 or 700 B.C., it does by no means follow that they represent, as it were, a complete stratum of Greek thought, still less that all we find in later times of Greek thought, language, myth, religion, and philosophy must have passed through that Homeric stratum. This would be taking far too narrow a view of the ancient growth of the Greek intellect. You know with what contempt some of the ancient philosophers of Greece spoke of Homer as one who had degraded the gods by what he sang of them. That shows that they at all events did not consider him as the only, as the earliest and truest representative of the ancient religion of the Greeks. And what applies to religion, applies to everything else. The Homeric poems are a splendid fragment, but they are a fragment only of ancient Greek thought. It is because they are the only fragment left to us of that ancient period, that we have so often been tempted to take them as a complete image of that period, and that we have forgotten that epic poetry in describing the wars and adventures of an heroic race, reflects chiefly the thoughts of one section of ancient society, and does not necessarily reflect the thoughts, the feelings, the customs, and superstitions of the people at large.

The Homeric poems, as you know, tell us very little about the state of the departed, except in that rhapsody of the Odyssey which is called the *Nekyia*, the journey of Odysseus to the realm of Hades. Many scholars in describing to us what the ancient Greeks thought about life after death, have taken that Nekyia for their chief, nay for their only guide. But this very rhapsody has by some excellent critics been considered as very peculiar and exceptional, and as being possibly the work of a different, probably a Boeotian poet.

These are points that admit of discussion, but there is nothing to lead us to admit that what Homer tells us about the state of the departed in Hades was all that the Greeks believed about a future life.

Take so simple a question as the disposal of dead bodies. If we took our information from Homer only, we should say that the ancient Greeks burnt the corpse. But there is a very well supported tradition that in the days of Cecrops the Athenians buried their dead [1].

I believe we may safely say that sacrifices in honour of the dead, the pouring out of blood on the grass, and the burning of victims dedicated to the departed, are all unknown in the Homeric poems. Nay, the same applies to Hesiod also. Whenever a general remark of this kind is made, it always provokes opposition, and great efforts are made to discover some traces in support of the opposite opinion. Thus in our case, the games celebrated by Achilles in honour of Patroklos, and again the pouring out of blood by Odysseus for the shades in Hades, have been pointed out to show that Homer knew of sacrifices for the dead, and of worship of ancestral spirits. But it is too easily forgotten that when such beliefs and customs are once recognised, they do not manifest themselves in a few isolated cases only, but pervade the whole atmosphere of a poem. The funeral honours paid to Patroklos stand by themselves. They are clearly an exceptional event. And the blood poured out by Odysseus to restore the shades of some departed heroes and heroines to life for a short time only, is something totally different from what is meant by ancestral worship [2].

But, in spite of this, I feel by no means inclined to

[1] Kirchmanni, *De Funeribus Romanorum*, Libri quatuor, 1672, p. 2 ; Cicero, de Legibus, 2, ' Nam et Athenis iam illo more a Cecrope, ut aiunt, permanuit hoc ius terra condendi.'

[2] What Rohde brings forward in his *Psyche* as proving the existence of ancestral worship in the Homeric poems, had been more fully treated before by P. Stengel in Fleckeisen's *Jahrbücher für Klass. Philologie*, 1883, p. 373, ' Einführung der in Homerischer Zeit noch nicht bekannten Opfer in Griechenland.'

say that these natural manifestations of human piety
were altogether absent in ancient Greece, and took
their origin in post-Homeric times only. We are
told in fact on very good authority that one of the
laws collected by Drakon was 'to honour the gods and
the local heroes [1]'. Drakon collected his laws in the
seventh century B. C., and even in his time this was
called a perpetual law.

I doubt even whether a rhapsody like the Nekyia,
treating of so lugubrious a subject, could ever have
become very popular either at private or public festivals. It was preserved, however, probably for the
same reason for which the catalogue of the ships was
preserved. It became something like the golden book
of the Venetian republic. To have the names of
certain heroes or heroines entered in the Nekyia,
became like a title of nobility to the families or
localities to which the most illustrious of the departed
heroes and heroines belonged, and there can be little
doubt that this very natural ambition led to the subsequent additions to the illustrious roll of the names
both of famous ancestors and of renowned cities.

If we keep all this in mind, we shall more easily
understand two things,—first, that the state of the
departed should be so rarely and only so vaguely
alluded to in the Homeric poems; and secondly, that
the Nekyia should in a less degree than other portions
of the Iliad and Odyssey, reflect the universal thoughts
of the Greeks on the mysterious subject of death and
life after death.

---

[1] Cf. Porphyrius, De Abstinentia, iv. 22, Ἐπεὶ καὶ Δράκοντος νόμος
μνημονεύεται τοιοῦτος, θεσμός αἰώνιος τοῖς Ἀτθίδα νεμομένοις, κύριος τὸν
ἅπαντα χρόνον, θεοὺς τιμᾶν καὶ ἥρωας ἐγχωρίους.

We know that this subject, the state of the dead, is at all times and in all countries one of the vaguest, one almost entirely determined by individual hopes and fears and imaginations, one on which the human heart is ready to believe almost anything, and one on which human wisdom can say nothing.   In the Homeric Nekyia we may see a picture of the lower world—if it is indeed a lower world—adapted to the great epic drama of which it forms a part; but I doubt whether we can accept it as a true representation of the ideas entertained by the fathers and mothers or children in the small homes of ancient Greece, as to the state of those for whom their hearts were bleeding and yearning.

Homer does not reflect popular Opinion on Death.

Let us consider a few points only, on which it seems to me quite clear that Homer does not reflect the general feeling of the Greeks with regard to the dead. One of the commonest names in Greek given to the dead is μάκαρες, the blest.   It is found in Hesiod, who knows of the islands of the blest, μακάρων νῆσοι, and in nearly all subsequent writers.   Homer, however, never speaks of the dead as blest, but represents them as utterly miserable.   You remember, how even Achilles, though honoured like a king among the departed, would rather be 'a serf on the land of a poor and portionless man than rule over all the dead who have come to nought' (Od. xi. 488).

If the Greeks at large had really shared Homer's idea that even the best of men were in the next world eidôla or shades, without energy, without real self-consciousness, incapable of action and enjoyment, though retaining their names and, so far, their identity (ἀμενηνὰ κάρηνα), they could never have called them the blest.

It might seem indeed from a passage in the Odyssey, beautifully, but yet not quite accurately, rendered by Mr. Gladstone, as if Homer had sometimes admitted in his heroes and heroines in Hades a continuance of their human feelings of love.   He translates the words of Penelope (Od. xx. 79):

> 'Would fair-haired Artemis had stayed my breath,
>   So might I pass below the hated earth,
> Yearn for Odysseus, even there in death,
>   Nor live to cheer a soul of meaner worth.'

But the true meaning is, not that she might yearn for Odysseus there, below the hated earth, but that looking, yearning for Odysseus, she might pass below the hated earth.   This may seem a small difference, but it involves important issues.

In spite of the popularity of the Homeric poems, I doubt whether the Greeks really believed that their favourite hero, Achilles, was such as Homer describes him, mourning his dreary fate in the realm of Hades. Their thoughts are more truly reflected, I believe, in the popular verses on Harmodius and Aristogiton, where we read :

> 'Dearest Harmodius, thou art surely not dead,
>   Thou dwellest, they say, in the isles of the blest,
> Where the swift-footed Achilles,
>   Where the son of Tydeus, the brave Diomedes, dwells.'

Here we see a very different Achilles from that of Homer, dwelling in the isles of the blest with Diomedes, the bravest of the brave, and with Harmodius and Aristogiton, who delivered Greece from her tyrants.

Small as Greece seems to us, it was always full of

life, full of individuality, full of variety. As a rule,
we may say, no doubt, that all the Greeks looked at
death as the greatest of misfortunes. Yet no one
was so ready as the Greek to give up his life for his
country, and to prefer death with honour to life with
dishonour. Some of the Greeks also had soon discovered the sorrow that is inseparable from life.
With all their enjoyment of life, even the Greeks
called mortal men δειλοί, wretched. Homer also calls
them frequently δειλοὶ βροτοί, miserable mortals!
And when we go a little further we find a poet like
Theognis in the sixth century proclaiming his conviction that it is 'best for man not to be born and to see
the rays of the burning sun, and, if born, then as soon
as possible to pass through the gates of Hades, and to
lie down, having heaped up much earth as his grave.'

> Πάντων μὲν μὴ φῦναι ἐπιχθονίοισιν ἄριστον
> Μηδ' ἐσιδεῖν αὐγὰς ὀξέος ἠελίου,
> Φύντα δ' ὅπως ὥκιστα πύλας Ἀίδαο περῆσαι
> Καὶ κεῖσθαι πολλὴν γῆν ἐπαμησάμενον.

Punishments.

And while Homer knows nothing of the blessedness
of the departed, he seems likewise ignorant of any
punishments inflicted on the dead for crimes committed in this life. This has often been denied, and the
sufferings of Sisyphos, Tantalos, and Tityos have been
quoted as instances of such punishments. But in all
these cases the sufferers are not ordinary mortals, nor
the crimes ordinary crimes. They are all crimes
committed against the gods, they belong to mythology
and not to ordinary life. Goethe [1] has called attention

---

[1] *Polygnots Gemälde in der Lesche zu Delphi.*

to the fact that the punishments are all of the same
peculiar character. 'The always returning stone of
Sisyphos,' he writes, 'the flying fruits of Tantalos, the
carrying water in broken vessels, all point to objects
not attained. Here there is no retribution corresponding to the crime, or any specific punishment.
No, the unhappy sufferers are all visited by the most
terrible of human fates, namely, to see the object of
serious and persevering endeavour frustrated.'

Post-Homeric Poets.

As soon, however, as we open the pages of post-
Homeric poets, whether of Pindar, or Aeschylus, or
Sophocles, all is changed. A belief in a continuance
of life after death, in rewards and punishments in
another life, meets us again and again. Even the idea
that the Departed receive their relatives and friends
when they come to die, is not unknown to Pindar.
We hear of sacrifices for the dead. Their spirits are
supposed to be capable of bringing blessings or misfortunes on those who survive them. Hence they
must be pleased and appeased by offerings which are
supposed to belong to the dead, and are not therefore
partaken of by the living, as in the case of festival
sacrifices offered to the gods. Pindar expresses even
a belief in a kind of transmigration of souls, though
always in human bodies. He describes the happy
life of the just after death, but he also paints the
sufferings of evil-doers in thrilling words, and he adds
that those who thrice were able to keep the soul far
from evil, will reach the isles of the blessed.

Aeschylus constantly appeals to the retribution in
Hades, for 'there also,' he says, 'another Zeus among

the departed gives the last judgment on crimes, as we are told[1].'

Plato.

Plato follows in the same strain. He even quotes Pindar in the Meno (81, 6), where he says: 'I have heard from certain wise men and women who spoke of things divine. . . . Some of them were priests and priestesses, who had studied how they might be able to give a reason of their profession. There have been poets also, such as the poet Pindar and other inspired men. And they say that the soul of man is immortal, and at one time has an end, which is termed dying, and at another time is born again, but is never destroyed. And the moral is, that a man ought to live always in perfect holiness; for in the ninth year Persephone sends the souls of those from whom she has received the penalty of ancient crime, back again into the light of this world, and these are they who become noble kings and mighty men, and great in wisdom, and are called saintly (ἀγνοί) heroes in after ages. The soul, then, as being immortal, and having been born again many times, and having seen all things that there are, whether in this world or in the world below, has knowledge of them all; and it is no wonder that she should be able to call to remembrance all that she ever knew about virtue, and about everything.' Here we see again a belief in something like metempsychosis.

Plato becomes even superstitious, when in the Phaedo (113) he describes the different rivers of the

---

[1] Supplices, 230, Κἀκεῖ δικάζει τἀμπλακήμαθ', ὡς λόγος, Ζεὺς ἄλλος ἐν καμοῦσιν ὑστάτας δίκας.

lower world, the Acheron, the Pyriphlegethon, and the Stygian river, and the sufferings which are inflicted on different classes of evil-doers. But even when he drops all mythological language, his belief remains that ' there is a world below in which either we or our posterity will suffer for our unjust deeds ' (Rep. 366),while his belief in a blessed life is eloquently expressed in the Phaedo (114) : ' Those who have been pre-eminent for holiness of life are released from this earthly prison, and go to their pure home which is above, and dwell in the purer earth; and those who have duly purified themselves with philosophy, live henceforth altogether without the body, in mansions fairer far than these, which may not be described, and of which the time would fail me to tell.'

The Mysteries.

There can be little doubt that in the so-called Mysteries also the fate of the soul in a future life formed the principal subject. Much has been written about these Mysteries. The most learned work on the subject is still Lobeck's *Aglaophamus*, published in 1829. For our own purposes it suffices to quote here the words of Cicero (Legg. ii. 14): 'Thy Athens,' he says, addressing Atticus, ' seems to have produced many other excellent and divine things, but nothing more excellent, and nothing better than those mysteries by which from a wild and savage life we have been tamed and raised to a higher humanity. They are truly called *initia*, for it is through them that we have learnt to know the beginnings of life. And we have received from them not only good reason why we should live with joy, but also why we should die with a better hope.'

The purely mythological conception of the punishments of the wicked in Hades becomes richer in horrible detail with every generation. That given by Plutarch can hardly be excelled by mediaeval moralists. 'There are three lakes there side by side,' he writes, 'one of boiling gold, the other extremely cold of lead, and the third of raw iron. Certain demons are standing by, like smiths, who with their instruments dip the wicked souls of the greedy and selfish alternately into these lakes.'

Plato's Influence.

There were, no doubt, in Greece, as elsewhere, philosophers who protested against the popular belief in these infernal regions, nay who openly denied the existence of souls after death. They either professed ignorance of anything that did not rest on the evidence of the senses, or they declared their belief that life after death was an impossibility. But the general convictions of the Greeks were not much influenced by these philosophic schools. It is true that even Sokrates and Plato often spoke hesitatingly, modestly, conditionally, when they touched on the topic of a future life. Plato, whose whole philosophy rests on a belief in the divine nature of the human soul, preserves nevertheless that intellectual reserve which is peculiar to the Greek mind, when he introduces Sokrates in the Apology as saying: 'If death is like sleep, even then I say that to die is gain: for eternity is then only a single night. But *if* death is the journey to another place, and there, *as men say* (εἰ ἀληθῆ ἐστι τὰ λεγόμενα), all the dead are, what good, O my friends and judges, can be greater than this? If, indeed, when the pilgrim arrives in the world below, he is delivered from the professors of justice in this world, and finds the true judges who are said to give judgment there, Minos and Rhadamanthus and Aeacus and Triptolemus, and other half-gods (ἡμίθεοι) who were righteous in their own life, that pilgrimage will be worth making. What would not a man give if he might converse with Orpheus and Musaeus and Hesiod and Homer? Nay, if this be true, let me die again and again. Above all, I shall then be able to continue my search into true and false knowledge; as in this world, so also in that; and I shall find out who is wise, and who pretends to be wise, and is not. . . . Besides being happier in that world than in this, they will be immortal, *if what is said is true* (εἴπερ γε τὰ λεγόμενα ἀληθῆ ἐστιν).'

In the imaginary funeral oration, however, which Sokrates delivers in the Menexenus[1], and which he professes to have learnt from Aspasia, he speaks very positively of the welcome which the departed ancestors will give to their descendants when the hour of their destiny has come (247). But immediately after he speaks conditionally, and says: ' But, if the dead have any knowledge of the living, they will displease us most by making themselves miserable and by taking their misfortunes to heart, and they will please us best, if they bear their loss lightly and temperately.'

It is well known that Thucydides in his Funeral Oration is altogether silent on the existence of the

[1] The Menexenus is a spurious dialogue, but is included in the Alexandrine catalogue of Plato's works.

soul after death, while others, such as Demosthenes (De Falsa Leg. 66), speak conditionally, like Plato, ' If the departed see us, if they know what we are doing, they will rejoice.'

Xenophon's Cyropaedia.

Another pupil of Sokrates, Xenophon, speaks in a similar strain when he introduces the dying Cyrus taking leave of his children : ' By the paternal gods, my sons,' he says, ' respect one another, if you care to please me. For you surely do not imagine that you know clearly that I shall be nothing, when I have finished with my human life. For even now you never saw my soul, but you knew its existence from what it did. And have you not seen, what terrors the souls of those who have suffered injustice bring upon the criminals ; what avenging spirits they send to the evil-doers? And do you believe that the honours paid to the dead would continue, if their souls had no longer any power? I, indeed, O sons, have never believed that the soul, while it is in a mortal body, lives, and is dead when it is free from it : for I see that even these mortal bodies live only so long as the soul is in them. Nor can I believe that the soul will be without reason ($\check{\alpha}\phi\rho\omega\nu$), after it has been separated from this unreasoning body ; but when the mind has been separated, unmixed and pure from the body, then it is likely that it will be most rational. When man is dissolved, it is clear that everything has gone to what is homogeneous, except the soul, which alone, whether present or absent, is never seen. Consider also that nothing is nearer to human death than sleep, and that the soul of man seems then most divine, and sees then something of the future, because it is then most free. If then these things are as I believe, and the soul leaves the body, do what I ask from reverence for my soul. But if it is not so, and if the soul remains in the body and dies, even then do not do or think anything impious or unholy for fear of the eternal, the omniscient, the omnipotent gods, who hold together this order of all things, flawless, unfading, unfailing, and inconceivable by its greatness and by its beauty.'

Influence of Philosophers.

These may be called purely philosophical speculations, confined to the schools, and not representative of public opinion in Greece. This is true, to a certain extent. No nation consists of philosophers only, but no nation escapes their influence. How few people read Kant, and yet such words as *Das Ding an sich*, the categories of the understanding, the categorical imperative, have become current coin in Germany, and not in Germany only. In Germany.Goethe's novel, *Werthers Leiden*, produced such an effect that the number of suicides from an unhappy love became alarming. In Greece we are told that Plato's Phaedo produced a similar effect. We read in Kallimachos (Epigram 25): 'With the words, Helios, farewell! Kleombrotos, the Ambrakiote, sprang from a high wall into death, without having suffered anything worthy of death ; he had only read one book, Plato's book on the soul [1].'

---

[1] Cic. Tusc. Quaest. i. 34 : 'A malis igitur mors abducit, non a bonis, verum si quaerimus. Hoc quidem a Cyrenaico Hegesia sic copiose disputatur, ut is a rege Ptolemaeo prohibitus esse dicatur illa in scholis dicere, quod multi, his auditis, mortem sibi ipsi con sciscerent. Callemachi quidem epigramma in Ambraciotam Cleombrotum est : quem ait, quum nihil ei accidisset adversi, e muro se in mare abiecisse, lecto Platonis libro.'

Funeral Inscriptions.

But though the popular mind is certainly enlightened and guided by those who were rightly
called men of light and leading, we must carefully
distinguish between the form which their teaching assumes in the language of the people, and the full and
accurate expression which they give to it themselves.

During historical times, if we may judge from
poetry, laws, customs, inscriptions, and all the rest,
the Greeks did not commit themselves to a belief in
a Homeric Hades, in a Tartaros, or in Elysian fields.
All this belonged to mythology and to the past.
What they really cared for, and what they expressed
when it was necessary to speak of the departed, was
that, though the body was burnt or buried, their soul
was not destroyed. On the monument of those who
had fallen in 431 B.C., in the battle of Potidaea, the
following inscription was engraved :

> Αἰθὴρ μὲν ψυχὰς ὑπεδέξατο, σώ[ματα δὲ χθῶν]
> τῶν δὲ, Ποτιδαίας δ' ἀμφὶ πύλας ἔδ[αμεν].

'The aether has received the souls, but the earth the bodies of
these men. They fell round the gates of Potidaea[1].'

The same sentiment is expressed again and again
with slight variations.

Thus a saying is ascribed to Epicharmos (Plat.
cons. Apoll. p. 110):

> συνεκρίθη καὶ διεκρίθη κἀπῆνθεν
> ὅθεν ἦνθεν πάλιν, γᾶ μὲν εἰς
> γᾶν, πνεῦμ' ἄνω· τί τῶνδε
> χαλεπόν ; οὐδὲ ἕν.

'It was mixed together and was separated, it went again from
whence it came, earth to earth, the spirit upwards. What is difficult
here ? Nothing.'

[1] Lehrs, *Aufsätze*, p. 341, conjectures σώματα τύμβος, and again,
σώματα δ' ἐσθλῶν τῶν δὲ Ποτιδαίας ἀμφὶ πύλας ἔδαμεν, or ἐδάμη.

Euripides, in the Supplices, 531, says :

> Ἐάσατ' ἤδη γῇ καλυφθῆναι νεκρούς,
> ὅθεν δ' ἕκαστον ἐς τὸ σῶμ' ἀφίκετο,
> ἐνταῦθ' ἀπελθεῖν, πνεῦμα μὲν πρὸς αἰθέρα,
> τὸ σῶμα δ' ἐς γῆν.

'Let now the dead bodies be covered by the earth, and each go away whence it came into the body ; the breath to the aether, the body into the earth.'

The collection of Greek inscriptions contains many lines inscribed on funeral monuments, all breathing the same spirit [1].

'The Moira seized him,' we read, 'who had been kind-hearted to his fellows, gentle to the good, an enemy to the wicked ; she gives the body here beneath the earth, the soul high above to heaven.'

A daughter who has been killed by lightning says to her mother :

'Mother, leave thy grief, remembering the soul which Zeus has rendered immortal and undecaying to me for all time, and has carried now into the starry sky.'

On a tomb of a drowned sailor we read :

'Breakers have broken bones and flesh, but the soul inhabits the aethereal roof' (αἰθέριον πόλον).

And again :

'My name is Menelas, but what lies here is my body, the soul dwells in the aether of the immortals.'

Again :

'Even if thou hurriest by, stop a moment, dear traveller ! The fate of death seized me, and the

---

[1] Many of these inscriptions, as here translated, have been collected by Lehrs, l. c., p. 342.

earth covers my body, taking back the gift which she had once bestowed. But my soul went to the aether and to the halls of Zeus; the unchanging law took my bones only into Hades.'

Sometimes we read that the soul 'is at home with the stars, and dwells in the sacred place of the Blest.' Sometimes, that the dead dwells in the place of life, by the side of the gods. A philosopher declares from his grave, 'I inhabit the sacred abode of the heroes, not that of Acheron; for such a goal of life is granted to the wise.'

I insert one more epitaph, taken from the Greek Anthology, of which it has truly been said that it is, as it were, a missing link between Paganism and Catholicism, and that its creed is Christianity without Christ.

Οὐκ ἔθανες, Πρώτη, μετέβης δ' ἐς ἀμείνονα χῶρον,
Καὶ ναίεις μακάρων νήσους θαλίῃ ἐνὶ πολλῇ·
Ἔνθα κατ' Ἠλυσίων πεδίων σκιρτῶσα γέγηθας
Ἄνθεσιν ἐν μαλακοῖσι κακῶν ἔκτοσθεν ἁπάντων.
Οὐ χειμὼν λυπεῖ σ' οὐ καῦμ' οὐ νοῦσος ἐνοχλεῖ,
Οὐ πεινῇς, οὐ δίψος ἔχει σ' ἀλλ'· οὐδὲ ποθεινὸς
Ἀνθρώπων ἔτι σοι βίοτος· ζώεις γὰρ ἀμέμπτως
Αὐγαῖς ἐν καθαραῖσιν Ὀλύμπου πλησίον ὄντος.

'Dying, thou art not dead !—thou art gone to a happier country,
And in the isles of the blest thou rejoicest in weal and abundance,
There, Proté, is thy home in the peace of Elysian meadows,
Meadows with asphodel strewn, and peace unblighted with sorrow.
Winter molests thee no longer, nor heat nor disease; and thou shalt not
Hunger or thirst any more; but, unholpen of man and unheedful,
Spotless and fearless of sin, thou exultest in view of Olympus;
Yea, and thy gods are thy light, and their glory is ever upon thee.'

(Translated by Hon. Lionel A. Tollemache,
Stones of Stumbling, p. 64.)

The Divinity of the Soul.

But while these expressions of faith and hope satisfied the great mass of mourners in Greece, while to them the departed were simply the Blest (μάκαρες, also μακαρίται, and ἥρωες), dwelling on high with the Blest or with the gods, a more philosophical, or, I should say, a more Platonic view of the soul manifests itself likewise in many places.

Plato's thoughts about the soul were not concerned only with its fate *after* death, he looked upon the soul as eternal, as pre-existent, as imprisoned in the body, and as really delivered from her prison by death. He himself does not call the soul a god, but he never doubts her divine nature. His followers, however, speak more boldly, perhaps more mythologically, and call the soul of man a god.

Cicero, who became the most active interpreter of Plato at Rome, speaks likewise of the soul as divine, because, as he adds, 'I do not dare, like Euripides, to call it a god[1].'

It is difficult to say what real difference there is between these two expressions. Can anything be divine, and yet not participate in the nature of a god? It is language that confuses us, and leads us to imagine that there is a difference, and that there can be different kinds of divinity, one belonging to the gods, the other to men. But if there is a divine substance, it can be but · one and the same, and differences can be differences of manifestation only.

---

[1] Cic. Tusc. Quaest. i. 26 : 'Ergo animus, ut ego dico, divinus est ; ut Euripides audet dicere, deus : et quidem, si deus aut anima aut ignis est, idem est animus hominis.'

Cicero himself seems to have felt this, and he speaks quite as boldly as Euripides when he relates the 'Dream of Scipio[1].'

Somnium Scipionis.

'Strive for that,' he says, 'and know that not thou art mortal, but this thy body. For thou art not what this bodily form shows, but the soul (*mens*) is what everybody really is, and not the figure which can be shown with the finger. Know therefore that thou art a god, for it is God who lives, perceives, remembers, judges, and who governs, leads, and moves this body over which he is placed, as the principal God governs, leads, and rules this world. As God himself moves this world which is partially mortal, thus the eternal mind (*animus*) moves this frail body. . . .

'As it is clear that that is eternal which is moved by itself, who would deny that this nature belongs to the mind (*animi*)? For mindless (*inanimum*) is everything which is moved by an external impulse, but what is living (animal) that is impelled by an inner movement which is its own, and this is the proper

---

[1] De Re Publ. vi. 24 : 'Tu vero enitere et sic habeto, non esse te mortalem, sed corpus hoc : nec enim tu es, quem forma ista declarat ; sed mens cuiusque is est quisque, non ea figura, quae digito demonstrari potest. Deum te igitur scito esse : si quidem deus est, qui viget, qui sentit, qui meminit, qui providet, qui tam regit et moderatur et movet id corpus, cui praepositus est, quam hunc mundum ille princeps deus : et ut mundum ex quadam parte mortalem ipse deus aeternus, sic fragile corpus animus sempiternus movet. . . .

'Quum pateat igitur aeternum id esse, quod a se ipso moveatur ; quis est, qui hanc naturam animis esse tributam neget ? Inanimum est enim omne, quod pulsu agitatur externo : quod autem animal est, id motu cietur interiore et suo ; nam haec est natura propria animi atque vis. Quae si est una ex omnibus, quae sese moveat, neque nata est certe et aeterna est.'

nature and power of the mind (*animus*). If then the soul alone of all things is moved by itself, it is certainly not born, and it is eternal.'

These are the words of Cicero, but the spirit, as you perceive, is the spirit of Plato—and, will not many of us add, the spirit of truth?

LECTURE XII.

WHAT DOES IT LEAD TO ?

A T the end of my Lectures on Physical Religion I felt it necessary to answer the question, What does it all lead to ? The same question presents itself at the end of these Lectures on Anthropological Religion ; and I shall try to answer it once more.

The Historical Proof.

You may remember how it was said that the fact that all human beings believed in gods and God was no proof whatever of the truth of that belief, and of the real existence of divine beings, or of *one* Infinite Being. I tried to show, on the contrary, that what I call the historical proof was really, if not the only, at least the strongest argument for the belief in the existence of God.

Leave man alone, I said, and he will believe in something beyond this world. This has been proved to be a fact by the modern study of the history of all religions. There are no exceptions anywhere, except those which arise from mental idiocy and moral degradation. But as little as we take into account the large number of inmates of lunatic asylums when we maintain that two and two make four, should we be obliged to consider the case of some degraded tribes, supposing they existed, who are said to be without a name for gods or God, and whose only sign of humanity is their language, a remnant and, at the same time, a witness of their former higher state.

History, no doubt, teaches us that much of what people in different stages of their historical progress believed to be true about the gods was not true, was, as they found out themselves, unworthy of the gods. That is perfectly true, but it only serves to confirm the lesson of all history, that truth is never the result of a sudden communication, but the reward of patient labour and honest search. The fact remains, that men, as Homer expresses it, Il. iii. 44, yearn for the gods. The metaphorical expression which Homer uses is full of meaning. As birds open their beaks to be fed, because they are hungry, men open, χατέουσι, their hearts and minds, because they are hungry, because they hunger and thirst after God, because they want to be fed. It is this hunger, this weakness, if you like, this incompleteness of human nature, attested by universal history, which is the best proof, nay more than a proof, which is the very fact of the existence of something beyond all finite knowledge, call it by any name you like in all the numberless languages and dialects and jargons of the world. Those who maintain that this is a delusion, must admit at all events that it is a universal delusion, and a really universal delusion must be accepted as true, in the only sense in which anything can be true to human beings such as we are. We may readily admit that our senses are imperfect; but for all that, all our knowledge must begin with the senses. We know that our senses have often deceived us; but for all that, we also know that our senses themselves have helped us to discover and correct their errors. What is quoted as one of the most glaring instances of universal delusion, the belief in the central position of the earth and the movement of the sun round the earth, was after all an imperfect expression only of the facts before us. In the same sense many of the ancient religions, many of our modern theologies also, may be called imperfect, and yet by no means utterly false. As the sun rises and sets and gives us light and warmth, whether we call it by central or eccentric names, the light of the world, the Infinite behind all finite phenomena, remains. Our vision may be clouded by human ignorance, nay the light that shines upon us may be so bright and fierce that, unless veiled in passing clouds, it would burn and blind the human eye. Yet the light is there; we feel and know it. Clouds, dark or radiant, may come and go, but the light, reflected in ever so many marvellous shapes, is, and remains our light.

The Two Lessons of History.

History teaches us two lessons. The Jews represent their God as jealous of all false or imperfect gods. This is the first lesson: Man ought to be jealous of all untruth in whatever form it meets him. The Hindus, on the other hand, represent their Supreme Being as saying, 'Even those who worship idols, worship me.' This is the second lesson, that we ought to be tolerant, and try to discover some grains of truth in all untruth, some honest endeavour in all failures; nay, what has been called a hidden and divine education of man in the whole history of the world.

If we confine our study of history, and especially of the history of religion, to one sacred book only, say the Old Testament, we can never learn from that single book, that a belief in God is universal, and that it becomes more and more pure and perfect, not by casual revelation, but by slow and irresistible evolution. Here is a lesson which nothing but a comprehensive study of the sacred books of the world, an exploration of all the religions of mankind, can possibly teach us. And yet that lesson seems to me the only safe and sound foundation of a belief in God. That belief may be very indefinite—and how can human belief in the Infinite ever be anything but indefinite? And yet, what can be more convincing than that simple argument, if it is not an intuition rather than an argument, which underlies all religions from beginning to end, and in every part of the world, viz. that where there is an act there must be an agent, where there is something finite, there must be something beyond the finite, by whatever name we like to call it. This then is the historical proof of the existence of God; this was the outcome of our Lectures on Physical Religion.

Recapitulation of Anthropological Religion.

If now we apply exactly the same reasoning to the facts placed before us by a study of what I call Anthropological Religion; if we ask once more, What does it all lead to? my answer is the same.

Man, if left to himself, has everywhere arrived at the conviction that there is something in man or of man besides the material body. This was a lesson taught, as we saw, not so much by life as by death. Besides the body, besides the heart, besides the blood, there was the breath. Man was struck by that, and when the breath had left the body, he simply stated the fact, that the breath or the *psyché* had departed. The speculations on the true nature of that psyché within, belong to the domain of Psychological Religion, which will form the subject of my next course of Lectures.

A mere study of language sufficed to show us how general, nay how universal, is the belief in something beside the body, in some agent within, or in what in Sanskrit is called by a very general name, the anta*h*kara*n*a, the agency within. Every kind of internal agency was ascribed to that something, which showed itself not only as simply breathing and living, but as feeling and perceiving, soon also as naming, conceiving, and reasoning.

In these Lectures on Anthropological Religion we have had chiefly to deal with the speculations which arose from that psyché as no longer *within,* but as after death *without* the body. Here also language began with the name of breath. The breath had gone, the psyché had departed. That psyché, however, was soon conceived, not as mere breath or air, but as retaining most of those activities which had been ascribed to it during life, such as feeling, perceiving, naming, conceiving, and reasoning.

So far I do not see what can be brought forward against this primitive and universal form of belief.

(3)   Z

If there was a something in man that could receive, perceive, and conceive, that something, whatever name we call it, was gone with death. But no one could think that it had been annihilated—*nusquam nihil ex aliquo.* So long, therefore, as the ancient philosophers said no more than that this something, called breath or psyché, had left the body and had gone somewhere else, I do not see what counter-argument could be advanced against them.

Even during life, the body alone, though it could live by itself, could not be said to see or hear or perceive by itself. The eye by itself does not see, it requires something else to receive and to perceive, and that something, though itself invisible, was as real as the invisible Infinite and the Divine behind the agents in nature, whom the ancient nations called their gods. It became in turn the soul, the mind, the agent, the subject, till at last it was recognised as the Infinite and the Divine in man [1].

The ancients knew all this as well as we do, nay, they saw it and pronounced it more clearly than we do. Thus Epicharmos said without hesitation:

Νόος ὁρῇ καὶ νόος ἀκούει· τἄλλα κωφὰ καὶ τυφλά.

'The mind sees, and the mind hears, all the rest is deaf and blind,'

—all the rest, including the body with eyes and ears and other organs of sense.

So long again as these psychés or souls were spoken of in the plural and were supposed after death to be somewhere, the argument would still remain unassailable. Remember, we are dealing here, not with schooled metaphysicians, but with the so-called

[1] Plut. de fort. 3, p. 98 ; see also Lucret. 3, 36 ; Cic. Tusc. i. 20 ; Hatch, *Hibbert Lectures,* p. 173.

sons of nature, though before these universal problems of the world, even the best-schooled metaphysicians are not much wiser than these so-called sons of nature. If the ancient nations had been satisfied with this simple faith that the psychés or souls of their departed friends continued to exist somewhere, there could have been no opposition of any kind to this as an article of the universal faith of mankind. It might have been called a self-evident proposition.

But man, as we say, does not only reason. He has also a heart, and that heart will believe many things that cannot be proved, if only they cannot be disproved.

First of all came the question, *where* do the souls of the departed exist? All the answers returned are equally natural, all are equally unobjectionable, but likewise equally not proven, because they are beyond the reach of proof. The best answer was perhaps that contained in the most ancient Greek language and mythology, that the souls had gone to the house of the Invisible, of *Aides*. No one has ever said anything truer. That house of the Invisible was placed, as we saw, either beneath the earth, or beyond the earth in the west, in the land of the setting sun; while others who looked upon heaven as the abode of the gods, placed the souls of the departed also in the same abode.

With regard to these fond hopes and imaginations, all we can say is that they may be true, that they may all be fulfilled, but that we are no better off than the Vedic poets or the lowest of savages for pronouncing a definite opinion.

Next came the question, *how* the souls fare after

Z 2

death.   We are inclined to smile at the idea that the
next life will be much the same as this, that there will
be hunting-fields, battle-fields, music, poetry, sweet
discourse with our friends, meditation, and adoration.
And yet there is again nothing utterly unreasonable
in all this.   It is a deduction, it is true, based on *one*
precedent only, namely, on the precedent of this
present life.   But as there can be no other precedent,
the belief so widely entertained that the next life will
be much like this, seems in reality the most reasonable conclusion at which man, whether in his childhood or in his old age, could have arrived.

This conclusion was strengthened by two influences,
one purely imaginative, the other, however, by no
means unreasonable.

It has generally been supposed that bows and
arrows, pots and pans, playthings and medicine
bottles, at last, even wives and servants, were burnt
or buried with the dead, because people believed that
the next would be some kind of continuation of the
present life.   I tried to show, on the contrary, that
what is here represented as the cause, may far more
likely have been the effect, that many things were
placed on the funeral pile, or in or on the grave, from
a mere desire to give up something to those whom one
had loved and served during life.   When afterwards
a reason was asked to account for what was originally
a mere impulse, an unreasoning act, a belief was
expressed and very soon defended against all gain-
sayers, that all these things, down to the dolls and
medicine bottles of children, were not merely thrown
away, but would for ever prove useful in another life.

And when these offerings to the dead took in time

a more settled form, and became part of the religious ceremonial among many nations, both civilised and uncivilised, the idea that the dead were cognisant of the honours paid to them, and could enjoy the gifts offered to them, grew stronger and stronger[1]. Soon also the thought arose that the dead resented the neglect of what was due to them, that they would find no rest till they had received their funeral honours, and that they would haunt the abodes of their relations and bring misfortune on their families. till their just demands had been fulfilled.

By this process of reasoning, if reasoning it may be called, the question how the souls of the departed existed in their new abodes, answered itself. They were of necessity supposed to be capable of knowing what passed in this life, of enjoying offerings, of appreciating praise, of rewarding those who cared for them, and punishing those who neglected them. Thus, without actually ascribing to them a body like the body that had been burnt or buried, they were supposed to be conscious, to retain their names, and to have what we call the faculties of feeling, perceiving, conceiving, and reasoning. We then saw how an even more powerful impulse sprang from the belief in a moral government of the universe, by whatever name it might be called. The mere conviction that no deed can die, that there must be an effect to every cause, would irresistibly lead to the conclusion that crimes, unpunished in this, will be punished in the next life, and that the good deeds unrewarded here, will receive their reward there. This idea soon received an enormous development. It led to the

---

[1] Xenophon, Cyrop. 8, 7, 18.

invention of sunny isles in the west, of a paradise in
the east, and of glorious abodes in heaven. It also
inspired both ancient and modern poets in their descriptions of the terrors of the lower world, the fire of
hell, and the tortures of the *Inferno*.

We can distinguish three stages in the growth of
this belief. With some people, as with the Jews, and
with some of the Greeks, life after death was hardly
more than mere existence, without joy, but likewise
without suffering, without rewards, and without
punishments. It was a sleep with their fathers.

With others, as the Vedic Indians, for instance, life
after death was conceived chiefly as a happy life, a
state of enjoyment in company with the gods.

Then, by the side of those who reaped the reward
of their virtues in heaven, was imagined another place
for the punishment of the wicked. This took place at
a later time both in India and in Greece.

And lastly, a more philosophical theory prevailed,
that by a succession of new births the soul would
assume new bodies, having thus an opportunity given
it for rising to higher and higher perfection, and
reaching in the end the supreme goal, nearness to,
nay, likeness, or even oneness or atone-ness, with
God.

In all these thoughts which we find not only in
India, Greece, and Italy, but scattered all over the
world, wherever human beings have been living
together, we can distinguish between what is true,
true for us to-day as it was for the earliest thinkers
and speakers on earth, and what is merely imagination, often quite harmless, but having no claim to be
called either true or untrue.

What is true to us, as it was to our earliest ancestors, is that the soul does not die.   In many languages
even the expression, 'He is dead,' is avoided, partly, it
may be, because it is an inauspicious expression, but
partly also because it is felt to contain an untruth.   I
am told that in some parts of Scotland also, you will
never hear that a person has died.   You are told that
he has been taken away.   Mr. Macdonald, a missionary,
remarked the same among the Zulus in Africa.   They
never say, 'He is dead,' they say, 'He is not here,'
and they speak of the departed spirits as 'ascending
to heaven,' or as 'gone home[1].'

It seems to me that they are right in this, at least
to a certain point.   To die applies to the body ; it has
really no sense as applied to the soul, if only we distinguish rightly between what we mean by body and
what we mean by soul.   The soul is neither born, as
the body is born, nor does it live, as the body lives ; nor
can it die, therefore, as the body dies.   We do not say
that the soul is blind, because the eyes of the body have
been injured, or that it is deaf, because the tympanum
has been pierced, or even that the soul is mad, because
the central organ, whether we call it heart or brain, has
been injured.   The soul is the witness only, it may be
the compassionate witness, of all that passes in the
body.   It perceives what it perceives without eyes
and without ears, and even madness is only like a
darkening of the light, like a deep sleep that falls on
the body and cannot be shaken off.

And what applies to the soul within, applies also to
the souls without, I mean, to the souls, after the decay

[1] Macdonald, *Journal of the Anthropological Institute*, Nov. 1890, p.
121.

and death of the body.   It is because the ancient, and
many of the modern philosophers also, cannot distinguish between what is body and what is soul,
because, in fact, they do not believe in a soul, but
only talk about it, that they become involved in
endless contradictions in their utterances about the
souls of the departed.   In our longings for the departed
we often think of them as young or old, we think of
them as man or woman, as father or mother, as husband
or wife.   Even nationality and language are supposed
to remain after death, and we often hear expressions,
'Oh, if the souls are without all this, without age,
without sex, without national character, without even
their native language, what will they be to us?'

The answer is, they will really be the same to us as
they were in this life.   Unless we can bring ourselves
to believe that a soul has a beginning, and that our
soul sprang into being at the time of our birth, the
soul within us must have existed before.

> 'Our birth is but a sleep and a forgetting,
>   The soul that rises with us, our life's star,
> Has had elsewhere its setting,
>   And cometh from afar.'

But however convinced we may be of the soul's
eternal existence, we shall always remain ignorant as
to how it existed.   And yet we do not murmur or
complain.   Our soul on awakening here is not quite a
stranger to itself, and the souls who as our parents,
our wives, and husbands, our children, and our friends,
have greeted us at first as strangers in this life, but
have become to us as if we had known them for ever,
and as if we could never lose them again.   If it were
to be so again in the next life, if there also we should
meet at first as strangers till drawn together by the

same mysterious love that has drawn us together here, why should we murmur or complain? Thousands of years ago we read of a husband telling his wife, 'Verily a wife is not dear, that you may love the wife, but that you may love the soul, therefore a wife is dear.' What does that mean? It means that true love consists not in loving what is perishable, but in discovering and loving what is eternal in man or woman. In Sanskrit that eternal part is called by many names; the best seems that which is used in this very passage, Âtmâ. We translate it by soul, but it is even higher and purer than soul, and it is perhaps best translated by the word *Self*. That which constitutes the true Self, the looker on, the witness within us, that which is everywhere in the body and yet nowhere to be touched, that which cannot die or expire, because it never breathed, that is the Infinite in man which philosophers have been groping for, though 'he is not far from every one of us.' It is the Divine or God-like in man.

Ka*tha*-upanishad.

It might seem as if such speculations belonged to modern times only, when there is leisure for the few at least, to think, not of this life only, but also of the next. But that is not the case. The curiosity as to what awaits us in the next life, is very old. We find among the Vedic Upanishads one that is entirely devoted to this subject. It is called the Ka*tha*-upanishad. We may, I believe, safely say that this Upanishad is older than Buddha, and that, for our present purposes, is enough. It is a strange mixture of mythology and philosophy. Some portions of it are probably later additions, and some scholars have attempted, more or less successfully, to separate these more modern from the more ancient parts. I shall only attempt to give you a short abstract, and to select those passages which are universally intelligible, and can appeal to our own sympathies.

The Upanishad consists chiefly of a dialogue between Yama, the ruler of the dead, who has become identified with Mrityu or death, and a young Brâhmanic student, of the name of Nakiketas.

We are told in the beginning that the father of this young Brâhman performed a sacrifice in which he professed to give away everything he possessed. The son is represented as taunting his father that, after all, he had not given away everything, because he did not give away his own son. The father becomes angry at last, and exclaims:

'Well, I shall give thee unto Death.'

The son at once accepts his fate, and says:

'Look back, how it was with those who came before, look forward how it will be with those who come after. A mortal ripens like corn, like corn he springs up again.'

It so happens that when the young Brâhman enters the abode of Death, Yama, the lord of the departed, is absent. For three nights no hospitality is shown to Nakiketas, and this was looked upon as so great an offence that Yama, when he returns, has to offer him three boons to avert his anger. Nakiketas asks as his first boon that his father may not be angry with him when he returns from the mouth of death. This is granted.

He then asks for the knowledge of a sacrifice by which he may attain immortality in heaven, where

there is no death, no old age, no hunger or thirst, and
no sorrow.   This too is granted.

And now it might be supposed that no more could
be asked for.   But Na*k*iketas is not satisfied with the
ordinary immortality in heaven, though it gives everlasting peace and happiness.   He wants to know more
and to have more, and says :

'There is that doubt, when a man is dead, some saying, he is ;
others, he is not. This I should like to know, taught by thee ;
this is the third of my boons.'

Then a fierce struggle begins between the young
Brâhman and Death.   Death offers him anything
rather than to tell him this mystery which, as he says,
even the gods do not know.   He offers him health
and wealth, children and chariots, fair maidens and
music, but all in vain.   Na*k*iketas will have his third
boon, he will know what happens to man after he is
dead, and Yama has at last to yield.

Then follows the answer of Yama or Death :

'Fools,' he says, 'dwelling in darkness, wise in their own con-
ceit, and puffed up with vain knowledge, go round and round,
staggering to and fro, like blind men, led by the blind.'

' The Hereafter never rises before the eyes of the careless child,
deluded by the delusion of wealth. "This is the world," he thinks,
"there is no other ; " and thus he falls again and again under my
sway (the sway of death).'   II. 5 seq.

Then follows the explanation of what constitutes
the true being and the true immortality of man, what
is called Âtmâ in Sanskrit, and is generally translated
by the soul, but which is better rendered by the self,
the self that lies behind the Ego, behind the mere personality of man, and which is really, when fully
known, the same as Brahman, the universal Self.

Yama continues :

'The knowing (Self) is not born, it dies not ; it sprang from nothing, nothing sprang from it. The ancient is unborn, eternal, everlasting, he is never killed, though the body is killed.' II. 18.

'The Self, smaller than small, greater than great, is hidden in the heart of the creature. A man who is free from desires and free from sorrow, sees the majesty of the Self by the grace of the Creator (or, through the tranquillity of the senses).' II. 20.

'That Self cannot be gained by the Veda, nor by understanding, nor by much learning. He whom the Self chooses, by him the Self can be gained. The Self chooses him as his own.' II. 23.

Then follows a parable which reminds one of a well-known passage in Plato's Phaedros :

'Know the Self to be sitting in the chariot, the body to be the chariot, the intellect (buddhi) the charioteer, and the mind the reins.'

'The senses they call the horses, the objects of the senses their roads. When he (the Highest Self) is in union with the body, the senses, and the mind, then wise people call him the Enjoyer.'

'He who has no understanding and whose mind (the reins) is never firmly held, his senses (horses) are unmanageable, like vicious horses of a charioteer.'

'But he who has understanding and whose mind is always firmly held, his senses are under control, like good horses of a charioteer.'

'He who has no understanding, who is unmindful and always impure, never reaches that place, but enters into the round of births.'

'But he who has understanding, who is mindful and always pure, reaches indeed that place, from whence he is not born again.' III. 3-8.

'Rise, awake! having obtained your boons, understand them! The sharp edge of a razor is difficult to pass over ; and thus the wise say that the path (that leads to the Self, or to Self-knowledge) is hard.' III. 14.

'He who has perceived that which is without sound, without touch, without form, without decay, without taste, eternal, without smell, without beginning, without end, beyond the Great, and unchangeable, is freed from the jaws of death.' III. 15.

Here ends the first chapter. Then follows a second which contains a collection of verses, all bearing on our subject, but full of allusions to minute points of Indian philosophy. It would require more time than we can spare to make their real meaning quite clear, and I must be satisfied with quoting a few of the more simple and telling verses :

'No mortal lives by the breath that goes up and by the breath that goes down. We live by another, in whom these two repose.' V. 5.

'He, the Highest Person, who is awake in us while we are asleep, shaping one lovely sight after another, that indeed is the Bright, that is Brahman, that alone is called the Immortal. All words are contained in it, and no one goes beyond. This is that.' V. 8.

'As the one fire, after it has entered the world, though one, becomes different according to whatever it burns, thus the one Self within all things becomes different, according to whatever it enters, and exists also without.' V. 9.

'As the sun, the eye of the whole world, is not contaminated by the external impurities seen by the eyes, thus the one Self within all things is never contaminated by the misery of the world, being himself without.'

'There is one ruler, the Self within all things, who makes the one form manifold. The wise who perceive him within their Self, to them belongs eternal happiness, not to others.'

'There is one eternal thinker, thinking non-eternal thoughts, who, though one, fulfils the desires of many. The wise who perceive him within their Self, to them belongs eternal peace, not to others.' V. 11–13.

'Beyond the senses is the mind, beyond the mind is the highest (created) Being, higher than that Being is the Great Self, higher than the Great, the highest Undeveloped.'

'Beyond the Undeveloped is the Person, the all-pervading and entirely imperceptible. Every creature that knows him is liberated, and obtains immortality.'

'His form is not to be seen, no one beholds him with the eye. He is imagined by the heart, by wisdom, by the mind. Those who know this, are immortal.' VI. 7–9.

'He (the Self) cannot be reached by speech, by mind, or by the eye. How can it be apprehended except by him who says : "He is ?"'

'By the words "He is," is he to be apprehended, and by (admitting) the reality of both (the invisible Brahman and the visible world, as coming from Brahman). When he has been apprehended by the words "He is," then his reality reveals itself.'

'When all desires that dwell in his heart cease, then the mortal becomes immortal, and obtains Brahman.'

'When all the ties of the heart are severed here on earth, then the mortal becomes immortal—here ends the teaching.' VI. 12–15.

We are then told that the young Brâhman, after

having received this instruction, became free and
obtained Brahman, and that everybody who knows
all this about his true Self, will be like him.

I doubt whether any literature, and more particularly any ancient literature, has produced anything to
match this Upanishad.   To those who can enter into
the spirit of its teaching, or, as Yama said, to those
whom the Self has chosen, it is perfectly marvellous.
But even those who shrink from following its doctrine, must admit that the discovery of such a work
among the so-called niggers of India, composed at
a time when neither Roman nor Saxon had as yet
set foot on these isles, is an important discovery,
as important at least as what has been discovered
in the hieroglyphic records of Egypt, and in the
cuneiform inscriptions of Babylon and Nineveh.   We
may not find in the Veda so many names of kings,
so many accounts of battles and conquests, so many
dates carrying us back to three or four thousand years
before our era.   But we find in the Veda, and more
particularly in the Upanishads, what has occupied the
thoughts of man at all times, what occupies them now
and will occupy them for ever—a search after truth,
a desire to discover the Eternal that underlies the
Ephemeral, a longing to find in the human heart the
assurance of a future life, and an attempt to re-unite
the bond which once held the human and the divine
together, the true atone-ment between God and man.
How this old problem was solved in certain religions,
we shall see in our next and last Lecture.

LECTURE XIII.

THE DIVINE AND THE HUMAN.

THE principal object of the study of *Anthropological Religion* in its historical development is to learn how man has been searching for the god-like element in human nature, just as a study of Physical Religion showed him to us as bent on discovering something divine or infinite in that objective nature by which he found himself surrounded. I have tried therefore to place before you the various attempts by which the human mind, whether in India, Greece, and Rome, or in Palestine and Egypt, or even in countries not yet illuminated by the rays of civilisation, arrived at the discovery of something more than human in human nature, of something immortal in mortal man, at a belief in a soul, and in the divine kinship of that soul. It required an effort, perhaps the greatest effort of which human nature is capable, to bring the two concepts of the human and the divine, which for a time seemed diametrically opposed to each other, into one focus again. It is the history of these efforts, and, at the same time, the justification of these efforts, that forms the second great division of

Natural Religion, nay of all religion—for what would religion be without this second article of faith—'I believe in my own soul and its divine sonship.'

Worship of the Departed leads to the Recognition of the Divine in Man.

We saw that one of the most powerful helps to bring the too widely distant concepts of the divine and the human together again, was derived from ancestor-worship. The worship of the spirits of the departed which, under various forms, was so widely spread over the ancient world, could not but accustom the human mind to the idea that there was something in man which deserved such worship. The souls of the departed were lifted higher and higher, till at last they reached the highest stage which existed in the human mind, namely that of divine beings, in the ancient sense of that word. The Romans had their *Divi Manes*, their divine ancestral spirits. In their ancient laws it was laid down that the rights of these gods should be sacred, *Deorum Manium jura sancta sunto;* and that our friends, when dead, should be held as gods. *Sos* (i. e. *suos*) *leto dato divos habento* [1].

In Greece the ancestral spirits of families became θεοὶ πατρῷοι, paternal gods, and the same name was given to the ancestors of a race and the founders of towns.

Among the Vedic Indians the Pit*ri*s or fathers became the companions of the Devas; in later times they are placed even above the Devas [2].

---

[1] Cic. De Leg. 2, 9, 22.
[2] *India, What can it teach us?* p. 372.

In ancient Persia the Fravashis, the Fravashis of the faithful, the awful and overpowering Fravashis, helped Ahura Mazda in all his works.

Apotheosis.

This idea of apotheosis or deification of man, as it meets us in many parts of the world, may seem very strange to us. It would be more than strange, it would be an idea simply impossible, unless there had been preparatory steps leading up to it. It is to all intents and purposes a transition *in alterum genus.* Nay, if there are two *genera,* which seem completely to exclude one another, they are those of gods and men. Gods might well have been defined as beings who, whatever else they may be, are not men ; men as beings who, whatever else they may be, are not gods. Yet from very early times we saw how both Greeks and Romans had accustomed their minds to the idea, that a man may become a god. That gods also may assume the form of men, and even appear to man disguised in human shape, is more intelligible. For after all, the gods, we are told, can do all things. But to conceive that human nature could ever be changed into divine nature, requires an effort that seems at first beyond the powers at all events of those whose idea of deity was represented by beings such as Zeus, Apollo, and Athene.

Let us try whether we may still discover how the Greeks, who must always remain a representative race in the evolution of human thought, were helped over this difficulty, how they came to reconcile their reason, which was always so keen and vigorous, to what must at first have appeared to them a contradic-

A a

tion in terms, an apotheosis of man, or an apanthro-
posis of God. Nowhere else, not even in India, can
we discover the vestiges of this transition more clearly
than in Greece. I propose therefore to examine it
more carefully, so that it may serve as an illustration
of similar processes which have taken place in other
countries also, but have not left us there the same
complete record which we find in the literature of
Greece.

Heroes as Διογενεῖς.

We saw how the Greeks were led to a belief in
Zeus, as the supreme deity of nature. When Zeus
had once been recognised as the father of gods and
men, it was natural and intelligible that the ancient,
powerful kings of Greece should have been called, in
a special sense, the offspring of Zeus. When we find
these kings called Διογενεῖς, this need not at first
have implied much more than what was meant by our
'Kings by the grace of God.'

The transition from this to actual sonship was very
easy. If Aeacus, for instance, was born in Aegina
or of Aegina, and if he was also a βασιλεὺς Διογενής,
a Zeus-born king, it was almost inevitable that in
more or less poetical language Aegina should be
represented as his mother, and Zeus as his father.
And while in this case we see a mortal woman
married to a god, there are other cases where a
goddess is married to a mortal man. Thus Achilles
is represented as the son of the goddess Thetis and
of Peleus.

In all these cases, whenever there was some
Olympian blood in the veins of human heroes, they

were supposed to be half-way between the gods and men, and in many cases they were believed not to die like ordinary mortals, but to live in the Isles of the Blest, in the Elysian Fields, or even with the Olympian gods. Menelaos, though only the son-in-law of Zeus, is told that it is not decreed for him by the gods to die, but that the immortals will send him to the Elysian plain, because he is the son-in-law of Zeus [1].

This apotheosis or deification of heroes, though purely mythological in its origin, may have helped towards the discovery of something divine in man. Only we must always bear in mind that these heroes of the Theban and Trojan wars were exceptional beings. In some cases it is almost certain that they were not real men, but purely mythological creations. If Dionysos, for instance, because he is the son of a mortal woman, is represented to us as a hero, who afterwards became a god, even an Olympian god [2], we must remember that Dionysos was probably an ancient deity, before he was represented as a human hero. He never died. Helena also was certainly a goddess [3], before she was represented as the wife of Menelaos, and the cause of the Trojan war. As to Herakles, even the ancients admitted that there was a mortal and an immortal Herakles. Herodotus, ii. 44, tells us that the one, the Olympian, received divine honours, the other ancestral honours only [4].

The introduction of these new beings, half human,

[1] Od. iv. 555.
[2] Diod. Siculus, 4, 15 ; Eurip. Bacchae, 767.
[3] Isocrates, 10, 61.
[4] Καὶ τῷ μὲν ὡς ἀθανάτῳ Ὀλυμπίῳ δὲ ἐπωνυμίην, θύουσι, τῷ δὲ ἑτέρῳ ὡς ἥρωϊ ἐναγίζουσι.

half divine, could not but modify the whole character of the religion of the Greeks. Religion is, no doubt, a very general term, and it is difficult to lay hold of it when, as in ancient Greece, it existed as yet in the minds of individuals, or families, or villages only. On this account Hesiod's works, containing the first attempt at a systematic treatment of Greek religion, deserve to be considered by students of religion quite as carefully as the works of Homer. It may be useful, therefore, before we proceed further, to cast a glance at his Theogony, and at what he considered the objects of religious belief and worship to have been among the Greeks of his own time.

Whether the system of Greek religion which we find in Hesiod, was entirely his own work or the work of the Greek people at large, is difficult to say. It is quite certain, no doubt, that neither Homer nor Hesiod 'made' the gods of the Greeks, but it is truer of Hesiod than of Homer that he reduced them to something like order.

Hesiod admitted gods and men, but he also admitted intermediate beings. He seems to have been the first to use the word and the concept of ἡμίθεος, half-god, which was probably unknown to Homer (Il. xii. 23). He applies it to those very heroes of the Trojan and Theban wars, of whom we have been speaking. But he never admits that an ordinary man could become a god or even a half-god. Between gods and men he placed the heroes, ἥρωες, or half-gods, ἡμίθεοι, and the Daimones, δαίμονες.

Heroes.

It is quite true, as I pointed out, that Hesiod's heroes were exceptional beings, not ordinary mortals. Yet the fact that these heroes were believed to have lived on earth, like ordinary mortals, and had, after their death, been transferred either to the isles of the blessed, or had been admitted to the society of the Olympian gods, made it easier in later times to imagine that a real mortal, distinguished above the rest, might share the same honours as those who were the direct descendants of the gods (ἐκ θεῶν γεγονότες, Isocr. 4, 84). We read of such men as receiving not only the usual ancestral worship, but as worshipped, like the heroes, and, in some cases, as worshipped like the gods. We read of the Chersonitae, for instance, sacrificing to Miltiades, the victor of Marathon, 490 B.C., after his death, as to their founder (Herod. vi. 38). In Greece, where the patriotic feeling was so strong, nothing was more natural than that national honours should be paid to those who had died for their country. Pausanias tells us (i. 32, 4) that the Marathonians worshipped all who had fallen in the battle of Marathon, calling them Heroes, and especially Marathon, from whom their Demos had its name.

Plutarch relates (Arist. 21) that after the battle of Plataea, 479 B.C., the inhabitants performed funeral sacrifices (ἐναγίζειν) every year to the Hellenes who had fallen and been buried there. And they do so still, he continues.

'On the 16th of the Attic month Maimakterion they have a great procession, preceded at day-break by a trumpeter who gives the sign to attack. Then follow carriages with myrtle and garlands, a black bull, and free-born boys, carrying libations of wine and milk

in amphoras, and oil and ointments in jugs. No slave is allowed
to take any part, because those Greeks once died for freedom. At
last follows the Archon of Plataea, walking through the town to the
graves. He is never allowed to touch a sword or to wear any but
white vestments, but on this occasion he is clothed in a red chiton,
carrying an urn which he has taken from the archive, and girded
with a sword. He takes water from a spring, washes the funeral
columns himself, and anoints them with sweet oil. After he has
killed the bull on the altar, and prayed to Zeus and to the chthonic
Hermes, he invites the brave who have died for Hellas to the meal
and the partaking of the blood. He then mixes a goblet of wine,
and while pouring out the libation, he says : " I drink to men who
died for the liberty of the Hellenes." This festival is kept by the
Plataeensians to the present day.'

Thucydides (v. 11) tells us that ' Brasidas, who died
after gaining the victory at Amphipolis (422 B.C.), was
buried in the city with public honours in front of
what is now the Agora. The whole body of the allies
in military array followed him to the grave. The
Amphipolitans enclosed his sepulchre, and to this day
they sacrifice to him as to a hero, and also celebrate
games and yearly offerings in his honour. They
likewise made him their founder, and dedicated their
colony to him.'

Many similar cases might be quoted, all showing
how the distance which originally separated men
from the heroes as well as from the gods, became
smaller and smaller in the eyes of the Greeks. When
Demosthenes speaks of those who have fallen for
their country, he says in so many words[1]: ' How
should one not consider men of such merit as blessed,
men who have received such recognition and honour ?
One may fairly say of them that they are the asses-
sors of the lower gods, and in the isles of the blessed
placed in the same rank as the brave men of former
times[2].'

[1] Demosth. epitaph. 1399, § 36, p. 590, t. ii. Bekk.
[2] Lehrs, Populäre Aufsätze, p. 332.

Plutarch (Vita Lys. 18) tells us that Lysander (died 394 B.C.) was the first to whom the Greeks actually erected altars and offered sacrifices as to a god. In later times even bodily strength, athletic power, nay mere physical beauty, might raise a man to the rank of heroes. Herodotus tells us that Philip of Croton, a contemporary of Lysander, obtained, on account of his beauty, what no one else had obtained, for the Egestans built a Heroion on his tomb, and honoured him by sacrifices (θυσίῃσι). This custom was continued till at last ἥρως became the received name for any departed spirit. On Boeotian tombstones nothing is more common than the inscription, ἥρως χαῖρε, hail, O hero!

If then we find that an ordinary mortal could be honoured like a hero, and a hero could be worshipped like a god, it is easy to see that the mere likeness would soon be forgotten, that the mortal would be honoured as a hero, and the hero worshipped as a god. And thus a transition was effected half-unconsciously between the human and the divine, and the existence of something divine in man would be admitted almost by necessity.

Daimones.

The conception of Daimones led by another road to the discovery of something divine in man. While the heroes were originally human, the Daimones were in the beginning purely divine beings with nothing human about them. Plutarch[1] tells us that Hesiod

---

[1] See Plut. Def. Orac. 10 : Ἡσίοδος δὲ καθαρῶς καὶ διωρισμένως πρῶτος ἐξέθηκε τῶν λογικῶν τέτταρα γένη, θεούς, εἶτα δαίμονας πολλοὺς κἀγαθούς, εἶτα ἥρωας, εἶτα ἀνθρώπους, τῶν ἡμιθέων εἰς ἥρωας ἀποκριθέντων.

was the first who divided all rational beings into four classes, namely *gods*, *daimones*, many and good, *heroes*, including the half-gods, and *men*.

It may be doubtful whether Hesiod had this fourfold division always clearly before his mind, and whether it ever formed the recognised foundation of the religion of the Greeks. His identifying the daimones with the men of the golden race seems at all events purely arbitrary. This name of Daimones is in fact one of the most difficult names in the religious phraseology of the ancient Greeks. We translate the word by demons [1], which gives of course a very imperfect idea of its import. At first δαίμων clearly meant a god, the same as θεός. Thus we read in Homer of Athene returning from the earth to the Daimones on Olympus. Δαίμων is used more especially when a god appears as an active power. It then comes very near to the Latin *numen*, a divine power, as distinguished from the more personal *deus*. Thus Helios, the sun, is called by Aristophanes a great demon among gods and men.

But we saw already how the same word δαίμων was used in another sense too. It was applied by Hesiod to the first or the golden race of men. This has caused much confusion.

Hesiod's Four Races.

Hesiod speaks of four races of men who lived before the present race, the *golden*, the *silver*, and the *copper* race, and lastly, the race of *heroes* or *half-gods*.

The first race, the golden, was made by the Olym-

[1] See H. Spencer, *Sociology*, p. 323.

pian gods under Kronos.   They lived a life of perfect
happiness ; and, without suffering from the evils of
old age, they passed away as in a sleep.   But
after they had been buried, Zeus changed them
into Daimones, and they now roam about on earth,
clothed in air, and watching over laws and crimes.

The second or silver race was given up to folly,
and neglected the worship of the gods.   After passing
away, they became the Blessed under the earth
(ἐπιχθόι ιοι μάκαρες θνητοὶ καλέονται).

Then Zeus made the third or copper race, in the
days when iron was not yet known.   It is said that
these men were made out of ash-trees (ἐκ μελιῶν), and
it is curious to observe that the Germans also had a
tradition that men were made out of such trees.
They were warriors of enormous strength.   After a
time they died and passed away.

After these three races, the golden, the silver, and
the copper races, we should expect the present or
iron race.   But here Hesiod interpolates the race
of the heroes, the heroes of the Theban and Trojan
wars, who are called by him ἡμίθεοι or half-gods.
These, after they died, did not, as Homer represents
them, descend into the house of Hades, but, according
to Hesiod, Zeus allowed them to live in the isles of the
blessed, ruled by Kronos as their king.

Daimon therefore meant originally god, and was
probably on Greek soil as old a word as theós.   Its
etymology is unfortunately uncertain, but its meaning differs from that of theós chiefly by its impersonal
and unmythological character.   Daimones were divine
agents, at first, without any proper names, without
temples and sacrifices.   Afterwards they were repre-

sented as the followers (Plat. Legg. viii. p. 848 D),
the messengers, and the servants of the gods (Plut.
Def. Orac. 13).

As these divine powers watch over man, it was
supposed after a time that every man had his own
daimon [1], likewise every family, and every town.
At first, these daimones were kind, tutelary beings.
Hence the ἀγαθὸς δαίμων, the good genius, of a man.
But we also hear of an evil daimon, who is account-
able for the misfortunes that befall a man. It is difficult for us to connect any clear ideas with these
daimones who determined the fates of man. But
how familiar this idea was to the Greeks, we see
from such expressions as δαιμόνιος. A δαιμόνιος ἀνήρ
was meant for a man possessed, strange, luckless,
wretched, sometimes also for an inspired and marvellous person [2]. Our awful comes often very near to
δαιμόνιος.

The Daimonion of Sokrates.

We shall now better understand what Sokrates
really meant by his Daimonion, and why he held
that a belief in this Daimonion involved a belief in
gods and even in sons of gods or heroes. This is
what Plato puts into the mouth of Sokrates in his
Apology (Apol. 27 D):

'You say that I teach and believe in δαιμόνια, new
or old, no matter for that. . . . But if I believe in
δαιμόνια, I must believe in δαίμονες; is not that
true? . . . Now, what are δαίμονες? are they not
either gods or the sons of gods? Is that true?'

'Yes, that is true.'

---

[1] Phokylides, Fragm. 17 B.
[2] Lehrs, *Aufsätze aus dem Alterthum*, p. 146.

' But this is just the ingenious riddle of which I was speaking : the δαίμονες are gods, and you say first that I do not believe in gods, and then again that I do believe in gods ; that is, if I believe in δαίμονες. Or, if the δαίμονες are the illegitimate sons of gods, whether by the nymphs or by any other mothers, as is thought, that, as all men will allow, necessarily implies the existence of their parents. You might as well affirm the existence of mules, and deny that of horses and asses. . . . But no one who has a particle of understanding will ever be convinced by you that the same man can believe in δαιμόνια and θεῖα, and yet not believe that there are δαίμονες, θεοί, and ἥρωες.'

This Daimonion or this Daimon became under various names more and more important in later philosophical systems, particularly in the widespread system of the Stoics. With them the rational part of the human soul was considered as a part of the divine reason, given to every man as the god within, or as his δαίμων.

All this is clear and intelligible. The only disturbing element in the history of the word δαίμων is the idea of Hesiod that the men of the golden race were raised by Zeus to the rank of daimones. It is hardly ever mentioned as an article of national belief by other representative thinkers of Greece, and it utterly perverts the original character of the daimones which is divine from the beginning and remains divine to the end, when it has been recognised as the Divine, dwelling in man.

The Three Roads leading to the Discovery of something Divine in Man.

We have thus discovered three roads on which the Greeks were conducted to the discovery of something more than human, something superhuman, something divine or infinite in man. The most important road was that of ancestor-worship, beginning with the honours paid to departed parents, grandparents, and great-grandparents, then leading on to the worship of the ancestors of a family, of a clan, of a town, and of a state, and ending in the recognition of a world of spirits, not far removed from the world of the gods.

The second road started from a kind of mythological belief in human heroes, as the offspring of Zeus. Afterwards ordinary mortals also were raised to the same level, and thus another approach was made to the discovery of something divine, or, at least, god-like in man.

The third road started from a belief in divine powers, called Daímones. These spirits were supposed to watch over the destiny of a man, then to become his destiny. A man being possessed by his daimon, was at last identified with it, and the divine in man was thus once more recognised as the δαιμόνιον of Sokrates and other philosophers.

Nearness, likeness, and oneness with the Divine are the three goals which the human mind reached in Greece. In each case we see that a belief in nature-gods is pre-supposed, nay that without that belief anthropological religion would be simply impossible.

Plato on Gods, Daimones, Heroes, and Ancestral Spirits.

We cannot find a better summing-up of the last

results of Greek religion than what is given us by Plato.

'First,' he says (Laws, 716 seq.), 'comes a belief in God, in that God who, as the old tradition declares, holds in His hand the beginning, middle, and end of all that is, and moves according to His nature in a straight line (*rita*) towards the accomplishment of His end. Justice always follows Him, and is the punisher of those who fall short of the divine law. Every man therefore ought to make up his mind that he will be one of the followers of God—and he who would be dear to God, must, as far as possible, be like Him and such as He is.'

Now this may seem a very philosophical religion, but this belief in God, quite apart from a belief in the many Olympian gods, can be discovered in Homer quite as much as in Plato. In the Iliad, ix. 49, Diomedes says[1]: 'Let all flee home, but we two, I and Sthenelos, will fight till we see the end of Troy: *for we came with God.*' In the Odyssey (xiv. 444; x. 306), the swineherd says to Ulysses: 'Eat and enjoy what is here, for God will grant one thing, but another He will refuse, whatever He will in His mind, *for He can do all things.*'

And Plato himself, after he has thus spoken of God, continues: 'This is the conclusion, which is also the noblest and truest of all sayings, that for the good man to offer sacrifices to the gods, and hold converse with them by means of prayers and offerings and every kind of service, is the noblest and best of all things, and also the most conducive to a happy life, and very fit and meet.'

[1] *Lectures on the Science of Language*, ii. 460.

He then continues: ' Next after the Olympian gods, and the gods of the state, honour should be given to the gods below.

' Next to these gods, a wise man will do service to the daimones or spirits, and then to the heroes, and after them will follow the sacred places of private and ancestral gods, having their ritual according to law.

' Next comes the honour of living parents, to whom, as is meet, we have to pay the first and greatest and oldest of all debts. . . . And all his life long a man ought never to utter an unbecoming word to them; for of all light and winged words he will have to give an account; Nemesis, the messenger of Justice, is appointed to watch over them. When they are angry and want to satisfy their feelings in word or deed, he should not resist them; for a father who thinks that he has been wronged by his son may be reasonably expected to be very angry.

' At their death, the most moderate funeral is best. . . . And let a man not forget to pay the yearly tribute of respect to the dead, honouring them chiefly by omitting nothing that conduces to a perpetual remembrance of them, and giving a reasonable portion of his fortune to the dead.'

Whatever in this account of Greek religion in its widest sense may be ascribed to Plato personally, one thing seems very clear, that at his time a belief in the Olympian gods, and a belief in the spirits of the departed, existed peaceably side by side, and that funeral ceremonies, and a continued commemoration of the dead were considered essential elements of a truly religious life, quite as much as the sacrifices and praises of the great gods of nature.

Our own Problems.

And now you will perceive how near these problems which occupied the ancient world, approach the problems of our own time. We need not look upon the struggles through which, as we saw, the Greek mind passed in its search for the divine in man, τὸ θεῖον ἐν ἀνθρώπῳ, as the immediate antecedents of our own struggles. These searchings after truth, whether in Greece and Rome, or in India and Persia, need not be more to us than parallel instances, historical lessons, showing us how others toiled at the same task at which we ourselves are toiling still. But even thus they are full of import, for, after all, the same heart beats in every human breast.

Belief in Immortality in the Old Testament.

But there is one religion, which forms not only a parallel, but is in one sense the real antecedent of our own religion, supplying the historical background of our faith, and still feeding the thoughts of many Christians. I mean, of course, the Jewish.

Now it is well known that in no religion is the abyss which separates the divine from the human greater than in that of the Jews. An idea such as that expressed in a verse ascribed to Hesiod (Opera et Dies, 108), ὡς ὁμόθεν γεγάασι θεοὶ θνητοί τ' ἄνθρωποι, could hardly be expressed in Hebrew.

The question therefore which we have to answer is, whether the ancient Jews ever bridged over that abyss, whether they also discovered something divine in man, whether they believed in a life after death or in the immortality of the soul. This question has been dis-

cussed by the most learned theologians for many
centuries, and, strange to say, they have not arrived
at a unanimous conclusion yet. Unfortunately this
question, like many others connected with religion,
has been dragged out of the quiet field of historical
research into the noisy arena of theological gladiator-
ship. Some theologians considered it orthodox to
deny the existence of a belief in immortality in the
Old Testament, because, if the Jews had believed in
the immortality of the soul, St. Paul could not have
said that it was 'Christ who abolished death and
brought life and immortality to light by the gospel'
(2 Tit. i. 10). Others equally eager to appear orthodox held the opposite opinion, because Christ Himself had appealed to the Old Testament, in which God
calls Himself 'the God of Abraham, and the God of
Isaac, and the God of Jacob, and God is not the God
of the dead, but of the living' (Matt. xxii. 31).

But quite apart from the delusive influence which
theological prepossessions always exercise on historical
research, the reason why these answers have hitherto
proved so unsatisfactory must be sought for in the
indefinite character of the question itself. First of
all, the Old Testament is a very general and be-
wildering term. The Old Testament, as is now generally admitted, comprehends a number of books,
written by different authors and at different times.
Secondly, even immortality, though it seem at first
sight a very simple and clear term, may mean many
things and requires therefore a very careful definition.

Meaning of Immortality.

If immortality is meant for no more than a continuance of existence, if by a belief in immortality on the part of the Jews is meant no more than that the Jews did not believe in the annihilation of the soul at the time of death, we may confidently assert that, to the bulk of the Jewish nation, this very idea of annihilation was as yet unfamiliar. Dr. H. Schultz, to whose learned work, *Alttestamentliche Theologie*, I feel greatly indebted, seems to think (p. 698) that it is the more highly developed races only who cannot conceive a personal being as absolutely coming to an end. But the fact is that the idea of absolute annihilation and nothingness is hardly ever found except among people whose mind has received some amount of philosophical cultivation, certainly more than what the Jews possessed in early times. The Jews did not believe in the utter destruction of the soul, but, on the other hand, their idea of life after death was hardly that of life at all. It was existence, without life. Death was considered by them as by the Greeks as the greatest of misfortunes. To rejoice in death is a purely Christian, not a Jewish idea. It may be that expressions such as ' Abraham was gathered unto his people' (Gen. xxv. 8), or the words of David, ' I shall go to my son, but he will not return to me ' (2 Sam. xii. 23), show that a certain degree of personal identity was supposed by the Jews also to remain after death. This is indicated also by the recalling of the ghosts of the dead, as in the case of Samuel. The very name given to these ghosts, *elohim*, seems to show that they were supposed to have retained their personal character, while the strict injunctions against such superstitious customs serve only to prove that they existed. But beyond this, all is vague and dark.

Sheol.

The place in which the departed were believed to dwell was called by the Jews Sheol (שְׁאוֹל), which seems originally to have meant no more than grave or cave. Assyrian scholars derive it from an Accadian word, *shual*, but it can hardly be considered as a foreign word in Hebrew. Sheol is not meant for an individual grave (*bor*, *keber*), though its first idea may have been borrowed from it, but for a vast space in the interior of the earth. It is the land of shadows, of the Rephaim, where there is no work, nor device, nor knowledge, nor wisdom. The dead lie down and are at rest. They have fewer interests than even the Greek shades in Hades. All distinctions are gone, though sometimes kings are mentioned as sitting there on thrones (Jes. xiv. 9). But though the Jews believed that the souls continued to exist in Sheol, they did not believe that the wicked would there be punished and the good rewarded. All rewards and punishments for virtue or vice were confined to this world, and a long life was regarded as the surest proof of the favour of Jehovah. It may, no doubt, be taken as a sign of wonderful humility that, with two exceptions, Enoch and Elijah, the greatest of the Jewish saints and heroes should have been satisfied with this meagre reward. But it was their conception of God, as infinitely removed from this world, that made a belief in true immortality almost impossible for them, and excluded all hope for a nearer approach to God, or for any share in that true immortality which belonged to Him and to Him alone.

Controversy as to the Jewish Belief in Immortality.

To most students of religion it seems, indeed, as if a religion without a faith in immortality was impossible. Many years ago (1865)[1], and in opposition to the very highest authorities, I ventured to say: 'Without a belief in personal immortality, religion surely is like an arch resting on one pillar only, like a bridge ending in an abyss. We cannot wonder at the great difficulties felt and expressed by Bishop Warburton and other eminent divines, with regard to the supposed total absence of the doctrine of immortality or personal immortality in the Old Testament, and it is equally startling that the Sadducees who sat in the same council with the high-priest, openly denied the resurrection. However, though not expressly asserted anywhere, a belief in personal immortality is taken for granted in several passages of the Old Testament, and it is difficult to think of Abraham or Moses as without a belief in life and immortality.'

For this passage I was severely taken to task by one of the greatest classical scholars of our age, Professor K. Lehrs. In his *Populäre Aufsätze aus dem Alterthum*, p. 304, he wrote: 'No one would be more disgusted than Lessing by the words boldly uttered by M. M., that, though not expressly asserted anywhere, a belief in personal immortality is taken for granted in several passages of the O. T.' This is as strong in language as weak in argument. Lehrs knew that Lessing had denied the possibility of any religion existing without a belief in a future life, future rewards and punishments. He likewise knew,

---

[1] *Chips from a German Workshop*, vol. i. p. 45.

or ought to have known, how disparagingly Kant[1] and Schopenhauer[2] had spoken of the Jewish religion on account of the very absence of that belief.

It was not likely, therefore, that I should have ventured to say what I said without having what I believed to be some good reason on my side. If, therefore, Professor Lehrs felt disgusted, the easiest way to get over his disgust would have been to read once more the book of which he spoke so rashly.

I quite agree with him, and other scholars, that a belief in immortality does not appear on the surface of the Old Testament, as it appears in the New Testament, and in the sacred books of other religions. We should look in vain in the Old Testament for such an utterance as 'He that believeth in me, though he were dead, yet shall he live.' We could not match the words of a Vedic poet, who exclaims: 'Who will restore me to the great Aditi, that I may see father and mother.' No heroine in the Old Testament would have said what Antigone is made to say : 'Departing hence, I strongly cherish the hope that I shall be fondly welcomed by my father, and by my mother, and by my brother.'

But though a belief in immortality does not pervade the whole organism of the Old, as it pervades that of the New Testament, I still hold that we can catch, by what I ventured to call a kind of microscopic analysis,

---

[1] Kant meint, da ohne Glauben an ein künftiges Leben gar keine Religion gedacht werden könne, so enthalte das Judenthum, als solches genommen, gar keine Religion.

[2] Schopenhauer, *Paral.* i. p. 137, writes : 'Die eigentliche Juden-religion, wie sie in der Genesis und allen historischen Büchern bis zum Ende der Chronica dargestellt und gelehrt wird, ist die roheste aller Religionen, weil sie die einzige ist, die durchaus keine Unsterblichkeitslehre, noch irgend eine Spur davon hat.'

hidden germs, at least, of that belief in many passages
of the sacred writings of the Jews. I shall mention
a few of these passages, in order to show that I did
not, like Professor Lehrs, speak at random.

I am well aware that certain passages which have
been most frequently quoted as showing a belief in
immortality in the Old Testament, have to be surrendered. The first is the passage from Job xix. 25.
This was formerly translated: 'For I know that my
redeemer liveth, and that he shall stand at the latter
day upon the earth.' Most scholars, however much
they differ on the exact interpretation of these difficult lines, agree now that they cannot mean what
they seemed to mean to former translators[1], and
that what is meant by a redeemer is a vindicator,
here God Himself, who will stand up for the inno-
cence of Job. Professor Schultz translates: 'For
I know my vindicator lives, and a revenger (Blut-
rächer) will rise up on the dust (the grave), and,
after this my skin has been devoured, and I am de-
nuded of my flesh, I see God (i. e. the revenger on
the dust), Him whom I see (fighting) for me, and my
eyes see Him—no longer angry; the heart in my
bosom fails. If ye say, how shall we persecute him,
and that the root of the matter is found in me, Be ye
afraid for yourselves of the sword, for sword-guilt in
anger—that ye know (the Almighty).'

Another passage, Psalm xvi. ver. 10, which was
formerly translated : 'Thou wilt not leave my soul in
hell,' is rendered in the Revised Version by 'Thou
wilt not leave my soul to Sheol,' that is, 'Thou wilt

---

[1] Schultz, l. c., p. 705 : *Voraussetzungen der christlichen Lehre von der
Unsterblichkeit*, Göttingen, 1861, pp. 219–223.

not surrender my soul to Sheol,' or ' Thou wilt not let
me die yet.'

As passages, however, which seem to me to contain
a silent recognition of something divine, and therefore
immortal in man, I should mention Gen. i. 26, ' And
God said, Let us make man in our image, after óur
likeness.' And again, Gen. ii. 7, ' And the Lord God
formed man of the dust of the ground, and breathed
into his nostrils the breath of life ; and man became a
living soul.' Now a God-like being that lives by the
breath of God, cannot have been conceived at the
same time as something totally different from God.
Nay, we are told distinctly that when the dust returns
to dust, the spirit or breath returns to God who gave it.

A verse like that in Psalm viii. 5, ' For thou hast
made man but little lower than the Elohim (angels),'
could hardly have been written by one who believed
man to be but dust, and no better than the beasts of
the field.

Again, when we read in Gen. iii. 22, that the Lord
sent Adam and Eve forth from the garden of Eden,
we are told that this was done, lest he put forth his
hand and take also of the tree of life, and eat, and live
for ever. This seems to imply that man, if he had
remained in the garden of Eden, would have been
capable of eternal life.

The two cases of Enoch and Elijah are, no doubt,
too exceptional to prove a belief in immortality, but
they show, at all events, that the mind of the Hebrews
was familiar with the idea of a human being returning to God, without suffering the penalty of death.

I do not mean to say that passages such as these
prove that the Jews had anticipated the Christian

belief in the immortality of the soul. I only maintain that they contain the germs of such a belief, and that they are incompatible with a belief in the utter annihilation of the soul, which Lehrs, Schopenhauer, and others would force on the religion of the Old Testament.

But it would be as easy, nay, much easier, to collect a number of passages from the Old Testament which seem to contain a distinct denial of immortality. To those who believe in a complete unity of the Old Testament, who ignore its composite character and its historical growth, and who look upon the whole of it as miraculously revealed, such contradictions must be perplexing, and can only be removed by a great effort of special pleading. In the eyes of the historian, however, they only serve to confirm the truly historical character of that collection of ancient and modern books. Thus the author of Psalm xxxix. 14, says, 'Before I go hence and am no more.' We read in the Book of Job, vii. 8–10, 'The eye of him that seeth me shall behold me no more : thine eyes shall be upon me, but I shall not be. As the cloud is consumed and vanisheth away, so he that goeth down to Sheol shall come up no more. He shall return no more to his house, neither shall his place know him any more.'

Job xiv. 7, 'For there is hope for a tree, if it be cut down—But man dieth and wasteth away, yea, man giveth up the ghost, and where is he? As the waters fall from the sea, and the river decayeth and drieth up ; so man lieth down and riseth not. Till the heavens be no more, they shall not awake, nor be roused out of their sleep.'

If we turn to Ecclesiastes, his utterances become
more and more despairing. 'That which befalleth
the sons of men befalleth beasts; even one thing
befalleth them: as the one dieth, so dieth the other;
yea, they have all one breath; so that man hath no
pre-eminence above a beast.'

Such sceptical utterances, however, could not but
provoke resistance. In the later history of the Jews,
whether from their own heart's desire, or from their
intercourse with foreign nations, we find that a belief
in a life after death became more and more prominent.

Thus, while at the very dawn of Christianity the
Sadducees openly denied that 'there was any resurrection' or spirit or angel,' the Pharisees, according to
Josephus, believed that 'the souls have an immortal
strength in them, and that in the under-world they
will experience rewards or punishments, according as
they have lived well or ill in this life.'

Still there always remained in the Jewish mind the
idea of the unapproachable majesty of Jehovah. The
souls might have their rewards and punishments in
the lower world, but true immortality, a communion
of the soul with God, was beyond the horizon of the
Jewish mind. The idea of anything approaching
apotheosis was, and remained to the last, blasphemy
in the eyes of the Jews. Adam, though created by
Jehovah, is never called the son of God, in a genealo-
gical sense, except once in the Gospel of St. Luke.
Here the genealogy of Joseph is traced back to David,
and that of David to Enos, Seth, and Adam, 'who
was the son of God.' If we may recognise Rabbinical
influences in this genealogy, they are at all events
very modern, and we know that at the very same

time the fact that Jesus called Himself the Son of God was enough to condemn Him to death.

Reaction.

But it is exactly among the Jews, where the two ideas of the Divine and the Human had been most widely wrenched apart, that we witness the strongest reaction. The desire for nearness to God, likeness to God, oneness or atone-ment with God, may be suppressed for a time. It may be silenced by the awe with which the majesty of the Divine fills the human heart. But it is always there. Though the Jew lies prostrate before Jehovah, yet his soul always panted for Him, as the hart panteth after the waterbrook ; and it was, after all, the Jew who, in the great history of the world, was destined to solve the riddle of the Divine in man.

But how was it to be solved? Not one of the three roads that led the Greek to the discovery of the Divine in man was open to the Jew.

The first road which led man through the worship of ancestral spirits to the recognition of something Divine in man was barred to the Jew. The ghosts of his departed friends were in Sheol, and to offer sacrifices to them was unlawful.

The second road was too mythological. The Jew knew no Διογενεῖς, no sons of Jehovah, like Herakles, or Dionysos, or Menelaos. Abraham was the friend, Moses was the servant, David was the anointed of God, and if they were never raised to a divine, or even half-divine rank, much less could ordinary mortals hope for such an elevation.

And yet there are passages, scattered about in the

Old Testament, in which some idea of a divine sonship seems very clearly expressed. Thus we read in
Deuteronomy, xiv. 1, 'Ye are the children of the
Lord, your God.' But the full meaning of these passages seems never to have been realised. 'Father and
son' were used in a poetical, often also in a moral
sense, as when we read in 2 Sam. vii. 14, the words
meant for David: 'I will be his father, and he shall
be my son. If he commit any iniquity, I will chasten
him with the rod of men, and with the stripes of the
children of men.' But we never see it used in the
Old Testament as St. John used it, when he wrote
(1 John iii. 1), 'Behold, what manner of love the
Father has bestowed upon us, that we should be
called the sons of God.'

The third road also was not likely to tempt the
Jewish mind. Their belief in angels might have
helped them, as the belief in daimones helped the
Greek, in their first faltering steps towards that goal.
But though the Jewish angels of the Lord might
indeed 'encamp round about them that fear him,
and deliver them[1],' they would never become indwelling spirits, like the daimonion of Sokrates, and
never point the way to the discovery of the Divine
in human nature.

Christianity, the Revelation of the Divine Sonship of Christ and Man.

And yet it was the soil of Jewish thought that in
the end gave birth to the true conception of the
relation between the Divine in nature and the Divine
in man. In what I am going to say, I shall pay little

[1] Psalm xii. 7.

regard to the miraculous events in which the birth of that concept is supposed to have been manifested. What are those miraculous wrappings to us? When the Divine in the outward world has once been fully recognised, there can be nothing more or less divine, nothing more or less miraculous, either in nature or in history. Those who assign a divine and miraculous character to certain consecrated events only in the history of the world, are in great danger of desecrating thereby the whole drama of history, and to make it, not only profane, but godless.

It is easy to call this a pantheistic view of the world. It is pantheistic, in the best sense of the word, so much so that any other view would soon become atheistic. Even the ancient Greeks suspected the ubiquity or omnipresence of the Divine, when, as early as the time of Thales, they declared that *all* is full of the gods. The choice here lies really between Pantheism and Atheism. If anything, the greatest or the smallest, can ever happen without the will of God, then God is no longer God. To distinguish between a direct and indirect influence of the Divine, to admit a general and a special providence, is like a relapse into polytheism, a belief in one and many gods.

What we call Christianity embraces several fundamental doctrines, but the most important of them all is the recognition of the Divine in man, or, as we call it, the belief in the divinity of the son. The belief in God, let us say in God the Father, or the Creator and Ruler of the world, had been elaborated by the Jews. It was ready to hand. Greeks and Romans, most of the civilised and uncivilised nations of the world had arrived at it.

But when the Founder of Christianity called God His Father, and not only His Father, but the Father of all mankind, He did no longer speak the language of either Jews or Greeks. To the Jews, to claim divine sonship for man would have been blasphemy. To the Greeks divine sonship would have meant no more than a miraculous, a mythological event, such as the birth of Hercules. Christ spoke a new language, a language liable, no doubt, to be misunderstood, as all language is; but a language which to those who understood it, has imparted a new glory to the face of the whole world. It is well known how this event, the discovery of the Divine in man, which involves a complete change in the spiritual condition of mankind, and marks the great turning-point in the history of the world, has been surrounded by a legendary halo, has been obscured, has been changed into mere mythology, so that its real meaning has often been quite forgotten, and has to be discovered again by honest and fearless seeking. Christ had to speak the language of His time, but He gave a new meaning to it, and yet that language has often retained its old discarded meaning in the minds of His earliest, nay sometimes of His latest disciples also.

The Divine sonship of which He speaks was not blasphemy, as the Jews thought; it was not mythology, as so many of His own followers imagined, and still imagine. Father and son, divine and human, were like the old bottles that could hardly hold the new wine; and yet how often have the old broken bottles been preferred to the new wine, that was to give new life to the world.

The Words Father and Son.

Let us first examine the words father and son a little more closely. They seem the best-known words of our language, and yet it would be difficult to find two words more full of mystery, even in their every-day acceptation. Again, nothing seems at first more natural than to apply these words to God and man. In many, if not in most religions, man has addressed God as his father, and has looked upon himself as his son. The expression has become so familiar that we hardly feel that it is, and can only be, a metaphor. And yet it is really the boldest metaphor in the whole of human language. The two words must be almost completely emptied of their contents, before they become fit to express the relation between God and man. Such is human language. We cannot help it, only we should not forget it.

Parable of the King's Son.

But now, let us go a step further. It can easily be seen that true sonship depends mainly on knowledge. A man may be the son of a king, but if he is brought up by an old shepherd with his other children, he is a shepherd-boy, and not a prince. And yet as soon as he discovers and knows that the king is his father, and not the shepherd, he at once becomes a prince, he is a prince, he feels himself a prince, the son of a king.

It is in the same way that man must discover that God is his father, before he can become a son of God. To know is here to be, to be to know. No mere miracle will change the shepherd-boy into a prince; no mere miracle will make man the son of God. That sonship can be gained through knowledge only, 'through man knowing God, or rather being known of God [1],' and till it is so gained, it does not exist, even though it be a fact.

If we apply this to the words in which Christ speaks of Himself as the Son of God, we shall see that to Him it is no miracle, it is no mystery, it is no question of supernatural contrivance;—it is simply clear knowledge; and it was this self-knowledge which made Christ what He was, it was this which constituted His true, His eternal divinity. This is not *Apotheosis*, a word which by its formation seems to imply a removal from the level of humanity to that of deity; it is rather, if I may be allowed to coin a new word, *Anatheosis*, a taking back, or a taking up of the human into the divine nature. What can be clearer than the words of Christ Himself: 'No man knoweth the Son, but the Father; neither knoweth any man the Father, save the Son, and he to whomsoever the Son will reveal Him' (Luke x. 22).

But we must remember that though Christ uses the homely words of father and son, He Himself warns His disciples against the wrong use of these words. 'Call no man your father upon the earth,' He says, 'for one is your father, which is in heaven' (Matth. xxiii. 9).— Can anything be clearer and stronger,? Instead of saying, as we should say, 'Call not God father, because father means your father upon the earth,' He says, 'Call no man father, for father has now assumed a new and higher meaning, and can no longer be used in its old familiar sense.'

[1] Gal. iv. 9.

The Position of Christianity in the History of the World.

If we have learnt to look upon Christianity, not as something unreal and unhistorical, but as an integral part of history, of the historical growth of the human race, we can see now how all the searchings after the Divine or the Infinite in man, which we watched in our former Lectures, were fulfilled in these simple utterances of Christ. His preaching, we are told, brought life and immortality to light. Life, the life of the soul, and immortality, the immortality of the soul, were there, and had always been there. But they were brought to light, man was made fully conscious of them, man remembered his royal birth, when the word had been spoken by Christ.

The Second Birth.

This was called a new birth, and it was so as much as it would be a new birth to the shepherd-boy, when he knew that he was a born prince. This expression, a new birth, or a second birth, which so staggered Nicodemus, is a very familiar expression in Sanskrit. One feels surprised at first when one sees Dviga, twice-born, as the regular name for the higher castes in India. The Brâhmans themselves, to judge from the various explanations they give of that title, seem to have forgotten its true meaning. But its original conception can hardly have been different from that of a new birth, that is, the recognition of something superhuman, divine, and immortal in man, which marks to every man the beginning of a new life.

For we must never forget that it was not the principal object of Christ's teaching to make others believe that He only was divine, immortal, or the

Son of God. He wished them to believe this for *their own* sake, for *their own* regeneration. Thus we read, 'As many as received him, to them gave he power to become the sons of God, even to them that believe in his name: which were born, not of blood, nor of the will of the flesh, nor of the will of man, but of God' (St. John i. 12). The same doctrine is repeated again and again. 'He that believeth in the Son, has everlasting life' (St. John iii. 36; vi. 47). 'He that heareth my word, hath everlasting life' (St. John v. 24). 'He giveth life unto the world' (St. John vi. 33). Can we doubt what was the meaning of that life? It was immortality, an immortality which need not wait for death, but has its surety even in this life. 'If a man keep my saying, he shall never see death' (St. John ix. 52). 'Whosoever liveth and believeth in me, shall never die' (St. John xi. 26). 'As thou, Father, art in me, and I in thee, that they also may be one in us' (St. John xvii. 21).

It might be thought, at first, that this recognition of a divine element in man must necessarily lower the conception of the Divine. And so it does in one sense. It brings God nearer to us; it brings the Divine from the clouds to the earth. It bridges over the abyss by which the Divine and the human were completely separated in the Jewish and likewise in many of the Pagan religions. It rends the veil of the temple. This lowering, therefore, is no real lowering of the Divine. It is an expanding of the concept of the Divine, and at the same time a raising of the concept of humanity, or rather a restoration of what is called human to its true character, a regeneration, or a

second birth, as it is often called by Christ Himself;
—'except a man be born again, he cannot see the
kingdom of God.'

Christ's Teaching and its Later Interpretation.

The endless theological discussions which, beginning
from the first, and not yet ended in the nineteenth
century, were meant to define the words of Christ
and to draw new limits between the Divine and the
human, have fortunately no interest for us. The
amount of learning spent on these speculations is
incredible. The Church has been rent asunder by
them. Hundreds, nay thousands, who thought too
freely and spoke too boldly on this subject were sent
to prison and to the stake; and, when all other arguments failed, the argument of the biggest battalions
has often been invoked for a final solution. These
are sad chapters in the history of the world, written
in blood and tears. They would never have been
written if the Church had been satisfied with the
words of Christ. We have not many of His own
words. We cannot even be certain that we always
have them exactly as He spoke them. Christ never
wrote, He never composed a treatise on the true
relation between the Divine and the human, either
with regard to Himself or with regard to humanity
at large. His utterances were always short and
complete. Nothing can be left out in them, and
nothing ought to be added. A truth does not gain
by many words. Often it is completely strangled by
them. You have only to read some of those heavy
folios of the so-called Fathers of the Church, or of the
great theological authorities of the middle ages, and

you will be appalled at the havoc which, with all
their logic and all their piety, these learned Rabbis
have wrought in the simple words of Christ. I do
not mean to say that His words are not full of
meaning, or that they would not supply texts for
thousands of sermons and commentaries. But we
must not forget that they were meant to be what
they are, that they were meant to say exactly what
they say, neither more nor less, and that to add one
jot or tittle to them, is often to destroy them altogether. As early a witness as Justin Martyr, when
speaking of the teaching of Christ, says: 'His speeches
were brief and cut short, for He was not a sophist, but
His speech was the power of God[1].'

It is quite true that to the student of history it is
of the deepest interest to discover the antecedents
and parallels of these short utterances, to watch the
previous struggles of the human mind, while searching
for the true expression of these nascent truths. But
when that expression has at last been found, it ought
to suffice. The historian may descend once more
into the shaft from which the ore has been raised,
and examine once more the ore from which the gold
has been extracted. But it is the small ounce of
precious gold, purified, weighed, and coined, that is
wanted for our daily life, and to tamper with it, or
to mix it up once more with the slags from which
it has been extracted, or cast it back into the shaft
from which it has been raised, would be sheer
madness. And yet that is what so many theological
writers, both in ancient and modern times, are con-

---

[1] Apol. i. 14: Βραχεῖς δὲ καὶ σύντομοι παρ' αὐτοῦ λόγοι γεγόνασιν· οὐ
γὰρ σοφιστὴς ὑπῆρχεν, ἀλλὰ δύναμις θεοῦ ὁ λόγος αὐτοῦ ἦν.

stantly doing. Christ, when speaking of Himself and His relation to God, expressed all He wished to say in a few words. 'I and my Father are one' (St. John x. 30), and 'My Father is greater than I' (St. John xiv. 28). And when addressing His disciples, and through them the whole of mankind, His words are again as short and telling as words can be: 'As thou, Father, art in me, and I in thee, they also may be one in us.'

And as if to protest once more against the too human interpretation of such purely symbolical words as father and mother, son and brother, you remember the words which sounded so startling to many ears. When His mother and His brethren were seeking for Him, 'He answered, saying, Who is my mother, or my brethren? And he looked round about on them which sat about him, and said: Behold my mother and my brethren! For whosoever shall do the will of God, the same is my brother, and my sister, and mother' (Mark iii. 32–35; Luke viii. 21).

These utterances are very short, but why will people imagine that short utterances contain less than long treatises? There are subjects on which but little *can* be said. When treating of Physical Religion, we found that after all had been said in different sacred books about God in nature, there remained in the end but that one short name, 'I Am that I Am.' In treating of Anthropological Religion we arrive at the same result. We see how, starting from different points, the deepest thinkers in every part of the world suspected in man something more than the body, something not mortal, soon something immortal; something not merely human, soon some-

thing superhuman, divine, and infinite. They called
it by ever so many names, the breath, the soul, the
spirit, the self; but in the end no words seemed to
express the relation between the Divine in man and
the Divine in nature better than that of father and
son, though even that expression had to be carefully
guarded against mythological corruption.

Objections considered.

I know full well the objections that will be raised
against the line of argument which I have followed in this course of Lectures on Anthropological
Religion.

It will be said on one side that I have deserted the
impartial standpoint from which the student of the
Science of Religion should never flinch, and that
my chief object has been to magnify Christianity, by
showing that it is the fulfilment of all that the world
has been hoping and striving for. In one sense that
is true. But if I hold that Christianity has given
the best and truest expression to what the old world
had tried to express in various and less perfect ways,
I have at least given the facts on which I rely. If
my facts can be proved to be wrong, my conclusions
will fall; and if any better expression can be given
to what the witness within calls the truth, I should
be most ready to accept it. Nor should I ever wish
to convey the impression that, because the teaching
of Christ is true, therefore all the teachings of other
religions are false. It has been, on the contrary, my
constant endeavour to show how much truth there
is in other religions, nay, to use the words of St.
Augustine, that there is not one which does not con-

tain some grains of truth. But because in Christian
countries Christianity has often been exalted by exaggerated and meaningless praise, there is no reason
why we should be ashamed to claim for it that place
which, not only the voice of our own heart, but the
voice of history, assigns to it among all the religions
of the world. At some times silence may be the
truest homage, but if there is a time to be silent,
there is also a time to speak.

When in my last course of Lectures on Physical
Religion I endeavoured to trace the various roads
which led to the discovery and the naming of the
Infinite in nature, I did not say that the different
names and concepts of the gods or agents in nature
which we find in non-Christian religions were all
wrong. On the contrary, I tried to show in all of
them the earnest endeavour to feel after God, if haply
they might find Him. I still hold therefore that the
whole of Physical Religion may best be summed up
in the words: 'I believe in God the Father Almighty,
maker of heaven and earth.' That language is religious, and, if you like, mythological, but it is nevertheless the highest expression that human language
can devise.

In the present course of Lectures I have likewise
endeavoured to describe the various attempts at discovering something infinite in man, and I have
shown that a belief in something within us, different
from the body, is universal. I hold to this till one
single language can be produced which is without a
name for soul. There is not the same jealousy here.
On the contrary, there is great readiness to accept
the different names for soul and the different forms of

belief in its perpetuity or immortality, as supports of our own belief in something immortal within us. I go even further, and am quite willing to admit that there are certain philosophies which have entered more deeply into this problem of the Divine in man or the immortality of the soul than any religion. But philosophy, we must remember, is not religion. Philosophy is for the few, religion for the many, nay for all, and the question which concerns us is whether any religion has discovered a truer expression for the relation between man and God than Christianity. Here also the words, ' I believe in Jesus Christ, the Son of God,' may, if properly understood, serve to sum up nearly all that has been thought on the Divine element in human nature, on the Infinite in man.

But while on one side I shall incur the displeasure of those who carry impartiality to the brink of injustice, I expect even stronger objections from the opposite side. So far from accepting the position which I have assigned to Christianity in the historical growth of religion, many theologians will hold that Christianity stands altogether outside the stream of history, and beyond the reach of any comparison with other religions. The true divinity which, as I tried to show, Christ claimed for Himself and for His brethren, would not satisfy them at all. They want, not a real, but a miraculous divinity, a divinity not very different, in fact, from that which, soon after his death, was ascribed to Plato, as the son of Apollo, or which was claimed for other founders of religions. If people are satisfied with such a belief, it probably contains all that they require, because it is all they can as yet comprehend. Nor do I deny that they have a warrant for their belief in some of the earliest documents of the Christian Church. But the very fact that by the side of the three Synoptical Gospels we find the Gospel according to St. John, should teach us that there is a natural progress and easy transition from the one to the other, and that the same lesson may be conveyed to some in parables, to others in all plainness of thought and speech.

I am prepared for these objections from two opposite quarters, and while I never notice mere abuse, I shall always feel most grateful if any of my opponents will point out when my facts are wrong historically, or my deductions faulty logically. I know but too well how easy it is to err in treating of the origin and history of religions, and no pioneer need be ashamed if he has sometimes missed the right road. But I may repeat at the end of this course what I said when I began it: ' Do you think it is possible to lecture on religion, even on natural religion, without giving offence either on the right or on the left? And do you think that a man would be worth his salt who, in lecturing on religion, even on natural religion, were to look either right or left, instead of looking all facts, as they meet him, straight in the face to see whether they are facts or not, and, if they are facts, to find out what they mean?'

It is possible that to some philosophers the subject which I have treated under the name of Anthropological Religion may seem to form no part of religion at all. It is true that 'I believe in the existence of the soul,' forms as yet no part of any creed; and yet what would it profit a man if he believed all the creeds, and did not believe in his own soul? But if I should not have succeeded in showing how the belief in something infinite, immortal, and divine in man forms an essential part of all religions, I may, in conclusion, appeal to three authorities in my support.

The first is Lord Gifford himself. His opinions have a right to be considered by those who have been entrusted with carrying out the intentions of his Will.

Lord Gifford, in his remarkable essay on Substance (p. 207), says: 'God must be the very substance and essence of the human soul. The human soul is neither self-derived nor self-subsisting. It would vanish if it had not a substance, and its substance is God.'

What Lord Gifford asserts simply as a fact, is expressed in more diffident language by one who had all his life been almost face to face with the workings of God in nature, and to whom, if to any one, the heavens had declared not only the glory, but the eternal wisdom of God. Kepler, the discoverer of the three laws on which our planetary system is founded, declared 'that it was his highest wish to find *within* the God whom he had found everywhere *without*[1].'

The third witness is Kant. He expresses the same thought, though again from a different point of view.

Before the tribunal of his own critical philosophy both the Divine in nature and the Divine in man were treated as transcendent, and as beyond the reach of our categories, while all the arguments for the existence of God, the cosmological, the teleological,

[1] *Philosophy and Theology*, by J. H. Stirling, p. 32.

and the ontological, were summarily dismissed. And yet he says, in a passage that has often been quoted:

'Two things fill the mind with ever new and growing admiration and awe, the more frequently and the more intensely we ponder on them: the starry firmament above me, and the moral law within me. Neither of them is hidden in darkness, so that I need look for it or could only suspect it in what is beyond. I see them both before me, and I connect them directly with the consciousness of my own existence. The former begins with the place which I myself occupy in the external world of sense, and enlarges my connection here into the infinitely great, with worlds beyond worlds, and systems of systems, nay, also into the unlimited time of their periodical motion, their beginning and their continuance. The latter begins with my own invisible self, my personality, and places me in a world of true infinitude, perceptible to the understanding only, with which I know myself to be connected, not, as before, by a casual bond only, but by a general and necessary union[1].'

The divine presence which Kant beheld in the starry firmament is the Infinite in nature. The divine presence which he perceived in his conscience or in his own invisible self is the Infinite in man.

The historical development of our belief in the Infinite in nature I tried to explain in my Lectures in 1890. The gradual growth of a belief in something infinite, immortal, and divine in man, formed the subject of my present course. If life and strength be spared I hope to treat of the true nature of

[1] *Works*, ed. Rosenkranz and Schubert, vol. viii. p. 312 seq.

the soul, and of the relation between the Infinite in
man and the Infinite in nature in my next and, what
will be, I am sorry to say, my last course of Lectures
before the members of the University and the citizens
of this busy town of Glasgow.

APPENDIX I.

P. 87.

INDRA OR AṆDRA.

THE reason why I protest against scientific levity is because it does real mischief in retarding the progress of our science. There is so much still to do, and there are, no doubt, so many real dangers lurking on every side, that we cannot afford to waste time in attending to false alarms. Some of these alarms are most objectionable. If a scholar comes forward and gives his facts and reasons why he differs from other scholars, he may be right or wrong, and, unless his objections arise from sheer ignorance, he may claim an answer. But a custom has sprung up of late which is much to be deprecated. We are told that A. says one thing, but B., often an unknown writer in an unknown journal, says quite another, and that therefore no one knows anything. If those who indulge in this kind of warfare would give their reasons why they consider A. wrong and B. right, that would be useful work. But simply to say B. differs from A., therefore A. is wrong, or B. differs from A., therefore both are wrong, is unworthy, if not of a scholar, at least of a logician. Here is an example of what I mean.

When we have an etymology which is invulnerable on phonetic grounds, and perfectly satisfactory so far as the meaning of the word is concerned, it requires very strong arguments to replace it by another.

The derivation of the name of Indra, a god who is constantly represented as bringing rain, from the same root which yielded ind-u, rain-drop, is beyond the reach of reasonable criticism. To say that we have in Sanskrit no verb ind or id, is saying no more than that there are hundreds of words in Sanskrit the root of which has not been preserved in a verbal base. But even supposing, what would be a mere guess, that Indra was derived from some unknown pre-Aryan or un-Aryan root, there can be no doubt that in the mind of the Vedic poets ind-u and ind-ra were inseparably connected[1]. However, a certain amount of free and easy scepticism might be tolerated, if some other very plausible etymology of Indra had been suggested, for with such ancient names as the names of Vedic gods it is not unfrequently difficult to decide which of two equally possible etymologies is to be considered as the real one. But what shall we say to the following criticism[2]? 'It is right to call attention to the fact that Indra is not said to rain in the sense in which Parganya, or Zeus, or Jupiter was said to rain; and the etymology which was supposed to prove his name to have made him a pluvial divinity has been superseded by a better one which has nothing to do with rain.'

No Vedic scholar, so far as I know, has ever maintained that Indra rained in the sense in which Parganya was said to rain; but no Vedic scholar, so far as I know, has ever denied that Indra conquered the rain and sent it down on the parched earth. An etymology, therefore, which has nothing to do with rain, cannot well be called a better one on that ground.

But what is this better etymology? It was suggested many years ago by Bezzenberger, and I should be surprised

[1] In the same manner as Soma is connected with suta, Indra is connected with indu, e. g. Rv. IX. 101, 5, Induh Indráya pavate; Rv. I. 139, 6, Vríshan Indra vríshapā́nâsah índavah imé sutā́h ádrisutâsah udbhídah; see also IX. 37, 6; 62, 15; 85, 4; 96, 9; 101, 5; 110, 11.

[2] *Hibbert Lectures*, by J. Rhys, p. 295.

if that conscientious scholar attached much value to it, and
would still wish to defend it, particularly when the reading
of the Zend Añdra for Iñdra has become more than doubtful[1]. This Zend form Añdra was supposed to be the Old
High-German *antra*, and this *antra* was supposed to mean
giant, and to be derived from a root *and*, standing for *nad*,
to howl. Now, first there is no such root as *and* for *nad*.
Secondly, there is no such word in Old High-German as
antra, but *antra* is a purely imaginary word, invented in
order to account for O. H. G. *antrisc* and *entrisc*, which
means old, strange, wild, &c. But by the side of *antrisc*
there is in O. H. G. another word, *antisc*. It is by no means
certain that these are two forms of the same word. It is far
better to keep them distinct.

Schade, in his *Altdeutsche Wörterbuch*, gives antisc, andisk,
entisk, entisch.

And antrisc, entrisc, eintrisk, endirisk, enderisk ahd.,
amhd. entrisch, adj. antiquus, priscus, antiquatus; barbarus,
fremd; befremdlich, sonderbar. N. H. G. bair. entrisch,
Schmeller 1, 77, Myth. 491.

Nor is it at all certain that either of these words has
anything to do with the Germanic word for giant, O. E. *ent*
(see Bosw.-Toller, p. 252), adj. *entisc* (Beow., l. 2980), German
Enz, and *enzerisch*, ungeheuer, pointing to a stem **ántiz*.

With such a form as O. H. G. **antra*, supposing it ever
existed, or **antiz*, we should never get at Sanskrit Indra;
we might possibly get at Andhra, an ancient Vedic race,
the name of which would be about as appropriate as that of
the Indi, which Mone is said to have connected with A. S.
ent, plur. *entas*[2]. When will people learn that vowels are
quite as important as consonants?

---

[1] Darmesteter, *Ormazd et Ahriman*, p. 263; v. Bradke, *Dyaus Asura*,
p. 84. See Vendidad X. 9; XIX. 43.

[2] For other etymologies of *ant*, see Grimm, *Deutsche Mythologie*,
p. 491.

This new etymology of Indra is therefore phonetically faulty, but it is likewise semantically untenable. If any Vedic Deva was ever a real Deva it was Indra, and to represent him as originally human, or as an old giant, is the wildest Euhemerism.

If the etymology which connects indu and indra had really been thought objectionable, several other etymologies far less objectionable than the O. H. G. *antra might have been quoted. For, as I say again, and as everybody familiar with these researches is aware of, it is by no means easy, in tracing ancient names of gods and heroes to their probable source, to exclude all other etymologies as simply impossible. Professor Ludwig[1], one of our best Vedic scholars, suggested the Old Slavonic jędrŭ, quick; Professor Roth seems still to be in favour of deriving Indra from in or inv, with an epenthetic d, so that it should have meant tamer or conqueror. But the epenthesis of d between n and r is possible in Greek, not in Sanskrit. Ever so many more guesses proceeding from ancient Sanskrit scholars may be seen in the Nirukta, X. 8. But none of them is so entirely free from objections, whether phonetic or semantic, as that which derives Indra from the same root which yielded indu, and thus vindicates for Indra the original meaning of the Rain-god. To say, therefore, that that etymology has been superseded by Professor Bezzenberger's ingenious but rash guess, is dealing in indolent assertions that can only be prejudicial to the interests of true scholarship.

Professor Jacobi in Kuhn's *Zeitschrift*, xxxi. p. 316, has proposed a new etymology of Indra, by comparing it with ἀνήρ, ἀνδρό-ς, and indirectly with Sk. nara, man. Apart from other objections, the phonetic difficulty pointed out before, the absence of an epenthetic d in Sanskrit, is decisive against this etymology.

[1] *Rig-veda*, vol. iii. p. 324.

APPENDIX II.

P. 88.

HEY DIDDLE DIDDLE.

In criticising the labours of comparative philologists, great stress has been laid on the fact that comparative philologists sometimes differ from each other. It is difficult to imagine a weaker, not to say a meaner, argument. It was the same argument that was used against the decipherers of hieroglyphic, cuneiform, Umbrian, and Oscan inscriptions. They were laughed at because they differed from each other, and they were laughed at because they differed from themselves; as if progress, or, as it is now called, evolution, were possible without scholars differing from themselves and differing from others.

When learned argument was impossible or troublesome, squibs have often had to take its place in order to throw ridicule on serious students. I still remember the time when the late Sir George Cornewall Lewis published his famous squib, ' *Inscriptio antiqua in Agro Bruttio nuper reperta : edidit et interpretatus est Johannes Brownius, A. M. Aedis Christi quondam alumnus, Oxoniae,* 1862.' All the laughers were then on his side, and comparative scholars were assured that an English Chancellor of the Exchequer had disposed of such men as Champollion, Bunsen, Burnouf, Rawlinson, Kirchhoff, Aufrecht, Mommsen, *et hoc genus omne,* in the short hours of leisure left him by his official duties. It seems to be a common failing of Chancellors of the Exchequer that they imagine that in the few hours of leisure left them by their arduous duties they can do infinitely more than ordinary mortals who spend all their time over Greek and Latin. I was truly sorry for Sir George Cornewall Lewis at the time, and I believe he lived long enough to be truly sorry himself for this *jeu d'esprit*, which, I confess, reminded me always of an elephant trying to dance on a

rope.   In his *Astronomy of the Ancients* he had tried to show
that, wherever the tradition of a language had once been
broken, it was impossible, by means of the comparative
method, to decipher an ancient inscription, whether in
Egypt, Persia, Italy, or anywhere else.   In his squib he
gave a practical illustration, showing that, by employing the
same comparative method, he was able to interpret any inscription, even the following, which he proved to be Umbrian:—

> HEYDIDDLEDIDDLE
> THECATANDTHEFIDDLE
> THECOWJUMPEDOVERTHEMOON
> THELITTLEDOGLAUGHED
> TOSEESUCHFINESPORT
> ANDTHEDISHRANAWAYWITHTHESPOON.

Often was I asked at the time—now nearly thirty years
ago—why I did not answer these attacks; but, with all
respect for Sir George Cornewall Lewis, I felt that no
answer was deserved.   Would an astronomer feel called
upon to answer, if the most learned Chancellor of the
Exchequer asked him, in his most solemn way, whether he
really thought that the sun did not rise?   Would a chemist
feel disturbed in his experiments if he were told, even by the
most jocular of journalists, that by profusely mixing oxygen
and hydrogen he had never succeeded in producing a single
drop of water?   It is no doubt the duty of a journalist to
give his opinion about everything; and if he does it with
real *esprit*, no one finds fault with him.   He may even, if he
is persevering, stir up a certain amount of what is called
public opinion: but what is public opinion to a scholar and
to a lover of truth?   Of course, if it can be shown that
Bopp and Grimm have completely changed their opinion, or
that those who followed after them have convicted these
great scholars of many an error, the ignorant crowd will
always say, 'Aha! aha!'   But those who are quiet in the

land would, on the contrary, be utterly disheartened if it were otherwise, and if, in spite of constant moil and toil, the best scholars were always to remain in the same trench, never advancing a step in the siege of the strong fortress of truth. What seems to me intolerable is that persons who avowedly cannot form an independent opinion of two views, the one propounded by Bopp, the other by Grimm, should think that they can dispose of two such giants by simply saying, ' Aha! aha! they contradict each other.'

It is strange that some of these ready critics, who, though ignorant of Sanskrit, pride themselves on their knowledge of Greek and Latin, should be unaware that fortunately in Greek and Latin philology also great scholars contradict themselves and contradict others quite as much as in Sanskrit, Zend, Gothic, or comparative philology. The Greek classics have been interpreted now for nearly two thousand years—at Alexandria, at Rome, at Constantinople, at Paris, Oxford, Cambridge, and Berlin. No doubt a schoolboy, when reading his Homer, imagines that the construction of every line is settled by his tutor, and the meaning of every word by his Liddell and Scott. But every true scholar knows how different the real state of the case is, how much uncertainty attaches to the meaning of many words ; how often scholars have changed their interpretation of certain lines ; and how fiercely the highest authorities contradict each other as to the true purport of Homeric poetry and Homeric mythology. Let us open the *Odyssey*, and in the very first line the best scholars differ as to the meaning of πολύτροπος and the grammatical analysis of ἔννεπε. Ennius was right in rendering ἔννεπε (i. e. ἔν-σεπε) by *insece*, an etymologically-identical form, identical also with the German *ansagen*, English *to say*. But, if he was right in this, it follows that we must change ἔσπετε, say, into ἔσπετε, because it stands for σε-σέπ-ετε, and there is no excuse for dropping the aspirate. As a matter of fact some of the MSS. read ἔσπετε. However, La

Roche and other Homeric interpreters differ on this point, as on many others.

But if Ennius was right in rendering ἔννεπε by *insece*, he was probably wrong in taking πολύτροπος in the sense of *versatus*, as if it were πολύμητις. Πολύτροπος in our passage means no more than ὅς μάλα πολλὰ πλάγχθη, according to a very common peculiarity of Homeric diction. Still this again is an open question.

The very next word, πλάγχθη, gives rise to a new controversy as to whether it means 'he was tossed' or 'made to wander.' I decidedly prefer the first meaning, but far greater authorities prefer the second.

And so we could go on from page to page, pointing out words and whole sentences on which doctors disagree, and yet without any scholar venturing to say that it is useless therefore to read Homer [1].

There are two classes of readers for Homer, as there are two classes of readers for the Vedas. One class must accept what either Indian or European commentators have laid down as the law, just as schoolboys must accept what their master tells them, whether out of Aristarchus or out of Merry and Munro. Another class of more advanced students must judge for themselves. But no one would even pass moderations by simply saying that Sâyana differed from Ludwig and Aristarchus from La Roche, and that therefore they were probably both wrong. If two doctors disagree, it is surely no proof of superior knowledge and judgment to smile at those who honestly try to form their own opinion. It does not follow that both are wrong, because an indolent looker-on cannot decide which of them is right. It rather follows

---

[1] What is the true meaning of ἀσπερχές, Od. I. 20; of ἀτρεκέως, Od. I. 169? How should we interpret θεῶν ἐν γούνασι κεῖται, Od. I. 267? how ἔεδνα in Od. I. 277; ἀνοπαῖα, Od. I. 320; ἀλφηστής, Od. I. 349; ἀργός, Od. II. 11; εὐδείελος, Od. II. 167; ἠλεός, Od. II. 243, &c.? Might we not say to some recent translators of Homer, *Hic Rhodos, hic salta*?

that the mere looker-on should keep at a respectful distance, and that he should not try to act as umpire, unless he knows the difference between a hit and a miss.   Squibs are amusing for the time, but they are very apt to turn into boomerangs.

APPENDIX III.

P. 126.

ON TOTEMS AND THEIR VARIOUS ORIGIN.

Mr. Hoskyns Abrahall gives a curious extract from a paper, written by an Ottawa Indian [1], where he states that 'the Indians to whom he himself belonged, were divided into tribes, and a tribe was again subdivided into sections, or families, according to their *ododams*, that is, their devices, signs, or what may be called, according to the usages of civilised communities, "coats of arms."   The members of a particular family kept themselves distinct, at least nominally, from the other members of the tribe; and, in their large villages, all people claiming to belong to the same *ododam*, or sign, were required to dwell in that section of the village set apart for them specially, and which, from the mention of gates, we may suppose was enclosed by wickets or some sort of fence.   At the principal entrance into this enclosure there was the figure of an animal, or some other sign, set up on the top of one of the posts.   By means of this sign everybody might know to what particular family the inhabitants of that quarter claimed to belong.   For instance, those whose *ododam* was the bear, would set up the figure of that animal at their principal gate.   Some of the families were called after their *ododam*.   For example, those who had the gull for their *ododam*, were called the Gull family, or simply,

---

[1] *Academy*, 1884, Sept. 27 ; *The Canadian Journal* (Toronto). New Series, No. 14 (March 1858).

the Gulls; they would, of course, put up the figure of that
bird at their gate. Others did not adopt this custom; for
instance, the family who set up the bear, were called the Big
Feet. Many of the village gates must have been adorned
with very curious carvings, in consequence of parts only of
different animals being frequently joined together to make up
the ensigns armorial of a family; for instance, the *ododam* of
one particular section consisted of a small hawk and the fins
of a sturgeon (pp. 119–120).'

Here, however, as in most cases, where we try to discover
the origin of certain customs [1], we ought to be on our guard
against supposing that, if we discover one plausible origin,
the whole problem is solved. Like rivers, most customs
have more than one source. We saw already how one clan,
called the Big Feet, had for their sign the Bear. Here the
Big Feet may have suggested the Bear quite as well as the
Bear might have suggested the Big Feet. When we meet
with a sign consisting of the wing of a hawk and the fins of
a sturgeon, it is difficult to imagine what couple of ancestors
this clan could have claimed. We know how many purely
accidental circumstances have led to the foundation of certain
armorial bearings among ourselves, and we must be prepared
for the same variety among the Red Indians.

If scholars can prove that early races really believed that
they were descended from bears, or dogs, and serpents and
birds, I have nothing to say, though to my mind such conceptions, far from being original, seem generally later
superstitions due to misunderstandings, and often to superstitions only. Even if it pleased a certain school to see in
such superstitions a recollection of our pre-historic animal
ancestors, no harm can be done so long as the door is left

---

[1] How the *totem* is only one out of many manifestations of Sign-
language (ideography), may be seen from an excellent paper by E.
Curtius, *Über Wappengebrauch und Wappenstil im griechischen Alterthum*,
Berlin, 1874.

wide open for other explanations. A student familiar with the customs of uncivilised races would probably consider these marks or names of clans so natural, and, at the same time, so much under the influence of historical events which baffle all conjecture, that he would abstain from attempting a general explanation of them, except where by some accident the key to one or other of these names had actually fallen into his hands. What could seem more natural than that, as we name and number our houses, people in their earliest settlements should have tried to distinguish their lairs or abodes by some visible signs. And if they marked their abode with a dead crow or a live wolf, would they not soon be called the Crows or the Wolves?

What could seem more natural than, for some reason or other, to call a man a donkey or a bear? And in this case also, might not his descendants have been called the Donkeys or the Bears?

Again, what could seem more natural than that people living in a country inhabited by snakes or bears, should themselves be called Nâgas (snakes), or Arkades (Ursini or Bears)? And as Bears could only be descended from some primitive or divine Bear, what is there irrational or even surprising in such myths as the descent of the Arcadians from a she-bear and Zeus?

All this, however, is only guess-work, and on closer examination we should find again and again that our guesses were wrong. The Shoshoni tribe, for instance [1], according to Bushmann, an offshoot of the northern branch of the Nahuatl linguistic division, goes by the name of Snakes, Gens des Serpents, Serpentine Indians. But there seems to be no trace of their worshipping a snake or claiming descent from a snake, and our author tells us that their name was taken from the Snake river flowing through the country of this

---

[1] *Proceedings of the American Philosophical Society*, April 1886, p. 206.

tribe, on account of the numerous puff-adders found upon its banks [1]. The gesture-sign by which the Shoshonis are known is formed by placing the closed right hand near the right hip, forefinger extended and pointing forward, palm down; then the hand is pushed to the front and toward the left, the hand is rotated from side to side, giving the index a serpentine motion, which is the sign for snake, as a reptile. The word Shoshoni, however, does not mean snake, and Dr. Hoffmann believes that the gesture-sign of snake refers to the weaving or building of the grass lodges in which these tribes lived. The question becomes still more complicated when we are told that the Shoshonis always ride on horseback, and that, if they lose their horse and have to walk on foot, they become Shoshocoes.

Another tribe is now called Tejon, a Spanish translation of the Indian word *Tin'liu*, a badger-hole. This name, however, does not originate with the many depressions found in the country occupied by this people, but from a myth having allusion to their origin in peopling the country by coming out of the earth through badger-holes, and consequently calling themselves *Badger-hole People*.

Another tribe is called the Crows, Absarokas, but the true Absaroka is said to have been white.

I only mention these few facts in order to show that if we want to know the real origin of totems we must study well-authenticated cases, such, for instance, as Mr. Brinton has placed before us in his valuable publications on American folk-lore.

Having shown why the White One, or the Rising Sun, and, in the end, the Creator of the World, was called the *Great Hare* or *Rabbit*, and having proved the prevalence of a belief among the Red Indians and other tribes that they were 'Children of the Sun,' Mr. Brinton finds no difficulty in

---

[1] In Malay *ular* is a snake, but *ular ular* a brook.

accounting for the Hare as a clan-mark, or for the great respect which was paid to that mark and to that clan [1].

If the Athapascan tribes west of the Rocky Mountains—the Kenai, the Kolushes, and the Atnai—claim descent from a raven, Mr. Brinton has shown that with them the Raven was the name of the mighty cloud-bird, who in the beginning of things seized the elements and brought the world from the abyss of the primitive ocean (p. 229). How different, and how much more real, is this explanation than the vague theory, lately propounded again by Lippert [2], that 'a totem is the same as a fetish in which the soul of some departed ancestor has taken up its abode.' What evidence is there that any Red Indian ever held such an opinion?

It may seem strange to us that the Dogribs, the Chepewyans, the Hare Indians, and also the west-coast Eskimos, with the natives of the Aleutian Isles, should claim descent from a Dog. But this animal again is known to have been the fixed symbol of the water-goddess from whom, as well as from the sun or the winds, all life on earth was supposed to spring [3] (p. 229). Need we wonder then that the Dog should have become one of the family signs !

'Though hasty writers,' as Mr. Brinton writes, ' have often said that the Indian tribes claim lineal descent from different wild beasts, probably . . . this will prove, on examination, to be an error resting on a misapprehension arising from the habit of the natives of adopting as their totem or clan-mark the figure and name of some animal, or else in an ignorance of the animate symbols employed with such marked preference

---

[1] In a Lecture, lately delivered by Dr. Brinton (1885, p. 9), he goes so far as to say : 'The word for rabbit in Algonkin is almost identical with that for light, and when these savages applied the word to their divinity, they agreed with him who said, " God is Light, and in Him is no darkness at all." '

[2] *Die Religionen*, p. 12.

[3] See also Horatio Hale, ' The Iroquois Sacrifice of the White Dog,' *American Antiquarian*, Jan. 1885.

by the red race to express abstract ideas. In some cases,
doubtless, the natives themselves came, in time, to confound
the symbol with the idea, by that familiar process of personi-
fication and consequent debasement exemplified in the history
of every religion ; but I do not believe that a single example
could be found where an Indian tribe had a tradition whose
real purport was that man came by natural process of descent
from an ancestor, a brute ' (p. 232).

How modern some of these so-called totems may be, can be
seen from a communication made to me by an English
traveller, who resided for a long time among the Red Indians.
He saw in the centre of a village belonging to the Mandans
as their totem, or object of tutelary worship, a boat, and their
head Priest or Medicine Man was called ' The Old Man of the
Boat.' The legend they told of the boat was exactly that of
Noah in the Old Testament, and so closely did they follow
it that they always kept two pigeons near the boat in commemoration of the service they had rendered during the big
flood.

Some scholars would no doubt feel inclined to use this
coincidence as a proof that the Red Indians brought this
legend away from the primeval centre of humanity ; but it is
by no means impossible that we have here a totem which is
due to a Christian Missionary, and perhaps not more than a
hundred years old. Such facts teach caution, however difficult
that lesson may be.

Totemism is one of those pseudo scientific terms which
have done infinite harm to the study of mythology. I have
often protested, but, I am afraid, in vain, against the habit of
using a name, which is applicable to certain objects in a certain
country and at a certain time, as a general appellation.

I protested many years ago against the custom of calling
all monuments, consisting of three stones and a fourth on
the top, *cromlechs*, in whatever part of the world they are
found. Cromlech is the Celtic name of Celtic monuments,

and to apply it to similar monuments found in Africa, Egypt, the Lebanon, in India or in Hawaii, is, to say the least, extremely misleading[1].

I protested once more against the slovenly use of the term *fetish*, a name assigned by Portuguese sailors to certain objects of worship (feitiços) among the negroes of the Gold Coast, but afterwards so widely extended that hardly any tangible object of worship can now escape the name of fetish, or any religion the byeword of fetishism[2]. The stone swallowed by Jupiter and afterwards preserved at Delphi, the anvils fastened to the feet of Hera, the stone found in the coffin of Alkmene, the stone which Jacob took for his pillow, and afterward consecrated as a Beth-el, the Coronation-stone at Westminster Abbey, all have lately been promiscuously labelled as 'fetishes,' as if that taught us anything, instead of making confusion only worse confounded.

All this is thoroughly unscientific. To take a foreign word, without accurately defining it, and then to add to it the magical termination of *ism*, may save a great deal of trouble, but what is here called trouble, is in reality accurate thought.

Totemism[3] is no doubt, a very convenient term. I have often used it myself, and should have been the last person to cavil at its barbarous form[4], if only its meaning were accurately defined. It was simply in order to hint at the danger of using such terms without knowing even their etymology and meaning, that I lately recalled the remarks of Father Cuoq. The word *totem* is properly *ote*, meaning 'clan-mark.' The possessive form is *otem*, and with the personal pronoun *nind otem*, 'my clan-mark,' *kit*

---

[1] *Chips from a German Workshop*, iii. p. 279.

[2] *Hibbert Lectures*, p. 54 seq.

[3] Waitz, *Anthropologie*, iii. p. 190 seq.; Bancroft, *Native Races*, p. 130 seq.   [4] *Selected Essays*, ii. p. 376, etc.

otem, 'thy clan-mark[1].' Nothing was further from my thoughts than to wish to abolish the old familiar term of *totem*, when it is used in its legitimate sense. There are much stronger reasons why we should abolish such terms as *Zend*, *Avesta*, *Pâli*, *Aryan*, and *Turanian*, yet if only we define clearly what we mean by them, it is far better to retain them. All I wish for is that those who write about *Totem* and *Totemism* should tell us exactly what they mean by those words, and that they should not take it for granted that religion must everywhere pass through the phases of fetishism, totemism, animism or any other ism.

APPENDIX IV.

P. 168.

DURGÂ.

Durgâ, as a goddess, occurs for the first time in one of the Khilas of the Rig-veda, if indeed we may assign to these poor compilations a greater antiquity than to the Âranyakas. This Khila is a hymn to Râtrî, the night. It is found in the MSS. of the Rig-veda after the 127th hymn of the 10th Mandala (see my edit. princ., vol. vi. p. 23). After four verses addressed to Râtrî, follow some verses addressed to Durgâ. I give the translation of the hymn, as far as it can be translated in its imperfect form[2]:

'O Night, the terrestrial air has been filled by the father's powers; thou, the mighty, traversest the mansions of the sky, and awful darkness returns.

'O Night, may thy man-beholding seers (the stars) be ninety-nine, eighty-eight, and seventy-seven.

'I approach the Night, the mother, who brings rest to all creatures, the kindly[3], holy, dark night of the whole world.

'I have approached the fortunate (sivâ) night, who quiets

---

[1] *Academy*, 1884, Sept. 20.   [2] See Muir, *Sanskrit Texts*, iv. p. 498.
[3] Some MSS. read Durgâm.

and composes (all things), adorned with a garland of plants and stars. O kind one, may we reach the other side! O kind one, may we reach the other side! Om, adoration!'

Now begins the hymn to Durgâ, though there is as yet nothing in these verses that points directly to this goddess as described in the Mârkandeya Purâna. We have had the epithets sivâ and durgâ in the preceding verses, as applied to Râtrî, we now see her called Durgâ, but without any definite mythological character.

'I shall eagerly praise the divine (devi) Durgâ, who yields a refuge, who is beloved by the Bahvrikas (priests of the Rig-veda), who is equal to a thousand[1]. Let us pour out Soma to Gâtavedas (Fire)[2].

'Thou art approached[3] by Rishis for the peace of the twice-born, thou art born in the Rig-veda. May she (or Agni) burn up the wealth of the enemy.

'Whatever Brâhmanas, learned or ignorant, approach thee, O Goddess (devi), the carrier of oblations, may she (or he) carry us over all obstacles (durgâni).

'Whatever twice-born men shall celebrate the fire-coloured, beautiful, gentle (goddess), she will carry them over obstacles, —Agni (carries) across all evils, as in a boat across a river.

'All who are bewildered in obstacles, in misfortune, in fearful war, in trouble from enemies, in visitations from fire or thieves, in escape from evil stars, in troublesome obstacles, in wars and wildernesses, approach thee. Give us security from these, give us security from these. Om, adoration!

'The long-haired (kesini), whose name among all creatures is Pañkamî (the Fifth, or Beautiful), may she, the good Night, the goddess (devi), preserve us always, may she preserve us always. Om, adoration!

---

[1] Could it be sahasra samgñitam, with a thousand names?
[2] The last lines in this and the three following verses are borrowed from Rv. I. 99.
[3] Samupâsritâ.

'I approach as my refuge Durgâ, the goddess, the fire-coloured, flaming with heat, the daughter of the sun (Viro-*k*ana), who is welcome for the rewards of good works. O thou well-speeding, adoration to thy speed !

'May Durgâ, the goddess (devî*h*), be propitious for our success !

'He who always recites this praise of Durgâ night after night [viz. â râtri, Ku*s*ika Saubhara, the poet, or Râtrî Bhâradvâ*g*î, praise of the Night, metre Gâyatrî], he who mutters the hymn to Râtrî, he succeeds at that very time.'

This is clearly a compilation made on purpose for a goddess Durgâ. What we can recognise behind her, are the night and the fire. The epithet durgâ, difficult to pass, or difficult to approach, would be applicable to both.

In the Taittirîya-âra*n*yaka, X. 7, we find a verse addressed to the same goddess, but under the name of Durgi*h*:

Kâtyâyanâya vidmahe, Kanyâkumârî dhîmahi, tan no Durgi*h* pro*k*odayât.

I doubt whether the text is correct. We expect the names Kâtyâyanî, the accusative Kanyâkumârîm, and Durgâ. The commentator, however, explains Durgi for Durgâ as linga-vyatyaya*s kh*ândasa*h*, and it has to be observed that all the preceding deities are masculine, namely, Rudra, Vinâyaka, Nandi, Kârtikeya, Garu*d*a, Brahmâ, Vish*n*u, Narasi*m*ha, Âditya, Agni, and lastly Durgi. In the text of the Mahâ-nârâya*n*a Upanishad, III. 12 (ed. G. A. Jacob, 1888, p. 4), the text is more correct:

Kâtyâyanyai vidmahe, Kanyâkumârîm dhîmahi, tan no Durgâ prakadayât.

Again, in Taitt.-Âr. X. 26 and 30, we find invocations addressed to Gâyatrî, which strongly remind us of Durgâ. In the 26th Anuvâka, Gâyatrî is called varadâ, boon-giving, and in the 30th Anuvâka she is spoken of as uttame *s*ikhare *g*âtâ (or devî) bhûmyâm parvata-mûrdhani, 'born on the highest peak, on the earth, on the summit of the mountain,' which epithets might refer to Pârvatî, but are by tradition referred to Gâyatrî or Sarasvatî.

Several of the names given to Rudra in the Taittirîya-Âra*n*yaka, point to him as the husband of Durgâ. Thus we read, X. 18 :

Namo hira*n*yabâhave, hira*n*yavar*n*âya, hira*n*yarûpâya, hira*n*yapataye, Ambikâpataye, Umâpataye, Pa*s*upataye, namo nama*h*.

'Adoration to the golden-armed, golden-coloured, golden-shaped, the lord of gold, the lord of Ambikâ, the lord of Umâ, the lord of cattle !'

This Ambikâ is mentioned as the sister of Rudra in Vâ*g*. Sa*m*h. III. 57, and his name Tryambaka is derived from strî-ambika (*S*atap.-Br. II. 6, 2, 9), because Ambikâ, his sister, shared the sacrifice with him. This Ambikâ is in Taitt.-Br. I. 6, 10, 4, identified with *S*arad, the autumn.

The name Tryambaka has also been explained as 'having three mothers, or sisters.' But this can hardly be, as his wife also is called Tryambakâ. Most likely it was meant as another expression for Trilo*k*ana, three-eyed, one of the most general names of *S*iva in later times.

APPENDIX V.

P. 180.

ON THE UNTRUSTWORTHINESS OF ANTHROPOLOGICAL EVIDENCE.

As it has been suggested that my representation of the untrustworthy character of much of the evidence on which students of comparative theology and of anthropology have to rely is exaggerated, I give here some of the *pièces justificatives*. I do not blame anybody. On the contrary, I highly appreciate the labours of those who have given us their accounts of what they have seen and heard among savage tribes.   Nor have I any right to find fault with others who in their study of language, customs, and religions have trusted these accounts, as I myself have but too often shared their fate.   All I say is that now that we have found out by sad experience how untrustworthy some of these accounts are, and how often they flatly contradict each other, we ought to discard all evidence that does not come to us either from a man who was able himself to converse with native races, or who was at least an eye-witness of what he relates. Even then, I know full well, there still remain many dangers.   Savages, when brought into conversational inter-course with white people, are generally very anxious to please.   They never like to disappoint or contradict their questioners.   Mr. Ellis in his charming *Polynesian Researches*, published many years ago, remarks that almost in the same breath a Malagasy will express his belief that when he dies he ceases altogether to exist, and yet confess the fact that he is in the habit of praying to his ancestors who are supposed to hover about their tombs.

It was Darwin, I believe, who remarked very truly, 'that the effects of false inferences are but of little moment, for every one feels a pleasure in setting them straight, but that false facts are most dangerous, because there may be but few who can point out their untruth[1].'   When we have to deal with the evidence taken from language or from literary works, everybody can form his own opinion, or, if he cannot, he can abstain.   But when we have to deal with evidence even of eye-witnesses from the Andaman Islands, and if these eye-witnesses not only differ, but contradict each other, what shall we do?   Shall we go to the Andaman Islands, before finishing a sentence?   And if we did go, would it not take years before we could learn the native dialects in order to be able freely to converse with the natives, and thus to guard

[1] *Journal of Anthropological Institute*, Aug. 1890, p. 43.

against the very mishaps that have befallen those who came before us ? All we can do is to follow strictly the two principles which I laid down in my Lecture, never to quote any but eye-witnesses, and never to trust even eye-witnesses unless they were familiar with the language. This, no doubt, will very considerably reduce the bulk of what has been written on anecdotic anthropology, and more particularly, on comparative theology, but what we lose in quantity we shall certainly gain in quality.

It is unfortunate that this subject cannot be discussed without exciting personal resentments. I sometimes wish that all learned works could be written anonymously. Whenever one scholar arrives at results different from those hitherto accepted, it is looked upon as a kind of slur thrown on those who hold the old opinion. It does not seem to be so in other sciences. If a new planet is discovered by one observer, the other astronomers do not consider themselves disgraced, or bound in honour to defend their old map of the stars. When spectral analysis showed that former theories on the constituent elements of the sun were imperfect and erroneous, no one felt ashamed of his former ignorance.

Why should it be different with scholars ? The difficulty of gaining a clear conception of a religion by addressing some questions on religious topics to a few savages is enormous. It is not easy, as we all know, to draw an intelligent answer on the most common subjects from a ploughboy. But a native of Australia stands on a much lower level than most English ploughboys. And if he is asked any question by a white man, he is frightened. He does not know why he should be asked such questions, and he is at once afraid of mischief. When he gives an answer, the questioner himself is often at a loss to understand, or, thinking he does understand it, he entirely misapprehends its real meaning.

Names of Places.

What can be simpler than to ask the name of a place?
But though wandering tribes may have names for any remarkable spot in their territories, they seldom feel the
necessity of naming larger areas, and when they are asked
their names, they are as much at a loss as if we were asked
the name of a long extent of downs or forests. Thus it is
extremely probable that the name of what is now called the
Manéra Plains arose from a Sydney black being asked the
name, and replying *manyer*, that is, *I do not know*. Ever
since the place has been called *Manera*.

Mr. Threlkeld, in his *Australian Grammar* (1834), tells us
that a naturalist one day requested the name of a native cat
from M'Gill, his aboriginal, who replied *minnaring*. The
person was about to write down the word '*minnaring*, a
native cat,' when Mr. Threlkeld prevented him, observing
that the word was not the name of the native cat, but a
question, namely, 'What' (is it you say? being understood),
the black man not understanding what was said.

A similar accident is said to have occurred with regard to
the inhabitants of the Andaman islands, the so-called Mincopies. When they were asked their name, they answered
Min kaich (come here), or *Kâmin kâpi* (stand here), and
this, according to Mr. E. H. Man (*The Andaman Islanders*,
p. 3), may have been corrupted to Mincopie.

A similar case is mentioned by Chamisso in his *Voyage
Round the World*. It is a well-known Polynesian custom to
exchange names in token of friendship. One of Chamisso's
companions, Dr. Eschholtz, wished to exchange his name with
a person sitting on the left of the chief. The chief being
asked his name, replied *Teridili*, 'he on the left?' i.e. 'Do
you mean him on the left?' This *Teridili* was, however,
mistaken for the man's name, and adopted by Chamisso's
friend. When Chamisso's friend, Dr. Eschholtz, was asked by
Teridili for his name, he did not quite understand either.

Chamisso interpreted, saying, *Dein Name*, i. e. ' he wants to know your name.' Upon which *Teridili* laid hold of *Dein Name*, and was called in future *Deinnam*[1].

These may seem extreme cases, but even as extreme cases, they are far more frequent than we should suspect. It is only by remembering this difficulty of a free exchange of ideas between civilised and uncivilised people that we can account for the constant contradictions between eye-witnesses who have spent years in Africa, Australia, or New Zealand, who have observed the same scenery and the same customs, who have even acquired a slight familiarity with the spoken dialects of the natives, and who nevertheless give the most conflicting accounts of what they have seen with their own eyes and heard with their own ears.

The Australian Blacks as described by Different Observers.

Mr. Curr's book on the *Australian Race* is a strong case in point. He has lived in Australia for many years. He seems to be a man of an observant mind, and free from any preconceived theories. He tells us that since the year 1866 he has been paying attention to the dialects spoken in Australia, and that he began his own collection of lists of words in 1873. He has had help from many quarters, and has been a diligent reader of the more important books that have been published on the languages, the customs, and religious opinions of the natives of Australia. He has had much intercourse with the blacks, though what that intercourse between Europeans and the natives of Australia amounts to, we may gather from a remark made by Mr. Curr (i. 26), that the conversation between the two is generally carried on with a vocabulary of probably not more than 250 words and 50 phrases.

---

[1] Chamisso, *Werke*, i. p. 247.

The Australian as the Lowest Savage.

The Australian is often supposed to be the nearest approach to primitive man. Leaving the so-called primitive man out of the question, for I am afraid we shall never know anything about him, it is certainly of extreme importance to know, how low a human being may sink, without ceasing to be a human being.

Are there Fireless Savages?

Let us begin with the question whether there are any human beings without a knowledge of kindling and keeping fire. Some anthropologists, it is well known, are as anxious to prove that primitive man must have been fireless as that he must have been godless. If then a missionary states that he has actually met with tribes that had no knowledge of kindling fire, no one surely would blame the anthropologist who accepts so welcome a statement in support of his own theory. But what is he to do, if another traveller asserts that he has seen the same tribe in the same locality kindling a fire? He can only turn away in disgust, or learn the lesson that from the days of Herodotus even to our own time 'the testimony of travellers is extremely doubtful.'

This is not an imaginary case. The natives of Tasmania, for instance, who, like the Australians, have often sat for the portrait of the primordial man, were declared by Calder in his *Journal*, pp. 19–20, to have been unacquainted with the art of kindling fire. Other authorities, such as Dove and Backhouse, confirmed this statement. However, it was proved by Fourneaux that the Tasmanians could not have been ignorant of fire, and that they knew at least two methods of kindling fire. For he found in one of their huts 'the stone they strike fire with, and tinder made of bark.' Others discovered flints and dried grass kept in baskets. Davies (p. 419) was informed that 'they obtained fire by rubbing round rapidly in their hands a piece of hard pointed stick, the pointed end being inserted into a notch in another piece of dry wood.' As this process was not always success-ful, they generally, as Melville states, p. 347, and especially in wet weather, carried on their peregrinations a fire-stick, lighted in their last encampment. Mrs. Meredith (p. 139) relates that when the natives crossed over to Maria Island, they provided a little raised platform on the raft, on which they carried some lighted fuel to kindle their fire when they arrived there. Is not that the rudimentary type of the ship that brought every year the sacred fire from Delos? It may be, but it may also be something totally different.

Prometheus-legend in Australia.

It would seem as if the Tasmanians possessed even a kind of Prometheus-legend, though in a very primitive form. It was related by a native of the Oyster Bay tribe.

'My father,' he said, 'my grandfather, all of them lived a long time ago, all over the country; they had no fire. Two black fellows came. They were seen by my fathers, my countrymen, on the top of a hill. They threw fire like a star—it fell among the black men, my countrymen. They were frightened, they fled away, all of them. After a while they returned, they hastened and made a fire, a fire with wood; no more was fire lost in our land.' The legend then goes on to say that the two black fellows are now in the clouds, and are seen in the clear nights like two stars. Mr. Milligan, who tells this story in the *Papers of the Royal Society of Tasmania*, vol. iii. p. 274, identifies these two stars with Castor and Pollux. And he adds another legend about some other stars near them, given him by the same black.

'The two black men,' he related, 'stayed awhile in the land of my fathers. Two women (Lowanna) were bathing; it was near a rocky shore, where mussels were plentiful.

The women were sulky, they were sad; their husbands were faithless, they had gone with two girls. The women were lonely; they were swimming in the water, they were diving for cray-fish. A sting-ray lay concealed in the hollow of a rock—a large sting-ray! The sting-ray was large, he had a very long spear; from his hole he spied the women, he saw them dive; he pierced them with his spear, he killed them, he carried them away. Awhile they were gone out of sight. The sting-ray returned, he came close on shore, he lay in still water, near the sandy beach; with him were the women, they were fast on his spear—they were dead.

'The two black men fought the sting-ray; they slew him with their spears; they killed him; the women were dead! The two black men made a fire—a fire of wood. On either side they laid a woman,—the fire was between: the women were dead! The black men sought some ants, some blue ants (puggany eptietta); they placed them on the bosoms (parugga poingta) of the women. Severely, intensely they were bitten. The women revived,—they lived once more. Soon there came a fog (mayen-tayana), a fog dark as night. The two black men went away, the women disappeared; they passed through the fog, the thick, dark fog! Their place is in the clouds. Two stars you see in the clear cold night; the two black men are there, the women are with them: they are stars above!'

Here you have the rudiments of a ballad, it may be of an epic poem. Nothing was wanting but a *vates sacer*, and instead of two black fellows we should have had a Prometheus; instead of two women, diving for cray-fish, another black Helen.

Let us now return to Australia, and examine a few cases in which Mr. Curr, as an eye-witness, contradicts other witnesses point blank, with regard to the black fellows of Australia.

Colour of Australians.

Are these black fellows black? No, says Mr. Curr, Australians have a dash of copper colour, never the sooty tinge of the African negro (p. 37).

Name of Australians.

Mr. Ridley says that Murri is the general name for Australian blacks. Mr. Curr says No, and maintains that it is confined to the eastern portion of the continent (p. 114). He also holds that this Murri must be carefully distinguished from Murrî, the name given to children in certain families (p. 114).

Moral Ideas.

Are they devoid of moral ideas? Most missionaries say Yes; Mr. Curr says No, and he ascribes their horror of consanguineous marriages to some undefined moral sentiment.

Property in Land.

There may be some excuse for a difference of opinion as to whether the Australians recognise land either as communal or as private property. It may have been the arrival of European settlers that served to arouse in the native mind the idea of personal property in land, while in former times, when there was enough and more than enough of land for all, every one took what he required, and defended it *vi et armis* against all intruders, as long as he liked to keep it. That the Australians did not till the soil before the arrival of Europeans, nor tried to domesticate any animals, seems admitted on all sides. But Mr. Curr does not consider this as a proof of savagery, but explains it by the fact that, like the Andamanese, they had abundance of food ready to their hands, and that there was hardly an animal or plant worth domestication and cultivation in Australia (p. 79).

Moveable Property.

With regard to moveable property, there is again conflict of evidence. Taplin, when describing the Narrinyeris, says (p. 66), that weapons, implements, and ornaments belong to the tribe in common. Mr. Curr maintains that they are private property without any exception. He also narrates that the man whose spear first wounds the animal, is considered as its owner when slain, according to a principle which is recognised by Manu also. Among other tribes traditional rules seem to fix the portion which different relatives may claim of a slain animal.

Tribal Customs.

Sir George Grey had maintained that if a man marries two or more wives, each belonging to a different family, his sons will often rise against each other, in fighting the battles of the families to which their respective mothers belong. Mr. Curr (p. 67) entirely denies the fact, and tries to show that it is impossible. No young man of a tribe, he says, could ever be at war with his brothers or fathers. Yet Mr. McLennan has built a whole social theory on the statement made by Sir George Grey.

It has often been said that some blacks gave the masonic sign to a white man. Again Mr. Curr denies it altogether.

We now come to the much discussed question, whether the Australians had any idea of a God.

Religious Ideas.

Again, most missionaries would say No, others Yes. But how can such a question even be asked? How could these blacks possibly have an idea of what we call God? One of the missionaries at New Norcia in Western Australia stated that the blacks in his neighbourhood have a very remote and vague idea of a Maker of all things, or rather of a great and strong man who made all things by the power of his word. The Rev. W. Ridley says that the tribes on the Namoi and the neighbouring rivers (who had long had missionaries among them) believe in a Creator, whom they call *Bayamê* or Maker; that he made man, whom he will judge, reward, and punish.

If a missionary asked some of the black fellows in our own mining districts, I doubt whether he would receive any better answer. The idea of all things being made by the power of his word, even though he be conceived as a great and strong man only, is far beyond the capacity of thousands of Christians.

But what does Mr. Curr say? He found that the people whom he asked whether they had a knowledge of God, were much surprised by the few simple questions which he put to them. And he expresses his conviction that the blacks, before they had come in contact with missionaries, had no knowledge of God, practised no prayers, and believed in no places of reward and punishment beyond the grave. 'As regards religion and morality,' he says, p. 105, 'passing over a little outward show, it seems to me that they do not exist among them.' Here he really contradicts himself, for on another occasion he accounts for their horror of certain marriages as dictated by moral principles[1].

Ghosts.

The Australians believe that man has a spiritual part. This is admitted even by Mr. Curr, who denies them every-

---

[1] See also p. 100, where Mr. Curr writes: 'Morality is but little regarded by the Australian black, though he is not by any means free from remorse consequent on infractions of the laws of that natural morality with the perception of which it seems every human being is born. From my own observations, I have no doubt that the black feels, in the commencement of his career at least, that murder, infanticide, adultery, lying, and theft are wrong, and also that their committal brings remorse.'

thing else that other authorities have allowed them, such as a belief in God as maker of the world, and as judge of men. ' When a man dies,' he writes, ' it is a very widely-spread custom for the relatives to tie up the limbs of the corpse securely, so as to prevent his coming out of the grave in the shape of a ghost. Even when the body of a relative or friend has been burnt to ashes, the same fear of seeing the deceased, or of being injured or frightened by him, still haunts the survivors, who always leave the spot at which a death has occurred, for a time at least. A man's ghost is accredited with all sorts of powers which the person himself did not possess while alive. Only the ghosts of men lately dead are feared.'

Social Institutions.

That the Australian, however savage in some respects, was under certain social restraints, could not be denied. ' The male (p. 51) must commonly submit, without hope of escape, to have one or more of his teeth knocked out, to have the septum of his nose pierced, to have certain painful cuttings made into his skin, and to other hardships which have to be undergone, before he is allowed the rights of manhood.' These restraints are not resisted. Boys who are not allowed to eat certain kinds of meat, are seldom tempted even by white people to break this rule. Where then is the controlling power to uphold these artificial restraints ? Mr. Brong Smyth in his work, *The Aborigines of Australia*, declares that it was done by regular councils of old men. Mr. Curr (p. 52) flatly denies the existence of such councils, and maintains that the delegation of authority to chief or council belongs notoriously to a stage of progress which the Australian race has not reached. Even when another writer, Mr. James Dawson, comes forward in his work entitled *Australian Aborigines*, as an additional witness to the existence of chiefs and councils, Mr. Curr declares that he was imposed on by the blacks, and that his statements are impossible. He himself appeals to his long and familiar intercourse with the natives, and to the account of one William Buckley, an escaped convict, who lived for thirty-two years with one of the Western tribes, and who states that the tribes acknowledge no particular chief as being superior to the rest, and that they have no chiefs claiming or possessing any superior right over the soil.

Next comes the Rev. George Taplin. In a work of his called *Folk-lore*, published in 1879, he maintains that the eighteen clans of the Narrinyeri are governed by a chief called *Rupulli*, or landholder, and that there is at the same time a supreme council.

Mr. Curr, however, again contradicts this statement, and quotes Mr. E. J. Eyre, who in his *Journals of Expeditions of Discovery in Central Australia* asserts that among none of the tribes yet known, have chiefs ever been found to be acknowledged, though in all there are always some men who take the lead, and whose opinions and wishes have great weight with others. . . . Each father of a family rules absolutely over his own circle. Mr. Curr finishes up by saying (p. 60) that he has made inquiries and received written replies from the observers of about a hundred tribes to the effect that no government, no habitual exercise of authority by one or a few individuals, exists anywhere in Australia. He himself ascribes all the restraints which exist to custom, education, and particularly to superstition and the fear of sorcery.

Marriage.

It seems almost incredible that there should be this conflict of witnesses on points which one imagines might be settled by the most direct evidence. But it is not only on the question of government that witnesses contradict each other flatly. We find even more of hard swearing with regard to marriage. And here a new element comes in. Several anthropologists in Europe and America have started the theory that marriage was originally communal, that is to say, that all the women of a tribe were the wives of all the men, and all the men the husbands of all the women. To call this marriage, even communal marriage, has always struck me as a bold euphemism. We may speak of polygamy, where one husband marries several wives, or of polyandry, where a wife is married to several husbands; but promiscuous intercourse between all the men and all the women of a tribe, between fathers, mothers, sisters, and brothers should hardly be spoken of as marriage. Whether such a state of things exists now anywhere, or whether it ever has existed, is a question that depends entirely on testimony. And here one would imagine that such a state of things, if it existed, could hardly be disguised. The exact form of government may withdraw itself from observation, and different facts may here be interpreted in different ways. A man might live many years in England without being able to give an intelligible account of the English constitution. But a state of promiscuous sexual intercourse prevailing among the members of a whole tribe, could hardly admit of misinterpretation. There are vague allusions to some such state of things in the epic poetry of the Indians. But when people are charged with living in a state of godharma, that is, with living like bulls and cows, that implies a charge of immorality, and it involves at all events a recognition of the lawfulness of marriage. This is very different from a supposed stage of civilisation in which the very idea of marriage was yet not known.

Now it is well known that among many savages, marriages, so far from being promiscuous, are under the most minute and complicated restrictions, restrictions so inexplicable, not to say irrational, that their very existence seems to require the admission of a long-continued tradition. In order to believe, therefore, that the same savages should at any time have been utterly ignorant of the meaning of marriage, would require the very strongest evidence.

Mr. Curr thinks that there is a very strong tendency in observers abroad, if they have become acquainted with a new and startling theory that has become popular at home, to see confirmations of it everywhere. In fact, if so many accounts of the life of savages are untrustworthy, the fault, according to Mr. Curr, lies with the whites quite as much as with the blacks. 'Every one acquainted with the blacks,' he writes, p. 131, 'will, I think, bear me out when I say that the greatest care is necessary in taking their statements; for their desire to please, and their disregard of truth are such that, if a white man making inquiries allows his views or wishes to be known, he is almost certain to find the aboriginal agreeing with him in every particular. . . . But it is not the evidence of the blacks only which requires to be cautiously sought and well sifted before acceptance; for it seems to me that, when a statement has been pronounced important in scientific circles, there are not wanting educated white men who will support it on very insufficient grounds.'

The system of intricate restrictions regulating the marriages of Australians has been the subject of most learned treatises. It was first pointed out by Sir George Grey (1841), but it was displayed in all its fulness by the Rev. Lorimer Fison and Mr. A. W. Howitt, in their work, *Kamilaroi and Kurnai*, 1880. It was headed by a preface from the pen of Professor Lewis M. Morgan, the well-known author of the *System of Consanguinity and Affinity of the Human Family*. We must remember that similar systematic restrictions on marriage had been discovered in Asia, Africa, and America, and hence, as Mr. Curr remarks, the inclination of later writers to discover among the Australian blacks as near an approach as possible to the marriage systems in other parts of the world. That inclination, no doubt, exists, and has to be carefully guarded against. But Mr. Curr assures us that what Mr. Fison has written, and what has been so largely utilised by anthropologists, 'contains important statements quite at variance with fact' (p. 119). Mr. Curr entirely denies the existence of what has been called communal or class marriage in Australia, as opposed to the very principle of Australian marriage, though he fully admits that the peculiar restrictions placed on marriage in Australia exhibit strong points of similarity with the restrictions accepted by uncivilised races in Africa, Asia, and America.

Every kind of evidence is made to tell by writers who have a theory to defend. Thus, because in the Australian language, the names for son and nephew are alike, it was argued that the system of communal marriage must have prevailed, which rendered it impossible for a man to distinguish his children from those of his brothers. But it was forgotten that women also call their own and their sisters' children by the same name. Was that because they did not know whether their own children were their own? That the use of such terms of endearment proves nothing as to the former existence of communal marriage is best shown by the fact, that in many dialects they are used in familiar conversation only, while if fathers speak *of*, not *to*, their nephews, they have a distinct name for each (p. 136).

ON THE UNTRUSTWORTHINESS OF THE ACCOUNTS OF THE RELIGIOUS IDEAS OF SAVAGES.

Tasmania.

If there is so much uncertainty as to what would seem to be clear and palpable matters in the life of savage races, we must not be surprised that, with regard to their religious ideas, the evidence even of eye-witnesses should be altogether confused and contradictory. There is one excuse for this which deserves consideration. Each witness can speak of those persons only with whom he has been brought into personal contact. What he relates, therefore, may possibly be true of a family, or of a clan, or of a whole tribe. But in a country like Australia, with so many tribes scattered about, it would seem to be impossible to say anything in general of the religious opinions of the Australians.

I have therefore chosen the small island of Tasmania, with its sparse and uniform population, and we shall find that even in this limited area accounts of different observers vary very considerably when they attempt to describe the religious customs and beliefs of the Tasmanian aborigines. I take a book lately published by Mr. H. L. Roth on the *Aborigines of Tasmania.* It is an honest, unpretentious, but very useful book. He first of all gives us on pp. 2–8 a very complete bibliography of all works treating of Tasmania, and then proceeds to place before us the quintessence distilled from that little library. In the fourteen chapters of his book Mr. Roth treats of the country, the form and size of its inhabitants, the psychology of the natives, their wars, their knowledge of fire, hunting, and fishing, their nomadic life, their personal habits, their scientific and artistic acquirements, their manufactures, their trade, their customs, good and bad, their language, their osteology, and lastly their origin.

It would be impossible to give an idea of the wealth of information on all these subjects which Mr. Roth has rendered accessible in this volume. It is well-arranged, and all his statements can readily be verified, for he always gives his references, and a complete index renders its use easy at all times. *O si sic omnes !*

I shall confine my remarks to one subject only, the Tasmanian religion, and, with the help of Mr. Roth, I shall undertake to show that there is not one essential feature in the religion of the Tasmanians on which different authorities

have not made assertions diametrically opposed to each
other.

No Religion.—Nothing staggers a savage—perhaps even
an educated man—so much as when he is asked what his
religion is. No wonder that many of the Tasmanians, when
asked that question, answered, with a broad grin, ' Don't
know.' What should we say if we were asked whether we
believe in *Raegoo Wrapper* or *Namma* ? Widowson, however,
assures us that the Tasmanians had really no religion at all.
' It is generally supposed,' he says, ' that they have not
the slightest idea of a Supreme Being.' Briton adds, ' They
do not appear to have any rites or ceremonies, religious or
otherwise.'

Dualism.—That the Tasmanians were Dualists, believing,
like the followers of Zoroaster, in a good and an evil spirit, is
attested by numerous authorities. Leigh says :—' Their
notions of religion are very obscure. However, they believe
in two spirits : one, they say, governs the day, whom they
call the good spirit; the other governs the night, and him
they think evil. To the good spirit they attribute everything
good, and to the evil spirit everything hurtful.' Jeffreys
says :—' They have but a very indistinct notion of their
imaginary deity, who, they say, presides over the day, an
evil spirit making its appearance in the night. This deity,
whosoever it is, they believe to be the giver of everything
good.' He adds, however, that they appear to acknowledge
no more than one god, thus furnishing an exact parallel to
the Parsis, who, though they admit two spirits, acknowledge
Ormazd only as their true god. Milligan confirms this view.
He admits that the Tasmanians believed in many spirits, but
he adds that ' they considered one or two spirits to be of
omnipotent energy, though they do not seem to have invested
even these last with attributes of benevolence.' Robinson
maintains that ' they were fatalists (whatever that may
mean in their language), and that they believed in the

existence both of a good and evil spirit. The latter they called *Raegoo Wrapper*, to whom they attributed all their afflictions, and they used the same word to express thunder and lightning.'

Nature-gods.—That the Tasmanians derived some of their ideas of the godhead from the great phenomena of Nature we have seen already from their identifying day and night with their good and evil spirits. Thunder and lightning were their names for the evil spirit, or their devil, as some observers call him. Besides day and night, thunder and lightning, the moon also is mentioned as an object of their worship. Thus, Lloyd tells us, 'that it was customary among the aborigines to meet at some time-honoured trysting-place at every full moon, a period regarded by them with most profound reverence.' Indeed, he adds, 'judging from their extraordinary gestures in the dance, the upturned eye and outstretched arm, apparently in a supplicating spirit, I have been often disposed to conclude that the poor savages were invoking the mercy and protection of that planet as their guardian deity.'

Devil-worship.—We now come to the testimony in support of an exclusive devil-worship. Davies asserts that the aborigines certainly believed in the existence of an evil spirit, called by some tribes Namma, who has power by night. Of him they are much afraid, and never will willingly go out in the dark. But, he adds, 'I could never make out that they believed in a good deity, for although they spoke of one, it struck me that it was what they had been told; they may, however, believe in one who has power by day.'

Backhouse speaks in the same hesitating tone:

'These people,' he says, 'have received a few faint ideas of the existence and superintending providence of God; but they still attribute the strong emotions of their minds to the devil, who, they say, tells them this or that, and to whom they attribute the power of prophetic communication. It is not clear that by the devil they mean anything more than a spirit; but they say he lives in their breasts, on which account they shrink from having the breast touched.'

If we could fully trust this statement, and it is confirmed to some extent by Horton, it would be most important as showing the germs of moral ideas among the Tasmanians. To believe in a devil, not simply with horns and hoofs, but living within our hearts, is an advance which, even in Europe, has as yet been made by a small minority only. The majority of Tasmanians evidently represented their devil in a more material form. Thus Dove says that, 'while they had no term in their native language to designate the Creator of all things, they stood in awe of an imaginary spirit who was disposed to annoy and hurt them. The appearance of this malignant demon in some horrible form, was especially dreaded in the season of night.'

Monotheism.—But while some authorities seem inclined to reduce the Tasmanian religion to a belief in a devil only, others seem to look upon it as almost monotheism. Thus Jeffreys, though he admits that the Tasmanians (like most Agnostics) have a very indistinct notion of their imaginary deity, relates that they have a kind of song which they chant to him. He knows that they believe in a good and an evil spirit, but he adds, that they believe the good spirit to be the giver of everything good, and that they do not appear to acknowledge any more than one god. That good spirit had, as we saw, no name, and this, which to some may seem to be a serious defect, is again a feature which the Tasmanian religion shares in common with the religion of far more advanced races.

Spirit-worship.—Those who hold that religion began everywhere with a belief in spirits may likewise find some support for their theory in the accounts given of the Tasmanians. Henderson states :

'A common belief prevails in Tasmania and New South

Wales regarding the existence of inferior spirits, who conceal themselves in the deep woody chasms during the day, but who wander forth after dark, with power to injure or even to destroy. Their rude encampments are frequently alarmed by these unearthly visitors, whose fearful moanings are at one time borne on the midnight breeze, and at another are heard mingling with the howling tempest.'

This does not prove as yet that these spirits are always believed to be the spirits of the departed. Milligan, however, after telling us that the Tasmanians were polytheists—that is, that they believed in guardian angels or spirits, and in a plurality of powerful but gererally evil-disposed beings, inhabiting crevices and caverns of rocks, and making temporary abode in hollow trees and solitary valleys, adds 'that the aborigines were extremely superstitious, believing most implicitly in the return of the spirits of their departed friends and relations to bless or injure them, as the case might be. To their guardian spirits, the spirits of their departed friends or relations, they gave the generic name *Warrawah*, an aboriginal term signifying shade, shadow, ghost, or apparition.'

Immortality of the Soul.—One point on which nearly all witnesses seem to agree is the belief of the Tasmanians in the immortality of the soul. They evidently had not yet advanced so far as to be able to doubt it. Milligan had ascertained that the aborigines of Tasmania, previous to their intercourse with Europeans, distinctly entertained the idea of immortality, as regarded the soul or spirit of man. Robinson, who was present at the burning of a dead body, received the following explanation from a native:—' Native dead, fire ; goes road England, plenty natives England. What he meant to say was that when a black fellow was dead and had been burnt, he went to England, where there are many black fellows. The name of England, *Dreany*, as a distant country, and the home of white people, had become with them the name of a new Elysium. Others expected to reappear on an island in the Straits, and to jump up white men. They anticipated in another life the full enjoyment of what they coveted in this. Backhouse declares that they have some vague ideas of a future existence. Dove remarks that they were persuaded of their being ushered by death into another and happier state, and he considers this as almost the only remnant of a primitive religion which maintained a firm abode in their minds. However, as if to show that no account of their religious persuasions should go uncontradicted, Davies remarks that, 'though it is hard to believe that the natives have no idea of a future state, yet from every inquiry, both from themselves and from whites most conversant with them, I have never been able to ascertain that such a belief exists.'

Prayers.—Of course those who maintain that the Tasmanians have no religion, maintain at the same time that they have no kind of worship, no sacrifices, no prayers. But Leigh tells us that, ' when any of the family are on a journey, they are accustomed to sing to the good spirit for the purpose of securing his protection over their absent friends, and that they may be brought back in health and safety.' Jeffreys relates that it frequently happens that the sealers . . . are compelled to leave their native women for several days together. On these occasions these affectionate creatures have a kind of song, which they chant to their imaginary deity.

Charms.—It is known also that the Tasmanians carried charms, mostly a bone, or even the skull of their relatives and friends. In some cases they ascribed healing powers to these bones, or at all events they put them by their side or on their head when they felt sick. This, after all, is no more than our preserving a lock of hair, and looking at it when we are in trouble or grief.

Negative evidence is always less trustworthy than positive.

Still it may be taken for what it is worth, that observers seem never to have discovered idols (p. 69), totems (p. 75), or fetishes, among the natives of Tasmania.

Such is the nature of the evidence bearing on the religious ideas of the Tasmanians, which Mr. Roth has collected so carefully and so conscientiously. Nothing can be more full of contradictions, more doubtful, more perplexing. With such materials anthropologists and sociologists have had to build up their systems, and yet they look down with contempt on the evidence supplied by the Veda, the Old Testament, and the Homeric poems, because they contain various readings and because some passages admit of different translations!

We saw that there is hardly any kind of religion that could not be proved to have been the original religion of the Tasmanians. If it were desired to prove that, prior to the advent of Europeans, they were atheists, without any religious ideas or ceremonial usages, we have several excellent witnesses to prove it. We could prove equally well that they believed in a devil only, that they were Dualists, believing in a good and an evil spirit, that they had deified the powers of Nature, that they had arrived at a belief in one God, that they were polytheists, that they believed in ghosts, in the return of the spirits of their friends, in the immortality of the soul, and in the efficacy of prayers and charms. Nay, if it were desired to produce perfectly unprejudiced evidence in favour of the descent of man from some higher animal, Lord Monboddo might have appealed to the Tasmanians. For, according to Mr. Horton, they believed 'that they were formed with tails and without knee-joints, by a benevolent being, and that another descended from heaven, and compassionating the sufferers, cut off their tails, and with grease softened their knees.'

APPENDIX VI.

P. 244.

RAJENDRALAL MITRA'S NOTES ON VEDIC FUNERALS.

NOTE 1. Rajendralal Mitra has collected the following rules from other Sûtras. Immediately after death of a person who has always maintained the sacrificial fires in his house, a homa should be performed, accompanied by a mantra. According to Bodhâyana four offerings should be made, while touching the right hand of the dead, to the Gârhapatya-fire, with a spoon overflowingly full of clarified butter. Bharadvâga prefers the Âhavanîya-fire, and is silent as to whether the offering should be fourfold or not. Âsvalâyana recommends the rite to be performed at a subsequent stage of the funeral.

Rajendralal Mitra makes here the following important remark ! Nothing is said regarding the taking of the dying to the river-side, or of the ceremony of immersing the lower half of the body in water at the moment of death, which forms so offensive a part of the modern ceremonial in Bengal.

NOTE 2. Rajendralal Mitra adds the following details : ' A cot of Udumbara wood is to be provided, and, having spread on it a piece of black antelope skin with the hairy side outwards and the head pointing to the south, the corpse is to be laid thereon with the face upwards. A son, brother, or other relative, or in his absence whoever takes the lead, should next address the corpse to give up its old clothing, and dress it in a new suit. The body is then covered with a piece of unbleached, uncut cloth, having fringes on both sides, the operation being performed while repeating a mantra. Then, wrapping it in its bedding or mat, it is to be borne on its cot to the place of cremation. The removal, according to some authorities, should be made by aged slaves ; according to others, on a cart drawn by two bullocks. The road from the house to the burning-ground used to be divided into three stages, and at the end of each, the procession used to halt, deposit the body on its cot on the ground, and address a mantra.'

NOTE 3. Rajendralal Mitra adds here again some details which are interesting. 'Leaving the funeral pile to smoulder, the chief mourner excavates three trenches to the north of the pyre, and lining them with pebbles and sand, fills them with water brought in an odd number of jars. The people who had followed the procession are then requested to purify themselves by bathing in them; which being done, a yoke is put up with three palâsa branches stuck in the ground and tied at the top with a piece of weak string, and they are made to pass under it. The chief mourner passes last, and then, plucking out the yoke, offers a prayer to the sun. Thereupon, the party proceed to the nearest stream, and without looking at each other, purify themselves by bathing and a prayer to Pragâpati.'

NOTE 4. Rajendralal Mitra adds: 'Subsequently, a proper place having been selected, a funeral procession should proceed to it in the morning, and the chief mourner should begin the operations of the day by sweeping the spot with a piece of leather, or a broom of palâsa wood. Then, yoking a pair of bullocks to a plough, he should dig six furrows running from east to west, and, saluting them with a mantra, deposit the urn in the central furrow. The bullocks should now be let loose by the south side, and water sprinkled over the place with an udumbara branch, or from a jar. The covering of the urn is then removed, some aromatic herbs, sarvaushadhi, are put into the urn, and subsequently closed with pebbles and sand; each of the operations being performed while repeating an appropriate mantra. A mantra should likewise be pronounced for every one of the operations which follow, and these include, (1) the putting of bricks around the urn; (2) the throwing thereon some sesamum seed and fried barley; (3) placing some butter on an unbaked plate on the south side; (4) spreading there some

darbha grass; (5) surrounding the tumulus with a palisade
of palâsa branches, and (6) crowning the whole by sticking on
the top of it a flowering head of the nala reed—arundo
karka.   The operator then anoints his body with old ghee,
and, without looking at the urn, places it on the spread
grass, invokes the manes, wipes the urn with a bit of old rag,
sprinkles some water with an udumbara branch, or from a
jar, having covered his own person with an old cloth, and
then buries the urn with bricks laid over it.

'Some karu rice is then cooked, sanctified by a mantra, and
while the chief mourner repeats five others, is put on the five
sides of the urn.   Sesamum seed and barley are now scattered
around, some herbs put on the mound, and more bricks added.
Water should subsequently be sprinkled on the place, a
prayer should be addressed to the gods, a branch of the
varuna tree and a lot of brick-bats, a sami branch and some
barley, should be placed on the mound, and the dead be
invoked to translate himself to whichever region he likes . . .
A few holes being dug round the mound, the ceremony of
burial is completed.'

APPENDIX VII.

P. 268.

FUNERAL CEREMONIES.

Let us examine a few cases in point.   Mr. A. Werner, in
the *Academy* of Dec. 28, 1889, called attention to what he
called 'Survivals in Negro Funeral Ceremonies.'   They were
collected among the Negroes in Cleveland, and traced back
to similar customs among the Negroes in Africa.   At a
funeral in Cleveland 'a stalwart Negro was seen to take
from one of the carriages a small coffin.   With the ceremony
of a short and simple prayer it was deposited in the earth.

Six or eight friends of the dead babe stood with tearful eyes during the few minutes occupied in filling the little grave. Then they re-entered the carriages and drove away. Just before leaving, a woman, whom I judged to be the bereaved mother, laid upon the mound two or three infant toys. Looking about among the large number of graves of children, I observed this practice to be very general. Some were literally covered with playthings. Upon inquiring I was told that this custom is almost universal among the coloured people in the South . . . Upon fully half the small graves, lying or standing, partly buried in the earth, were medicine-bottles of every size and shape. Some were nearly full, and all contained more or less of medicine which had no doubt been used in the effort to ward off the visit of death . . . One old woman who was loitering about the cemetery said, in answer to my question: " I kain't tell ye why, mister, but dey allers does it. When I was a chile, I libed down in ole Virginny, an' it was jes de same dar. I d'no, but mebbe dey t'inks de medisun 'll he'p de chil'en arter dey's buried, but I don't see no good in it nohow." ' Mr. Werner then proceeds to show that this custom is clearly a continuation of the native West-African one (mentioned by Burton, Stanley, and others) of placing crockery and other household utensils on the grave for the use of the deceased . . . ' The American negroes,' he concludes, ' while continuing the practice, have evidently forgotten its origin—which is perhaps not to be wondered at, seeing that most of them are two or three generations removed from contact with African soil.'

Now, first of all, there is a peculiar Nemesis that seems to track the steps of lorists in all parts of the world. While Mr. Werner asserts that this custom exists widely among the coloured people in the South, Mr. W. J. Brown in the *Academy* of June 29, 1890, states that his inquiries have only resulted in finding that, so far as the persons questioned, both white and coloured, knew, no such custom as leaving medicine-bottles or playthings on the graves of children had been heard of or seen in the Valley of Virginia. But in a visit to Petersburg, Virginia, he came across a coloured burial-ground, and noticed upon the children's graves, medicine-bottles, dolls, tea-sets, a psalter, and ornaments of various kinds. When he pressed the people for an explanation, some said it was done that the dead might see what they had taken, others said it was to mark the site of the grave (some kind of totemism), others again that it was mere foolishness.

Of course, if we press for an answer, we generally receive an answer. But is there any necessity to ask for an explanation? You know that to imagine fondly, means to imagine foolishly, and when the custom was called mere foolishness, it might with equal truth have been called mere fondness.

APPENDIX VIII.

P. 312.

(From the *Athenæum*.)

THE 'KALEVALA.'

Oxford, Oct. 1, 1888.

Looking through some of the recent numbers of the *Athenæum*, my eye was caught by the name of Dr. Krohn, of Viborg. I had been for some time expecting a letter from him, and now I see that he has been drowned. He was engaged in translating my *Hibbert Lectures*, 'On the Origin and Growth of Religion,' into Finnish, to be published by the Finnish Literary Society. Dr. Krohn was an excellent Finnish scholar, and, as you mention in your notice, he obtained a prize from the French Academy in 1881 for his *History of Finnish Literature*. Finnish literature has been a subject of interest to me ever since I met my friend Kelgren at Paris, nearly forty years ago. He also is dead long ago, but the impulse which he gave at Helsingfors to a comparative study of Finno-Ugric and Aryan traditions has continued to the present day. I deeply regret that I have not been able myself to continue the study of Finnish, but my interest in the subject has never flagged. In one of my earliest courses of lectures delivered at Oxford, I gave a full account of the now famous Finnish epic poem, the 'Kalevala,' and I pointed out the important collateral light which the collection of these songs from the mouths of the people by Lönnrot and others might throw on the collection of other epic poems, whether in Greece or Germany or Persia or India. I felt most anxious that a full and accurate account of Lönnrot's labours should be published before it was too late, and I was carrying on a correspondence with Dr. Krohn on this very subject, little suspecting that, like so many delightful correspondences, this, too, was to be cut short by death.

I send you a few extracts from Dr. Krohn's last letter, which will show you how much important information on some of the most interesting questions of what I may still call the Wolfian controversy we might have expected from Dr. Krohn's labours.

I had asked whether no more various readings had been discovered, and whether the separate ballads always began and ended in the same way. After telling me that a large collection of various readings existed in the archives of the Finnish Literary Society, Dr. Krohn continues:

'It is a mistake to imagine that the "Kalevala" is sung without a settled division of ballads. The ἀοιδός does not sing to-day, say from *a* to *d*, and to-morrow from *c* to *f*. Though there is unity in our epic poem, it consists, nevertheless, of separate songs, and these are always repeated from the same beginning to the same end. When, however, they are transferred from one place to another, their skeleton, so to say, may be considerably modified.

'The component elements of the "Kalevala" are all independent short poems, and whatever people may say about the impossibility of such short poems growing into a complete poem, here are the facts to show how it can be and has been done. The poems, often originally very short, grow longer and longer by the singer inserting short pieces known to him from other poems. Sometimes whole episodes are thus added, but very seldom does the singer add anything of his own. He will sometimes join two quite isolated poems, and this can be shown to have been done in many parts of the "Kalevala." Some of these rhapsodies thus joined together remain afterwards as a complete and independent poem, and attract further additions. Sometimes poems referring to different heroes are combined, and what was said and sung originally of different heroes is now said and sung of one and the same. For instance, in the song of Lemminkainen's second expedition to Pohjola (songs 26–29), the original hero Kauko has been superseded by Lemminkainen, who originally was killed in his first expedition to Pohjola, though afterwards called back to life (songs 12–15). When, however, several songs have thus been united into one, passages are often omitted or abbreviated, for the memory of the Finnish rhapsodes is not very strong and cannot hold beyond a certain number of verses. We can clearly see that the separate epos of Kullervo has been added to the Sampo epos, which forms the principal subject of the "Kalevala." In doing this the bad wife of the smith, against whom Kullervo had vowed vengeance, has received the name of the hostess of Ilmarinen. Into one account of the wooing of the rivals Wäinämöinen and Ilmarinen certain verses have been introduced by which the daughter of Pohjola declares that she would follow him, whoever he was, who had made the Sampo. Here, therefore, the song of the Sampo is pre-supposed, though the two songs are but seldom sung as outwardly joined. Many such instances might be added, but they would require long extracts from the "Kalevala."

'Our Finnish rhapsodes are generally void of all poetic gifts, and they proceed in their work almost mechanically. One of the best of them received some years ago a small pension from Helsingfors, but the verses in which he conveyed his thanks were miserable both in thought and form.

'In some respects this is fortunate. Much, however, depends on their memory. A strong memory preserves the poems intact; a weak memory causes variation, and in consequence further development. Nothing is ever changed on purpose, but in a weak head poems get mixed, and a trait from one poem may travel into another unawares. By repetition such mistakes may become permanent, particularly in localities in which the poem from which the singer has borrowed is not known.

'Again, when a certain hero becomes very popular in one locality many stories are attracted towards him. If he has achieved one great exploit why should he not have achieved others? The same applies to events. The description of the Päivölä feast was evidently a favourite subject, and in order to spin it out many traits have been added from Scandinavian and Russian songs—nay, even from the feast of Cana in the Bible.

'Thus we can see how originally in his dialogue with Anni (eighteenth song), Wäinämöinen spoke only of his intention to go fishing. But afterwards he is made to add that he means to shoot geese, or that he is on the war-path. Again, in the original Finnish poem the creator was represented as being assisted by a bird. But if there was once a bird, it was supposed that the bird ought to lay an egg, and thus the Lituanian legend of the mundane egg was superadded. Thus we can watch the gradual genesis of the "Kalevala."

Much of the ancient Finnish poetry has, no doubt, been lost, but what survived was what was most liked by the people, possibly, therefore, what was the most beautiful. If a nucleus had once been formed, such as the story of the Sampo, everything else was drawn into the same vortex. It is generally supposed that some popular excitement produced by great political events is favourable to the growth of epic poetry. If so, it must have been when the Fins migrated into their present seats and came in contact for the first time with an entirely new civilisation, the Scandinavian, that the growth of their epic poetry took place. Many of their legends betray Scandinavian influences. This contact with new ideas and new characters may even have told on the characters of the ancient Finnish heroes. Thus we see in the charm-songs, in the song of Sampo, and in the creation story how the old Wäinämöinen is only a kind of wise and brave prophet. In some of the later songs he appears as shrewd and tricky, and his amorous propensities make him ridiculous. Some passages, such as the touching answer which his mother gives to her despairing son Kullervo, or the charming reply of the Pohjola maid, "that she cared far more for the brightness of the forehead than for the brightness of her wooers' gold," can be explained by individual poetical genius only, but the names of those true poets are lost for ever. Other passages, again, are bare of all poetic beauty, unmeaning, even absurd. Yet they are listened to with the same reverence, and are never exposed to any disparaging criticism.

'The first work of uniting separate ballads into an epic story must be done by the people themselves. Where this has not been done, attempts made in the same direction by individual collectors or scholars have generally proved failures. This was the case with Macpherson; with Avenarius, who tried to unite the Russian popular songs into an epic poem; and even with Kreutzwald, who has given us a more or less artificial collection of the Estonian ballads about Kalevipoeg. But when, as in Finland, the people had performed the first sifting of the floating materials, a scholar like Lönnrot had no difficulty in imparting to these materials the last finishing touch. It cannot be denied that our Lönnrot has in several passages made the somewhat loose unity of the poem more perfect. He has drawn certain songs into the general frame of the poem which had as yet been left outside by the rhapsodes. He has added also a number of interpolations taken from other songs, which were meant to render the story more complete, and has arranged the songs in order, so that the unity of the whole poem should become more apparent. All this should be known in order to prevent misunderstandings. It is a mistake to imagine that Lönnrot learned the songs of the " Kalevala " as a child. In his native place they had long been forgotten. He began his studies with a small collection which had been made by Topelius, but afterwards collected so many, and knew them so well by heart, that he claimed for himself the privileges as other rhapsodes. " As I am convinced," he said, " that not a single rune-singer knows more songs than I do, I used the right, which every rhapsode claims, of joining the songs as they seemed to require it." How right his judgment was in these matters, and how sure his tact, is proved by the fact that the rhapsodes afterwards united the same songs. Nor can this be ascribed to their acquaintance with Lönnrot's printed edition, for the simple reason that in Russian Karelia and Ingerman-land, where these songs are found, the population is as yet ignorant of reading and writing. It is fortunate also that Lönnrot himself was not a poet any more than other rhap-. sodes, though no doubt his taste, cultivated by classical studies, was more refined than theirs.

' Thus, though a certain influence exercised by the final collector of the Finnish runes cannot be denied, we seem to possess these poems in a far more primitive form than the

Homeric poems or the epic poem of the Nibelungs. The *diaskeuasts* of these two epics have reduced the popular elements to a far more artificial unity than Lönnrot attempted in dealing with the Finnish ballads. We have only to compare the "Nibelungenlied" of the twelfth century with the few remaining ballads of the "Edda" in order to see how much we have lost.'

While I was waiting for fuller information, especially with regard to Lönnrot's *collectanea*, and the exact manner in which he learnt these songs by heart and afterwards reduced them to writing, my kind informant was snatched away. Let us hope that the Société Finno-Ougrienne at Helsingfors, which has done such excellent work already, may soon give us a complete history of the discovery and collection of the Finnish epic ballads by Lönnrot and others. It will be one of the most important contributions to a comparative study of epic literature, and may throw light on some of the darkest problems of the Wolfian controversy. May I also express a hope that such essays as are meant to be read by scholars all over Europe might be written in French or German, and not in Finnish or Swedish?

F. MAX MÜLLER.

INDEX.

———

THE END.